FORTRAN 77: A
Structured, Disciplined
Style Based on 1977
American National Standard
FORTRAN and Compatible
with WATFOR, WATFIV,
WATFIV-S, and M77
FORTRAN Compilers

FORTRAN 77: A Structured, Disciplined Style Based on 1977 American National Standard FORTRAN and Compatible with WATFOR, WATFIV, WATFIV-S, and M77 FORTRAN Compilers

Second Edition

Gordon B. Davis
Thomas R. Hoffmann
University of Minnesota

McGraw-Hill Book Company

New York St. Louis San Francisco Auckland
Bogotá Hamburg Johannesburg London Madrid
Mexico Montreal New Delhi Panama
Paris São Paulo Singapore
Sydney Tokyo
Toronto

FORTRAN 77: A Structured, Disciplined Style
Based on 1977 American National Standard FORTRAN and Compatible
with WATFOR, WATFIV, WATFIV-S, and M77 FORTRAN Compilers

4 5 6 7 8 9 0 S E M S E M 8 9 8 7 6 5 4

ISBN 0-07-015903-3

This book was set in Baskerville by Progressive Typographers.
The editors were James E. Vastyan and Jonathan Palace;
the designer was Ben Kann;
the production supervisor was John Mancia.
New drawings were done by J & R Services, Inc.
Semline, Inc., was printer and binder.

Library of Congress Cataloging in Publication Data

Davis, Gordon Bitter.
 FORTRAN 77.

 Rev. ed. of: FORTRAN. c1978.
 Includes index.
 1. FORTRAN (Computer program language)
I. Hoffmann, Thomas Russell, date   . II. Ti-
tle.   III. Title: FORTRAN seventy-seven.
QA76.73.F25D385 1983   001.64′24   82-8251
ISBN 0-07-015903-3

Contents

Preface

Why another FORTRAN book? The first edition of this text was written for three reasons:

1 The 1977 changes in the American National Standard FORTRAN made existing FORTRAN texts obsolete.

2 Developments in programming style and programming discipline made most existing FORTRAN texts inappropriate.

3 In the past, the teaching of FORTRAN had generally emphasized individual statements; we felt a better method is to teach students to write complete programs in a disciplined, clear style.

The first edition has been used by students of various backgrounds—undergraduate, graduate, and nondegree students. The response from this diverse group of students to the approach and content of the text has been very encouraging. We have observed that students write well-designed, readable programs by following the patterns and procedures presented in this text.

The second edition follows the basic teaching approach of the first edition but incorporates suggestions made by professors and students. Changes also reflect a much wider availability of FORTRAN compilers for 1977 standard FORTRAN. Major changes include:

1 Introduction of the type statement in Chapter 2. This is required in order to present character output. It also is desirable for those who follow a programming style of explicit typing of all variables.

2 Presentation of the 1977 standard character output instructions in Chapter 3. This reflects the general availability of the 1977 standard.

3 Expansion and clarification of instructions for use of files.

4 Expansion and clarification of additional features.

5 More explanation and comments for students doing interactive programming from terminals.

6 Additional material on debugging in each chapter.

The text adheres to the 1977 American National Standard (ANS) FOR-TRAN. Most of the newer FORTRAN compilers will meet this standard, but many small computers will implement only a simplified version of the 1977 Standard FORTRAN called Subset FORTRAN. The full 1977 FORTRAN is presented in the text, but features not included in the 1977 Subset FOR-TRAN are noted in the chapters and summarized in Appendix C.

During the period from 1966 when FORTRAN was first standardized to 1977 when the revised FORTRAN standard was adopted, there were important changes in FORTRAN compilers for student use. The most significant development was a student-oriented FORTRAN in three versions—WAT-FOR, WATFIV, and WATFIV-S. Intended primarily for use on IBM computers, these versions added a number of useful features to FORTRAN that were not part of the 1966 standard. MNF was a similar student-oriented FOR-TRAN for users of large-scale Control Data computers. The revised 1977 FORTRAN standard incorporates most of the WATFOR, WATFIV, and MNF innovations. The 1977 FORTRAN also adds other features not included in the 1966 standard, but makes almost no changes in the 1966 features. In other words, programs written in 1966 FORTRAN will generally work under the new standard.

Although this text is based on the 1977 American National Standard FOR-TRAN, users of older versions of FORTRAN may employ the text very effectively, keeping in mind that the text covers fundamental features of FOR-TRAN in Chapters 1–5, file processing in Chapter 6, and other features in Chapter 7. In general, students may use older versions of FORTRAN with this text as follows:

WATFOR/WATFIV version   The material in Chapters 1–5 is compatible, with minor exceptions that are presented in Appendix C. Sequential file processing (Chapter 6) and most features of Chapter 7 (such as character processing) are also the same in WATFOR/WATFIV as in the 1977 Standard FORTRAN.

WATFIV-S version   Of the six structured programming instructions introduced by WATFIV-S, only the block IF instruction is implemented by the 1977 Standard FORTRAN; otherwise, WATFIV-S has the same compatibility as WATFIV.

M77 version   All of the features presented in Chapters 1–5 are allowed by M77, the replacement for MNF.

1966 Standard FORTRAN version   The major problem affecting the use of Chapters 1 and 2 is the lack of the list-directed (free format) input and output with the 1966 version. A FORMAT statement must be used. A short section at the end of Chapter 1 explains how to introduce the needed FORMAT statement without changing the flow of instruction. The CHARACTER type explained in Chapter 2 and used in Chapter 3 is new with 1977 FORTRAN. Other differences are explained in Appendix C.

Other versions of FORTRAN   The major compatibility question is the existence of list-directed input and output. Some versions have it; others do not. If not included, a FORMAT statement can be introduced with Chapter 1, as explained above.

Sequential file processing instructions in Chapter 6 do not represent significant changes over past standards; however, there are major changes for direct-access processing. The student who is doing file processing with direct-access files will therefore need to have the reference manual for the compiler being used.

The text supports both traditional batch submission of programs on cards and interactive programming from a terminal. Appendix A describes the use of a card punch, and Appendix B describes procedures for programming in FORTRAN at a terminal.

The philosophy of the text is that the students should, from the beginning, learn to write programs in a disciplined style using a well-developed program structure. Programming that is done in a structured, disciplined manner is more productive and results in programs that have fewer errors, are simpler to debug, and are more easily maintained (altered and updated) than programs written without this approach. This text does not simply teach the rules for FORTRAN; it teaches by explanation and by example how to apply the rules of the FORTRAN langauge to write clear, structured programs.

Many students are able to learn a programming language with little assistance; others require lectures to reinforce the language text. Recognizing the need for both instructional approaches; this text was written so that it may be used in a self-instructional mode without lectures. This also makes it suitable for in-company training. When the lecture method is preferred, the text is still well suited because the organization of each topic chapter into an A and B part facilitates lecture presentation. Part A presents language features. An instructor can amplify and illustrate these features in an accompanying lecture. Part B contains two sample programs and the programming exercises, one of which will normally be assigned. An instructor may wish to use the sample program as the subject of a lecture, adding comments on style and usage.

FORTRAN courses (and students taking courses) have differing learning objectives. These range from "getting a feel for this important language" to learning to be a good FORTRAN programmer. The text is suitable for a wide range of objectives by selective use of part or all of the material. An objective of introducing students to the elements of the FORTRAN language and the structure of FORTRAN programs can be achieved by Chapters 1–4 (and perhaps 5). Students needing to understand the entire range of capabilities for the language will also use Chapters 5, 6, and 7. The text may be used alone if the objective is only to learn FORTRAN; it may be used as the language text for a course that also introduces students to computer science or computer data processing.

A large number of students have provided feedback that has been incorporated in the text. Graduate teaching assistants have provided ideas and pointed out sections needing improvement. Timothy Hoffmann reviewed the manuscript and validated the problems by writing solution programs. Alison Davis reviewed the manuscript. Janice DeGross did an outstanding job of typing it.

The features of this text that we feel are especially useful in teaching and learning FORTRAN are:

1   The division of each chapter into Part A, a language explanation, and Part B, containing complete programs and accompanying documentation to illustrate features in Part A.

2   An emphasis on programming style with an example of a recommended style being used throughout.

3   Reference material easily accessible—list of functions on inside front cover and list of features following the index.

4   A method for recording and easily referencing the specifications for the FORTRAN compiler being used (inside back cover).

5   The use of list-directed (free format) input and output for the first two chapters. This allows a student to write programs without learning the FORMAT statement.

6   Where alternative FORTRAN features exist, emphasis on the use of features that are less error-prone, such as apostrophe editing and logical IF.

7   A large number of problems suited to different disciplines. At the end of each chapter, there are 15 problems divided into five different categories. This allows the text to be used for students with different backgrounds and interests. Solutions have been written for all of the problems. These solutions are available in an Instructor's Guide.

8   An explanation of keypunching in Appendix A and terminal entry in Appendix B.

We appreciate receiving suggestions for corrections or changes and ideas for additional exercises from readers. Comments may be sent to Gordon B. Davis or Thomas R. Hoffmann, Department of Management Sciences, School of Management, University of Minnesota, Minneapolis, Minnesota 55455.

Gordon B. Davis
Thomas R. Hoffmann

FORTRAN 77: A Structured, Disciplined Style Based on 1977 American National Standard FORTRAN and Compatible with WATFOR, WATFIV, WATFIV-S, and M77 FORTRAN Compilers

chapter **1A**

Programming discipline, the FORTRAN language, and FORTRAN statements to write a simple program

This chapter introduces the concept of a programming language, and explains the value of programming discipline. The chapter describes the FORTRAN language, explains general procedures for preparing a FORTRAN program, and introduces five FORTRAN statements needed to code a simple FORTRAN program. Two complete FORTRAN programs are contained in Chapter 1B. Using these example programs as guides, you will be able to code and prepare a simple FORTRAN program for processing. Chapter 1A thus provides concepts necessary for understanding the nature of FORTRAN programming and Chapter 1B provides an introductory experience in preparing a FORTRAN program. The program written as the assignment for Chapter 1B is also used to provide experience in following the procedures by which a FORTRAN program is submitted to the computer center and processed.

Instructing a computer

Before starting the explanation of the FORTRAN language, it may be helpful to review how a computer is instructed. A computer system requires both hardware and software. The *hardware* consists of all the equipment; the *software* includes the programs of instructions that direct the operations of the computer equipment.

Hardware and software

A hardware computer system, shown in Figure 1-1, has input units (such as a card reader), a central processing unit (CPU), and output units (such as a printer). It also has external storage devices, such as magnetic disks or magnetic-tape units (also called secondary or auxilliary storage). In a typical processing job, data comes from the input unit (and perhaps from external storage) into the central processor where computation and other processing is performed. After processing, the results are sent to the output device (say a printer) or to a secondary storage device to be held for later output or further processing.

The CPU can perform operations such as read, write, add, etc., but the sequence in which these operations are to be performed and the specific input

Figure 1-1
Hardware in a computer system. Illustrations from IBM/370 equipment. (*Courtesy of International Business Machines Corporation.*)

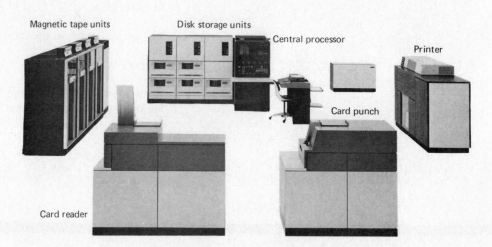

Magnetic tape units   Disk storage units   Central processor   Printer

Card punch

Card reader

and output units to be used are specified by a set of instructions stored in the computer memory. The general term applied to these computer processing instructions is *software.* The instructions are organized into sets called routines and programs. A *routine* refers to a set of instructions that directs the performance of a specific task, such as calculating the square root of a quantity or producing an error message when an error is encountered in input data. A *program* consists of one or more routines that direct the solution of a complete problem.

There are several major types of software. Three types especially relevant to the study of FORTRAN are application programs, compilers, and operating systems.

1 *Application programs* Programs that direct the processing for an application of computers, such as preparing payroll, preparing checks, calculating a rate of return for a proposed project, calculating stress factors for a building structure, etc. The FORTRAN examples in this text are application programs. Application programs may be written by personnel in organizations needing them, or they may be purchased from software vendors who prepare and sell programs for frequently encountered applications.

2 *Compilers* Programs that translate instructions written in a high-level language, such as FORTRAN, into a set of machine instructions specific to the computer being used.

3 *Operating system* A set of routines that directs and manages the operations of the computer. The operating system supports and directs the running of application programs. For example, if an application program has an instruction to read a card from the card reader but the card reader is not operable, the operating system sends a suitable message to the computer operator.

Operating systems and compilers are generally obtained from either the hardware vendor or independent software vendors. Programs being executed are stored in the internal (main or primary) storage or memory, which is part of the central processing unit. Programs not currently being executed but which need to be available are stored in external storage. Some parts of the operating system remain in main storage all of the time. Based on job control instructions to be described later, these operating system routines bring into internal memory the routines and programs to be executed and direct their execution. The programs to be run may be compilers, application programs, or other software.

Machine-level languages

A program in main memory must be in machine language to be executed. A machine language instruction is represented as a string of binary digits called *bits* (represented by 1s and 0s), which identify the operations to be performed and the data, etc., to be used. The machine-level instructions differ for different series of computers and different manufacturers. As an example, a typical instruction for a large IBM computer has the following form (with 1 standing for a 1-bit and 0 for a 0-bit in storage):

010110100011000010111010001000000

Even though the internal machine representation is in this form, it would be very difficult and could lead to error if a programmer were required to deal with such instructions. In cases when machine instructions are printed for operator or programmer use, a condensed notation is employed. For example, the preceding instruction would be printed out for operator/programmer inspection as 5A30BA40. .

Although more usable than the machine representation, this condensed notation is still difficult to use. Therefore, if a program is to be written in machine-level instructions, the programmer generally uses a symbolic assembly language. Symbolic assembly languages as a class are often referred to as *low-level languages*. These languages are machine-oriented because each symbolic assembly instruction is converted into one machine-language instruction. The preceding machine-language instruction coded in symbolic assembly language might be: A   3,PAY where, for example, A means "add." The computer cannot directly execute the symbolic instructions, so these must be translated into machine-language instructions. This is done by a program called a *symbolic assembly system* which converts each symbolic instruction into an equivalent machine-level code instruction. Machine-oriented programming is very useful for some applications because instruction coding can be very machine-sensitive and thus obtain very efficient use of the computer. However, an assembly language program is relatively difficult to code, and logic errors are difficult to find. It is also difficult and time-consuming to change. A program in a low-level, machine-oriented language also has limited transferability (portability) from one computer to another.

High-level languages

A *high-level language* is oriented to problem solution or processing procedures rather than to the machine-level instructions of a particular computer. The instruction statements use words, phrases, and symbols that are similar to those commonly used to describe solution or processing procedures. Another major difference between a high-level instruction and a symbolic assembly instruction is that one high-level instruction is translated into many machine-language instructions.

There are a number of different high-level languages for different types of problems. Each of these languages consists of a grammar (set of rules) and predefined words for writing instructions. A program called a *compiler* is used to translate the program written in the high-level language (the source program) into machine-level instructions (the object program) for the computer on which the program is to be run. Since machine-level instructions differ among computer series, there must be a unique compiler program for each computer series. For example, there is a FORTRAN compiler written for the IBM 3300 computers, another written for the UNIVAC 1100 series computers, and yet another written for the Control Data Cyber computers.

There are two important advantages of high-level languages over symbolic assembly languages: They are machine-independent in the sense that programs written in a high-level language can be compiled and run on any computer (for which there is a compiler) with few or no changes, and they are relatively easy to learn. Today, these languages are generally so powerful and efficient that they have virtually eliminated the need for symbolic assembly language coding except for a few specialized applications. It is also relatively easy to standardize methods of programming with high-level languages. Organizations having a concern with program accuracy and a desire for programming discipline have strongly influenced the trend toward use of high-level languages.

The two most common high-level languages are FORTRAN and COBOL, FORTRAN is best suited for formula-type mathematical problems while COBOL is the dominant language in business data processing. Other high-level languages having significant use are BASIC, Pascal, PL/I, Ada, and APL.

The FORTRAN language

FORTRAN (an acronym for FORmula TRANslator) is the most widely used of a class of high-level languages called scientific or algebraic languages. It is available for use on almost all computers. Although not limited to mathematical problems, it is especially useful for problems that can be stated in terms of formulas or arithmetic procedures. This covers a wide range of problems. For example, FORTRAN is suitable for such diverse problems as analysis of sales statistics in a business and analysis of structural stress for designing a building.

Development of FORTRAN

FORTRAN was developed in 1957 by IBM in conjunction with some major users, but it is now used by all computer vendors. FORTRAN has changed and evolved. This evolutionary process resulted, during the development period, in several FORTRANs of increasing complexity. Major versions were called FORTRAN, FORTRAN II, and FORTRAN IV. Each new version made a few changes in the basic instructions and included additional features. In 1966, a voluntary FORTRAN standard, American National Standard (ANS) FORTRAN, was adopted. The International Standards Organization (ISO) also defined standard FORTRAN.

A revised American National Standard (ANS) FORTRAN was adopted in 1977. This 1977 standard adds features to the previous 1966 standard FORTRAN, clarifies some ambiguities, and makes a few minor changes. The new standard also defines two different levels for FORTRAN implementation: Subset FORTRAN and full FORTRAN. Subset FORTRAN is a compatible subset of the comprehensive full FORTRAN. This text is based on the 1977 standard, although differences between the 1977 standard and the 1966 standard will be noted because many compilers may not accept the added 1977 features. The text concentrates on the most-used features of FORTRAN; some advanced or little-used features will be summarized in less detail in Chapter 7.

Concurrent with the development of standard FORTRAN has been the development of special teaching-oriented FORTRAN compilers. The best known of these, developed at the University of Waterloo (Waterloo, Ontario), are termed WATFOR and WATFIV. Similar compilers for large Control Data computers are MNF and M77. WATFIV-S is a version of WATFIV containing six special structured programming instructions (see Appendix C). The teaching-oriented compilers were designed to provide excellent error-diagnostic messages for students, do fast execution of small student programs, and relax some error-prone features of FORTRAN. The new 1977

FORTRAN standard adopted the most significant features of the teaching-oriented FORTRANs, so the American National Standard FORTRAN is recommended as the basis for all FORTRAN programming, by students as well as by professional programmers.

How to study FORTRAN using this text

FORTRAN is a machine-independent language for instructing a computer. In other words, the programmer writing FORTRAN does not need to know any machine-level details for the computer being used. The language is procedure-oriented—designed for instructing the computer in a problem-solving procedure. The language consists of a vocabulary of symbols and words and a grammar of rules for writing procedural instructions. The symbols, words, and rules utilize many common mathematical and English-language conventions so that the language is fairly easy to learn and to understand. The rules are, however, precise and must be followed with care. In other words, learning FORTRAN is like learning a special-purpose language. There are rules of construction and vocabulary to learn, and one becomes proficient by doing rather than by much reading.

The objective of the text is to assist you in learning to write clear, understandable, error-free FORTRAN programs. To achieve this objective, you need to do each of the following:

1 Learn the instructions and other elements of the language.

2 Learn how to apply the language rules and to use the FORTRAN instructions to compose a clear, understandable program.

3 Learn how to submit a program to be compiled and executed (using the computer that is available to you).

The first objective is met by part A of each chapter. There is a description of instructions or rules, and illustrations of their use are provided. To assist in learning, there are self-testing exercises after every major unit in each chapter. At each self-testing exercise, answer the questions and check your responses against the answers at the end of the chapter.

The second objective is achieved by part B of each chapter, which contains complete programs. You should study the example programs, noting the style, the error-control features included in the program, and the documentation describing the programs. These examples of good programming style provide a pattern to follow in writing your programs.

The third objective requires the programming of a problem, carrying out the procedures to keypunch the program (or enter it at a terminal), submitting the program to be run, and removing errors. A variety of different programming problems is provided with each chapter. In carrying out the writing, coding, running, etc., of a program, the text provides the following aids:

1 A reference list of all FORTRAN language features. (List of 1977 American National Standard FORTRAN Statements and Specifications follows index).

2 A place to record specifications and features you need to know about the compiler for the computer you will use. The form to record these is on the inside

of the back cover. The specifications should be filled in from material furnished by your instructor or obtained by consulting the FORTRAN reference manual for your computer.

3　A reference list of all FORTRAN intrinsic functions on the inside of the front cover. Check off those functions that are available to you (you can wait to do this until after completing Chapter 2).

4　An appendix (Appendix A) describing how to use the keypunch to punch instructions and data. Also, Appendix B describes procedures for programming in FORTRAN from a terminal.

The text is based on the latest 1977 American National Standard FORTRAN, but because the fundamental features of all versions of FORTRAN are the same or nearly the same, it is possible to use this text with FORTRAN versions that are based on the older 1966 standard and on teaching-oriented implementations of FORTRAN. Appendix C assists in understanding differences in these versions of FORTRAN. Before proceeding, scan the front and back endpapers, the three appendixes, and the List of 1977 ANS FORTRAN Statements and Specifications (follows index).

A structured, disciplined style in FORTRAN programming

The title of this text indicates that there can be a structured, disciplined style in writing FORTRAN programs. Since the text follows this approach, it will be useful to understand the reasons for the approach and the basic methods to implement it.

Computer programs frequently do not meet user requirements, are not produced on time, cost considerably more than estimated, contain errors, and are difficult to maintain (to correct or change to meet new requirements). These difficulties have been observed with such frequency that many organizations have attempted to change the practice of programming in order to improve performance. The revised approach can be termed *programming discipline*—well-defined practices, procedures, and development control processes. A student should not merely learn to code FORTRAN statements. It is equally important to learn how these statements are combined into a high-quality program—one which is easy to understand (and change, if necessary) and which uses computer resources efficiently.

Objectives of a disciplined approach to programming

Because programming discipline is an underlying philosophy for this text and because of the importance of programming discipline to industry, it will be useful to summarize the major objectives of this approach to programming:

1　*Meet user needs*　A program has a purpose, such as to produce an analysis or to compute a set of statistics. An assignment to prepare a program is a failure if the program is not used because the potential users of the application find it too complex or too difficult. A disciplined approach to program design includes a careful analysis of user requirements before programming.

2   *Development on time within budget*   Estimates of time and cost for writing computer programs have frequently been substantially in error. By using a more structured, disciplined approach, installations have achieved dramatic improvements in productivity and have improved their ability to estimate time to complete.

3   *Error-free set of instructions*   It is generally considered that all large-scale computer programs contain errors, and it may be impossible to remove every single error from a large set of programs. However, using a disciplined, structured approach, programs may be designed and developed in a manner that minimizes the likelihood of errors and that facilitates detection and correction of errors in testing. The result can be virtually error-free programming.

4   *Error-resistant operation*   A program may produce erroneous results, due either to program errors or to incorrect input. The program should be designed so that errors will, whenever possible, be detected by the program itself during execution. The design features to assist in detecting errors are:
   (*a*) Input validation. This is a process of testing all input data items to determine whether or not they meet the criteria set for them. For example, data input may be tested for:

   Existence of necessary input data items

   Data item values within acceptable range

   Incorrect class of data (for example, alphabetic characters in a data item that should be numeric)

   (*b*) Tests of correctness during processing. These generally take the form of tests for reasonableness of results and checks of logical relationships among different results.

5   *Maintainable programs*   Computer programs change, especially when first placed into use. Programs should be written with the maintenance activity in mind. The program documentation and the style in which a program is written should allow another programmer to understand the logic of the program and to make a change in one part of the program without unknowingly introducing an error into another part of the same program.

6   *Portable programs*   A tested program, written in FORTRAN, should be transferable without substantial change to another computer having a FORTRAN compiler. This means that all nonstandard FORTRAN instructions should be avoided. Straightforward, well-documented instructions that follow a disciplined, structured approach are portable with little difficulty; programs with intricate or poorly documented logic are not.

Modular design of programs

One of the key concepts in the application of programming discipline is the design of a program as a set of units referred to as *blocks* or *modules*. A program module is defined as the part of a program that performs a separate function such as input, input validation, processing of one type of input, etc. A program module may be quite large (in terms of logic and instructions required), so that it may be further divided into logical submodules. The process of subdivision continues until all modules are of manageable size in terms of complexity of logic and numbers of instructions. In practice, a FORTRAN module with more than 60 statements (takes more than one page to list) is too large.

Although computer programs differ greatly in purpose and processing, it is possible to identify types of functions that are commonly needed in programs. Programs can be logically separated into the following functional modules.

Functional module	Description
Initialization	Establishes initial values for some variables, prints headings, messages, etc. May not be necessary.
Input	Performs input of data required by the program.
Input data validation	Performs validation of input data to detect errors or omissions.
Processing	Performs computation or data manipulation.
Output	Performs output of data to be provided by the program.
Error handling	Performs analysis of error condition and outputs error messages. For small programs, error handling may be included in other modules.
Closing procedure	Performs procedures to end the execution of the program.

These modules reflect a logical flow for a computer program. After initialization, processing proceeds logically with input, input validation, various processing modules, and output. Error handling may be required during execution of any of the modules. At the conclusion of processing, the closing procedures to complete the program are performed. Although all of the functions of these logical modules are normally found in well-written programs, they are not always defined as separate program modules; they may be combined or rearranged to suit the flow of a particular program.

Structured programming

One method of achieving the objective of accurate, error-resistant, maintainable programs is to code (write) each module in a simple, easily understood format.

A useful starting point for understanding how to code the modules in a computer program in a clear, easily understood format is the fact that all computer program processing can be coded by using only three logic structures (patterns) or combinations of these structures:

1 Simple sequence
2 Selection
3 Repetition

The three basic patterns should be understood, since these structures have general applicability to computer programming.

The simple sequence structure consists of one action followed by another. In other words, perform operation A (Figure 1-2), and then perform operation B.

The selection structure consists of a test for a condition followed by two alternative paths for the program to follow. The program selects one of the program-control paths depending on the test of the condition. After performing one of the two paths, the program control returns to a single point.

Figure 1-2
Simple sequence and selection program structures.

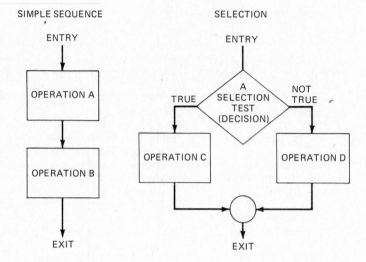

This pattern can be termed IF . . . ELSE because the logic can be stated (for condition P and operations C and D): IF P (is true) perform C ELSE (otherwise) perform D (Figure 1-2).

The repetition structure can also be called a *loop*. In a loop, an operation (or set of operations) is repeated while (as long as) some condition is satisfied. The basic form of repetition is termed DO WHILE (Figure 1-3) in the literature of structured programming. Using FORTRAN terminology to be explained in Chapter 4, it might be termed a DO loop. In the DO WHILE pattern, the program logic tests a condition governing the continued operation of the loop; if it is true, the program executes the operation (called E in Figure 1-3) and loops back for another test. If the condition is not true, the repetition ceases. In other words, DO the loop WHILE (as long as) the loop repetition condition is true.

One of the objectives in using the three basic structures is to make programs more understandable to those concerned with design, review, and mainte-

Figure 1-3
The DO WHILE repetition structure.

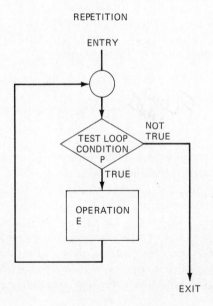

Figure 1-4
Nesting of coding structures.

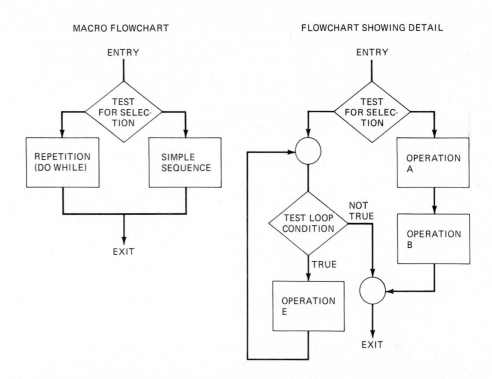

MACRO FLOWCHART

FLOWCHART SHOWING DETAIL

nance. It is possible to combine the three simple structures to produce more complex coding while maintaining the simplicity inherent in the three patterns. For example, the logic of the program may involve a selection between two program paths. If one path is chosen, there should be a repetition loop; if the other is selected, there is a simple sequence. The combination of the structures is illustrated in Figure 1-4. Note that there is still a single entry/single exit for the entire structure.

This short explanation of the three structures provides some insight into their value in a disciplined programming approach. The structures are useful because:

1   The program is simplified. Only the three building blocks are used. There is a single point of entry into each structure as well as a single point of exit.
2   The three coding structures allow a program to be read from top to bottom, making the logic of the program more visible for checking and maintenance.

The FORTRAN language was not designed for structured programming, but it is possible to follow the ideas reasonably well. Rules for doing this will be explained in the text as they become relevant.

Planning a FORTRAN program

A FORTRAN program should be planned before the program instructions are written. Before planning the program, there will have been a recognition of the need for the program and some definition of what the program aims to accomplish (the requirements). The program planning process designs a program to meet the requirements. It is usually desirable to first design the overall structure of the program and then to work on the detailed logic. Tools and techniques that assist in planning the program and the program logic include program design language (pseudocode), flowcharts, and layouts. Program design language and flowcharts are explained in this chapter; layouts are explained in Chapter 3.

Planning overall program structure

Planning a program is similar to planning a building such as a home. First, there is an overall layout showing the different rooms (different functions to be performed) and their relationship to other rooms. Detailed design of each room follows. Likewise, there needs to be an overall structure for the computer program. This consists of the modules for the different program functions. When the modules are defined and relationships among modules specified, the individual modules can be designed and coded. The need for a systematic approach to design is more apparent with large programs, but the basic skill can be developed by applying planning techniques to small programs.

An orderly approach to overall planning can follow a sequence such as the following:

1 Define requirements in terms of outputs
   (a) Define fundamental requirements in terms of outputs to users of the application. The output desired can be:

   A single number, such as the rate of interest for a finance proposal.

   A set of numbers, such as a set of descriptive statistics.

   A report, such as a financial statement.

   (b) Define additional outputs required so that recipients of the output understand it and have assurance it is correct and complete. These requirements include:

   Dates, version numbers, etc., that distinguish variations of the output.

   Headings, titles, and labels on the data items in the output.

   Identification of (or list of) data used as input, the factors used in computations, and totals (where these can be compared to related totals to demonstrate completeness). These are included as needed to assure users that the results are correct and complete.

   (c) Define error message outputs to explain errors in input or processing and to explain what recipients of the output can (should) do to correct the errors.
2 Based on the outputs, define inputs required for the application.
3 Define the validation procedure to check that data items being input are correct and complete. Define procedures for handling data items identified as having errors.
4 Define procedures for transforming input data into output:
   (a) Transforming valid input data into the desired output.
   (b) Converting invalid data into error outputs.

If the transformation procedure has many steps, it may need to be factored into several component procedures.

5 Define the program structure in terms of major modules. The planning analysis should help to clarify why, as explained earlier, a program is likely to contain one or more modules for:

Input

Input data validation

Processing

Output

Error handling (and error outputs)

The other two modules, initialization and closing procedures, are frequently needed to set up processing and ensure complete termination.

Program design language in program planning

A program design language consists of abbreviated statements in English (or other natural language) that specify the procedures the program is to perform. These program design language statements are also termed *pseudocode,* and the terms will be used interchangeably in the text. The statements are independent of the FORTRAN language but tend to recognize the features of the language. For example, a program to read input data from punched cards, compute the sum of the two input values, and print the input values and their sum might read as follows:

READ values for x and y from card

Compute sum = x + y

PRINT x, y, and sum

STOP

In this simple case, each line of program design language (PDL) results in one line of FORTRAN, but in other cases a single line of PDL may require many lines of FORTRAN. PDL tends to be quite useful in planning the general flow of a program.

There are no standard rules for program design language; the main objective is an understandable description of the program logic. A useful approach to PDL will be illustrated in the descriptions of sample programs in part B of each chapter.

Program flowchart in program planning and documentation

FORTRAN is well suited to the use of flowcharts in planning and documenting programs because the language is oriented toward procedural logic. Some programmers find flowcharts very useful; others do not use them. We find flowcharts are less useful than PDL for planning the general flow of a program but are more useful in planning and documenting detailed logic. In any case, flowcharts are found frequently enough that a FORTRAN programmer should be familiar with them. Therefore, we recommend their use in the problems in this text.

Flowcharts are a means of symbolically depicting the (1) logic and procedures of programs and (2) the elements and flows of systems. The American National Standards Institute has defined standard flowcharting symbols and their use in data processing.[1] The following are the most common symbols used in flowcharting FORTRAN programs:

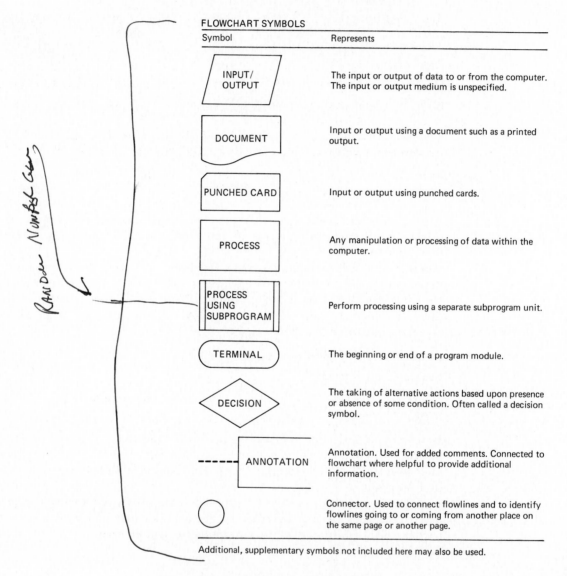

FLOWCHART SYMBOLS

Symbol	Represents
INPUT/OUTPUT	The input or output of data to or from the computer. The input or output medium is unspecified.
DOCUMENT	Input or output using a document such as a printed output.
PUNCHED CARD	Input or output using punched cards.
PROCESS	Any manipulation or processing of data within the computer.
PROCESS USING SUBPROGRAM	Perform processing using a separate subprogram unit.
TERMINAL	The beginning or end of a program module.
DECISION	The taking of alternative actions based upon presence or absence of some condition. Often called a decision symbol.
ANNOTATION	Annotation. Used for added comments. Connected to flowchart where helpful to provide additional information.
◯	Connector. Used to connect flowlines and to identify flowlines going to or coming from another place on the same page or another page.

Additional, supplementary symbols not included here may also be used.

The symbols are connected with flowlines in order to indicate the direction or sequence of processing. Flowcharts are written to be read from top to bottom and from left to right. If the flow is right to left or bottom to top, arrowheads must be used on the flowlines to indicate direction of flow. Otherwise, arrowheads are optional but recommended. The flowchart symbols were used in Figures 1-2, 1-3, and 1-4 to describe basic program structures. Review these figures as examples of how the symbols are put together. The design of flow-

[1] American National Standards Institute, X3.5-1970, "Flowchart Symbols and Their Usage in Information Processing."

charts for FORTRAN programs will be explained in the text by example and by explanations associated with programming exercises.

Self-testing exercise 1-1

There will be frequent self-testing exercises to help you test your comprehension of the material just explained. The answers are at the end of the chapter.

1 Distinguish between hardware and software.

2 What is the difference between machine language and symbolic assembly language?

3 What are the advantages of high-level languages over symbolic assembly languages?

4 FORTRAN stands for _____.

5 What has been the role of the American National Standards Institute (ANSI) in the development of FORTRAN?

6 Name six objectives of a disciplined approach to program design.

7 Name the functional modules in a program.

8 Name and describe the three basic program structures.

9 Match the flowchart symbol with its definition.

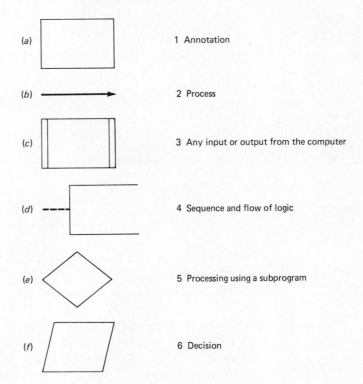

10 If a program is transferable to another computer having a compiler for that language, without substantial change, the program is _____.

11 The most common tools for planning the logic for a FORTRAN program are _____ and/or _____.

12 Explain an orderly set of steps for planning overall program structure.

Coding a FORTRAN program

When FORTRAN program design is completed, the next step is to code the program by writing FORTRAN instruction statements. These statements are then input to the FORTRAN compiler in the computer in one of two ways: (1) entered at the keyboard of a computer terminal; or (2) keypunched into cards for reading by the card reader attached to the computer. In either case, it is useful to write the FORTRAN program statements on specially designed coding paper (Figure 1-5). The columns of the coding paper are marked to aid correct coding. Some rules for using the coding paper are presented. Review them now and then return to them when you start coding your first program. There are 80 columns that are used as follows:

Column	How used
1	Comments and special options. An asterisk (*) or the letter C in column 1 (or C only in older versions) indicates that what follows on the line is not an instruction translated by the FORTRAN compiler. The line is printed as part of the program listing and is therefore used for explanatory comments in the program listing.
1–5	Statement label. Used as an identifier for referencing the statement. Can be written anywhere in the five columns (spaces are ignored), but it is usually right-justified (extra spaces to left). In other words, reference number 349 is usually written as bb349 instead of 349bb (where b stands for a blank).
6	If a FORTRAN statement is too long for one line, it may be continued on succeeding lines by putting a nonzero character (say 1, 2, etc.) in column 6 of each continuation line. The initial line to be continued may have a blank or a 0 in column 6. Clarity of coding is enhanced if the FORTRAN statements on the continuation lines are indented to, for example, column 11.
7–72	FORTRAN statement. The statement can begin anywhere from 7 to 72. Indentation and spacing may be used to improve readability.
73–80	When the statements of a program are punched into cards, each statement will be punched onto one 80-column card utilizing only columns 1 to 72. The last eight columns of the program statement cards either are not used or are used for identification. They are not translated. (Note, however, that all 80 columns of a data card can be used for data.)

In coding FORTRAN statements, certain conventions reduce the possibility of error when the lines of coding are punched into cards or entered at a terminal:

1   Use the FORTRAN coding paper. Each space on the coding form corresponds to a column on a punched card, so that one character is written in each space. This reduces errors in keypunching.

2   Code only in printed capital letters because the printed capitals are easier to read.

3   Clearly differentiate between numbers and letters that are similar. The letter O and the zero are the biggest problems, but S and 5, Z and 2, and I and 1 are often confused. Various methods are used for differentiating, such as underlining or slashing either the letter or the number. It is very common for FORTRAN programmers to slash the alphabetic O. The American National Stan-

Figure 1-5
FORTRAN coding form.

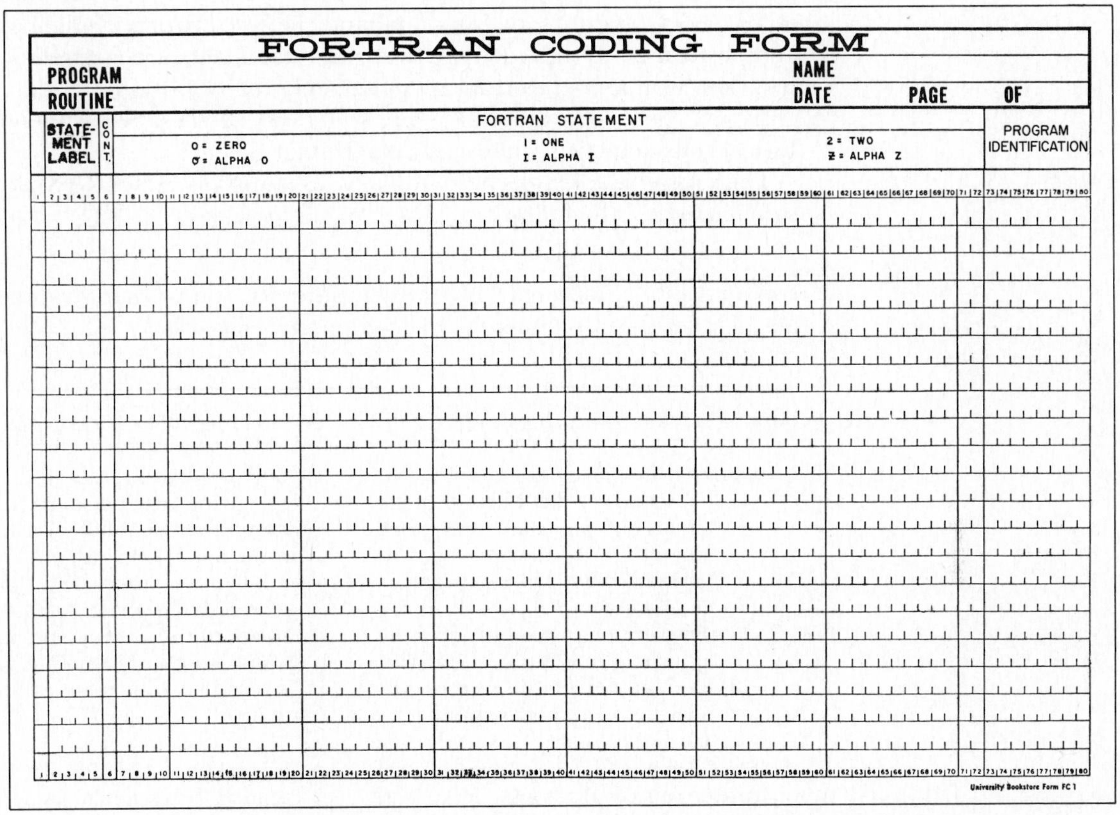
FORTRAN CODING FORM
PROGRAM NAME
ROUTINE DATE PAGE OF
STATEMENT LABEL | CONT. | FORTRAN STATEMENT | PROGRAM IDENTIFICATION
0 = ZERO Ơ = ALPHA O | 1 = ONE I = ALPHA I | 2 = TWO Ƶ = ALPHA Z
University Bookstore Form FC 1

dard coding convention (shown below) is to put a line through the letter Z and to add a loop to O, leaving the related numbers as they are usually written.

Letter	Number
Ơ	0
Ƶ	2
I	1
S	5

In reading printer or terminal output, it is also possible to make a mistake between the letter O and the zero. Many new typestyles emphasize the difference. Another approach to differentiation used with many printers is to slash the zeros. The printouts in this text follow the zero slash convention.

Compiling and executing a FORTRAN program

After coding (writing) a FORTRAN program (called the *source program*), the next steps are to input the program statements into the computer for compilation, to compile, to make corrections as needed (debug), and to execute the program using data required by the program. The steps from compilation and execution of a program may use either batch processing or terminal input and interactive processing. Batch processing means that each job to be processed on the computer is submitted as a set (batch) of punched cards (or other media), and that the job is "in hand" before any processing is scheduled and performed. In interactive processing, statements are entered at a terminal. Compilation and execution immediately follow program entry, and data entry may be at the terminal as the program executes. See Appendix B for special considerations when using a terminal.

The entire process of compiling and executing a FORTRAN program is summarized in the following steps:

1 Input program statements into the computer for compilation (translation into machine-level instructions for the computer being used).

Punched cards/batch processing	Terminal input/interactive processing
(a) Source deck preparation (1) Punching of FORTRAN statements into punched cards—one line of coding into one card to produce the source program deck. (2) Preparation of input data by punching into punched cards. (3) Preparation of job control instructions and punching into cards. (b) Submit job (consisting of job control cards, source program deck, and data deck) for compilation and execution.	(a) Log onto the computer at the terminal giving data as required, such as, user number and access security code. Specify that a FORTRAN program is to be entered. There is a place in the sheet facing the back cover for recording log-on instructions and other commands for using a terminal with your computer system. (b) Enter FORTRAN statements one at a time at the terminal. Generally, each statement is preceded by a line number (independent of the FORTRAN statement labels).

2 Compile and debug.

(a) Normally, the job is compiled and immediately executed if there are no errors in the program. If errors are present, a program listing is printed giving error messages to aid debugging. (b) Errors are identified, corrections made in the job deck, and the job resubmitted.	(a) After all program statements have been entered, a command is entered to compile and execute. If there are errors, messages are printed or displayed identifying the FORTRAN statement line number and the type of error. (b) Each erroneous statement is corrected by typing a corrected statement having the same line number as the erroneous one, or statements to be added may be inserted at appropriate locations. When the command is given to compile and execute, the compiler first replaces the error statements with the corrected statements and inserts any new statements in line number sequence.

3   Execution.

(a) The program will be executed if no program code errors are detected. The data deck submitted with the job deck will be used in the execution (although other methods will be described in Chapter 6).	(a) The program will be executed using a data file entered previously or data entered at execution time in response to requests (prompts) from the program.
(b) The output will usually be a listing of the program and the output specified by the program.	(b) The output will be in the form specified by the program. If a program listing is desired, it is obtained by a separate command.

Step 1b for punched card/batch processing needs some explanation. Every job to be run on the computer from punched cards must have job control instructions along with it. These instructions, punched into cards, provide specifications for the operating system (the software that manages the compilation and execution of the program). For example, one of the job control instruction cards will specify that the job is a FORTRAN program to be compiled. The operating system will interpret the job control card and bring the FORTRAN compiler into the main storage of the computer. The operating system then turns control over to the compiler program, which reads and translates the FORTRAN program statements, etc. The job control cards are different for each computer. A job control manual for the computer being used provides the programmer with the necessary specifications and instructions. For the common case of compilation and immediate execution, a complete source deck is composed of:

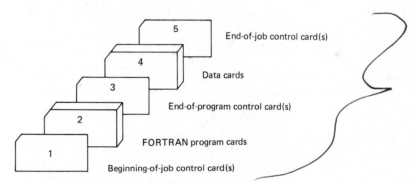

Computer centers running student jobs normally prepare a short description of the job control cards usually required for student programs. The inside back cover of this text provides a space for you to summarize these requirements.

The output from compilation of a FORTRAN program will vary depending on (1) whether or not the job ran successfully to completion or was aborted because of an error and (2) what output options have been selected by the job control cards. The output from compilation may have a first or top sheet with data required for returning the job (job number, name of programmer, etc.) as well as summary job statistics and an end-of-job message. Following this output, there is a listing of the FORTRAN program along with error messages, if any. The last output will be the results from the execution of the program, if any. There are optional elements used by advanced programmers as aids in debugging program errors that may not have been detected by the compiler. Since most errors made by beginning programmers are detectable by the compiler, the beginning programmer can generally rely on messages generated during attempted compilation and can ignore the optional debugging output.

Compilers will detect most errors made by student programmers because most student errors are made in program statement syntax—errors in punctuation, spelling, spacing, and omission of necessary elements. Two methods of indicating the location of error entries are used: (1) the compiler numbers each source program line and generates at the end of the program a list of the numbered lines having errors, with related error messages, or (2) as errors are detected, the diagnostic messages or codes are printed close to the source program lines. Many compilers also print warning messages that alert the programmer to possible errors.

A program may be compiled without error diagnostics and yet not be correct; it may still have incomplete or incorrect program logic. Completion of the program requires testing of program logic and removing errors. Documentation of the program also needs to be completed. Testing and documentation will be explained in subsequent chapters.

Self-testing exercise 1-2

1 What is the purpose of coding a C or * in column 1 of a line on the FORTRAN coding form?

2 Every batch job run on the computer must have job control instructions (cards) that provide specifications for the _____

_____.

3 For a common computer program job of compilation and immediate execution, what is the order of the following elements of the job deck (assuming input via punched cards)?
(a) Data cards
(b) End-of-job cards
(c) FORTRAN program cards
(d) Beginning-of-job cards
(e) End-of-program control cards

4 Compilers will detect errors made by student programmers because most errors they make are _____ (punctuation, spelling, etc.) rather than program logic errors.

Five FORTRAN statements for writing a simple program

In order to get started, five FORTRAN statements will be explained. These are sufficient to write a simple but complete FORTRAN program.

1 List-directed input (free format READ)
2 List-directed output (PRINT in preset format)
3 Arithmetic assignment statement

4   STOP

5   END

In using these instructions, it will be necessary to refer to data items. Data items can be constants, which have the same value throughout the program, or variables, which can assume different values. Therefore, before explaining the five statements, the FORTRAN rules for writing and referencing data items will be discussed.

Variables and constants

In simple formulas and computations, there are two classes of data—constants and variables. These terms are used in FORTRAN in the same sense as in mathematical notation.

1   A *constant* is a quantity that does not change; thus, the value itself can be written. Examples are 3.1416, 5, and 0.06.

2   A *variable* is a representation for a quantity which is not known or can vary in different problems. In mathematics, a variable is represented by a one-character name, such as a, α, χ. In FORTRAN, a variable quantity is represented by a name from one to six characters, such as A, ALPHA, X1.

There is a direct correspondence between constants and variables in a mathematical formula and in the coding of a computation in FORTRAN.

Mathematical formula

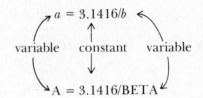

$$a = 3.1416/b$$

variable   constant   variable

FORTRAN statement   A = 3.1416/BETA

Thus, in general, if a variable is used in the mathematical formula, a variable name is used in FORTRAN; if a constant is used in the mathematical formulation, a constant is written in the FORTRAN statement. In some cases, a constant is given a name (such as k) in a mathematical formula to make the formula more general. In FORTRAN, such a constant can be represented by the constant value itself, or a variable name can be defined and given the constant value.

In a mathematical formula, the variable represents an abstract number. In FORTRAN, the variable name identifies the contents of a storage location. The storage location can be thought of as a box or pigeon hole in which data may be placed. When the variable is specified in a FORTRAN statement, the contents of the box are used (but not altered by the use). When a new value for the variable is computed, it replaces the previous contents. This distinction between the abstract mathematical variable and the FORTRAN variable name as identifier for the contents of a storage location is not important at this point. It will, however, be useful in understanding some FORTRAN programming practices to be presented in later chapters.

21

In solving problems, there is frequently a need to distinguish between data having only integer values and real data, which may have a fractional part. In FORTRAN, the distinction between integer-type and real-type data is important.

1 *Integer-type data* Data having only integer (whole number) values. Examples are 3, 719, and 64; note that no decimal point is used because no fractional part is to be represented.

2 *Real-type data* Data having a fractional part. Examples are 3.17, 46.5, 15.0, 11., and .091. Note that a decimal point is used even if the fractional portion is zero and not shown (such as 11. above). It is good practice to use the explicit zero in writing real quantities without a fractional part; for example, use 11.0 instead of 11. and 0.2 instead of .2 where there is no integer part. It is also good practice to code zero as 0.0 instead of 0 alone to reduce misperception by readers of the program.

There are both mathematical and practical reasons for the distinction between integer values and real values. An integer value is given an exact representation in the computer; a real value is an approximation because the computer binary coding of decimal values in some cases does not give an exact representation. This will be discussed in more detail later. For most problems, the distinction is simply whole numbers only for integer-type data and fractional part allowed for real data. A practical reason for integer data is that many procedures require integer values. Repeating a computation is done 3, 4, or N times (integers), but not a fractional number of times, such as 3.1

FORTRAN has specific rules for differentiating between names for real variables and names for integer variables. These are summarized below. There are also specific rules for integer and real constants.

Before describing the rules for writing constants, the use of exponent notation in FORTRAN will be explained. The use of exponent notation is com-

RULES FOR SYMBOLIC VARIABLE NAMES

Purpose of variable name
To associate a symbolic name with an unknown or variable value.

Rules for forming
1 First character must be alphabetic.
2 No special characters are allowed (that is, the names can contain only letters and numbers, not &, $, #, etc.). Blank spaces in a name are ignored.
3 The total number of characters must not exceed 6.

Implicit type for variables
The first letter of a variable name identifies the type of numeric data to be associated with the variable name. This implicit typing can be altered by such statements as the explicit-type declaration to be defined later.

Integer variable names
Start with one of the letters I, J, K, L, M, or N. (*HINT:* The first two letters in the word INTEGER are the bounds for the integer variable names, which are from I through N.)

Real variable names
Start with one of the letters other than I, J, K, L, M, or N. In other words, names starting with A through H and O through Z are real variable names.

EXAMPLES

Quiz

Variable name	Valid or not valid	If valid, integer or real	If not valid, why
X	Valid	Real	
X123	Valid	Real	
XY	Valid	Real	
ALPHA	Valid	Real	
BETA-3	Not valid		(-) is special character
$134	Not valid		$ is special character
X19.1	Not valid		(.) is special character
NUTS	Valid	Integer	
MOTHERS	Not valid		Too many characters
MOM	Valid	Integer	
RATE	Valid	Real	
1455A	Not valid		Does not start with alphabetic character
PAY DAY	Valid (equivalent to PAYDAY since blanks are ignored)		

mon in mathematics. For example, 315 billion (315,000,000,000) can be written as 315×10^9. The exponent notation is used whenever very large or very small numbers are to be written, but not all digits need be represented. In FORTRAN, the letter E as a separator between the number and the exponent ($\pm$nn) is used instead of 10. In other words, 315 billion may be written in FORTRAN as 315.0E + 09. The zero following the decimal, the plus sign in front of the exponent, and the zero in front of the 9, are optional; for example, 315.E + 9 is also correct. A decimal point is not required in the value; for example, 315.E + 9 and 315E + 9 are both correct forms of a real constant. In writing a quantity in E format, the significant digits of the number (sometimes referred to as the fraction or characteristic) can have any scaling desired, but the exponent ($\pm$nn) must reflect the scaling. For example, the following are identical in value.

31.5E + 10

3.15E + 11

.315E + 12

A negative 315 billion would have the sign in front (-315.0E + 9). Note that E does not mean exponentiation of the constant by the value following E, but means to scale the constant by powers of 10. Thus, 3.0E2 does not mean 3^2; it means 3.0×10^2, or 3.0×100, or 300. To interpret any E form, multiply the fraction by the power of 10 ($\pm$nn) following E. This is the same as moving the decimal point nn places to the right for a positive exponent and nn places to the left for a negative exponent. The plus sign on the exponent is optional, but we recommend it be used for clarity.

Number in E format	Stated in mathematical form	Quantity being represented
1.31756E + 10	1.31756×10^{10}	13175600000.
1.31756E - 5	1.31756×10^{-5}	.0000131756

RULES FOR CONSTANTS

Purpose of constant
To write a specific number in the program. Two types are used—integer (fixed point) and real (floating point).

General rules for forming constants
1 The decimal digits 0 and 9 are used to form a constant.
2 The minus sign must be used for a negative constant; an unsigned constant is considered positive; a plus sign is optional.
3 The size of a constant is limited to either a maximum number of digits or a maximum magnitude. There is a considerable range in allowable sizes for different computers.
4 Spaces within a constant are allowed, but their use is discouraged because it can be error-prone.

Rules for forming an integer constant
1 A constant *without* a decimal point.
2 Size limit ranging from 6 to about 10 digits. All processors accept at least six digits and most allow more.

Rules for forming a real constant
1 A constant *with* a decimal point.
2 All processors accept real constants with up to eight digits. Most processors accept more digits.

Rules for exponent form of real constant
If the quantity to be represented is larger or smaller than the allowed number of digits can represent, a special exponent form is used. The form consists of a number with or without a decimal point in it followed by the letter E and an optionally signed integer exponent. A positive exponent means the actual decimal point should be moved the number of places to the right specified by the integer. A minus exponent moves the decimal point to the left. This corresponds to scientific exponent notation. The limits of the exponent vary with different computers, but all accept E forms with a magnitude between 10^{38} 10^{-38} and most allow much larger exponents.

EXAMPLES

Constant	Valid or not valid	If valid, integer (I) or real (R); if not valid, why
123	Valid	I
123.	Valid	R
123.0	Valid	R
12 3	Valid, but blank not recommended (and may be invalid in older versions of FORTRAN)	I
123.E + 13	Valid	R (exponent form)
123.E − 13	Valid	R (exponent form)
3.141769984376432	Uncertain	May have too many digits
987.4E + 299	Uncertain	Exponent may be too large

As indicated by the rules for constants and variables, different FORTRAN processors may have different limits for the number of characters in a constant, the size of the exponent in the exponent form, etc. The inside back cover of this text provides a place to record the specifications and limits for the FORTRAN compiler you are using.

Self-testing exercise 1-3

1 What is the purpose of the variable name in FORTRAN and what is the difference between a variable and a constant?

2 What are the rules for naming a real variable?

3 What is the purpose of the E format for expressing quantities in FORTRAN?

4 In mathematical notation, *ab* means $a \times b$. What does AB stand for in FORTRAN?

5 Fill in the following table for constants and variables. If a form is invalid for most implementations but may be valid for some, note this difference.

	Valid or not valid	If valid, constant or variable	Integer or real type	If invalid, why
(a) FATHERS				
(b) DAD-O				
(c) FICA				
(d) INTR				
(e) F145				
(f) ABLE				
(g) X-14				
(h) 19E25				
(i) 18.47				
(j) 19876.45110				
(k) 98				
(l) 19875694315				

List-directed input statement

The FORTRAN program, if it needs data not included in the program statements, must read data. The data to be read may be part of a job deck submitted with a batch job, part of the data entered at a terminal, or part of a data file previously prepared and stored by the computer. The data items are not provided automatically to the program; the program must read them as needed. There are a number of instructions for use in reading data; the simplest is the list-directed input statement.

List-directed input will be used in Chapters 1 and 2. Additional input features will be explained in Chapters 3 and 6. The basic format of the list-directed input statement (also called free format READ) is shown in the box.

> **LIST-DIRECTED INPUT STATEMENT**
>
> READ *, v_1, v_2, . . . , v_n
>
> where v_1 = variable name that references first input data item, v_2 the second input data item, etc. The input data items must be separated by a comma or spaces. Integer values should have no decimal point; real values without a fractional part may have a decimal point, but it is not required (although we recommend it). Large values or very small values may be input in E exponent form.
>
> In some limited versions of FORTRAN, list-directed input may not be implemented. (If not available to you, see the section at end of this chapter.)

In order to understand how the list-directed READ works, assume three data items are to be read from a punched card. When data items are to be read, the programmer assigns each data item a symbolic variable name, say A, B, and I. A program statement to read the three values is written as follows:

This statement reads the three values from the punched card and places them in the storage locations reserved by the program for values of A, B, and I. Note that the first two values are real (with decimal points), and that the third is integer type. The space between the word READ and the asterisk is optional; we favor it for the sake of clarity. Additional spaces could be added between items in this list, but this is not usually done.

The order of the variable names in the READ statement must correspond to the order in which the data appears in the data card. The data items are punched into a punched card with either a comma or one or more spaces between them (Figure 1-6). Decimal points are also punched for real quantities, as are minus signs in front of negative quantities. Leading zeros and/or plus signs may be used in front of the first digit (but are not required). Large numbers or very small numbers may be input in exponent form.

List-directed output statement

The results of a FORTRAN program are not automatically printed. The program must include statements to specify the data items to be printed, the

Figure 1-6
Punched card with three data items to be read by list-directed READ.

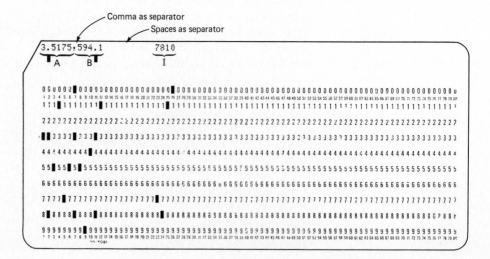

order in which these are to be printed, and labels, headings, etc., to identify output. The simplest instruction for printing output is the list-directed output statement. Other, more flexible output statements will be explained in Chapter 3.

The list-directed output statements specifies the variables whose values are to be printed out by listing the symbolic names for the variables. The values are printed in a standard preformatted way—generally in preset positions on the printer paper. Decimal points and minus signs will be printed where necessary. The basic form of the list-directed output is shown in the box.

LIST-DIRECTED OUTPUT

PRINT *, v_1, v_2, . . . , v_n

where v equals a variable name associated with a stored quantity or is a set of characters enclosed in apostrophes. The values are printed in preset areas on the output line. A preset maximum number of digits is printed. Trailing zeros may be printed with real data to make the preset number of digits. Exponent (E) form is used to represent values too large or too small for the output area. The first column on each print line is left blank.

In some limited versions of FORTRAN, list-directed output may not be included. (If not available to you, see the section at end of this chapter.)

Since the print positions available for output of a quantity are preset, a large number requiring more digits than are available for output is represented by the E format, in which the symbol E is used to indicate a powers of 10 exponential notation. As explained earlier, the digits following E, if positive, mean the decimal should be moved to the right that many places; if negative, to the left.

In the list-directed output instruction, a heading or label is printed by including it in the list of variables to be printed, preceded and followed by an apostrophe. For example, PRINT *, A, B will print as follows if A = 13.17 and B = 1.09.

```
13.1700     1.09000
```

The statement PRINT *, A, 'SUM', B will print:

```
13.1700     SUM  1.09000
```

To understand the typical operation of the list-directed output statement PRINT*, imagine that each line of output consists of a blank space in the first position as well as a set of areas or print fields for the rest of the line. All fields of the same type are of the same size. Each of the numeric data items being output is printed within the area of a fixed-size field. The computer automatically positions the value being printed in the field. Unused spaces in the field are left blank.

Spaces in the field are left blank.

Blank

Output line with fixed-size fields for use in printing numeric data items.

The size of the field places a limit on the number of digits that can be printed for a value. The maximum number of digits, the field size, and positioning within fields are not standardized. These may differ among implementations of FORTRAN. Observe the results from your compiler. As an example, a reasonable specification, assume a field size of 13 and a maximum of six significant digits that are printed for each numeric data item. Positioning within a field may be performed using rules such as the following (for a 13-position field):

1 *Integer data* Right-justify and leave six extra spaces at the left side of field.
2 *Real data* Start at the left of field with a blank divider space plus one space for a sign. The real value being printed takes seven spaces (six digits and a decimal point), leaving four blank spaces to the right of the field.
3 *Exponent form* Leave one blank divider space to the left, a position for sign, six digits with a decimal, one space for letter E to indicate exponent, sign of exponent (+ or −), and a two-digit exponent.

As an example of a preset maximum of six significant digits and a preset field size of 13 spaces, the following statement causes printing in columns as shown (assuming IX = 57, X = − 19.7764, and Y = 6.87580E + 06):

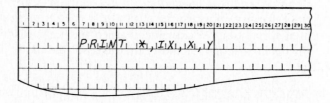

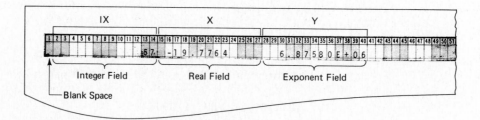

The preceding explanation for numeric data items did not include character output for labels, headings, etc. Characters are specified for printout by their inclusion in the output list before or after the variable they are to precede or follow. As noted, characters are enclosed in apostrophes, which are not printed. As with numeric data, there are no standards for positioning list-directed character output. But, in general, character data will use only the number of spaces required for the characters to be printed. If character data is printed before any numeric data, it will start in the second position on the line (because the first position is left blank in list-directed output). If character data follows numeric data, the characters are printed after the end of the numeric field. For example, using b to indicate a space,

```
PRINT *, 'HOW NOW'
bHOW NOW
PRINT *, X, 'PROFIT'
[if X = 1317.05]
bbb1317.05bbbbPROFIT
PRINT *, IDATE, 'PROFIT', X
[if IDATE = 1982]
bbbbbbbbbb1982PROFITbb1317.05
PRINT *, IDATE, 'bPROFIT', X
bbbbbbbbbb1982bPROFITbb1317.05
```

The third example illustrates the effect of right justification of integer output with no space before (or after) character data output. In the fourth example, a space is inserted between the integer data and the character output by including the space as a character output.

Prompting of input from a terminal

When a program is entered from a terminal and executed interactively, input data must also be entered from the terminal. But how does the terminal operator know when and in what form to enter data? In general, a READ statement that would read data from a punched card in batch operation is interpreted in interactive terminal operation as accepting an input from the terminal. The computer prompts the terminal operator to input the data by printing a prompt character or message. Generally, this is a question mark. The computer then waits for the operator to enter the data and hit the return key to indicate that the data is ready to enter. The program accepts and processes the input data. The difficulty is that the operator may not know or may have forgotten the specifications for the inputs. Or, there may be more than one input and the general prompt character does not specify the one that is required. As a general practice, it is desirable to print a message before an input prompt to describe to the terminal operator the input to be entered. For example, if the operator enters the date and the latest interest rate being paid by the government for Treasury bills, the program might contain PRINT and READ statements as follows.

```
PRINT *, 'ENTER TODAY'S DATE IN FORM YYMMDD.'
PRINT *, 'ENTER MOST RECENT T-BILL RATE IN FORM XX.XX.'
PRINT *, 'SEPARATE INPUTS BY SPACES OR BY A COMMA.'
READ *, IDATE, TRATE
```

When the program executes, it prints the message and then gives the prompt character.

```
ENTER TODAY'S DATE IN FORM YYMMDD.
ENTER MOST RECENT T-BILL RATE IN FORM XX.XX.
SEPARATE INPUTS BY SPACES OR BY A COMMA.
```

29

The terminal operator enters the data following the prompt character.

? 820118 13.05   (Hit RETURN key to send data to computer)

In summary, an important difference in good programming practice when programming for interactive execution as compared to batch execution is the use of messages before input prompts to describe the data to be entered and its form (if not clear from the context). See Appendix B for further suggestions for interactive programming.

Arithmetic assignment statements

Having described how to use a list-directed **READ** statement to input data items and a list-directed **PRINT** to output values, the next requirement is to process the input data to produce values for output. The basic statement for describing arithmetic operations is the assignment statement. Such a statement is of the general form:

$v = e$

where v stands for a variable name and e stands for an arithmetic expression. The expression consists of one or more variable names and/or constants connected by operation symbols.

Examples

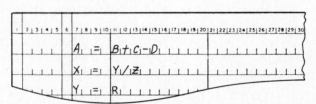

The form $v = e$ does not necessarily mean that v is equal to e. It directs the computer to replace the previous value of the variable on the left side of the equals sign with the results of the expression on the right. Or, in other words, it assigns the value of the expression on the right to the variable name on the left of the equals sign. Thus, a statement $X = X + 1.0$ means that the value of X is increased by the constant 1.0, and that this new value is assigned to (stored at) X. If X is referred to later in the program, the new value is the one made available. Because the computer executes the expression on the right side of the equals sign and then stores the result at the location of the variable on the left, having anything but a variable name to the left of the equals sign is illegal.

The operation symbols used in an assignment statement are those normally used in mathematics, except for multiplication and exponentiation, which make use of the asterisk.

The compiler ignores spaces before or after operation symbols and before or after the variable names and other operands. Thus, $K=A+B+C$ is equivalent to $K = A + B + C$. The use of spaces may add clarity for the reader. The multiplication operator must be used; it cannot be implied as is often done in mathematical notation; for example, ab meaning $a \times b$ must be written in FORTRAN as $A * B$.

In a mathematical expression, there is an accepted notational form that spe-

OPERATION SYMBOLS

Symbol	Stands for	Example
+	Addition	A + B
−	Subtraction	A − B
	or negation	− A
/	Division	A/B
*	Multiplication	A * B
**	Exponentiation	A**B

cifies the order in which the operations are to be performed. For example, $X + (Y/Z)$ is not the same as $(X + Y)/Z$. In the first instance, Y is divided by Z, and the result is added to X; in the second, X is added to Y, and the result is divided by Z. In some cases, the order of operation is not important because operations are commutative. Thus, $X = A + B + C - D$ can be performed in any order, and the results will be identical. The most common mathematical notation uses parentheses to specify the order of computation.

FORTRAN uses both a precedence rule and a parentheses rule to specify the way an arithmetic expression is to be handled. The *precedence rule* states that all exponentiation will be performed first, all multiplication and division next, and all addition and subtraction last. Where the precedence of operations is the same, such as in multiplication and division, the operations will be performed in order from left to right.

The *parentheses rule* states that operations will be performed in the inner-most set of parentheses first (using the precedence rule where appropriate) and then in the next set, etc., until all operations inside parentheses have been performed. Then the remaining operations in the expression are carried out according to the precedence rule.

Parentheses should be used freely. If redundant, they do no harm, and they improve the readability and maintainability of the program. It is better to be explicit by using parentheses than to rely on the precedence rule. Parentheses are also used to avoid having two operation symbols together. It is illegal to write A* − B, where the minus sign is a sign relating to B. Using parentheses to separate the two operation symbols makes the expression valid: A*(− B). Parentheses are always used in pairs. A common error in writing FORTRAN is to forget the closing parenthesis.

EXAMPLES

Know

No implied function

FORTRAN	Formula
X = A + B/C − D**2	$x = a + \dfrac{b}{c} - d^2$
X = (A + B)/(C + D)	$x = \dfrac{a + b}{c + d}$
X = (A + B)/C + D	$x = \dfrac{a + b}{c} + d$
X = A * B * C + 1.5	$x = abc + 1.5$
X = (A * B * C) + 1.5	$x = abc + 1.5$
X = (A * B) * (C + 1.5)	$x = (ab)(c + 1.5)$
X = A**Z + 1.0	$x = a^z + 1.0$
X = A**(Z + 1.0)	$x = a^{z+1}$

The rules for forming arithmetic expressions and statements can now be summarized. The student should pay particular attention to the precedence rules.

RULES FOR FORMING ARITHMETIC STATEMENTS

1 The general form of an arithmetic statement is $v = e$, where v stands for any variable name and e stands for an arithmetic expression.

2 The portion of the arithmetic statement to the left of the equals sign is a variable name. It must not be a constant nor contain arithmetic operations.

3 The equals sign means "assign as the value of the variable on the left the result of the expression on the right." It is not an equality sign in the mathematical sense.

4 Two operation symbols may not be used next to each other (except for two asterisks, which mean exponentiation).

5 Spaces may be used whenever desired to improve readability. The compiler ignores them.

6 Parentheses are used to specify order of operation and to avoid the two-operation symbol restriction. Operations inside parentheses are performed first. Parentheses must always be used in pairs.

7 In the absence of parentheses, the precedence rule for performing arithmetic operations specifies the order. Within one of the precedence levels, the operations are performed from left to right. The precedence rule is exponentiation first, multiplication and division second, and addition, subtraction, or negation third.

As explained earlier, real-type variables or constants may have a fractional part; an integer variable or integer constant cannot have a fractional part. In arithmetic operations involving integer data, the result cannot have a fractional part. This will receive further explanation in Chapter 2, but it suggests that mixing data of different types must be done with caution. For this chapter, the student should avoid possible problems in writing the assigned program by not using any integer variables or integer constants in arithmetic assignment statements. Make all variables and all constants real. An exception may be made in the case of exponents that are whole numbers. In other words, X**2 or X**N can be used, but write X**0.2 instead of X**(1/5). There are no restrictions on integer data used for identification purposes and not included in an arithmetic expression.

STOP and END statements

The STOP statement is used to specify that the program execution is to be terminated. The END statement is the last statement in the program. It signals the end of the program unit, and consists only of the word END.

The difference between STOP and END is that STOP is an instruction to stop the program when it is being executed, whereas END is an instruction to the compiler that there are no more statements in the program unit.

In a simple program the next to last statement will be STOP, the last statement will be END.

STOP and END STATEMENTS

STOP   Stops execution of the program

END   The last statement in a program

Blank spaces in FORTRAN statements and data

The use of blanks or spaces in writing FORTRAN is sometimes confusing to beginning programmers. Rules and recommended practices are therefore summarized for review.

BLANKS IN FORTRAN

Blanks are ignored in the following situations:

1 Blanks imbedded in a constant

   X = 3.1751   and   X = 3.1   751

are interpreted the same. However, for clarity of programming, do not imbed blanks.

2 Blanks in a statement number field (columns 1–5)

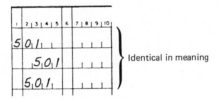

Identical in meaning

Recommended form is right-justified (blanks to left) as in the second example.

3 Blanks before or after FORTRAN words, parentheses, and symbols. Use or omit blanks to improve readability. The following pairs are identical to FORTRAN:

Blanks	No blanks
X = Y / Z	X=Y/Z
PRINT *, X, Y	PRINT*,X,Y

4 Blanks imbedded in a variable name are ignored, but we recommend they not be used.

Blanks are important in the following cases:

1 For list-directed input, one or more blanks or a comma are used to separate data items. The following are identical input data:

   93.17, 45

   93.17 45

2 For input, blanks cannot be imbedded in a data item. The value 93.176 cannot be input as 93.1   76

3 For character input or output, blanks are treated the same as other characters. For example, in the following statement, the blanks inside the apostrophes are characters the same as N, O, etc.

   PRINT *, 'NOW IS THE TIME'

Self-testing exercise 1-4

1 Write FORTRAN statements for each of the following formulas, using sufficient parentheses to make the statement execution precedence very clear.

(a) $x = \dfrac{a}{b} + c$

(b) $x = \dfrac{3y^2}{z^2}$

(c) $x = a^b + \dfrac{d}{e}$

(d) $x = \left(\dfrac{a}{b}\right) cd$

(e) $x = \dfrac{a + b}{c + d}$

2 Rewrite the following FORTRAN statements, eliminating the redundant parentheses used for clarity:

Formula	FORTRAN
(a) $x = \dfrac{a + b}{ef}$	X = (A + B)/(E * F)
(b) $x = abc + 1$	X = (A * B * C) + 1.0
(c) $x = \left(\dfrac{ab}{c}\right) d$	X = ((A * B)/C) * D

3 Write FORTRAN statements to perform the following:
(a) Read the values for A, B, and D from a punched card.
(b) Print the values for A, B, and D but in the order B, A, D.
(c) Print the value for A plus the words IS ALL.
(d) Stop the program.
(e) Identify the end of the program statements.
(f) Read values for C and D from an input data card. Print the inputs for visual inspection along with a label C before the value of C and a label D before the value of D.

Summary

FORTRAN is one of the most-used high-level languages for programming a computer. It is used primarily for formula-type problems, such as mathematical solutions, engineering analysis, statistical processing, and economic analysis. In designing and writing FORTRAN programs, the result will generally be improved if a disciplined style of design and coding is used. This will include the division of the program into logical modules and adherence to coding rules that emphasize the program structure. The program will generally contain logical modules to perform initialization, input, input validation, processing, normal output, error output, and termination procedures.

Overall program structure can be planned by considering the outputs to be prepared, the inputs needed to produce the outputs, and the processes to produce outputs from inputs. The design of a FORTRAN program logic can usually make effective use of a program flowchart and/or program design language. Special coding paper is recommended for use in writing FORTRAN statements, and it is recommended that standard conventions for handprinting be followed.

In order to compile and execute a FORTRAN program on punched cards, it will be necessary to obtain the job control cards to place with the program and data. If programming is done with a terminal, special terminal instructions must be followed.

Five FORTRAN statements were explained in the chapter: list-directed input, list-directed output, arithmetic assignment, STOP, and END. These five statements are sufficient for writing simple but complete FORTRAN programs.

Answers to self-testing exercises

Exercise 1-1

1 Hardware is the computer equipment; software consists of the operating system, compilers, application programs, and other sets of computer routines to direct the operation of the equipment.

2 A program exists in primary storage in machine language. This is the language the computer actually uses. A symbolic assembly language is a language for symbolically describing the parts of a machine-language instruction. The symbolic assembly language is easier to code and read than machine language and is directly translatable into machine-language instructions by the symbolic assembly system. (Generally, one symbolic assembly instruction is translated into one machine-language instruction.)

3 Compared to symbolic assembly languages, high-level languages such as FORTRAN are machine-independent (in the sense that they can be compiled and run with little or no changes on any computer having a compiler for the language); they are relatively easy to learn because they use formula-like instructions, require fewer instructions, provide more understandable documentation, and are easier to test and debug.

4 FORmula TRANslator

5 ANSI has established a standard language set for FORTRAN, divided into two different levels of implementation.

6 (a) Meet user needs
(b) Development on time within budget
(c) Error-free set of instructions
(d) Error-resistant operation
(e) Maintainable programs
(f) Portable programs

7 (a) Initialization
(b) Input
(c) Input data validation
(d) Processing
(e) Output
(f) Error handling
(g) Closing procedure

8 (a) Sequence. One action followed by another.
(b) Selection. Test for a condition followed by two alternative program paths.
(c) Repetition. A set of operations is repeated while some condition continues to be true.

9 (a) 2   (b) 4   (c) 5   (d) 1   (e) 6   (f) 3

10 Portable

11 Flowcharts and/or program design language (pseudocode)

12 An orderly sequence of steps can consist of the following:
(*a*) Define requirements in terms of outputs.
(*b*) Based on the outputs, define inputs.
(*c*) Define input validation and input error handling.
(*d*) Define procedures for transforming input data into output.
(*e*) Define the program structure in terms of major modules.

Exercise 1-2

1 The character C or * in column 1 means that the line is a comment line in the program and not an instruction to be translated.

2 Operating system

3 d, c, e, a, b

4 Syntactical (or syntax)

Exercise 1-3

1 The variable name is used to specify a value that can change with each execution of the program. The variable name identifies the location where the value is stored. Whereas a variable represents a quantity that is unknown or may change in value during the program, a constant is used to write a specific, unchanging value in the program.

2 The name begins with the letter A to H or O to Z and may contain up to six alphabetic characters and numeric digits. No special characters are allowed.

3 The E format is used to represent very large and very small numbers.

4 AB is a FORTRAN variable name for a real variable.

5

Valid or not valid	If valid, constant or variable	Integer or real type	If not valid, why
(*a*) Not valid	—	—	Too many characters
(*b*) Not valid	—	—	Special character not allowed
(*c*) Valid	Variable	Real	
(*d*) Valid	Variable	Integer	
(*e*) Valid	Variable	Real	
(*f*) Valid	Variable	Real	
(*g*) Not valid			Special character (-) not allowed
(*h*) Valid (decimal point and sign optional with exponent form of real constant)	Constant	Real	
(*i*) Valid	Constant	Real	
(*j*) Not valid (for most implementations)			Too large
(*k*) Valid	Constant	Integer	
(*l*) Not valid (for most implementations)			Too large

Exercise 1-4

1 (a) X = A/B + C

(b) X = 3.0 * Y**2/Z**2 but better as X = (3.0 * (Y**2)/(Z**2)

(c) X = A**B + D/E or X = A**B + (D/E)

(d) X = A/B * C * D but better as X = (A/B) * C * D

(e) X = (A + B)/(C + D)

2 (a) All are necessary.   (b) A * B * C + 1.0   (c) A * B/C * D

3 (a) READ *, A, B, D

(b) PRINT *, B, A, D

(c) PRINT *, A, 'IS ALL'

(d) STOP

(e) END

(f) READ *, C, D

PRINT *, 'C' , C, 'D' , D

If C has a value of 12.1 and D has a value of 98.13, the output will be:

C 12.1000 D 98.1300

Questions and problems

1 Define the following terms:

(a) application program

(b) compiler

(c) flowchart

(d) hardware

(e) high-level language

(f) job control cards

(g) machine-oriented language

(h) object program

(i) program module

(j) program design language

(k) routine

(l) software

(m) source program

(n) structured program

(o) symbolic assembly system

2 What are the hardware elements of a computer system?

3 What is the main difference between a machine-oriented language and a high-level language?

4 List and describe the main steps in developing a FORTRAN program.

5 Fill in the following table.

	Valid or not valid	Constant or variable	Integer or real type	If not valid, why
(a) MAN				
(b) WOMAN				
(c) X − 19				
(d) RATE				
(e) I				
(f) OUTPUT				
(g) 9FOUR				
(h) DOLL				
(i) 18.97				
(j) BETA				
(k) J19				
(l) 134.1E19				
(m) 1.9E − 20				

6 Assume three variables A, B, C. Indicate whether each of the following statements is valid. If not valid, explain.

(a) `READ *, A, B, C`
(b) `PRINT ABC`
(c) `READ A, B, C`
(d) `PRINT *, A, TOTAL IS, B`
(e) `PRINT 'THE SUM IS' , A`

7 Rewrite the following as FORTRAN statements. Use sufficient parentheses to make the order of operations clear.

(a) $x = \dfrac{a + b}{c}$

(b) $x = \dfrac{c + d}{f + g}$

(c) $x = (a^c)(d + f)$

(d) $x = (a^c)(b^d)$

(e) $x = a + b - c$

Section only for those using FORTRAN versions without list-directed input and output

Chapters 1 and 2 use only list-directed input and output because this simplifies the learning of the language. However, many older FORTRAN versions (or restricted versions, such as 1977 Standard Subset FORTRAN) do not include the list-directed input and output. For those students using compilers without these list-directed instructions, the problems in Chapters 1B and 2B require a change in the input and output instructions. Each input or output will require a pair of instructions, the first being an input or output instruction in a slightly different form and the second a FORMAT statement. The general form is:

READ(*u,fs*) list of variables separated by commas

fs FORMAT(list of specifications)

WRITE(*u,fs*) list of variables separated by commas

fs FORMAT(list of specifications)

where u is a unit number assigned by the installation to the card reader or printer and fs is a statement number.

Since these instructions will be explained fully in Chapter 3, two pairs of general-purpose statements will be given here for use with programs in Chapters 1B and 2B.

1 Statements to be used with problems having no integer variables to input or output:

To read:		READ(5,8001)	*list of real variables*	
	8001	FORMAT(18F10.0)		
To write:		WRITE(6,8002)	*list of real variables*	
	8002	FORMAT(18E16.8)		

To use these statements, the input data must be punched with a decimal point in fields of 10 in the input card, that is, the first data item is in columns 1 to 10, the second in columns 11 to 20, etc. The unit numbers 5 (for card reader) and 6 (for printer) may be different for different computers (for example, 1 and 3). The instructor will furnish the unit numbers for you to use. Output will all be in E format with no provisions for descriptive labels. These statements apply to all problems in Chapter 1B except 2 and 13, and for all problems except 2 and 6 in Chapter 2B. (Both this and the next set of statements apply to 9, 11, 13, 14, and 15 in Chapter 2B.)

2 Statements to be used with input or output of one integer variable as the first variable in the list and the remaining variables as real variables:

To read:		READ(5,8003)	*integer variable, real variables*	
	8003	FORMAT(I10,17F10.0)		
To write:		WRITE(6,8004)	*integer variable, real variables*	
	8004	FORMAT(I10,17E16.8)		

On input, the first data item must be in columns 1 to 10 without a decimal and with any extra spaces to the left. The remaining variables are in fields of 10 with a decimal point in each data item. The first output item will be an integer variable; the remaining items will be in E format. There is no provision for descriptive labels on the output. These statements apply only to problems with one integer input and one integer output. Since all variables may be given real names and input as real numbers, these statements are optional but fit the nature of the problem for 2 and 13 in Chapter 1B and for 2, 6, 9, 11, 13, 14, and 15 in Chapter 2B.

chapter **1B**

Example programs and programming exercises to read, compute, and print

Chapter 1A contained a descriptive and conceptual introduction to programming, programming discipline, and the FORTRAN language. Five FORTRAN instructions were explained. These instructions are sufficient to write simple programs using the sequence programming structure.

Chapter 1B consists of two complete examples of programs (using the features and the five statements explained in Chapter 1A) as well as programming exercises. The programming exercises provide a learning experience in following the procedures for writing a FORTRAN program and getting it to run on a specific computer. The student assignment is to:

1 Design a program using both a program design language and a flowchart. Both techniques are assigned to provide experience in these two alternatives.

2 Code the instructions on FORTRAN coding paper. Also code a set of input data.

3 Enter the program into the computer either by (*a*) entering statements at a terminal, or (*b*) keypunching program statements, data for execution, and job control instructions into punched cards and submitting them as a job deck for batch processing.

4 Remove all errors detected during compilation.

5 Execute the program using the data prepared for it.
   (*a*) In a batch job, cards containing the data are included in the job deck.
   (*b*) In a timesharing terminal execution, data items are input during execution.

The emphasis of Chapter 1B is on learning by examining complete example programs and by doing a complete program. This first programming problem not only provides experience with coding a simple FORTRAN program but also assists the student in learning the specific job control instructions and FORTRAN job submission procedures. Because the program is a simple one, the student can concentrate on the structure of a well-written program, on the submission procedures, and interpretation of the output.

General comments on the example programs

There are two example programs for two somewhat different types of problems:

1 *General program 1* Compute an employee paycheck.
2 *Statistical program 1* Calculate the ordinates of the normal curve for two values of the abscissa.

The two programs provide insight into the use of FORTRAN for two different types of problems. Also, some students may be more familiar with one problem area than the other; the two examples allow the student to concentrate on the example in which the problem context is best understood.

Before examining the example programs, the use of line numbers needs to be understood. Two types of line numbers may be encountered:

1   *Statement labels to identify certain statements during execution of the program*   When needed, the statement label is coded in columns 1–5 of the line. The statement label will be explained in Chapter 2. For now, it is sufficient to understand that statement labels, when used, are an integral part of the program.

2   *Line number for identification purposes*   These are not required by the FORTRAN language but are used for convenience or because of operational needs. Two examples are (see Figure 1-7):

(a)   In programming FORTRAN from a terminal, each statement is given a line number because interactive programming requires such an identifier (separate from statement labels). If you enter statements at a terminal, you will need to put a line number before each one, including all comment lines.

(b)   Printouts of the FORTRAN program from the compilation process frequently have line numbers added as a convenience in referring to statements. As examples of this practice, the listings in this text contain line numbers that were added in compilation. Note that the compiler used added line numbers only for executable lines. It did not assign line numbers to the comment lines used for documenting the programs. If you are coding a program to be punched into cards for batch processing, do not code the line identification numbers; these are added by the compiler (in most cases).

Example program structure

Note the structure of the example programs. The structure makes extensive use of comment lines. As explained, a comment line has an asterisk or the letter C in column 1. The * convention is new with 1977 FORTRAN; thus, some older versions of FORTRAN may allow only the C for a comment line.

The structure used in the example programs is recommended for the programs you are to write. This structure is not required by the FORTRAN language; it is recommended as a matter of style in writing clear, understandable,

Figure 1-7
Differences between line numbers and statement labels.

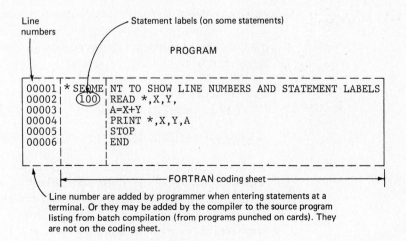

well-documented programs. The style issue becomes more significant as programs become larger and more complex; the style should be followed even in small programs as a learning experience and as a matter of programming discipline. The programs consist of the following blocks of coding:

1 *Program identification*   This block of comments describes the program and identifies the author and the date written. Any special comments regarding the program can be placed here.

2 *Variable identification*   Variable names in FORTRAN are short, and thus have limited capability to describe the variables. In order to fully document the program, there needs to be additional description of the data associated with each variable name. The names themselves should be as descriptive as possible to help the reader of the program remember the purpose of the variable. In addition, every variable name used in the program should be described in a comment statement. When coding a program, a description is written and placed in the variable identification block each time a new variable is used. This will result in the variable identification list being arranged in order by the first use of a variable. It is also a relatively simple matter to rearrange these statements so as to have the list in alphabetical order. Alphabetical arrangement is optional but useful, especially with long lists. For readability, we have chosen to start names in column 11 and to start the definitions in column 21. The variable identification block is for clear program documentation; it does not affect program execution. In large programs, note that the concept of variable identification may be altered slightly. Global variables may be described in a variable identification block for the program; variables applying only within a block may be described in the block description itself.

3 *Constant identification*   It is frequently useful to name constants rather than to employ them directly in the program. It sometimes makes the program easier to understand. Also, changeable constants (such as tax rates) are more easily changed if the constant value is named. This block may be omitted if no constants are named. The block is for documentation purposes.

4 *Initialization*   If constants are named, the values are set by arithmetic assignment statements before any processing. There will be additional instances where initial values need to be set, such as setting variables to zero. This block may be omitted if no initialization is performed.

5 *Processing blocks*   In the simple program, a single processing block may be sufficient. In later programs there will be several separate blocks, such as to read data, validate input data, process, output normal values, output error messages, and terminate the program.

As a matter of style to achieve a readable program, each block is identified by a name, set off by asterisks.

```
**********   PROGRAM IDENTIFICATION   **********
```

We have chosen to have the title for each block begin in column 21 so that it is somewhat centered and stands out. Blank comment lines to visually separate parts of the program begin in column 1 with an asterisk (or C) and end in column 72 with an asterisk. The end of the block is set off by a solid line of asterisks. Other conventions could be used; these are recommended and will be followed in this text.

Comments should be used freely within the processing modules. In order to differentiate comment lines from executable statements, we have chosen to have each set of one or more comment lines preceded and followed by a blank comment line having only an asterisk (or C) in column 1 and an asterisk in column 72. The comment line(s) have asterisks in columns 1 and 72, as well as the comment that begins in column 11. Additional program style conventions will be given in subsequent chapters.

Pseudocode and program flowcharts for example programs

The documentation for each program includes a program design language (pseudocode) description of the program and a program flowchart. Since these programs use only the sequence program structure, the pseudocode description and flowchart are simple and perhaps unnecessary. However, preparation of these forms of documentation in simple situations will provide practice in understanding them and in applying them in more complex programming situations. A programmer would probably not use both a pseudocode description and a program flowchart, but both are included to provide experience in using these alternatives. For this chapter, it is important to read all material for general program example 1 because it contains explanations having general applicability.

General program example 1 — compute employee pay

Problem description for general example 1

The program is to compute an employee's gross pay, taxes, net pay, and average net pay per hour based upon the following factors:

Total hours worked

Wage rate in dollars per hour

Taxes at the rate of 15 percent of gross pay

Pension contribution at the rate of 5 percent of gross pay

Miscellaneous deductions (an input given in dollars)

The input will consist of the employee identification number, hours worked, wage rate, and amount of miscellaneous deductions. The output should show gross pay, taxes, net pay (paycheck), and average rate of net pay per hour. The basic arithmetic operators and list-directed input and output are to be used in this program. Appropriate labels are to be used to identify the outputs. The program is to follow good programming practice for control of input errors. The input is to be checked (validated) by printing out (echoing) the input data for visual inspection.

Program documentation for general example 1

Both forms of program planning documentation are given here—a pseudocode program description (Figure 1-8) and a program flowchart (Figure 1-9).

Figure 1-8
Pseudocode description for planning general program 1—compute employee pay.

```
READ, id, hours, wage rate, deductions
PRINT input variables for visual validation
Gross pay = hours × rate
Taxes    = pay × tax rate of 15%
Net pay  = pay − taxes − misc. deductions − pension contribution of 5% of pay
Av. pay  = net pay ÷ hours
PRINT headings to identify outputs
PRINT gross pay, taxes, net pay, ave. net pay per hour
STOP
```

Figure 1-10 gives a program listing, a sample input, and sample output. Remember that the line numbers are not part of the program as written by the programmer; these were added by the FORTRAN compiler as statement references. Students learning to program frequently find it hard to visualize the steps that produce the results shown in Figure 1-10. Figure 1-11 summarizes the flow of inputs, processes, and outputs for solving a problem using FORTRAN.

Figure 1-9
Flowchart for planning general program 1—compute employee pay.

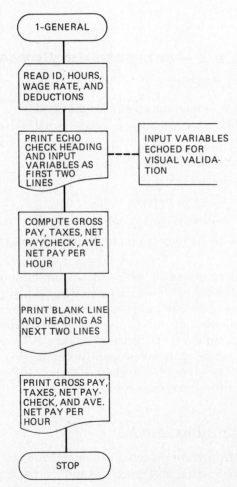

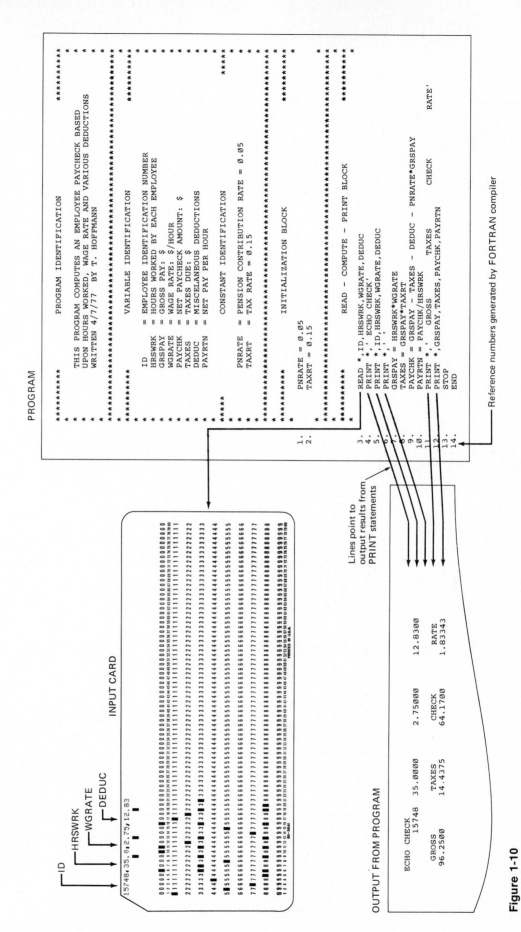

Figure 1-10
Program listing, sample punched-card input, and resulting output for general program 1—compute employee pay.

47

Figure 1-11
Flow of inputs, processes,
and outputs for a
FORTRAN program.

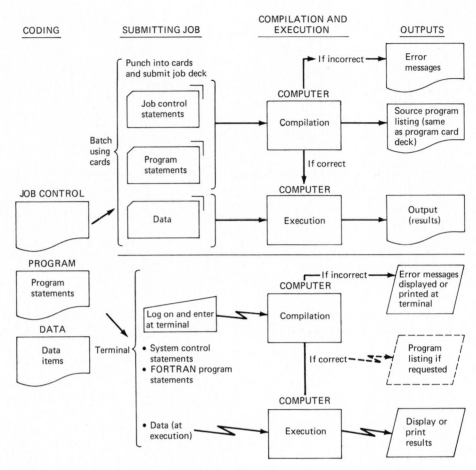

Planning program logic using a program design language

The pseudocode for general example 1 will be used to illustrate the use of a program design language as part of program planning and design. The resulting pseudocode is also useful as documentation of the program. Program planning and design using a program design language is an iterative process starting with a few general statements and expanding these statements as more program details are planned. When program planning and design are completed, program coding is begun. The process is illustrated for general example 1.

1   The major steps in the normal flow of processing by the program are described by general pseudocode statements. In other words, the programmer first plans for normal output with processing of normal, required inputs with no erroneous data or exceptions. Four statements are sufficient to describe the general flow of processing for general example 1:

Read input data
Calculate pay amounts
Print pay amounts
Stop

More detail can be added in the pseudocode if desired. For example, the general pseudocode statements describing the flow of processing can be replaced by statements showing more detail or by sets of statements. The relationship between the pseudocode statements and planned FORTRAN coding may be made explicit by using capital letters for pseudocode words that correspond to actual FORTRAN instruction words.

General pseudocode statement	Detailed pseudocode
Read input data	READ id, hours, wage rate, deductions
Calculate pay amounts	Gross pay = hours × rate
	Taxes = gross pay × tax rate of 15%
	Net pay = gross pay − taxes − deductions − (pension contribution of 5% of pay)
	Ave. net pay per hour = net pay ÷ hours
Print pay amounts	PRINT headings to identify outputs
	PRINT gross pay, taxes, net pay, ave. net pay per hour
Stop	STOP

2   The pseudocode program plan is expanded to include processing that is required in order to validate input data and to handle errors in input data and other exceptions. In the case of general example 1, the input data is to be printed out to allow visual validation. A pseudocode statement to reflect this requirement is:

PRINT input variables for visual validation

The statement is inserted after the statement to read the input variables. The completed plan for the program, written in pseudocode, is shown in Figure 1-8.

There are no standard rules for a program design language for use in planning a FORTRAN program. However, the following suggestions may be useful and will be followed in the text:

1   Each pseudocode statement describes one or more processing steps to be performed. The line is written in a condensed English-like form that also reflects the FORTRAN coding to be done.

2   Pseudocode statements referring to a specific FORTRAN instruction word (such as READ or PRINT) can include the FORTRAN word, which is then written in all capital letters.

3   A reference to a variable can describe it in words (such as sum or sum of pay amounts) or can use a descriptive name that is to be a program variable name (such as SUM or SUMPAY). The variable name in such cases is written in all capital letters. All other words in the pseudocode statement line are lowercase.

Additional pseudocode notation will be explained in later chapters.

Planning program logic using a flowchart

The process of planning and designing a program using a flowchart is similar to the process with a program design language. The major steps and logic of processing can be defined and then expanded. A major difference in using a flowchart compared to pseudocode is that the flow of processing is visually defined by symbols and lines. The symbols may indicate the media or equipment to be used. For the simple processing flow of general example 1, there is little difference between the flowchart and the pseudocode.

The steps in planning a program using a program flowchart are:

1 Define the general flow of the program for achieving desired output from normally expected input data. Use general processing symbols for input, processing, and output. Expand the description to a suitable level of detail.

2 Add processing boxes and processing flow to perform validation of input data and to handle exceptions.

Figure 1-9 shows the flowchart at the end of step 2. The amount of detail to be shown in the boxes should be enough to clearly define what is to be done. The flowchart boxes for reading and printing contain the words READ and PRINT. These words are not necessary because the symbols imply reading from cards or printing on paper; we include them to improve the readability of the flowcharts.

Notes on general example 1

The variable names for this program illustrate the need to choose names that as clearly as possible identify the quantity they represent. Other names might have been used (for example, GROSPY for GRSPAY or IDNUM for ID).

Even in a beginning program there are alternative ways to code statements. For example, each data output could have been printed on a separate line. Note the printing of a space to create a blank line between outputs (line 6 written as PRINT *,' '). The statement PRINT* without the blank enclosed in apostrophes will also print a blank line. Either method is acceptable.

The program also illustrates a good programming practice. Simple input data validation is provided by having a printout (echoing) of all input data. The reader of the output can then visually validate the input data. Other forms of input validation will be explained in a later chapter; but echoing of input data and visual input validation should always be considered in program design.

Another interesting feature of this program is the naming of the two constants—rates for tax and pension. These are constants and need not be named except that rates such as these are subject to change. By naming them, a single change in the initialization block will change the rate throughout the program.

Statistical program example 1 — calculate ordinates of the normal curve

Problem description for statistical example 1

Calculate the ordinates (y values) of the normal curve for two values of the abscissa (x values) and print them out with a simple heading using list-directed input and output. Use approximate values for π and e.

Equation: $y = \dfrac{1}{\sqrt{2\pi}} e^{-(X^2/2)}$

where π is the value for pi and the expression $1/\sqrt{2\pi}$ has an approximate value of 0.3989. e is the base for natural logarithms—a value of 2.7183 can be used for this problem.

Program documentation for statistical example 1

There are a pseudocode description (Figure 1-12), a program flowchart (Figure 1-13), and a program listing (Figure 1-14) with sample output. Input data is printed as part of the output of the results rather than having a separate printout of input data for visual validation.

Two outputs from running the program using two different compilers are shown. These illustrate that the format and precision (number of digits in output) of the result printed by list-directed output will vary among compilers. Precision will be explained further in Chapter 2, and methods for program control of precision in the output will be described in Chapter 3.

Notes on statistical example 1

The names for the values on the ordinates and abscissas could have been more descriptive: for example, ORD1 and ABSC1 might have been used in place of X1 and Y1. However, the equation used X and Y and thus those names were selected. The first X was called X1, the second X2. The second variable is called YTWO (whereas the corresponding X variable was called X2). This was done merely to illustrate alternatives in naming variables. Y2 would have been just as good as YTWO.

There are different ways to write the $e^{-(X^2/2)}$ portion of the equation using only the instructions in Chapter 1A. Four representative ways are shown below; two are used in the example program. Another way, using computer generated values for e instead of 2.7183, will be explained in Chapter 2A.

1 2.7183**((X**2)/(−2.0))

2 2.7183**((−X * X)/2.0)

3 2.7183**(−(X**2)/(2.0))

4 1.0/(2.7183**((X**2)/2.0))

In other words, there are different ways to code the equations, all of which are correct. It is generally preferable to use a straightforward, easily understood formulation.

Figure 1-12
Pseudocode description for planning statistical program 1—compute ordinates of normal curve.

```
Identify values (from math tables) of e and 1/√2π
READ X1, X2
Compute Y1 and Y2
PRINT heading
PRINT X1, Y1
PRINT X2, Y2
STOP
```

Figure 1-13
Program flowchart for planning statistical program 1—compute ordinates of normal curve.

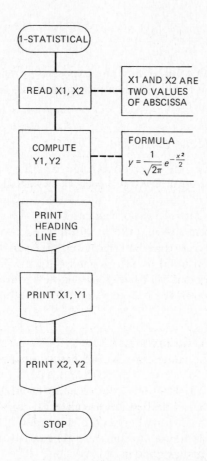

Summary of suggestions for programming style

After having reviewed the two example programs, a set of guidelines for programming style may be summarized. Additional guidelines will be added in later chapters.

GUIDELINES FOR PROGRAMMING STYLE

1 Analyze the problem before beginning to code instructions. If you do not understand the problem and the solution procedure, you cannot tell the computer what to do. Useful design and planning methods are a program design language and program flowcharts. In planning the program logic, follow a systematic approach:
   (*a*) Plan the general logic of processing for producing normally expected output from normally required inputs. Expand to the desired level of detail.
   (*b*) Add processing logic for input validation instructions.
2 Use FORTRAN coding paper to aid in writing instructions in proper format.
3 Use a block structure to divide the program into logical segments. Include an identification block and a list of variables block. The style selected for this text to identify a block is to have a block name line consisting of 10 asterisks, 10 blanks, name of block starting in column 21, and 10 asterisks starting in column 63.
4 Use explanatory comments. Use comments freely inside the blocks. Set off each group of one or more comments by a blank comment line before and after the comment lines. In the text style, the comment is indented to column 11.
5 Use parentheses to avoid ambiguity. Do not rely upon unfamiliar precedence rules.
6 Consider printout (echo) of input data as a visual check against incorrect input.
7 Print headings or labels to clearly identify all output values.

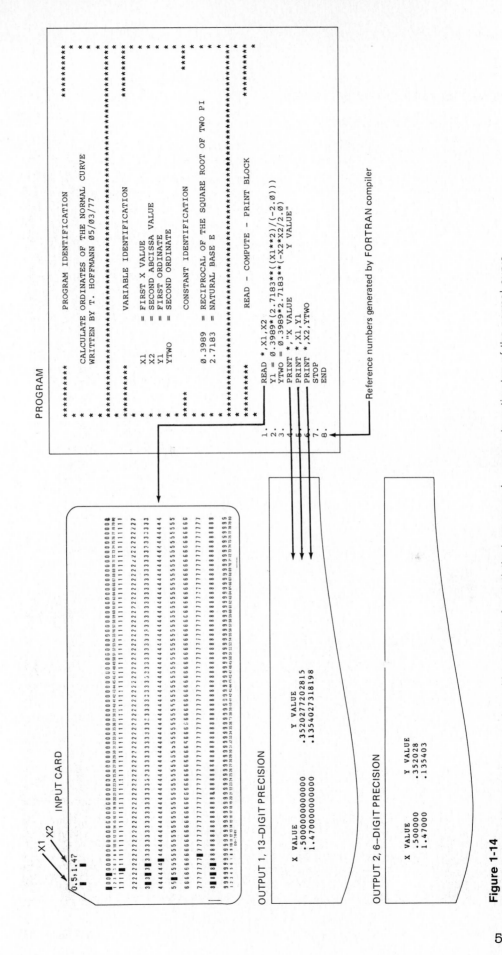

Figure 1-14
Program listing, sample input, and resulting outputs for statistical program 1 —compute estimates of the normal curve.

Programming exercises

Description of assignment

Select one or more problems (or take the problems assigned to you by the instructor). Use only the five statements presented in Chapter 1A. Write the program so that either input value specified in the problem can be used (even though only one input value is to be read and processed). Follow the style guidelines in Chapters 1A and 1B in doing the assignment.

1 Write a pseudocode description of the program you design. Plan for only one set of input data; provide for validation by printing (echoing) the input data.

2 Draw a program flowchart.

3 Code the program. Use only real variables and real constants in assignment statements. Do not use any integer variables or integer constants in computations.

4 Debug and execute with a set of data.
Hint: If a problem requires a value of e (the base for natural logarithms) or π (the ratio of the circumference of a circle to its diameter), use an approximate value of 2.7183 for e and 3.1416 for π. If a square root is required, exponentiate to the 0.5 power (i.e., 1.0/2.0 power). Use only real constants for exponents requiring computations (e.g., 1.0/3.0 instead of 1/3). Feel free to label variables with real names even when the formula gives letters such as n.

Mathematics and statistics

1 For an input value of r compute the volume of the corresponding sphere.

$$v = \frac{4}{3}\pi r^3$$

Use input values for r of 10 or 26.5 inches.

2 A geometric progression is of the following form:

$$a \quad ar \quad ar^2 \quad ar^3 \quad \ldots \quad ar^n$$

The sum of the terms of such a progression is:

$$s = a\frac{r^n - 1}{r - 1}$$

Use one of the following two sets of data as input values for a, r, and n and compute the sum.

a	r	n
1	3	6
1	0.5	7

3 The pythagorean formula can be stated as follows:

$$h = (a^2 + b^2)^{0.5}$$

where h is the hypotenuse and a and b are the sides of a right triangle. Compute h using one of the following two sets of input values a and b.

a	b
5.0	5.0
3.0	4.0

Business and economics

4 When interest compounds q times per year at an annual rate of i percent for n years, the principal p compounds to an amount a as follows:

$$a = p\left(1 + \frac{i}{q}\right)^{nq}$$

Write a program to compute the compound amount. Use either of the following two sets of input data:

p	i	q	n
1000	0.07	4	7
18.75	0.045	12	5.25

5 Various methods are used in depreciating capital goods; one of these is the declining balance method. The value of the item at the end of year n (v_n) is given by the following relationship:

$$v_n = v_0(1 - r)^n$$

where v_0 is the initial value and r is the depreciation rate. Compute v_n using either set of input data.

n	r	v_0
5	0.2	10,000.00
4	0.275	5,000.00

6 The economic order quantity (EOQ) is a function of annual usage a, interest rate i, the costs of setup s, and the cost of the item itself c. These are related as follows:

$$\text{EOQ} = \left(\frac{2as}{ci}\right)^{1/2}$$

Compute the EOQ using either of the following sets of values as input data.

a	s	c	i
8750	1.75	0.55	0.15
4000	1.55	0.45	0.25

Science and engineering

7 The earth is not a sphere; it is slightly flattened at the poles and is therefore more of an oblate spheroid. The formula for its volume is

$$v = \frac{4}{3}\pi a^2 b$$

Compute the volume of the earth for input values of $a = 7927$ and $b = 7900$ miles or input values of $a = 3963$ and $b = 3950$.

8 An eraser falling out of a window is timed in its fall. Use an input for time to fall of either 5 or 6.4 seconds. Calculate and print the height of the windows in feet and in meters as well as the floor from which the eraser fell (18 feet = 1 floor). The relationship between free-fall distance d in feet and time t in seconds is

$$d = 16t^2$$

(Hint: 1 foot = 0.3048 meters)

9 An empirical study has shown that the relationship between pressure and volume for superheated steam is

$$p = 1000\ v^{-1.4}$$

where v = volume.
For an input for v of 1.6 or 2.0, compute the pressure.

Humanities and social sciences

10 Empirical studies have shown a relationship between the time to perform a task and its frequency of repetition:

$$t_x = px^{-l}$$

where x = number of repetitions
$\quad\quad t_x$ = cumulative average task time for x th repetition
$\quad\quad p$ = time to perform task first time
$\quad\quad l$ = a learning factor

Compute the cumulative average time. Use one of the following sets of data as input.

x	p	l
100	3.4	0.465
50	3.4	0.93

11 A study was made of different groups of people to determine the number of males, females, orientals, and nonorientals. Use either set of input data. Compute the percentage of each category.

Study number	Male	Female	Oriental
1	256	244	302
2	108	492	413

12 Assuming towns are approximately circular and area equals πr^2, compute the population density of a town. Use either set of input data.

Town	Radius in miles	Population
1	0.6	65
2	1.7	395

General

13 Students are awarded points toward their grades based upon a weighted average of their quizzes, midterm exam, and final exam. The weighting is the average of three quizzes (Q_1, Q_2, Q_3), the midterm grade (MT), and twice their final exam grade (F). Compute total weighted points using as input either set of data.

Student ID	Q_1	Q_2	Q_3	MT	F
64358	45	95	87	74	83
17651	50	89	76	71	85

14 Cars can be rented on either a daily or weekly basis. The cost for daily rental is number of days N_d times daily rate R_d plus miles driven m times rate per mile R_m. The weekly cost is a weekly charge w plus cost of buying your own gas. The latter is a function of miles driven m, gas consumption mpg, and cost of gasoline per gallon C_g. Compute both the daily and weekly costs for a rental. Use one of the sets of data as input.

Situation	N_d	R_d	m	R_m	w	mpg	C_g
1	5	$25	200	$.18	$110	20	$1.37
2	4	$37	150	$.24	$140	16	$1.43

15 The relationship between Celsius and Fahrenheit temperatures is given by

$$c = \frac{5}{9}(f - 32)$$

Convert a Fahrenheit temperature to Celsius. Use either 50° or 92° as input data.

chapter **2A**

Intrinsic functions, integer-type data, type statement, if selection, data validation, and introduction to program testing

This chapter will explain a convenient method of programming common operations using a FORTRAN feature called intrinsic functions. It will explain the use of integer data and how the characteristics of integer data affect FORTRAN statements. Type statements to explicitly declare variables to be integer, real, or character are introduced. Three basic program coding patterns were described earlier: sequence, selection, and repetition. Sequence was presented in the previous chapter; statements for programming selection are explained in this chapter. The chapter continues the description of good programming practices with a survey of input validation, simple repetition loops, and program testing. It concludes with some suggestions for programming.

Basic intrinsic functions

The five operation symbols for addition (+), subtraction (−), multiplication (*), division (/), and exponentiation (**) were presented in Chapter 1A. In addition to these five operation symbols, FORTRAN provides prewritten program modules that perform common mathematical functions. These built-in functions are termed *intrinsic functions*. The use of an intrinsic function is specified by writing the function name followed by the expression to be operated upon (the argument) inside a set of parentheses. This is illustrated by four commonly used intrinsic functions:

SQRT	Take the square root of the expression
ABS	Take the absolute value of the expression
EXP	Exponentiate e to the power represented by the expression
AMAX1	Take the largest value from the list of real values in the argument

Examples

Problem	FORTRAN expression
$x = \sqrt{y}$	X = SQRT (Y)
$x = \sqrt{y + b}$	X = SQRT (Y + B)
$x = \lvert y - b \rvert$	X = ABS (Y − B)
$x = e^{y+b}$	X = EXP (Y + B)
$x = \max(a,b,c)$	X = AMAX1 (A, B, C)

The expression for a function can include another function. As an example, X = SQRT(ABS(Y − 7.0)) takes the square root of the absolute value of (Y − 7.0) and assigns it to X.

The FORTRAN standard specifies a generic name for each intrinsic function as well as specific names for use with different data types (integer, real, etc.) in the arguments and results. (The implications of the distinction between the real and integer functions will be made clear in the next section.) If the generic name is used, the compiler examines the type of the arguments and selects the correct function type. In other words, either the generic or type-specific function name may be used. In the older versions of FORTRAN, only the specific names were used. Therefore, specific names are more com-

TABLE 2-1   TRIGONOMETRIC FUNCTIONS IN FORTRAN*

Simple trigonometric functions		Arc functions		Hyperbolic functions	
Name	Function	Name	Function	Name	Function
SIN	Sine	ASIN	Arcsine	SINH	Hyperbolic sine
COS	Cosine	ACOS	Arccosine	COSH	Hyperbolic cosine
TAN	Tangent	ATAN	Arctangent	TANH	Hyperbolic tangent

* Generic and real argument names are the same; integer arguments are not allowed.

mon in older programs. For the sake of FORTRAN portability, the text will generally use specific names. A few commonly used functions are summarized in Table 2-1; additional functions are explained in Chapter 7. A list of all functions for reference purposes appears on the inside of the front cover. There are boxes to check off the functions available to you on your computer.

There is a set of trigonometric intrinsic functions (Table 2-2) to calculate the sine, cosine, etc., of angles. The argument for a simple trigonometric function is stated in radians of an angle, and can have a fractional part (which means it is real-type data); the result of the use of the function is also a real quantity.

Self-testing exercise 2-1

1   Write the FORTRAN statements for the following formulas:

(a) $X = \sqrt{a + b}$

(b) $X = \sqrt[3]{\dfrac{a}{b} + 2}$

TABLE 2-2   SELECTED FORTRAN INTRINSIC FUNCTIONS

Generic name	Specific name	Type of argument	Type of function result	Function performed on expression
ABS	IABS	Integer	Integer	Take absolute value
	ABS	Real	Real	
MAX	MAX0	Integer	Integer	Take largest value from list of integer values
	AMAX1	Real	Real	Take largest value from list of real values
MIN	MIN0	Integer	Integer	Take smallest value from list of integer values
	AMIN1	Real	Real	Take smallest value from list of real values
SQRT	SQRT	Real	Real	Take square root
EXP	EXP	Real	Real	Exponentiate e to power represented by expression
LOG	ALOG	Real	Real	Take natural log (to base e)
LOG10	ALOG10	Real	Real	Take log to base 10

(c) $Y = e^x$

(d) $X = \sqrt{|y + 5|}$

(e) $Y = \log_e x$

(f) $r^2 = x^2 + y^2$ (find r)

(g) $A = \max\ (x^2, y^2)$

2 Write the formulas for the following FORTRAN statements:

(a) `X = ALOG (Y + Z)`

(b) `Y = SIN(ABS(A))`

(c) `DISCR = ABS(B**2 - 4.0 * A * C)`

(d) `Y = EXP(-(X**2))`

(e) `RHO = A * COS(THETA)`

(f) `X = SQRT(A + B / C**D * E * F + 1.0)`

3 Rewrite a FORTRAN statement making use of intrinsic EXP function for the formula used in statistical problem example 1 (see page 53).

Use of integer-type data and mixed-type arithmetic

In Chapter 1A, two types of variables and constants were identified—real constants and variables, which can have a fractional part, and integer constants and variables, which cannot have a fractional part. Real constants, for example, always have a decimal point (4.0, 3.1, 39.) even if the fractional part is zero. Integer constants have no decimal point (4, 7, 39). The distinction between the two types is useful in programming but can cause errors if the programmer does not understand internal representation and operational differences related to the types.

Internal representation differences for real and integer data

An integer data item is always an exact representation of an integer value. It may assume only an integral value, such as 1, -1, 45, 18, 0, or -18. A real data item is a computer approximation of the value of a real number. In other words, for integer data, the computer has a method of representing the value exactly (using the binary number system). For real data, the internal computer representation is sometimes exact and in all cases is very close, but there are some real fractions that cannot be represented exactly. The problem is similar to that of representing certain common fractions as decimal numbers. The fraction $4/3$ cannot be represented exactly as a decimal number, but only reasonably close as 1.3333. . . .

Since an integer-type variable can only represent integer values, any fractional part of a data item is lost when it is processed or stored as an intger variable. For example, when division is performed with integer-type data and a fractional part remains in the answer, the fractional part is dropped. The result of $7 \div 4$ when both 7 and 4 are integers is 1 (instead 1.75); the result of $1 \div 3$ is 0 (instead of 0.3333).

The approximate rather than exact representation of some real fractions is not normally a problem, and a programmer could write many programs without noting the result of approximate representation. Difficulty is most likely

61

to occur when the program converts real data to integer representation or divides two integer variables.

Conversion of data between real and integer types

There are two major reasons that data items may need to be converted from real to integer or from integer to real:

1 In some computations, only the integer portion of a value is desired. Converting from real to integer retains the integral portion and drops the fractional part.

2 Expressions cannot be executed with data having mixed types, because integer data items are represented in the computer differently than the real data items. In an expression having variables with mixed types, type conversions must be made before the computations in the expression can be processed. Note that a real expression may have an integer exponent without requiring conversion, but an integer variable with a real exponent is a mixed-type expression and one of them must be converted.

If the preceding reasons apply, why are the variables not defined as the needed type rather than converted from one type to another? The reason is that a variable may need to be used in different expressions with variables of different types.

Any conversion from one type to another can be handled in one of three different ways: (1) across the equals sign; (2) with an explicit intrinsic conversion function; or (3) during execution of mixed expressions using default procedures. Type conversion will occur when different types are mixed in expressions. The only issue is whether or not to program the conversions explicitly rather than to rely on default conversion procedures that might lead to unexpected results.

In conversion across the equals sign, the expression on the right is evaluated and an answer obtained in the type used in that expression (real or integer). The answer is then converted and stored according to the type of the result variable on the left of the equals sign. Thus, $I = X * Y$ will compute the product of X and Y, convert the result to an integer, and store it in the location assigned to the integer variable name I. Any fractional part from $X * Y$ is lost.

The intrinsic function method is an explicit programming of conversion using intrinsic functions. As shown in Table 2-3, there is a function REAL (or FLOAT) to convert from integer to real and a function INT (or IFIX) to con-

TABLE 2-3   INTRINSIC FUNCTIONS TO CONVERT DATA TYPES

Generic name	Specific name	Type of argument	Type of function result	Function performed on expression
REAL	FLOAT	Integer	Real	Convert from integer to real type
INT	IFIX	Real	Integer	Convert from real to integer (truncating the fractional part)

INTRINSIC FUNCTIONS, INTEGER-TYPE DATA, TYPE STATEMENT, IF SELECTION

vert from real to integer. REAL and INT are generic names, and FLOAT and IFIX are specific names for the intrinsic conversion functions.

Examples

Statement	Result
I = 3.1417	I contains 3
R = 75	R contains 75.0
JIX = X * PRICE	JIX contains 3
where X = 3.5 and PRICE = 1.1	because result of X * PRICE = 3.85

Statement	Result
I = IFIX(3.1417)	I = 3
or I = INT(3.1417)	
R = FLOAT(75)	R = 75.0
or R = REAL(75)	
JIX = IFIX(X * PRICE)	JIX = 3
or JIX = INT(X * PRICE)	

If an expression contains mixed types and there is no explicit conversion, FORTRAN performs conversions as part of the execution of the statement. Integer variables in the mixed expression are converted to real values. It is generally not a good idea to rely on the automatic default conversion, since the programmer may not perceive the consequences of a mixed-type expression. It is much better to code the conversion explicitly using the conversion functions. Note the following examples:

Desired expression	Coding
X = A + K	X = A + FLOAT(K)
	or X = A + REAL(K)
I = K + A	I = K + IFIX(A)
	or I = K + INT(A)
X = I**A	X = FLOAT(I)**A
	or X = REAL(I)**A

Although the discussion has taken several paragraphs, the rules for integer and real types in expressions are fairly simple. These are summarized below.

RULES FOR INTEGER AND REAL TYPES IN EXPRESSIONS

1 If integer and real data types are mixed in an expression, integer variables or constants will be converted to real. Good programming practice is to explicitly code these conversions rather than rely upon default.
2 In the statement $a = b$, if a is of a different type than b, the results of b will be converted to the type of a. If the conversion is from real to integer, the fractional part of the expression results will be truncated and discarded.
3 Fractional parts from division of integer variables are truncated.
4 The allowable combinations of types in exponentiation are (a) integer expression with integer exponent, (b) real expression with real exponent, and (c) real expression with integer exponent. The exponent may be any arithmetic expression meeting these type restrictions.
5 An integer expression to a real exponent is a mixed-type expression. If used, the integer expression will be automatically converted to a real expression. Some older compilers will reject this form.

Self-testing exercise 2-2

1 Complete the following table:

Expression or statement	Valid or not valid; note if mixed type	If not valid, why; if mixed type, how converted
(a) A**2 + 1		
(b) A**(2 + 1)		
(c) A**(B + C / D)		
(d) A / B + D / 3		
(e) IX + JX + 4		
(f) KX = A + BI		
(g) FUN = SQRT(A + AXEL / BETA)		
(h) X = (A + B) / ((C + D) * E * IX)		
(i) X + Y = Z * ALPHA		
(j) JX = IX**A		
(k) X = A**I		

2 If A = 3.0, B = 2.5, IX = 3, and JX = 2, what will be the result of the following statements?
(a) X = A/B
(b) K = IX/JX
(c) KIX = JX/IX
(d) NIX = IX + 2/JX

3 Write statements using both intrinsic functions: generic and type-specific.
(a) Take the absolute value of integer value KDATA.
(b) Find the minimum for values of I, J, and K.

4 Convert the following by using the generic intrinsic function, then the specific intrinsic functions, and finally by coding a new variable name across the equals sign.
(a) JIX to a real variable
(b) DATA1 to an integer variable

5 Remove mixed mode by using explicit coding of conversion.
(a) X = I * B**I
(b) X = B + (C / J) + K**D

Explicit-type statements

In Chapter 1A, it was explained that any variable name beginning with the letters I through N is assumed to represent an integer variable with names having any other first letter representing real variables. Defining the type of variable by the first letter is termed *implicit typing*. There is also a need for explicit typing to:

1 Define variable types other than integer and real.
2 Override the implicit first-letter typing.
3 Specify type explicitly rather than to rely on implicit typing.

There are several types of variables in FORTRAN other than integer and real, and each has a unique representation in the computer. One of these additional types (character type) will be explained in this chapter; the remaining types will be described in Chapter 7. The explicit type statement has two forms: (1) the form for integer, real, and all other types except character type, and (2) the form for character type. These are summarized in the box and explained below.

TYPE DECLARATION

The explicit type statement is required for character-type variables and types other than real or integer.

1 *Other than character-type data* type v, v, ... Declares all variables in list to be of specified type.

  type = REAL, INTEGER, and others explained in Chapter 7. The explicit type statement for real and integer variables overrides the implicit typing based on the first letter of the variable name.

2 *Character-type data* CHARACTER v*len, v*len, . . . , where v is the variable name declared as storing character data and len is the maximum length of the string of characters to be stored. If the string being stored is less than maximum length, the string will be left-justified in the storage spaces and extra spaces at right will contain blanks. If len is not given, a length of one character is assumed.

  CHARACTER *len v, v, ... All variable names in list are declared as storing character and have the same length, len. A comma is optional following len.

Real and integer type statements

The form of the explicit type statement for real and integer types is:

type v, v, . . .

where type is the type name. The names for integer and real types are INTEGER and REAL. For example, if ALPHA and IRATE are to be declared as real (IRATE would otherwise be integer), and TIMES and RATE to be declared as integer, the following statements are written:

```
REAL ALPHA, IRATE
INTEGER TIMES, RATE
```

The fact that the type declaration is required for some types but is optional for integer and real variables (that can use implicit typing) leads to two alternatives for programming style.

1 Explicit declaration of the type of all variables, including integer and real variables. Ignore implicit typing.

2 Use implicit typing for real and integer variables. Use explicit declaration only for variables requiring it.

Those arguing for complete explicit typing say that this eliminates all ambiguity as to type. It also eliminates the restrictions on naming based on implicit typing. In this text, we will follow the second alternative and declare types only when necessary, because implicit typing is a significant feature of the FORTRAN language and has been followed in most existing programs. Therefore, we reason that a person learning FORTRAN should develop a good command of implicit typing. On the other hand, we recognize the logic for doing complete explicit typing declaration.

In the coding style followed in the text, type declarations will be placed in a program block following the program identification and variable identification blocks. The block can be titled TYPE DECLARATION AND STORAGE ALLOCATION BLOCK.

Character-type statement

Printing characters to label output was explained in Chapter 1A in connection with the list-directed print statement. The string of characters to be printed was defined as a character-type constant by enclosing it in apostrophes. In the following statement, TOTAL PAYMENTS is a character-type constant:

```
PRINT *, 'TOTAL PAYMENTS', T
```

There is frequently a need to have a variable name that refers to character data. This allows character data to be read, stored, manipulated, and output. This is done by assigning a variable name to reference each string of characters. But since characters will have a form different than numbers used in computation, the FORTRAN program must define all variable names associated with character data as being character type. This is done with a character-type statement. The basic character-type statement is in the form:

```
CHARACTER v*length, v*length, . . .
```

As an example, if HEAD1 references 15 characters and LABEL2 has 8 characters, the two names would be declared as referencing character data by the following:

```
CHARACTER HEAD1*15, LABEL2*8
```

In other words, a variable to be declared as character type must have a length (in characters) associated with it. Each character in the string of characters is counted (including blanks).

If all of the character variables in the list have the same length, the length specification need be stated only once before the variable list.

```
CHARACTER *length v,v,v, . . .
```

As an example, if character variables H1, H2, and H3 are all of length 12, they can be declared by:

```
CHARACTER *12  H1,H2,H3
```

When a character variable name has been declared, character data can be read by a list-directed input statement using the variable name. The character string being input must be enclosed in apostrophes. For example, a 12-character heading (called HEAD4) in the form 'XXXXXXXXXXXX' is to be read and then printed. The following statements are required:

```
CHARACTER HEAD4 * 12
READ *, HEAD4
PRINT *, HEAD4
```

Self-testing exercise 2-3

1   For a program, each set of input data is in the form 'XXXXXXXXXXXX', nnn, where the Xs represent a character string and each n a digit of an integer number. Write statements to declare a character name for the string, read the data, and print the character string and integer number. Use LABEL1 and NSHARE for variable names.

2   The programmer wrote an entire program using the variable name INTRST to refer to a real number and PYMNTN to refer to an integer value. Write type declarations to achieve the desired type.

3   Declare variables A, B, C, and D to be two characters in length.

4   Explain the difference between the following declarations:

```
CHARACTER * 1,G,H,I,J
CHARACTER G,H,I,J
```

Selection among alternative processing paths using the block IF statement

As explained in Chapter 1A, program logic is simplified by using only three program-coding structures:

1   Simple sequence
2   Selection
3   Repetition

Simple sequence was explained and used in Chapter 1; selection and simple repetition will be explained in this chapter; and repetition will be described in greater detail in Chapter 4.

Selection among alternative processing is programmed with the IF statement. There are essentially three forms of IF statements:

1   Block IF
2   Logical IF
3   Arithmetic IF

Each statement will be explained, but style preferences exist regarding usage. The block IF is preferred except for simple selection; in this case, the logical IF is used. The block IF statement is new with the 1977 FORTRAN standard and may not be available in older versions of FORTRAN. In such cases, the logical IF provides a good alternative. Although the arithmetic IF is presented for comprehensiveness, its use is discouraged because it is error-prone.

Figure 2-1
Flowchart of selection
program structure.

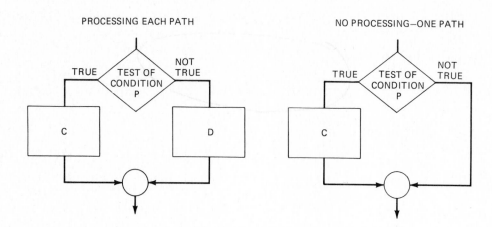

Selection structure

The selection structure consists of a logical expression that tests for a condition or a relation followed by two alternative paths for the program to follow. The program selects one program control path, depending on the results of the test (that is, the truth or falsity of the expression). After executing the instructions in one of the two program paths, the program continues with the statement following the two blocks of alternative instructions. This coding pattern can be termed IF. . .THEN. . .ELSE because the logic can be stated in if-then-else terms. For example, assume a condition P and sets of statements called C and D, as shown in Figure 2-1. The selection is described as follows: IF P (is true), THEN perform statements C; ELSE (if P is not true) perform statements D. The flowchart for the selection process consists of a decision symbol followed by two branches or paths, each with one or more process symbols to specify the processing to be performed for that branch. A frequent variation is to have one of the branches contain no processing. In that case the logic is: IF P (is true), THEN perform statements for C; ELSE continue with the processing that follows the selection statements.

Describing the selection coding structure in the pseudocode of a program design language will follow the basic idea of if-then-else. Using the conventions of this text, the pseudocode statements for a selection include the following:

```
A statement of the test to be performed
    IF (statement of condition to be tested) THEN
        (processing to be performed if condition is satisfied)
    ELSE (processing to be performed if condition is not satisfied)
```

The use of the capitalized words follows the convention explained earlier of capitalizing words that correspond to FORTRAN coding words. The indentation visually shows the parts of the selection structure.

Block IF statement

The FORTRAN statements to code a block IF selections structure consist of the following:

```
IF (logical expression) THEN
        statements to be processed for true block
ELSE
        statements to be processed for false block
ENDIF (or END IF)
```

The statements to be executed if the logical expression is true follow the THEN and are termed the *IF Block;* the statements to be executed if the logical expression is false follow the ELSE and are termed the *ELSE block.* The ELSE and the ELSE block can be omitted if no processing is to occur if the expression is false. The ELSE, when used, should be the only statement on the line. Each IF. . .THEN. . .[ELSE]. . . must end with an ENDIF. Indentation is recommended for statements in the IF block and the ELSE block to show the parts of the selection structure. Before illustrating the block IF, the programming of the logical expression will be explained.

Logical expressions

In the simplest type of logical expression, two arithmetic expressions (which may be only variable names) are separated by a relational operator that defines the nature of the condition or relation to be tested. The relational operators are shown below:

RELATIONAL OPERATORS

Operator	Representing
.LT.	Less than
.LE.	Less than or equal to
.EQ.	Equal to
.NE.	Not equal to
.GT.	Greater than
.GE.	Greater than or equal to

Note that a period precedes and follows the operators to differentiate them from variable names. The following are two examples of how a relation test is used in coding a logical expression in a selection structure.

```
IF (A .GT. B) THEN
    PRINT *, 'BIG IS', A
ELSE
    PRINT *, 'BIG IS', B
ENDIF

IF (SQRT(Y) .LE. 5.0) THEN
    RESULT = 5.0
ELSE
    RESULT = SQRT(Y)
ENDIF
```

Character strings may also be compared by using relational operators. If the names are of unequal length, the shorter one is assumed to be made of equal length by adding blank space characters to the right end. For example, if two names are stored in NAME1 and NAME2 and the computer is testing to see if they are in alphabetical order, the instruction could be:

```
IF (NAME1 .LE. NAME2) THEN
    PRINT *, 'NAMES ARE IN ORDER'
ELSE
    PRINT *, 'NAMES OUT OF ORDER'
ENDIF
```

A character constant may be used in making the comparison. For example, a test to see if an input is the word END would read:

```
IF (WORD .EQ. 'END') THEN
    PRINT *, 'END OF DATA'
ELSE
    PRINT *, 'NOT END OF DATA'
ENDIF
```

If two or more relational expressions are to be compared, logical operators may be used. The basic logical operators are .AND., .OR., and .NOT.; additional logical operators are explained in Chapter 7.

BASIC LOGICAL OPERATORS	
Operator	Expression is true when
.AND.	Both relations are true
.OR.	One or both of the relations are true
.NOT.	Opposite is true

A statement with the operator .AND. is true only if both relations connected by .AND. are true; a statement with the operator .OR. is true if either or both of the relations connected by .OR. are true. True means that the relationship is satisfied; for example, X .GT. Y is true if X is greater than Y. The operator .NOT. is used to indicate negation (opposite) of the relation. Statements can contain a number of relations connected by more than one logical operator. When more than one .AND. and .OR. are used in the same expression, the parenthesis rule (inside parentheses first) and a precedence rule can be applied. In the absence of parentheses, the following precedences are applied:

1   Arithmetic operations (using the precedence rule for them)
2   .NOT.
3   .AND.
4   .OR.

Operations having the same precedence are executed from left to right. For a clear program style, parentheses should be placed around the portions of the expressions connected by .AND. and .OR. even though they are not required.

The use of logical operators as part of a logical expression is illustrated by the following examples:

```
IF ((PAY .GT. 45.0) .AND. (AGE .LE. 17.0)) THEN
    TALLY = TALLY + 1.0
ENDIF
```

Add 1 to TALLY only if PAY is greater than 45 and age is less than 17. Both must be true. If either or both are not true, the program continues with statements following the selection structure. There is no ELSE block.

```
IF ((HRS .LE. 60.0) .AND. (HRS .GT. 0.0) .OR. (KODE .EQ. 1)) THEN
    RATE = PTRATE
ELSE
    RATE = QSRATE
ENDIF
```

The variable RATE will be set to either PTRATE or QSRATE, depending on the results of the test. If HRS is less than or equal to 60.0 and greater than zero, or if KODE is equal to 1, then set RATE to the value of PTRATE; otherwise (else), set RATE to the value of QSRATE.

The following example illustrates the use of more than one processing statement in the IF and ELSE blocks. In the example, RPAY (regular pay) is

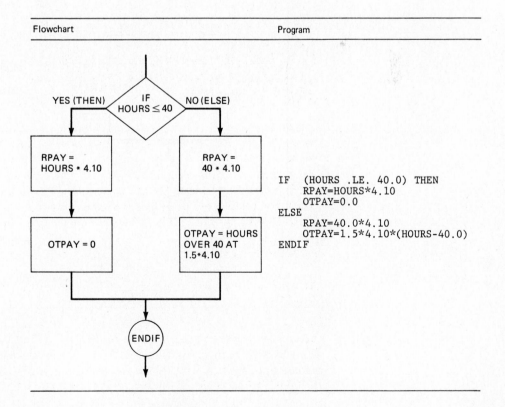

Flowchart	Program

```
IF  (HOURS .LE. 40.0) THEN
    RPAY=HOURS*4.10
    OTPAY=0.0
ELSE
    RPAY=40.0*4.10
    OTPAY=1.5*4.10*(HOURS-40.0)
ENDIF
```

computed at $4.10 per hour; for hours greater than 40, the OTPAY (over-time pay) is 1.5 times the $4.10 rate.

Nested block IFs

In some programming situations, a succession of tests determines the action to be taken. It is possible to have an if-then-else selection within an IF block or an ELSE block. Within an IF block (but not within an ELSE block), a sequence of tests can be programmed with an ELSEIF (or ELSE IF) statement.

Placement of an if-then-else coding structure within an IF or ELSE block is illustrated by the following example. In computing wages, if the shift code is greater than 1.0 (for other than day shift), the pay rate is $6.00 per hour. For the day shift (shift code = 1.0), the rate is $4.15 per hour; but if the day is Sunday (DAY = 7.0), there is a special premium of $3.00 per hour.

Flowchart	Program

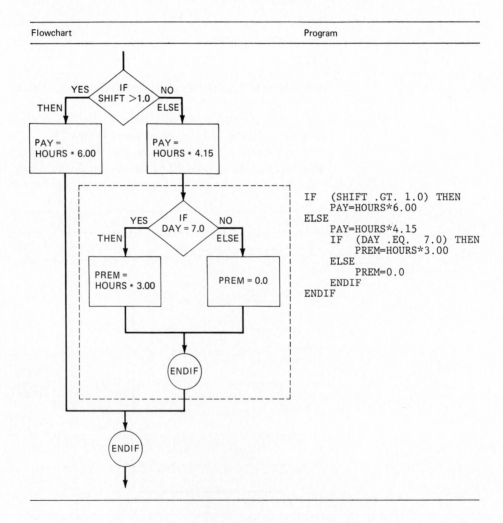

```
IF  (SHIFT .GT. 1.0) THEN
        PAY=HOURS*6.00
ELSE
        PAY=HOURS*4.15
        IF  (DAY .EQ.  7.0) THEN
            PREM=HOURS*3.00
        ELSE
            PREM=0.0
        ENDIF
ENDIF
```

As a style comment, the first test of (SHIFT .GT. 1.0) is satisfactory except when SHIFT is in error (say SHIFT = 6.0 even though there is no shift greater than 4). It is wise to test for a value being within valid limits before making a test in which all other values are assumed to be valid. The test in this case might be IF (SHIFT .LE. 0.0 .OR. SHIFT .GT. 4.0) THEN error-handling statement.

The ELSEIF. . .THEN statement is used to code a sequence of one or more additional tests within the IF block before the ELSE result. ELSEIF is part of the IF block and does not use a separate ENDIF. The ELSEIF statement may be repeated for a series of tests, each with a separate action if the test result is true. When a set of ELSEIF statements are used, the program tests each logical expression in turn. If the expression is not satisfied, the next test is performed; however, if the test is true, the action specified for that ELSE IF is taken and the program goes to the END IF at the end of the selection structure. If none of the IF or ELSEIF conditions or relations is true, the action specified in the ELSE block is processed. In other words:

```
IF (logical expression) THEN processing to be performed if logical expression is true
    (and skip rest of selection structure); if false, continue with next test.
    ELSEIF (logical expression) THEN processing to be performed if true (and skip
        rest of selection structure). If false, continue with the next ELSEIF. If all the IF
        and ELSEIF tests turn out to be false, execute the statements in the ELSE
        block.
ELSE
Statements to be executed only if none of the IF or ELSEIF logical expressions were
    evaluated as being true.
ENDIF
```

The use of ELSEIF in programming a series of tests in which testing need not continue if an expression is true is illustrated on the following page by a program segment that prints student grades based on exam scores:

90 to 100	A
80 to 89	B
70 to 79	C
Below 70	See instructor

Note that once a score is identified as being in a range, the remaining tests are not used.

By way of style comment, the tests of scores were written to test only greater than or equal to, since previous tests had logically eliminated the upper limit. But a good procedure would be to test explicitly for a score greater than 100.0 (an error). The other tests could also have been written to test for the entire range, as for example, IF (SCORE .GE. 80 .AND. SCORE .LE. 89) THEN. . . . The test following the .AND. is redundant, but the program logic is made clearer. Unless efficiency is an important consideration, the full coding is preferred.

The various features of the block IF statement are summarized in the box on page 75.

Flowchart	Program

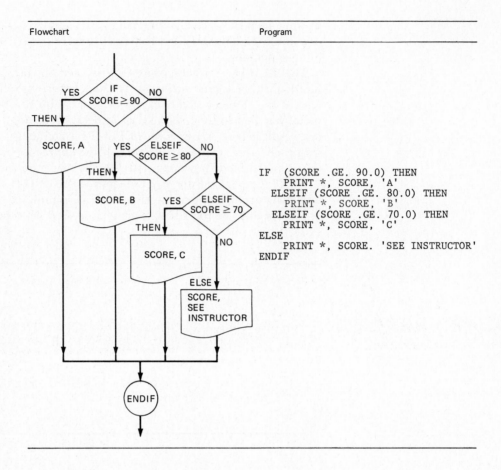

```
IF  (SCORE .GE. 90.0) THEN
    PRINT *, SCORE, 'A'
  ELSEIF (SCORE .GE. 80.0) THEN
    PRINT *, SCORE, 'B'
  ELSEIF (SCORE .GE. 70.0) THEN
    PRINT *, SCORE, 'C'
ELSE
    PRINT *, SCORE. 'SEE INSTRUCTOR'
ENDIF
```

Self-testing exercise 2-4

Write selection coding structures using the block IF for the following problems.

1 If the square root of $X^2 + Y^2$ is less than 100.0, the answer (ANSWR) is to be 12.0 ∗ X. If it is greater than or equal to 100.0, the value of ANSWR is to be X^2. Print the answer.

2 Find the largest quantity represented by three variables: ALPHA, BETA, and GAMMA. Call the largest quantity BIG. If two are equal, either value may be used.
(*a*) First write statements without using the AMAX1 (or MAX) function.
(*b*) Then write statements using the AMAX1 function.

3 Two variables, NIX and KIX, should be unequal. Find the largest in absolute value (without regard to sign). Print out the largest. If they are equal, stop the program.

4 Find out if $-550 \le X \le 1000$. If X falls within these limits (between -550 and $+1000$), print out YES. If not, print out NO. Then halt the computer.

5 Test whether A is greater than B and greater than C, or whether A is less than D and equal to E. If so, print TRUE. If false, print FALSE.

6 If a code number (ICODE) is equal to 1 or 2, pay is computed as 3.75 times regular hours and overtime is set to zero. If the code is 3, pay is 4.15 times regular hours and overtime is 1.5 times 4.15 times overtime hours. If code is more than 3, ICODE ERROR and its value are printed.

BLOCK IF STATEMENT

IF (logical expression) THEN statements for IF block	Logical expression is a relation or condition that can be true or false (satisfied or not satisfied).
	All statements in the IF block are executed if the expression is true; statements in the ELSE block are executed if the expression is false.
ELSE statements for ELSE block	The ELSE should be the only word on the line. The ELSE and ELSE block statements are optional and may be omitted.
ENDIF (or END IF)	Each IF . . . THEN . . . [ELSE] must end with an ENDIF statement.
ELSEIF (logical expression) THEN statements for ELSEIF block	ELSEIF (or ELSE IF) statement is used to program a sequence of tests within the IF block. The IF logical expression is tested first; if true, the statements for the IF condition are executed and the remaining statements through the ENDIF are ignored. If false, the ELSEIF expression is tested. If it is true, the statements for the ELSEIF are executed and the remaining statements are ignored. If the IF and ELSEIF logical expressions are all false, the ELSE block statements are executed. The ELSEIF is part of the IF block and does not use a separate ENDIF. *Note:* If coded as ELSE IF instead of ELSEIF, the words ELSE and IF must appear on the same coding line; otherwise, ELSE is considered to be the keyword for the ELSE block and an error condition exists.

Transferring control within a program

The block IF statement allows selection among two sets of instructions. In some cases, the program logic requires that the next instruction to be executed appear in another part of the program. In order to do this, FORTRAN uses statement labels to identify statements to which control should be transferred. The statement that transfers control is the GOTO (or GO TO) statement.

Statement labels in FORTRAN

FORTRAN statements may have a statement label, which is a number written in columns 1–5 of the coding sheet. The label is in a fixed position; it is never indented to the right of column 5 even if the statement it labels is indented. The statement label may be from one to five numeric digits. If there are less than five digits, it is customary to right justify them (leave the blanks at the left) within columns 1–5. The statement label numbers are coded by the programmer and used by the program; there is no connection with the line reference numbers required for each statement in a program entered at a terminal or the line numbers added to the program listing by many compilers.

Any FORTRAN statement may be labeled, but only those statements that are referenced by another program statement *must* be labeled. For example, in Chapter 1B, none of the statements were labeled. A good practice is to use statement labels only when they are needed for reference or documentation, because excess statement labels make it more difficult to locate the statement label being referenced. The rules of the language allow the statement labels to be in any order, and they need not be sequential. In other words, the statement label numbers are identifying labels; they do not specify sequence. However, having statement label numbers in sequence or approximate sequence makes it easier to locate a referenced statement label number.

As explained, a disciplined style for a FORTRAN program will divide the program into logical blocks of code. A useful approach to labeling is to have each block of code start a new set of numbers. For example, the first block will be labeled with numbers in the 100s. In fact, it is often useful to label the first statement in the block with 101. The second block will use 200s, with the first statement being labeled with 201, etc. This has the advantage that whenever a

Figure 2-2
Outline of program form with block numbering.

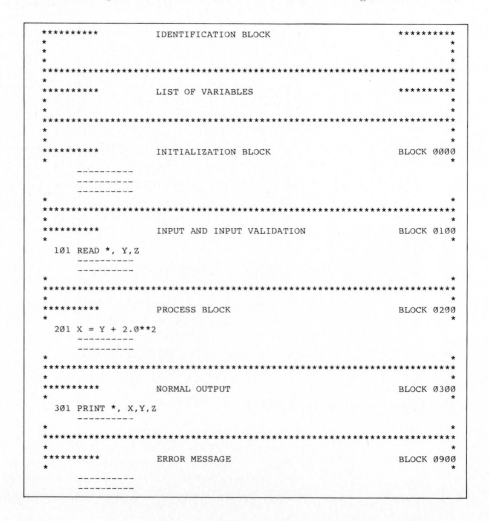

```
**********              IDENTIFICATION BLOCK                    **********
*                                                                        *
*                                                                        *
*                                                                        *
*************************************************************************
*                                                                        *
**********              LIST OF VARIABLES                       **********
*                                                                        *
*                                                                        *
*************************************************************************
*                                                                        *
**********              INITIALIZATION BLOCK          BLOCK 0000 *
*                                                                        *
      ----------
      ----------
      ----------
*                                                                        *
*************************************************************************
*                                                                        *
**********              INPUT AND INPUT VALIDATION    BLOCK 0100 *
*                                                                        *
   101 READ *, Y,Z
      ----------
      ----------
*                                                                        *
*************************************************************************
*                                                                        *
**********              PROCESS BLOCK                 BLOCK 0200 *
*                                                                        *
   201 X = Y + 2.0**2
      ----------
      ----------
*                                                                        *
*************************************************************************
*                                                                        *
**********              NORMAL OUTPUT                 BLOCK 0300 *
*                                                                        *
   301 PRINT *, X,Y,Z
      ----------
*                                                                        *
*************************************************************************
*                                                                        *
**********              ERROR MESSAGE                 BLOCK 0900 *
*                                                                        *
      ----------
      ----------
```

statement is referenced, its location in the program and the logical block to which it belongs are also identified. This is illustrated in Figure 2-2.

GOTO statement

The GOTO statement is used to branch around one or more statements. The branching is unconditional; that is, it does not depend on any test or condition.

> **GOTO STATEMENT**
>
> GOTO s (or GO TO s)
>
> where s is a statement label

When a GOTO is encountered, the next statement to be executed will be the one labeled with the statement number s. After statement s is executed, control continues with the statements following s. Because GOTOs may make a program difficult to debug and maintain, they should be used with care. To aid in understanding the logic of a program, we have chosen to place a set of comments before most GOTOs explaining the nature of the branching as shown by the following example:

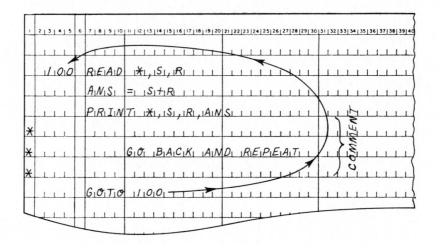

Selection of alternative processing paths using the IF statement

Block IF was added to FORTRAN in 1977. FORTRAN also contains two other IF statements that can be used for selection among alternative program paths: the logical IF statement and the arithmetic IF statement. The logical IF is the more important of the two; in fact, we do not recommend use of the arithmetic IF statement. It is only explained so that you can understand FORTRAN programs that use it.

Logical IF statement

The logical IF consists of a test of a logical expression followed by an executable FORTRAN statement. The logical expression to be tested is, for example, a relation between two variables or two arithmetic expressions. The relation is coded by one of the relational operators or logical operators explained earlier in the chapter. The FORTRAN statement in the IF statement following the logical expression is executed only if the logical expression is true (is satisfied). Following execution of that statement, processing continues with the next statement after the IF statement. If the logical expression is false, the executable statement in the logical IF is not executed; the program goes to the following statement. The logical IF can be used to code the same logic as a block IF. The block IF is preferred if the two branches of the selection have different sets of actions; the logical IF is the simpler construction if only one action is required for one branch.

> **LOGICAL IF STATEMENT**
>
> IF (e) st
>
> where e is a logical (relational) expression and st is almost any executable statement. If the relation is true, execute the statement; otherwise, do not execute the statement and continue with the statement following the IF statement.

The use of the simple logical IF statement in coding selection is illustrated by coding to find the largest of two real quantities A and B and to assign the largest value to BIG. This problem was illustrated earlier with the block IF. Since it may be helpful to compare the block IF coding, this is included.

In the example, there are two alternative processing statements for the two branches. The logical IF requires a GOTO; the block IF does not. The exam-

Flowcharts	Coding

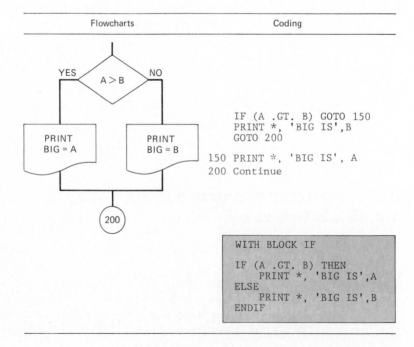

```
IF (A .GT. B) GOTO 150
PRINT *, 'BIG IS',B
GOTO 200

150 PRINT *, 'BIG IS', A
200 Continue
```

> **WITH BLOCK IF**
>
> ```
> IF (A .GT. B) THEN
>     PRINT *, 'BIG IS',A
> ELSE
>     PRINT *, 'BIG IS',B
> ENDIF
> ```

ple illustrates one possibility of making an error in coding a logical IF that is not likely to occur with a block IF. Unless the action of the statement following the logical IF is to be executed in both cases, there must be a GOTO statement for one of the branches to go around it. For example, if the program was coded

```
IF (A .GT. B) PRINT *, 'BIG IS', A
PRINT *, 'BIG IS', B
```

the result would be that PRINT *, 'BIG IS', B is always executed since this statement is executed whether A or B is larger. To avoid such errors and to write clear coding when using the simple logical IF, it is sometimes desirable to have a set of two or more logical IF statements even though this causes some redundant processing. For example, the problem of finding the larger of A or B could be coded with a set of two logical IF statements. The clarity of the logic more than offsets the additional processing:

```
IF (A .GT. B) PRINT *, 'BIG IS' A
IF (B .GE. A) PRINT *, 'BIG IS' B
```

Note that the coding causes B to be printed if the two variables are equal in value.

The logical expression can include logical operators. Examples of statements that include both relational and logical operators are shown below.

Examples

```
IF ((PAY .GT. 45.0) .AND. (AGE .LE. 17.0)) TALLY = TALLY + 1.0
```

Add 1 to TALLY only if PAY .GT. 45 and also AGE .LE. 17 (both are true).

```
IF ((HRS .GE. 60.0) .OR. (OT .EQ. 10)) GOTO 10
```

Transfer control to statement 10 if either of the relational statements is true.

Arithmetic IF statement

The arithmetic IF is not recommended because it tends to be error-prone. It is never necessary because the logical IF can be used. However, it was frequently used in older FORTRAN programs. Therefore, it will be explained so that FORTRAN programs written by those employing the feature can be understood.

ARITHMETIC IF STATEMENT

IF (expression) s_1, s_2, s_3

where the expression may be a variable name or arithmetic expression. If the expression, when evaluated, is negative (that is, less than zero) control goes to the first statement label listed; if zero, to the second statement label; and if positive, to the third. Statement labels are separated by commas.

Two examples illustrate the arithmetic IF:

IF Statement	Explanation
IF (X - 2.0) 100, 200, 400	IF X is less than 2.0, go to 100; if X equals 2.0, go to 200; if X is greater than 2.0, go to 400. By subtracting 2.0 from X, a negative condition is obtained in the first case, a zero for X equals 2.0, and a positive condition for anything greater than 2.0.
IF (X - 6.0) 113, 113, 210	If X $\leq$ 6.0, go to 113; if greater than 6.0, go to statement 210.

Validating input data

The selection structure programmed by the IF statements allows the coding of an important program block: validation of input data. Perhaps the most error-prone part of using a computer program is the preparation of the input data. Good program design suggests, therefore, that a program include features that are useful in detecting erroneous or incomplete input data. Two techniques should be employed where feasible.

1 Print out (echo) the input data for visual review. There may be a printout especially for validation purposes, or the input data may be printed as part of the final output. Printout of input data was used in the example programs in Chapter 1B.

2 Test the input data to check for data items that do not meet the criteria for valid data.

The testing for valid data is based on the fact that it is possible, in many cases, to specify criteria for input data. For example, the data for hours worked might be specified as not negative or zero and not greater than 65.0. A test for validity could consist of three separate tests or a single, composite test, such as:

```
IF ((HOURS .LE. 0.0) .OR. (HOURS .GT. 65.0))
    PRINT *, HOURS, 'HOURS ERROR'
```

During processing, it is sometimes desirable to program a test to avoid possible division by zero. For example, a computation of pay as a percentage of bonus would, if bonus were zero, produce a machine execution error and abort the job. Coding to prevent this execution error might read:

```
IF (BONUS .EQ. 0.0) THEN
    PRINT *, 'ERROR. BONUS IS ZERO.'
ELSE
    PRATE = PAY / BONUS
ENDIF
```

Self-testing exercise 2-5

Use a simple logical IF statement (not a block IF) to code the following operations.

1 If the square root of $X^2 + Y^2$ is less than 100.0, the answer (called ANSWR) is to be 12.0 * X. If it is greater than or equal to 100.0, the value of ANSWR is to be X^2. Print the answer.

2 Find out if X is between -550 and $+1000$ ($-550 \le X \le 1000$). If so, print 'yes'; otherwise, print 'no'. Then halt the computer.

3 Write a combined input and input validation block to test input data and reject (with a message) a negative or zero rate (RATE) or a rate greater than 15 percent. Stop the processing if there is an error.

4 Rewrite problem 3 with a block IF.

Processing more than one set of input data

The sequence program structure used in Chapter 1 works well for a single set of input data, but it is very cumbersome if more than one data card is to be read and processed. Since each READ statement reads only one card (using the statements explained so far), processing 10 different sets of input data on 10 different cards requires 10 sets of processing statements each with a READ statement, and each set of data has unique variable names. A more efficient program design is to write the program so that the READ statement and its related processing statement are used over again for each set of input data. This method is called *repetition* or *looping,* a fundamental technique in programming. A preferred method of repetition using the DO statement will be explained in more detail in Chapter 4; the repetition procedure described in this chapter is a simple IF loop that provides an introduction to repetition.

A simple IF loop

Assume a program segment that is to read values called X and Y from a card, compute the sum (called Z), and print the values assigned to X, Y, and Z. This is to be repeated for several sets of X and Y inputs. The repetition could be programmed with a GOTO statement to transfer control back to the first statement in the set as shown in the flowchart at the top of the next page.

The logic repeats the processing over and over using a new input card for each execution. The difficulty is that the repetition never terminates—it is an endless loop because there is no logic to cause it to stop looping. A program written in this way will eventually be abnormally terminated by the operating system, but this is not a satisfactory way to come to a stop.

A simple method for coding the end of a repetition is to use an IF statement to test whether or not the set of statements has been executed the appropriate number of times. Two methods of coding the test for termination when reading input data illustrate the concept.

1 Use a unique termination value for the input data item following the last set of data to be processed. Examples of such values are a negative value (if no regu-

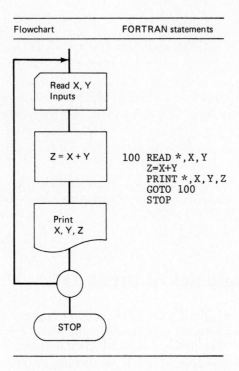

Flowchart	FORTRAN statements

```
100 READ *,X,Y
    Z=X+Y
    PRINT *,X,Y,Z
    GOTO 100
    STOP
```

lar value will be negative) or 999 (if no regular input would have this value). The coding and flowchart for a negative value are:

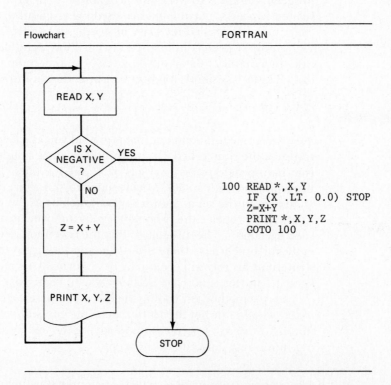

Flowchart	FORTRAN

```
100 READ *,X,Y
    IF (X .LT. 0.0) STOP
    Z=X+Y
    PRINT *,X,Y,Z
    GOTO 100
```

2   Establish a counter for input items. Keep track of the items read and terminate when the required number have been processed. For example, if the

input data card counter is called ICOUNT and 10 items are to be processed, the flowchart and coding could be as follows:

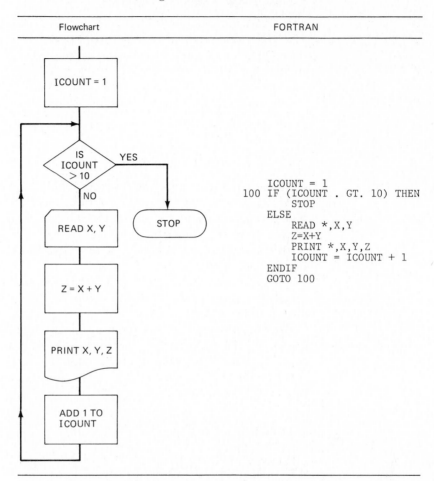

Flowchart	FORTRAN

```
      ICOUNT = 1
100   IF (ICOUNT . GT. 10) THEN
         STOP
      ELSE
         READ *,X,Y
         Z=X+Y
         PRINT *,X,Y,Z
         ICOUNT = ICOUNT + 1
      ENDIF
      GOTO 100
```

These two methods are illustrated in the example programs in Chapter 2B — a counter is used in general example 2 and a negative value test is used in statistical example 2. There are many variations on loop design. In the preceding use of a counter, the test for termination was placed at the beginning of the loop; it can also be placed at the end of the loop.

First- and last-time-through logic

In coding both simple loops and the more complex repetitions explained in Chapter 4, a major source of program logic errors occurs in the processing of the first data item through a block of code that will be used repeatedly and in the handling of the last data item.

The first-time-through errors generally result from failing to initialize properly. Logic that works perfectly once started will not give correct results if begun incorrectly. Two programming situations illustrate the need for first-time-through logic.

1   *Obtaining the largest value so far*   If, as each data item is processed, the program tests it to determine if it is the largest value so far and stores the largest value,

the instructions might read:

```
PLARGE = AMAX1 (DATA, PLARGE)
```

This instruction stores the larger of DATA and the previous PLARGE in PLARGE (which is then the largest so far). But what is PLARGE the first time the comparison is made? To ensure that the test will work properly at the first comparison, PLARGE must be initialized so that the first data item will be larger. This can be done by initializing PLARGE with a small value such as $-1.0E10$ that is less than any possible value of DATA.

2 *Adding to previous sum* In many programs, a sum is accumulated by a statement of the form:

```
SUM = SUM + DATA
```

In essence, this statement adds current value of DATA to the previous value of SUM. In order for the logic to work properly, SUM must be zero the first time through. If the first data amount is 5.0, then the SUM after the first execution will be 5.0 (but only if SUM is zero the first time through). Some (but not all) compilers set all storage to zero before the programming execution, but do not depend on it.

These two situations reflect a large class of first-time situations. These are usually relatively simple to analyze and program if the programmer is alert to the first-time problem.

The last-time problem occurs at termination when the last data item may not be processed or may be processed incorrectly. For example, refer to the previous example 2 with a termination test based on a card count of 10 and a count (ICOUNT) that started at 1. If the test read as shown below, only nine cards would be read.

```
IF (ICOUNT .GE. 10) THEN
    STOP
ELSE
```

As with first-time-through logic, the problem is easily solved if recognized.

Planning and design of a program with multiple cases and exceptions

In Chapter 1B, the explanation of the use of pseudocode and a program flow-chart in program planning described a two-step planning and design process based on a single case (a single set of input data). In this chapter, statements have been introduced that allow the program to repeat the processing using more than one set of input data (multiple cases); the statements also allow more computer input validation and more complete handling of exceptions. The logic of program planning and design is therefore expanded as follows to include these more complex problem situations.

1 Plan the general logic of processing for the simple case (one set of output from one set of normally expected data) to the level of detail useful for the specific problem.

2 Add a control structure to the simple case to handle multiple cases (multiple sets of input). Include logic required for first- and last-time-through processing.

3 Modify control structure and add logic for input validation and handling of input errors.

4 Add logic for handling exceptions and unusual cases, including cases in which zero or negative data values are exceptions.

This expanded program planning and design procedure is illustrated in Chapter 2B in connection with the pseudocode for general example 2.

Introduction to testing and quality assurance for a program

Having written a program, the programmer (and user) needs assurance that the program is correct and performs as expected. Testing and quality assurance of programs can use a variety of techniques. This section will describe the nature of the testing and quality-assurance process, explain the development and use of a set of test data—data designed specifically to test the program—and introduce debugging during compilation.

Testing and quality-assurance process

With a very simple FORTRAN program, testing is quite simple. However, for larger and more complex FORTRAN programs, there is a need for a process of testing and quality assurance that proceeds concurrently with the program design, programming, and debugging.

Programming	Testing and quality-assurance process
1 Problem recognition and algorithm selection	1 Check literature for existence of tested algorithm. Use a tested algorithm, if available.
2 Program design (for example, flow-charting and/or pseudocode)	2 Develop testing strategy and design of initial set of test data.
3 Program coding	3 (a) Desk checking. The programmer manually traces a few data items through the program (at the desk before compilation)
	(b) Program reading (peer review). It is frequently helpful to have other programmers (or fellow students who are programming) read a program to check for errors in logic, lack of good style, etc.
4 Compilation	4 Use compiler diagnostics to identify coding errors.
5 Debugging	5 Make corrections in design and code.
6 Testing	6 Use test data to identify logic errors and provide assurance of program correctness.

Development and use of test data

Data for testing a program should be designed to test all paths through the program. If a program consists of a simple sequence (such as the programs in Chapter 1B), a single set of data will test the program. In a program with selection structures, a separate set of test data needs to be provided for each path through the program. For example, assume a program with the following structure (shown in Figure 2-3). With one selection structure, there are two paths through the program. If these two paths are two processing paths for a payroll program that has one computational procedure for less than or equal to 40 hours and another procedure for over 40 hours, one set of test data should test for 40 hours and a second set of test should test for over 40 hours. Two sets of test data would be satisfactory except that a frequent source of error in programs is at the boundary value specified in the decision block; in the example, the boundary value is 40. It might be quite easy for the programmer to code IF (HOURS .LT. 40.0) rather than IF (HOURS .LE.

Figure 2-3
Paths through a simple payroll program for testing the program.

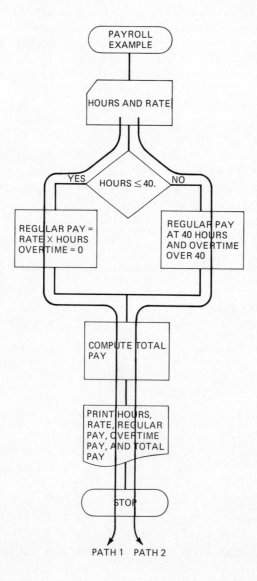

40.0). If the boundary value itself is not tested, this easily made error would not be detected. For this reason, it is recommended that test data include data at the boundary value, the boundary value minus one, and the boundary value plus one. In the simple example, this will require three sets of test data with hours data of 39, 40, 41.

The testing of all processing logic includes the use of invalid data to test the data validation logic. In other words, a complete set of test data will include:

1 Normal case testing of all boundary values and boundary values plus one and minus one.
2 Abnormal or invalid cases.

Debugging programs during compilation

The output from compilation is useful in removing coding-type errors (and keypunching errors that may not have been noticed in checking the FOR-TRAN deck before submission). The errors that can be detected by the compiler are language-use errors. However, a student should be aware that the error message from the compiler correctly identifies the existence of an error, but in a significant number of cases the computer is unable to specify the true cause of the error and may instead specify an incorrect cause.

Precision and accuracy in computing

Accuracy has to do with measurement. For example, suppose we wish to measure a large wooden table. Using three methods of measurement, we arrive at different accuracy.

Method of measurement	Accuracy
By eye	Within 1 foot
By using a hand span	Within 3 inches
By using a measuring tape	Within $1/16$ inch

Precision refers to the way the result is recorded: how many digits can be recorded. If the common fraction $4/3$ is to be recorded as a decimal, there is no limit to the trailing 3s; the limit imposed by the recorder (or by the computer structure) is the precision:

1.3	2-digit precision
1.333	4-digit precision
1.33333	6-digit precision

To understand the nature of precision, assume that only a fixed number of places is available for hand computation. Using only three or six places, solve $1/6 + 30$. The decimal point (shown by $\wedge$) will be allowed to float, and there will be rounding before digits are dropped. The results are shown at the top of the next page.

In hand computation, the person doing the computing will usually vary the precision from problem to problem, but a computer is generally designed to operate with a fixed precision. High-level-language compilers generally re-

Three-place precision	Six-place precision
$1/6 =$ | 1 | 6 | 7 |	| 1 | 6 | 6 | 6 | 7 |
$30 + 1/6 =$ | 3 | 0 | 2 |	| 3 | 0 | 1 | 6 | 6 | 7 |

flect the precision of the computer for which they are written. The precision can and does vary among computers. FORTRAN programs that can benefit from large precision will often have different results when compiled and executed on a computer with smaller precision. For example, Peter Minuit paid Indians $24 for Manhattan Island in 1626. If the Indians had invested the $24 at 6 percent compounded quarterly (6.0/4.0 percent per quarter), what sum would the Indians have had in 1976 after 350 years? The FORTRAN statement is:

```
    AMT = 24.0 * ((1.0 + (.06 / 4.0))**(350.0 * 4.0))
or  AMT = 24.0 * (1.015**1400.0)
```

Exponentiation to the 1400th power is done by logarithms, but the result is so large that it is very much affected by the precision used by the computer. The results obtained from two different computers illustrates the concept.

Computer	Result
IBM 370/158 (medium precision)	27,058,163,712
CDC CYBER 74 (high precision)	27,081,355,025

The IBM 370/158 result was rerun with a larger double precision specified (explained in Chapter 7); the result was 27,081,351,168, which is closer to the precision obtained on the large CDC computer.

This example should not be a cause for alarm. There are only a few problems where precision will be a significant factor. But the FORTRAN programmer should be aware of precision for those cases in which it is important.

The maximum precision obtainable inside the computer is not necessarily the precision obtained at output. In the case of list-directed output, the output precision is defined by the compiler writer; the programmer has no control over it. As noted in Chapter 1, the precision of list-directed output will vary for different implementations of standard FORTRAN.

Suggestions for the FORTRAN programmer

Because so much emphasis is placed in the text on good programming style, it may be useful to review the concept of a good program. Writing a good program is not merely writing language statements in correct form. The statements need to code a suitable solution procedure (a computing algorithm) that has been carefully designed. The coding should be done in a clear manner following a disciplined style. The statements need to be coded correctly, i.e., use the language correctly. These three important requirements can be understood by two analogies:

Analogy 1

A term paper on "Privacy and the Computer" has (assuming appropriate knowledge of the subject has been acquired by the student writer) three elements that affect the result:

1 The planning of an organization for the paper. This should have logical parts, each part with an objective, and able to fit the overall structure of the paper. This design is reflected in a clear outline of the topics to be included. This phase is similar to the development of a computer solution procedure which meets the needs posed by the problem.

2 The organization of the paper into paragraphs with headings, subheadings, indentation, underlining, etc. This is similar in concept to computer programming style.

3 The writing of sentences in correct grammatical form. This is the same as coding of correct statements in the program.

Analogy 2

A student is to develop a computer solution procedure for finding the square root of a number. The three steps in the process are:

1 Find or develop a solution procedure. The student finds that the Newton-Raphson algorithm is already known and well defined. This method can be described for this problem in a flowchart or in pseudocode. Organize the solution procedure for program clarity.

2 The program for the Newton-Raphson method can be divided into logically separate functions. For example, the separate activities in the solution procedure might be identified as:
    (a) Read input value and validate; that is, test for invalid values such as negative or zero.
    (b) Initialize all values for the computational procedure.
    (c) Perform the iterative procedures to find the square root.
    (d) Print out the input value and the square root.

3 The algorithm is coded in correct FORTRAN statements.

The programming style suggestions from Chapters 1 and 2 are listed below. The first seven suggestions summarize the guidelines described in Chapter 1, which should be reviewed; the remainder summarize good practice as explained in this chapter.

1 Analyze the problem and design the program before beginning to code instructions. If you do not understand the problem and the solution procedure, you cannot tell the computer what to do. Useful alternative design and planning methods are program design language (pseudocode) and program flowcharts. A suggested four-step process in planning and designing a program is:
    (a) Plan the general logic of processing for one simple normal case to the level of detail useful for the problem.
    (b) Add a control structure to the simple case to handle multiple cases. Include logic required for first-time-through and last-time-through processing.

(c) Modify the control structure and add logic for input validation and handling of input errors.

(d) Add logic for handling exceptions and unusual cases, including negative or zero values (if not allowed).

2   Use FORTRAN coding paper to aid in writing instructions in proper form.

3   Use a block structure to divide the program into logical segments. Include an identification block and a list-of-variables block for clear documentation. The style selected for this text is to have a block name line consisting of 10 asterisks, 10 blanks, name of block starting in column 21, and number of block (BLOCK nnnn) starting in column 63. To be manageable, blocks should be less than 60 statements.

4   Use explanatory comments at the beginning of each logical block. Use comments freely inside the blocks. Following the text style, set off each group of one or more inside-block comment lines by a blank comment line before and after. The inside-block comment lines are indented to column 11.

5   Use parentheses to avoid ambiguity. Do not rely upon unfamiliar precedence rules.

6   Consider a printout (echo) of input data as a visual check against incorrect input.

7   Print labels to clearly identify all output values.

8   Validate input data to make sure it falls within the limits assumed for the program. Provide suitable error messages and correct or reject bad data.

9   Use the block IF whenever appropriate. Also, use the logical IF. Do not use the arithmetic IF.

10   Check for incorrect logic following a basic logical IF. Remember that unless the action of the IF is to transfer control, the statement following the IF will be executed for both selection paths.

11   When coding tests of conditions, do not assume a value for any remaining condition. Make an explicit test.

12   Provide explicit error stops or error messages for instances when conditions that should never occur actually do occur.

13   Code for clarity, not for a minimum number of coding lines.

14   Explicitly initialize variables where needed for first-time-through processing.

15   A program should be checked out by running it with comprehensive test data for which the results are known. Test carefully the first-time-through and last-time-through logic, logic at and around boundary values, input validation, and handling of exceptions.

Summary

The basic intrinsic functions were explained. These reduce coding requirements for common operations. The intrinsic functions have a generic name as well as specific names that identify the type of data being produced (such as integer or real). Integer data is important in FORTRAN because there are situations where integer data is needed and because the characteristics of integer arithmetic are often useful. Modern FORTRAN compilers allow mixed types in an expression but convert them to a compatible type before execution. Good programming style is to code the conversions with intrinsic conversion functions rather than to rely upon automatic conversion. There are type statements to override the implicit first-letter typing of integer and real variables and to declare variable names for character data.

The selection structure is coded by the IF statement. The block IF and simple logical IF are preferred but many programs, especially older programs, make use of an arithmetic IF.

The IF statement provides the basis for understanding data validation. This should normally be included in well-written programs. A simple IF loop can be used to perform repetitive processing. When loops are used, it is important to carefully code the logic so that the program will work correctly the first time through and the last time through. The program should be tested using desk checking and test data. The concepts of precision and accuracy in computing are explained and contrasted. Style guidelines for Chapters 1 and 2 are summarized.

Answers to self-testing exercises

Exercise 2-1

1 (a) X = SQRT (A + B)

(b) X = (A / B + 2.0)**(1.0 / 3.0)

Exponentiating to the $1/3$ power is the same as taking the cube root. As was explained more fully in the chapter, the exponent must be real or it would turn out to be zero. The parentheses around the exponent are necessary. Why?

(c) Y = EXP (X)

(d) X = SQRT (ABS (Y + 5.0))

(e) Y = ALOG (X)

(f) R = SQRT (X**2 + Y**2)

Note that the square root of the right side was taken, since no expression is allowed on the left side.

(g) A = AMAX1 (X**2, Y**2)

2 (a) $x = \log_e(y + z)$

(b) $y = \sin|a|$

(c) $d = |b^2 - 4ac|$

(d) $y = e^{-x^2}$

(e) $p = a \cos \theta$

(f) $x = \sqrt{a + \dfrac{b}{c^d} ef + 1.0}$

3 Y = 0.3989 * EXP ((- X**2) / 2.0)

Exercise 2-2

1

Valid or not valid; note if mixed type	If not valid, why; if mixed type, how converted
(a) Valid, mixed	Will be converted to A**2 + 1.0
(b) Valid (integer arithmetic for integer exponent is valid)	
(c) Valid real type	
(d) Valid, mixed	Converts to A / B + D / 3.0
(e) Valid integer type	
(f) Valid, mixed	Result is converted to integer type

Figure 2-5
Continued.

```
27.          PRINT *, ' TOTAL          TOTAL         LARGEST'
28.          PRINT *, ' PAY            TAX          GROSS PAY '
29.          PRINT *,TOTPAY,TOTTAX,LARGEP
30.          STOP
      *                                                                    *
      **********************************************************************
      *                                                                    *
      *********          ERROR MESSAGE BLOCK                      BLOCK 0900
      *                                                                    *
31.   901 PRINT *,' NET PAY IS NOT POSITIVE. DO NOT ISSUE CHECK.'
      *                                                                    *
      *         GO BACK TO NORMAL PROCESSING                               *
      *                                                                    *
32.          GOTO 103
      *
33.     905 PRINT *,' ERROR IN INPUT DATA.'
      *
      *             DO NOT COMPUTE PAY.  GO BACK FOR MORE DATA.
      *
34.          GOTO 101
35.          END
```

ID   HRSWRK
     WGRATE
     DEDUC   SAMPLE INPUT

```
35746, 55.5, 7.24, 30.68
69587, 10, 2.67, 27.50
35649, 22, 2.75, 35.98
15768, 37, 6.28, 24.68
27543, 40, 3.57, 27.95
```

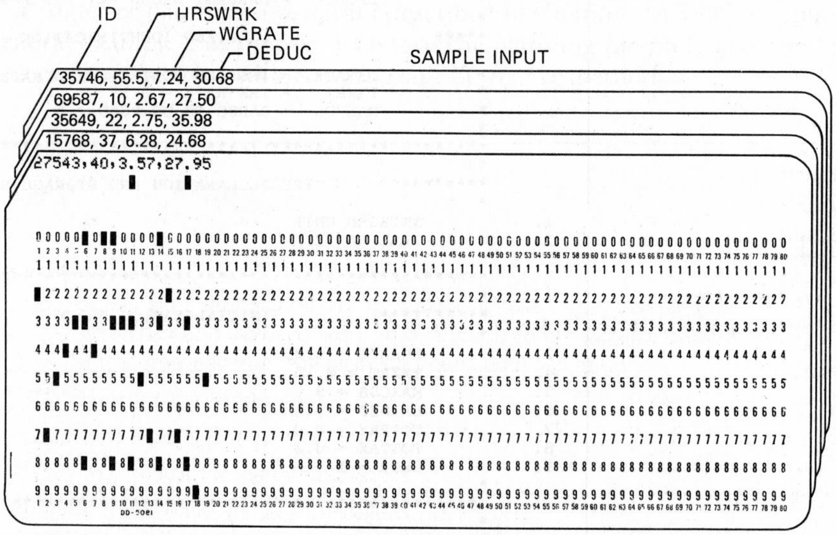

OUTPUT

```
      ECHO      27543  40.0000       3.57000      27.9500
      NET PAY =   86.2900    GROSS PAY =   142.800

      ECHO      15768  37.0000       6.28000      24.6800
      NET PAY =  161.208    GROSS PAY =   232.360

      ECHO      35649  22.0000       2.75000      35.9800
      ERROR IN INPUT DATA.

      ECHO      69587  10.0000       2.67000      27.5000
      NET PAY =  -6.14000    GROSS PAY =    26.7000
      NET PAY IS NOT POSITIVE. DO NOT ISSUE CHECK.

      ECHO      35746  55.5000       7.24000      30.6800
      NET PAY =  290.776    GROSS PAY =   401.820

      TOTAL         TOTAL       LARGEST
      PAY           TAX         GROSS PAY
      803.680       120.552      401.820
```

statements to override the implicit first-letter typing of integer and real variables and to declare variable names for character data.

The selection structure is coded by the IF statement. The block IF and simple logical IF are preferred but many programs, especially older programs, make use of an arithmetic IF.

The IF statement provides the basis for understanding data validation. This should normally be included in well-written programs. A simple IF loop can be used to perform repetitive processing. When loops are used, it is important to carefully code the logic so that the program will work correctly the first time through and the last time through. The program should be tested using desk checking and test data. The concepts of precision and accuracy in computing are explained and contrasted. Style guidelines for Chapters 1 and 2 are summarized.

Answers to self-testing exercises

Exercise 2-1

1 (a) `X = SQRT (A + B)`
(b) `X = (A / B + 2.0)**(1.0 / 3.0)`
Exponentiating to the $1/3$ power is the same as taking the cube root. As was explained more fully in the chapter, the exponent must be real or it would turn out to be zero. The parentheses around the exponent are necessary. Why?
(c) `Y = EXP (X)`
(d) `X = SQRT (ABS (Y + 5.0))`
(e) `Y = ALOG (X)`
(f) `R = SQRT (X**2 + Y**2)`
Note that the square root of the right side was taken, since no expression is allowed on the left side.
(g) `A = AMAX1 (X**2, Y**2)`

2 (a) $x = \log_e(y + z)$
(b) $y = \sin|a|$
(c) $d = |b^2 - 4ac|$
(d) $y = e^{-x^2}$
(e) $p = a \cos \theta$
(f) $x = \sqrt{a + \dfrac{b}{c^d} ef + 1.0}$

3 `Y = 0.3989 * EXP ((- X**2) / 2.0)`

Exercise 2-2

1

Valid or not valid; note if mixed type	If not valid, why; if mixed type, how converted
(a) Valid, mixed	Will be converted to A**2 + 1.0
(b) Valid (integer arithmetic for integer exponent is valid)	
(c) Valid real type	
(d) Valid, mixed	Converts to A / B + D / 3.0
(e) Valid integer type	
(f) Valid, mixed	Result is converted to integer type

Valid or not valid; note if mixed type	If not valid, why, if mixed type how converted
(g) Valid real type	
(h) Valid, mixed	Better to code as X = (A + B) / ((C + D) * E * FLOAT(IX))
(i) Not valid	Expression (X + Y) to left of equals sign not allowed
(j) Mixed	Integer may not have real exponent, so compiler will convert to: JX = FLOAT(IX)**A or some older compilers will reject it)
(k) Valid (integer exponent allowed)	

2 (a) 1.2   (b) 1   (c) 0   (d) 4

3 (a) J = ABS(KDATA)
      J = IABS(KDATA)
   (b) M = MIN(I, J, K)
      M = MINO(I, J, K)

4 (a) REAL(JIX)
      FLOAT(JIX)
      AJIX = JIX
   (b) INT(DATA1)
      IFIX(DATA1)
      IDATA1 = DATA1

5 (a) X = FLOAT(I) * B**I   or   X = REAL(I) * B**I
   (I in exponent need not be made real because an integer exponent does not cause a mixed-type expression.)
   (b) X = B + (C / FLOAT(J)) + FLOAT(K)**D   or
      X = B + (C / REAL(J)) + REAL(K)**D

Exercise 2-3

1
```
CHARACTER LABEL1 * 12
READ *,LABEL1,NSHARE
PRINT *,LABEL1,NSHARE
```

2
```
REAL INTRST
INTEGER PYMNTN
```

3
```
CHARACTER *2,A,B,C,D
```

4 They both declare variables G, H, I, J to be variable names for character data of one character each.

Exercise 2-4

1
```
IF (SQRT(X**2 + Y**2) .LT. 100.0) THEN
    ANSWR = 12.0 * Y
ELSE
    ANSWR = X**2
ENDIF
PRINT *,ANSWR
```

2 (*a*)
```
IF (ALPHA .GT. BETA .AND. ALPHA .GT. GAMMA) THEN
      BIG = ALPHA
    ELSEIF (BETA .GT. ALPHA .AND. BETA .GT. GAMMA) THEN
      BIG = BETA
  ELSE
      BIG = GAMMA
  ENDIF
```
(*b*) `BIG = AMAX1(ALPHA,BETA,GAMMA)`

3
```
IF (NIX .EQ. KIX) THEN
    STOP
  ELSEIF (ABS(NIX) .GT. ABS(KIX)) THEN
    PRINT *, NIX
ELSE
    PRINT *, KIX
ENDIF
```

4
```
IF ((X .GE. -550.0) .AND. (X .LE. 1000.0)) THEN
    PRINT *,'YES'
ELSE
    PRINT *,'NO'
ENDIF
STOP
```

5
```
IF((A .GT. B .AND. A .GT. C) .OR. (A .LT. D .AND. A .EQ. E)) THEN
    PRINT *,'TRUE'
ELSE
    PRINT *,'FALSE'
ENDIF
```

6
```
IF (ICODE .EQ. 1 .OR. ICODE .EQ. 2) THEN
    RPAY = RHRS * 3.75
    OTPAY = 0.0
    ELSIF (ICODE .EQ. 3) THEN
    RPAY = RHRS * 4.15
    OTPAY = 1.5 * 4.15 * OTHRS
ELSE
    PRINT *, 'ICODE ERROR', ICODE
ENDIF
STOP
```

(Annotations: IF block / IF... ELSE with ENDIF; ELSEIF block; ELSE block)

Exercise 2-5

1
```
IF (SQRT(X**2 + Y**2) .LT. 100.0) ANSWR = 12.0 *X
IF (SQRT(X**2 + Y**2) .GE. 100.0) ANSWR = X**2
PRINT *,ANSWR
```

The above answer is clear and complete but does repeat processing of the test. An alternative answer which is more efficient but more complex is:

```
      IF (SQRT(X**2 + Y**2) .LT. 100.0) GOTO 110
      ANSWR = X**2
      GOTO 120
110   ANSWR = 12.0 * X
120   PRINT *,ANSWR
```

2
```
IF ((X .GE. -550.0) .AND. (X .LE. 1000.0)) PRINT *,'YES'
IF ((X .LT. -550.0) .OR. (X .GT. 1000.0)) PRINT *,'NO'
STOP
```

3 Without block IF

```
READ *, RATE
IF ((RATE .LE. 0.0) .OR. (RATE .GT. 0.15)) GOTO 150
120 normal input processing
    GOTO 200 (to skip around next statements)
150 PRINT *, RATE, 'RATE NEG, ZERO, OR LARGE'
    STOP
200 continue with normal processing
```

4 With block IF

```
READ *, RATE
IF ((RATE .LE. 0.0) .OR. (RATE .GT. 0.15)) THEN
    PRINT *, RATE, 'RATE NEG, ZERO, OR LARGE'
    STOP
ENDIF
```
(continue with normal processing)

Questions and problems

1 Define the following terms:
(a) compilation
(b) desk checking
(c) input validation
(d) intrinsic function
(e) program reading

2 Describe two methods of input validation.

3 Describe the testing and quality-assurance procedures that accompany the development of a FORTRAN program.

4 A program is coded with one simple selection. How many sets of data are necessary to test the program fully? How many are necessary if the program has two simple selections?

5 Write the FORTRAN expressions for the following:
(a) X^a
(b) X^i
(c) X^{i-1}
(d) e^x
(e) $X^{1/3}$
(f) X^{-4}
(g) $X^{i/j}$
(h) $\dfrac{1}{X^2}$

6 What is the result of each of the following statements, given the stated values for the variables?
(a) $X = Y + Z/A$
(b) $IX = Y + Z/A$ $\Bigg\}$ $Y = 3.0, Z = 4.5, A = 2.0$

(c) $I = J/K$
(d) $I = L/J + K$ $\Big\}$ $J = 3, K = 9, L = 10$
(e) $I = J + L/K - L$

7 Write the formulas, given the following FORTRAN statements:
(a) `Y = SQRT (X**2 + 2.0) / (1.0 - X**N)`
(b) `X = THETA + SIN(THETA)`
(c) `Y = 1.0 / X`
(d) `E = ((A**2 + B**2)**(1.0 / 2.0)) / A`
(e) `X = A**B * C + D * E / F * G**2`

8 Write the FORTRAN statement to solve the formula for each of the following:
(a) $j = \sqrt{v}$
(b) $a = |x + y|$ where $|\ |$ means the absolute value
(c) $x = \dfrac{a(-b)}{c(-d)}$
(d) $s = \dfrac{p}{q} + \dfrac{3r}{s}$

9 Eliminate mixed-mode arithmetic in the following by the use of intrinsic functions:
(a) `IX = A + JX`
(b) `N = XK + JX`
(c) `X = IX**K`
(d) `X = X**I`
(e) `X = R**X + NIX`

10 Write a program segment to find the value of COST when COST is a step function of volume (a) first without a block IF and then (b) with a block IF.

If VOL is between 0 and 100	`COST = 200 + 0.3  × VOL`
If VOL is over 100 but not 1000	`COST = 300 + 0.3  × VOL`
If VOL is over 1000 but not over 5000	`COST = 350 + 0.25 × VOL`

11 Identify and correct the logical errors in the following:
(a)
```
      IF (A .GT. B) SMALL = A
      SMALL = B
```
(b)
```
      IF (HOURS .LT. 0.0 .OR. HOURS .GT. 65.0)GOTO 150
      PAY = HOURS * 2.5
  150 PRINT *, HOURS, 'ZERO OR NEG INPUT'
      STOP
      PRINT *, 'HOURS', HOURS, 'PAY', PAY
```

12 Write data validation statements for the quadratic formula—read the necessary variables from cards and validate the data as suitable for processing; that is, validate that $b^2 - 4ac$ is not negative (which would result in an error in attempting to take the square root). Print the input variables (with labels). Print error messages if data is invalid. The formula is:
$$\frac{-b \pm \sqrt{b^2 - 4ac}}{2a}$$

13 Write a program segment to validate an input data item PRICE. If it is zero, negative, or greater than 30.0, it is to be rejected. Print an error message that gives the value and specifies the reasons for rejection.

chapter **2B**

Example programs and programming exercises using intrinsic functions, IF selection, and data validation

The two example programs are for the same applications as the two example programs in Chapter 1B, but additional requirements have been added that utilize the features presented in this chapter. The two examples again provide variety in the type of applications being illustrated: a general example of payroll computation and a statistical example of calculating the ordinates of the normal curve. The example programs illustrate a disciplined style using principles of structured programming. The documentation contains both a pseudocode description and flowcharting to provide experience in the two techniques. Following the examples are programming exercises.

General notes on Chapter 2 examples

The two examples utilize intrinsic functions, IF selection, and data validation. Statement numbers are also used as labels on some statements. Additional style considerations are the use of more than one logical (numbered) block of processing statements, the use of pointer comments with backward GOTOs, a convention for GOTOs in pseudocode, and a type declaration and storage block. The examples use simple IF loops to read and process several sets of input data.

Numbered processing blocks

As the number of processing statements becomes larger and the number of processing functions increases, it is good programming style to divide a program into more than one group of statements. These groupings (logical blocks) are identified with a heading. It is also useful to assign a number to each of the blocks. The number also identifies the number series allowed for statements in the block. We have chosen to number the initialization block as 0000. The first block after that is numbered 0100, and any statements in the block are between 101 and 199; the next block is 0200 and the statements, if numbered, use labels ranging between 201 and 299. The block number can be placed anywhere in the block heading; we have placed it in the ten columns (63–72) at the right side of the block heading line as BLOCK nnnn.

It is frequently useful to have a separate block for error messages. A convention we have chosen is to assign 900 (or 9000 for larger programs) as the error block number. This means that any reference to a 900 or 9000 number is to an error message.

The advantage of the block number and block number series is in clearly identifying the statement to which a GOTO (or other transfer statement) transfers control. A statement GOTO 310 anywhere in the program is immediately understood as transferring control into block 300.

Pointer comments for backward GOTOs

The most understandable design for a computer program is usually a program that has no backward transfers of control, that is, no GOTOs transferring to earlier program statements. It is virtually impossible to achieve such a program design for all FORTRAN programs. Many FORTRAN programs will need to transfer backward (essentially a GO BACK statement). It is necessary, for example, when the program is to be repeated with new input data. This case is illustrated in both example programs.

In order to make a backward GOTO very clear, we include a comment line just before the GOTO describing what the GOTO is to accomplish (with a blank comment line on either side of the GOTO comment). The words GO BACK may be used in the comment to clearly mark a backward GOTO.

In the flowcharts, some of the backward GOTOs use a connector to avoid too many lines on the chart. The small circle has an identifying letter in it. The GOTO point has an arrow as well as a circle ──────▶(A) and the point A to which control is going has the same letter as well as an arrow to the entry point

(A)──────▶

Terminating the program

The two example programs read more than one set of data. They read and process input data until termination is indicated (usually by reaching the end of the data to be processed). There are several ways to program tests for end-of-data termination. Two simple ways are illustrated in the two example programs:

1 Test for the maximum number of input data items that should be read (general example 2).

2 Test for a data value that terminates the program (statistical example 2).

In the first example (general example 2), the maximum number of input items (MAXCDS) is initialized at 5 (in line 5). A card counter (CNTR but declared as integer type) is set to 1 in line 9. Each time a card is read, the counter is incremented by 1 (line 11). The counter is tested and, if less than or equal to the maximum, the program goes back to read new input data (line 25). In flowchart form, the logic of using a counter is given below:

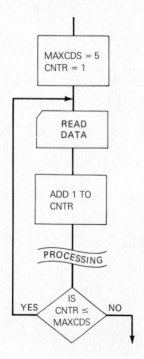

The second example program (statistical example 2) tests for an input data item that is negative (line 7). The input data must contain a data item with a negative value following the last data item to be processed.

In general, a program will be abnormally terminated by the operating system when the program attempts to read data and no more data is available. However, this default option is not good programming practice. It is better to provide for explicit termination with end-of-program messages as in the example programs. Another method will be explained in Chapter 3.

A GOTO pseudocode convention

The pseudocode description needs to provide for transfer of control (same principle as GOTO). The convention used in this text is to use a descriptive name in front of a block of pseudocode description. Any transfer of control in the program is planned with the pseudocode by writing transfer-type pseudocode with the name being the transfer point. The name is underlined. For example, a block of code might be named Summary; a pseudocode GOTO Summary is sufficient description for planning and documenting a program.

The pseudocode convention in the text for an IF test uses the IF block concept. IF and ELSE are used to identify the possible branches. If a branch has no processing, it is written as Else continue.

Type declaration and storage block

As a matter of style, type declarations are coded in a separate program block placed in the program after the variable identification block. In the two example programs, this block illustrates type declaration for declaring variables as being integer even though the first letter specifies real (or, alternatively, real even though the first letter indicates integer). The variables could have been altered by using a different first letter, but we choose to declare them as real or integer to show the use of type declarations.

General program example 2 — payroll computation

Problem description for general example 2

Paycheck amounts are computed for a specified number of employees. For data validation, input data is printed (echoed). Input data is also validated as being within suitable limits. After calculations, net pay and gross pay are printed, net pay for each employee is checked for a positive pay amount, and negative net pay is noted by an error message. After all employees are processed, the total gross pay and total taxes for all the employees are printed along with the largest single gross pay amount. Values for the following variables are input for each employee:

Identification number

Hours worked

Wage rate

Miscellaneous deductions

Chapter 2B

The pension rate is 5 percent of gross pay, and taxes are 15 percent of gross pay. The number of employees is specified as 5.

Program documentation for general example 2

The documentation consists of a pseudocode description (Figure 2-4), a program listing with simple output (Figure 2-5), and a program flowchart (Figure 2-6). Each symbol on the flowchart has at the upper right of the symbol the corresponding line numbers of the listing. This is primarily to aid you in reading the flowchart and comparing it to the program, but in some cases it may be a useful addition to the flowchart documentation.

Planning and designing the program for general example 2 with pseudocode

The logic for planning a program described in Chapter 2A will be applied to general example 2 using pseudocode as the planning method. The same process can also be used with the program flowchart method.

Figure 2-4
Pseudocode description of program for general example 2—payroll processing.

	Program line numbers
Declare types	1
Initialize pension rate at 5%, tax rate at 15%, totaling variables for gross pay and taxes at zero, largest value so far at zero, maximum number of cards at 5, and card counter at 1.	2–9
READ data for an employee	10
Increment card counter by 1	11
PRINT input data for visual validation	12–13
Validate input data for out-of-range conditions:	
Hours worked negative or greater than 60	14
Wage rate negative or greater than 10.00	15
Miscellaneous deductions negative or greater than 35.00	16
If input data invalid, print error message and go to test card counter	33–34
Else continue with processing of input data	
Compute gross pay, taxes, and net pay	17–19
Select and store largest gross pay so far	20
PRINT net pay and gross pay values for this employee	21
Check for negative net pay	22
If negative net pay, print warning message and continue with processing	31–32
Else continue with processing	
Add gross pay and taxes to accumulating totals	23–24
Test card counter against value for maximum number of cards to determine if more cards should be read	25
If yes, go back to READ another data card	25
Else continue to ending of program	
PRINT summary totals for gross pay and taxes plus largest gross pay	26–29
STOP	30

100

Figure 2-5
Listing of FORTRAN program, sample input, and output for general example 2—payroll processing.

PROGRAM

```
*********          PROGRAM IDENTIFICATION               *********
*                                                               *
*       THIS PROGRAM COMPUTES PAYCHECK AMOUNTS FOR EMPLOYEES     *
*       AND COMPANY TOTALS. IT ALSO FINDS THE LARGEST GROSS      *
*       PAY AMOUNT USING AN INTRINSIC FORTRAN FUNCTION.          *
*       WRITTEN Ø4/12/77 BY T. HOFFMANN   REV. 12/16/81          *
*                                                               *
*****************************************************************
*                                                               *
*********          VARIABLE IDENTIFICATION              *********
*                                                               *
*       ID      = EMPLOYEE IDENTIFICATION NUMBER                *
*       HRSWRK  = HOURS WORKED BY EACH EMPLOYEE                  *
*       GRSPAY  = GROSS PAY: $                                  *
*       WGRATE  = WAGE RATE: $/HOUR                             *
*       PAYCHK  = NET PAYCHECK AMOUNT: $                        *
*       TAXES   = TAXES DUE: $                                  *
*       DEDUC   = MISCELLANEOUS DEDUCTIONS                      *
*       TOTPAY  = TOTAL GROSS PAY FOR COMPANY : $               *
*       TOTTAX  = TOTAL TAXES FROM ALL EMPLOYEES :$             *
*       CNTR    = COUNTER TO LIMIT CARDS READ                   *
*       LARGEP  = LARGEST GROSS PAY FOR ANY EMPLOYEE            *
*                                                               *
*****          CONSTANT IDENTIFICATION                  *****
*                                                               *
*       PNRATE  = PENSION CONTRIBUTION RATE = Ø.Ø5              *
*       TAXRT   = TAX RATE = Ø.15                              *
*       MAXCDS  = CARDS TO BE READ = 5                         *
*                                                               *
*****************************************************************
*                                                               *
*********          TYPE DECLARATION AND STORAGE BLOCK   *********
*                                                               *
  1.          INTEGER CNTR
  2.          REAL LARGEP
*                                                               *
*****************************************************************
*                                                               *
*********          INITIALIZATION BLOCK        BLOCK ØØØØ       *
*                                                               *
  3.          PNRATE = Ø.Ø5
  4.          TAXRT = Ø.15
  5.          MAXCDS = 5
  6.          LARGEP = Ø.Ø
  7.          TOTPAY = Ø.Ø
  8.          TOTTAX = Ø.Ø
  9.          CNTR = 1
*                                                               *
*****************************************************************
*                                                               *
*********          READ-COMPUTE-PRINT DETAIL   BLOCK Ø1ØØ       *
*                                                               *
 1Ø.    1Ø1 READ *,ID,HRSWRK,WGRATE,DEDUC
 11.          CNTR = CNTR + 1
 12.          PRINT *,' '
 13.          PRINT *,' ECHO',ID,HRSWRK,WGRATE,DEDUC
 14.          IF((HRSWRK .LT. Ø.Ø) .OR. (HRSWRK .GT. 6Ø.Ø)) GOTO 9Ø5
 15.          IF((WGRATE .LT. Ø.Ø) .OR. (WGRATE .GT. 1Ø.Ø) ) GOTO 9Ø5
 16.          IF((DEDUC .LT. Ø.Ø) .OR. (DEDUC .GT. 35.Ø) ) GOTO 9Ø5
 17.          GRSPAY = HRSWRK*WGRATE
 18.          TAXES = GRSPAY*TAXRT
 19.          PAYCHK = GRSPAY - TAXES - DEDUC - PNRATE*GRSPAY
*                                                               *
*             SELECT LARGEST GROSS PAY SO FAR                  *
*                                                               *
 2Ø.          LARGEP = AMAX1(LARGEP,GRSPAY)
*                                                               *
*             CHECK FOR VALID PAYCHECK AMOUNT                  *
*                                                               *
 21.          PRINT *,' NET PAY = ',PAYCHK,' GROSS PAY = ',GRSPAY
 22.          IF(PAYCHK .LE. Ø.Ø) GOTO 9Ø1
 23.    1Ø3 TOTPAY = TOTPAY + GRSPAY
 24.          TOTTAX = TOTTAX + TAXES
*                                                               *
*          IF CARDS READ IS LESS THAN MAXIMUM, GO BACK TO READ ANOTHER *
*                                                               *
 25.          IF(CNTR .LE. MAXCDS) GOTO 1Ø1
*                                                               *
*****************************************************************
*                                                               *
*********          PRINT SUMMARY AND TERMINATE  BLOCK Ø2ØØ      *
*                                                               *
 26.          PRINT *, ' '
```

101

Figure 2-5
Continued.

```
27.            PRINT *, ' TOTAL            TOTAL          LARGEST'
28.            PRINT *, ' PAY              TAX          GROSS PAY '
29.            PRINT *,TOTPAY,TOTTAX,LARGEP
30.            STOP
     *                                                                        *
     **************************************************************************
     *                                                                        *
     *********          ERROR MESSAGE BLOCK                        BLOCK Ø9ØØ
     *                                                                        *
31.      9Ø1 PRINT *,' NET PAY IS NOT POSITIVE. DO NOT ISSUE CHECK.'
     *                                                                        *
     *          GO BACK TO NORMAL PROCESSING                                  *
     *                                                                        *
32.            GOTO 1Ø3
     *
33.      9Ø5 PRINT *,' ERROR IN INPUT DATA.'
     *
     *              DO NOT COMPUTE PAY.  GO BACK FOR MORE DATA.
     *
34.            GOTO 1Ø1
35.            END
```

ID   ─HRSWRK
          ─WGRATE
             ─DEDUC   SAMPLE INPUT

```
35746, 55.5, 7.24, 30.68
69587, 10, 2.67, 27.50
35649, 22, 2.75, 35.98
15768, 37, 6.28, 24.68
27543,40,3.57,27.95
```

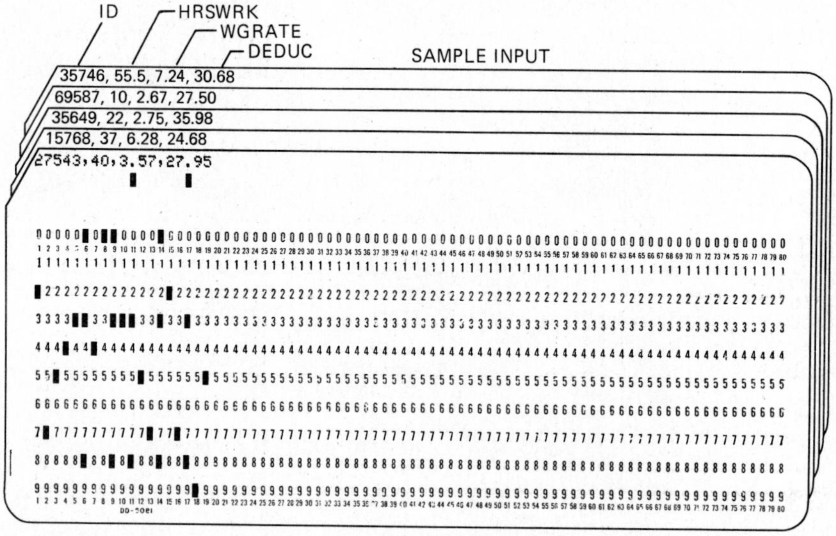

OUTPUT

```
ECHO        27543  40.0000        3.57000        27.9500
NET PAY =   86.2900       GROSS PAY =   142.800

ECHO        15768  37.0000        6.28000        24.6800
NET PAY =   161.208       GROSS PAY =   232.360

ECHO        35649  22.0000        2.75000        35.9800
ERROR IN INPUT DATA.

ECHO        69587  10.0000        2.67000        27.5000
NET PAY =  -6.14000      GROSS PAY =    26.7000
NET PAY IS NOT POSITIVE. DO NOT ISSUE CHECK.

ECHO        35746  55.5000        7.24000        30.6800
NET PAY =   290.776       GROSS PAY =   401.820

TOTAL              TOTAL          LARGEST
PAY                TAX          GROSS PAY
803.680          120.552          401.820
```

Figure 2-6
Program flowchart for general example 2—payroll processing. (Numbers beside symbols refer to line numbers on program listing.)

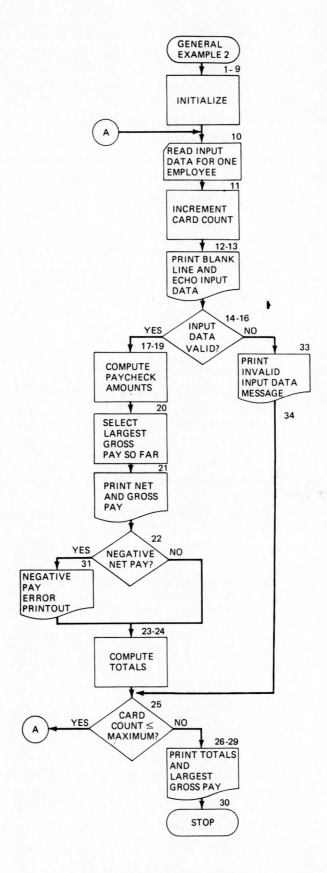

1   Plan the general logic of processing to produce one set of output from nor-
     mally expected input. Plan to the level of detail needed for the specific prob-
     lem. For example 2, the appropriate level of detail might be as follows:

     READ data for an employee

     Compute gross pay, taxes, and net pay

     Select largest gross pay so far

     PRINT net pay and gross pay values for this employee

     Add gross pay and taxes to accumulating totals

     PRINT summary totals for gross pay and taxes plus largest gross pay

     STOP

2   Add a control structure to handle multiple cases. Include logic required
     for first- and last-time-through processing. As an aid in reading the fol-
     lowing explanation, the statements from step 1 are at the margin and the
     statements added for multiple-case control are indented.

Statements from step 1
  ↓ Statements added to handle
    ↓ multiple cases

	Explanation
Initialize pension rate at 5% and tax rate at 15%	As a matter of style, these constants are named instead of the constant values being used in the formula statement. Therefore, they must be set to the desired values.
Initialize totaling variables for gross pay and taxes at zero	Totaling variables must be at zero for first-time-through logic.
Initialize largest value so far at zero	Largest value so far must be less than or equal to gross pay for first-time-through logic. Gross pay will be greater than or equal to zero, so largest value so far initialized at zero.
Initialize maximum number of input cards at 5 and a card counter at 1	Maximum number of inputs is given a variable name and set at 5. Alternatively, the constant 5 could have been coded directly in the IF test. Card counter to keep track of the number of repetitions of input reading must be set at 1 for the first-time-through logic of this program.
READ data for an employee	As a pseudocode convention for this text, underlining one or more words at the beginning of a line means the line of code will be referenced by a transfer of control in another pseudocode statement.
Increment card counter by 1	For first-time-through processing, the card counter is set at 1. After each reading of a card, the card counter is incremented by 1.

Statements from step 1
    Statements added to handle
      multiple cases
	Explanation

Compute gross pay, taxes, and net pay	
Select largest gross pay so far	Current gross pay is compared with the largest gross pay so far and the largest of the two is made the new largest gross pay so far. Note the need to initialize for first-time-through with this logic.
PRINT net pay and gross pay values for this employee	
Add gross pay and taxes to accumulating totals	Since current value for gross pay and taxes are being added to accumulated amounts, the totaling variables are set to zero for first-time-through logic.

Test card counter against value for maximum number of cards to determine if more cards should be read
    If yes, go back and READ another card
    Else continue
	The test determines whether the reading of input cards should continue. If the card counter is less than or equal to the maximum, another card should be read and processed. Underlined READ refers back to the pseudocode statement to 'READ data for an employee.'

PRINT summary totals for gross pay and taxes plus largest gross pay	
STOP	

3   Modify control structure and add logic for input validation and handling of input errors. The logic for this is placed after the two statements to read data and increment card counter. The input validation consists of two major steps:

PRINT input data for visual validation

Validate input data for out-of-range conditions

   If input data invalid, print error message and go to test card counter

   Else continue with processing of input data

If a programmer desires to specify more detail for the second validation step, the second pseudocode statement can be expanded to:

Validate input data for out-of-range conditions:

   Hours worked negative or greater than 60

   Wage rate negative or greater than 10.00

   Miscellaneous deductions negative or greater than 35.00

4   Add logic for handling exceptions and unusual cases, including cases in which data may be zero or negative. In this example, a net pay of negative is an unusual case and needs to be provided for. After printing net and gross pay, a test for negative net pay is inserted.

Check for negative net pay

  If negative net pay, print warning message and continue with processing

Else continue with processing

    Note that the program logic allows the negative net pay to be printed, but a warning message is also printed.

The complete pseudocode for the planning of general example 2 is shown in Figure 2-4. Review the complete pseudocode for the program and then read carefully through the FORTRAN program in Figure 2-6 noting the relationship of the pseudocode statements to the FORTRAN program. To aid in this comparison, the pseudocode statements are followed by the corresponding program line reference numbers from the program listing.

Notes on general example 2

This payroll program is more complex than the one in Chapter 1B and requires additional features. The usual identification blocks are given. A type declaration and storage block is added for two type declarations that override the implicit first-letter type. For example, it allows us to call the largest gross pay LARGEP and have the name reference real data. Since the program is more complex, the computation has been divided into several blocks. The first block contains all the initialization instructions; given a block number of 0000, it is executed only at the beginning of the program. The grouping of initialization in a separate block assists the review of this important step. There are additional blocks for read, compute, and print (block 0100), print summary and terminate (block 0200), and error messages (block 0900). Note we have written the block numbers at the right of the block name comment line.

Referring to the program listing in Figure 2-5, the output requirements of the program are met as follows:

1   The output for each employee consists of three or four lines:
    (a) A blank line to separate each employee output (line 12).
    (b) An echo of input data labeled 'ECHO' (line 13).
    (c) Net pay and gross pay (line 21) or an error message if input is invalid (line 33).
    (d) If net pay is negative, a message to not issue a paycheck (line 31).

2   After all five cards have been read and processed, a summary is printed (lines 26–29). The summary line headings consist of two or three words over each value. To line up the headings with the list-directed output for the computer being used, the heading line was written as two outputs (lines 27 and 28).

The AMAX1 intrinsic function is used to select the maximum employee gross pay. The generic MAX name could have been used (if available). Note the program style in the use of the IF statements in lines 14, 15, 16, 22, and 25. Simple logical IFs are used because there is only one action. The IFs are constructed so that the block of code that is normally expected to execute is placed after the IF and the error condition is a GOTO out of the normal flow.

As alternatives for coding this program, block IFs could have been used and the error messages included in the statements in the IF blocks. For example, the coding for lines 14–16, 33, and 34 could have been replaced by:

```
IF((HRSWRK .LT. 0.0) .OR. (HRSWRK .GT. 60.0)) THEN
    PRINT *, 'ERROR IN INPUT DATA'
    GOTO 101
  ELSEIF((WGRATE .LT. 0.0) .OR. (WGRATE .GT. 10.0)) THEN
    PRINT *, 'ERROR IN INPUT DATA'
    GOTO 101
  ELSEIF((DEDUC .LT. 0.0) .OR. (DEDUC .GT. 35.0)) THEN
    PRINT *, 'ERROR IN INPUT DATA'
    GOTO 101
ENDIF
```

The code for lines 22, 31, and 32 could have been replaced by:

```
IF(PAYCHK .LE. 0.0) THEN
    PRINT *, 'NET PAY IS NOT POSITIVE. DO NOT ISSUE CHECK.'
ENDIF
```

The use of the error message block may make the code easier to read since normal processing flow is not interrupted by error messages; however, placement of messages in the block IF where the error test is made may sometimes be preferred.

Statistical program example 2 — tables of ordinates of the normal curve

Problem description for statistical example 2

Calculate tables of the ordinates for the normal curve. Output from this is a table of X (abscissa) and Y (ordinate) values. Input for each table consists of a starting abscissa, an incrementing value, and the number of ordinates to compute. The program is to produce a table for each input until a negative input is read for the number of ordinates. The negative value terminates the program. The intrinsic function for exponentiation of e is to be used (EXP). The number of ordinates (table size) should not exceed 50.

$$\text{Equation: } y = \frac{1}{\sqrt{2\pi}} e^{-(x^2/2)}$$

where e is the base for natural logarithms and π has an approximate value of 3.1416.

Program documentation for statistical example 2

The documentation consists of a pseudocode description of the program (Figure 2-7), a program flowchart (Figure 2-8), and a program listing (Figure 2-9).

Figure 2-7
Pseudocode description for statistical example 2— tables of ordinates of normal curve.

Declare type
Initialize constant for $1/\sqrt{2\pi}$ and set problem number counter to 1
PRINT heading
READ starting abscissa value for table (XFIRST), abscissa increment (XINCR), and
    number of ordinates (NVALUS) to be computed
Test for end of job (that is, negative or zero value for number of ordinates)
  IF (number of ordinates is negative or zero) print end-of-program message and
    STOP
  Else continue
Validate input values for number of ordinates to be computed:
    IF (number of ordinates is greater than 50) print error message and go back to
      READ new data
    Else continue
Set abscissa value (XVALU) to starting value (XFIRST)
Set values counter (CNTR) for values in this problem to 1
Compute ordinate (YVALU) as function of abscissa value XVALU
PRINT abscissa value (XVALU) and ordinate value (YVALU)
Increment abscissa value (XVALU) by abscissa increment (XINCR)
Increment values counter by 1
Check to see whether more ordinates should be computed — values counter is less
    than or equal to number of ordinates to be computed
  If yes, go back to Compute ordinate
  Else PRINT end-of-problem message, increment problem number counter, and
    go back to READ

As in the general example, the line numbers of program statements are placed at the upper right of flowchart symbols as a cross-referencing aid.

Notes on statistical example 2

In this program, the value of $1\sqrt{2\pi}$ is computed, using the square root function (line 2) and a constant value of 6.2832 for 2π (see the constant identification following the list of variables). The structure of the READ-COMPUTE-PRINT block is essentially the same as in statistical problem 1 except that a counter has been inserted to limit the table length to a particular number of values. In addition, the intrinsic exponential function is used (line 11) in place of the constant value for e. A type declaration and storage block has been added to illustrate its use. Two variable names, CNTR and PROBN, are declared as referencing integer data.

The initialization block contains the printing of the heading that applies to the output (a global heading rather than a heading that applies to a single output or single set of outputs). The first-time-through situation is found in the use of a problem number. Each output table contains as the last line 'END OF PROBLEM problem number'. The problem number is initialized at 1 (line 3) and incremented after printing the END OF PROBLEM message but before the next card is read (line 18) for a new problem.

Backward GOTOs are used in the program but are clearly marked by comments before the GOTO statement (lines 15, 19, and 24). Note the use of explicit messages for the end of each table and for the end of the program. The end-of-program message makes it clear that program execution is complete. The input data could be echoed, but it is not necessary in this program since

Figure 2-8
Program flowchart for statistical example 2—tables of ordinates of normal curve. (Numbers beside symbols refer to line numbers on program listing.)

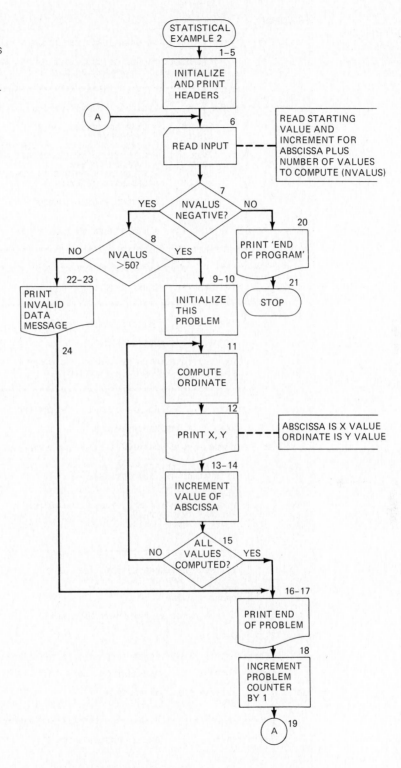

Figure 2-9
Listing of FORTRAN program, sample input, and output for statistical example 2—tables of ordinates of normal curve.

PROGRAM

```
*********          PROGRAM IDENTIFICATION                *********
*                                                                *
*       CALCULATE TABLES OF ORDINATES OF THE NORMAL CURVE        *
*       WRITTEN BY T. HOFFMANN 05/03/77  REV. 12/16/81           *
*                                                                *
******************************************************************
*                                                                *
*********          VARIABLE IDENTIFICATION               *********
*                                                                *
*       XFIRST    = STARTING VALUE FOR X                         *
*       XINCR     = INCREMENT OF X                               *
*       NVALUS    = NUMBER OF VALUES TO COMPUTE                  *
*       CNTR      = COUNTER TO LIMIT AGAINST NVALUS              *
*       PROBN     = PROBLEM NUMBER                               *
*       XVALU     = VALUE OF X TO USE TO COMPUTE YVALU           *
*       YVALU     = ORDINATE OF XVALU                            *
*                                                                *
*****              CONSTANT IDENTIFICATION               *****
*                                                                *
*       6.2832    = 2*PI                                         *
*       PIROOT    = 1.0/SQUARE ROOT OF 2*PI                      *
*                                                                *
******************************************************************
*                                                                *
*********     TYPE DECLARATION AND STORAGE BLOCK         *********
*                                                                *
1.            INTEGER CNTR,PROBN
*                                                                *
******************************************************************
*                                                                *
*********          INITIALIZATION BLOCK            BLOCK 0000
*                                                                *
2.            PIROOT = 1.0/SQRT(6.2832)
3.            PROBN = 1
4.            PRINT *,'ORDINATES OF THE NORMAL CURVE'
5.            PRINT *,' X VALUE        Y VALUE'
*                                                                *
******************************************************************
*                                                                *
*********          READ - COMPUTE - PRINT BLOCK    BLOCK 0100
*                                                                *
6.        101 READ *,XFIRST,XINCR,NVALUS
*                                                                *
*         NVALUS BEING NEGATIVE SIGNALS END OF DATA              *
*                                                                *
7.            IF(NVALUS .LE. 0) GOTO 201
8.            IF(NVALUS .GT. 50) GOTO 901
9.            XVALU = XFIRST
10.           CNTR = 1
11.       120 YVALU = PIROOT * EXP(-XVALU*XVALU/2.0)
12.           PRINT *,XVALU,YVALU
13.           XVALU = XVALU + XINCR
14.           CNTR = CNTR + 1
*                                                                *
*         IF NVALUS NOT YET COMPUTED, GO BACK FOR NEXT PAIR.     *
*                                                                *
15.           IF(CNTR .LE. NVALUS) GOTO 120
16.       130 PRINT *,' END OF PROBLEM',PROBN
17.           PRINT *,' '
18.           PROBN = PROBN + 1
*                                                                *
*            GO BACK AND READ NEXT DATA SET                      *
*                                                                *
19.           GOTO 101
*                                                                *
******************************************************************
*                                                                *
*********          TERMINATION BLOCK               BLOCK 0200
*                                                                *
20.       201 PRINT *,' END OF PROGRAM.'
21.           STOP
*                                                                *
******************************************************************
*                                                                *
*********          ERROR MESSAGE BLOCK             BLOCK 0900
*                                                                *
22.       901 PRINT *,' '
23.           PRINT *,' NVALUS TOO LARGE',NVALUS
*                                                                *
*            GO BACK TO END OF CURRENT PROBLEM AND READ NEXT DATA SET *
*                                                                *
24.           GOTO 130
25.           END
```

Figure 2-9
Continued

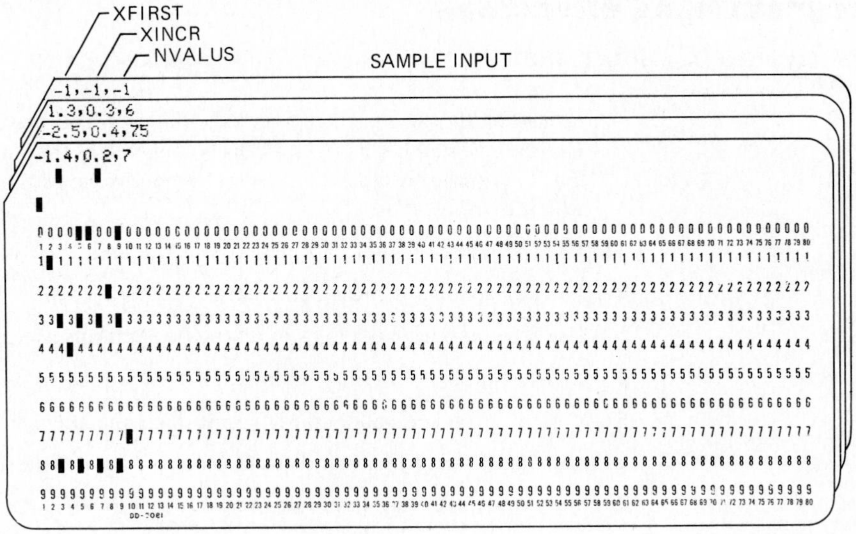

SAMPLE INPUT

OUTPUT

```
   X VALUE        Y VALUE
  -1.40000        .149727
  -1.20000        .194186
  -1.00000        .241970
  -.800000        .289691
  -.600000        .333224
  -.400000        .368270
  -.200000        .391042
  END OF PROBLEM


  NVALUS TOO LARGE           75
  END OF PROBLEM              2

   1.30000        .171368
   1.60000        .110921
   1.90000        .656157E-01
   2.20000        .354746E-01
   2.50000        .175283E-01
   2.80000        .791544E-02
  END OF PROBLEM              3

  END OF PROGRAM.
```

the starting value, increment, and number of entries are apparent from the table output.

The error message block could have been omitted and the single error message included in an IF block. Lines 8 and 22–24 would be replaced by:

```
IF(NVALUS .GT. 50) THEN
    PRINT *
    PRINT *, 'NVALUS TOO LARGE',NVALUS
    GOTO 130
ENDIF
```

In this problem either method appears satisfactory.

111

Programming exercises

Description of assignment

Select one or more problems (or take the problems assigned to you by the instructor). Use the five statements from Chapter 1 as well as the statements explained in Chapter 2A. The program should be written in good style using the following features (except where inappropriate):

1 Use the block IF where appropriate or the logical IF statement.

2 Use at least one intrinsic function.

3 Use sensible variable names and type declarations as appropriate.

4 Echo input data for visual validation if it is not printed out as part of the normal output.

5 Use programmed validation of input data when specified in the problem.

6 Use an IF loop to read and process more than one set of input data.

7 Check carefully first- and last-time-through logic.

The documentation should consist of the following:

1 Pseudocode description of program and/or program flowchart

2 Program listing

3 Results of program testing using both valid and invalid input

Chapter 3 will use these same problems but with additional requirements for formatting of output and handling of end and error conditions.

Mathematics and statistics

1 For the angles given below, compare the value given by the intrinsic sine function with the value obtained using the five terms of the following series expansion for the sine. (*Hint:* x must be in radians—1 degree equals $\pi/180$ radians.) Limit computations to positive angles less than $\pi/2$ radians.

$$\sin(x) = x - \frac{x^3}{3!} + \frac{x^5}{5!} - \frac{x^7}{7!} + \frac{x^9}{9!} - \cdots$$

Angle in degrees
15
95
60
45

2 For each of the following sets of sample data, compute the standard deviation and mean absolute deviation (average of the absolute deviations from the mean). The means are 2, 8.8, 40.0, and 10.7 for set A, B, C, and D. *Hint:* Read the mean and number of data points in a set and then read each data point in the set from a separate card.

A	B	C	D
−6	1.6	37.25	12.3
−12	6.3	39.4	8.0
8	12.4	45.61	17.4
14	9.3	38.0	6.5
13	8.0	35.78	9.3
7	7.7	42.65	
9	11.6	41.03	
−8	13.5	39.12	
10		43.66	
−15		37.5	

The formula for standard deviation is

$$\sqrt{\frac{\sum_{i=1}^{n} (X_i - \overline{X})^2}{n - 1}}$$

where X_i are the data items and $\overline{X}$ is the mean.

3 The number of combinations c of n things taken m at a time is

$$c = \frac{n!}{m!(n - m)!}$$

For large values of m or n (say k), the factorial can be approximated by Stirling's formula:

$$k! = e^{-k}k^k \sqrt{2\pi k}$$

where $e = 2.7183$ and $\pi = 3.1416$. *Note:* This is valid only for positive, nonzero values of k. Compute c for the following using Stirling's approximation formula. Use the FORTRAN function for e.

n	m
6	4
0	5
40	30
50	70

Business and economics

4 The formula for computing compound interest is

$$p = a \left(1 + \frac{i}{q}\right)^{nq}$$

where a = initial amount
 i = annual interest rate
 n = number of years

q = number of times compounded each year

p = value at end of n years

When q approaches infinity (continuous compounding) the equation becomes:

$$p = ae^{in}$$

where $e = 2.7183$.

For each of the following initial amounts and an interest rate of 7 percent, compare the values after 1 and 10 years for compounding quarterly and continuously. Use the FORTRAN exponential function for e.

$a = 1000, 565, 2045$

5 The economic order quantity (EOQ) is given by the following:

$$EOQ = \sqrt{\frac{2as}{ic}}$$

where a = annual usage

s = cost of placing an order

c = unit cost

i = annual carrying rate

For each of the following sets of data, compute the EOQ. Note that negative quantities or division by zero inside the square root are errors.

Set	a	s	c	i
1	10,000	11.75	.75	.20
2	1,000	3.50	1.25	.25
3	8,750	15.00	2.00	0
4	7,400	37.40	−1.30	.25
5	6,000	20.00	1.00	.20

6 Sales commissions c are computed as a multiple f of sales s in excess of quotas q. If goals are not met, no bonus is paid.

$$c = f(s - q)$$

For each of the following persons, compute the bonus and determine which one is the largest. Print a special message if quotas are not met.

Sales-person	Name	Goal	Actual	Bonus factor
1764	C. JONES	$400	$380	.2
2031	A. WHITE	300	340	.1
1885	X. SMITH	375	395	.17
0773	J. ADAMS	380	420	.15
2114	K. JAMES	325	367	.19

Science and engineering

7 The area of a triangle can be computed by the sine law when two sides of the triangle (a,b) and the angle θ between them is known.

Area = $\frac{1}{2} ab \sin \theta$

Given the following four triangular pieces of property, find their areas and determine which is largest. Omit computation if the angle is outside the range of 0 to 180 degrees.

Plot number	a	b	θ(radians)
1	137.4	80.9	.78
2	145.3	91.6	1.35
3	130.4	100.0	4.00
4	128.3	125.4	1.95

8 A projectile fired at an angle θ has a horizontal range R given by the following:

$$R = \frac{2v^2 \sin \theta \cos \theta}{g}$$

where v = initial velocity and g = 32.2 ft/sec². Compute R for each of the following (limit angles to 0 to $\pi/2$ radians and v to positive values):

v	θ
200	20
200	70
200	45
175	160
1750	60

9 The period p of a pendulum is given by the following formula:

$$p = 2\pi \sqrt{\frac{L}{g}} \left(1 + \frac{1}{4} \sin^2 \frac{\alpha}{2} \right)$$

where g = 980 cm/sec²
      L = pendulum length
      α = angle of displacement

Compute the periods of the following pendulums:

Pendulum number	L(cm)	α(degrees)
1	120	15
2	90	20
3	60	5
4	74.6	10
5	83.6	12

Humanities and social sciences

10 From the empirical study of learning, the following relationship was observed:

$$t_x = px^{-1}$$

where x = number of repetitions
t_x = cumulative average task time for the xth repetition
p = time to perform task the first time
l = learning factor

From this:

$$l = \frac{\log p - \log t_x}{\log x}$$

Compute l for each of the following situations (print warning if l is negative):

t_x	p	x
2.7	3.4	100
0.34	1.8	50
0.15	1.4	20
0.74	1.0	500
1.06	.8	400

11 Population growth is often either geometric (for example, doubles every 10 years) or exponential (increases at an increasing rate). For geometric growth, the equation for population size p in year n is:

$$p = a(1 + r)^n$$

where a is the initial population and r is the annual growth rate. For exponential growth a possible equation is:

$$p = ae^{rn}$$

Given $a = 10,000$, for the following situations compute the population in year 10 and the relative increase for both formulas.

Situation number	r
1	.1
2	.2
3	.5
4	.67
5	.7

12 Air pressure is a function of altitude h. For each of the following locations, compute the air pressure p given that the relationship is

$$p = 14.7e^{-0.000038h}$$

Location	Elevation h (in feet)
1 Denver	5280
2 Dead Sea	-1292
3 New York	55
4 New Delhi	760
5 Katmandu	4223

General

13 Given the currency exchange rates, compute the equivalent of each of the following amounts to U.S. dollars (or vice versa). Use a coding scheme such that:

Code	$US.	=	Alternate currency
1	1	=	2.2785 German marks
2	1	=	.5356 English pounds
3	1	=	219.65 Japanese yen

and negative codes mean opposite conversion (alternate currency to U.S. dollars). Identify which amount is the largest in U.S. dollars. Use the current rates (from *The Wall Street Journal*).

Data	
Code	Currency value
1	6.50
3	8.95
2	6.42
-3	12.44
6	8.95
-2	6.43
-1	8.88
4	2.95
1	7.50

Identify erroneous data cards (illegal codes).

14 A customer goes to a food market to buy groceries. Compute item costs and the total grocery bill, and find the most costly purchase for the following purchase list:

Items	Unit cost	Number of units
1 Beef	1.95	1.40
2 Potatoes	.85	6.75
3 Coffee	3.95	1.00
4 Candy	.15	12.00
5 Fruit	.98	7.95

15 Calculate the average temperature for each of the following weeks and determine which is warmest. Omit temperatures greater than 100 or less than 60 degrees Fahrenheit and print a warning message.

Week		Daily temperatures, °F				
1	July 4–8	85	70	83	77	75
2	July 11–15	90	78	77	80	77
3	July 18–22	999	77	85	84	73
4	July 25–29	77	85	78	0	88

chapter **3A**

Format-directed
input and output

The list-directed input and output instructions explained in Chapter 1 are very simple to use but very limiting. FORTRAN provides for more flexible input and output using format-directed input and output. The format-directed method for input and output is frequently the only method available because list-directed input and output is not supported by some older compilers and is not a part of Subset FORTRAN. The commonly used features of format-directed input and output are explained in this chapter; additional features for external files of data on magnetic tape and magnetic disks are explained in Chapter 6.

Format-directed instructions

In format-directed FORTRAN, obtaining data from an input device or writing data on an output device requires a pair of statements: the input/output statement and the FORMAT statement. The input/output statement specifies what is to be done, what device (unit) is to be used, and what variables are involved. The FORMAT statement specifies the form of the data being read in or written out. The input/output statement and the FORMAT statement are identified as belonging together by assigning a unique statement label to the FORMAT statement and referencing it in the input or output statement. Following the style recommended in this text, the FORMAT statement label will be part of the number series for the block in which it appears. For example, a pair of statements might appear as follows (where 5 is a device number and 700 is a statement label number):

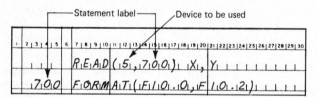

Input/output statements for format-directed input or output

The basic input/output statement with format-directed input/output describes (or implies) four specifications necessary for input or output:

1   The operation (read or write).
2   The device to be used (card reader, printer, disk storage, etc.). FORTRAN assumes these devices have been assigned unit numbers (1,2,3, . . . ,n).
3   The statement label of the FORMAT statement, which describes the format of the data to be input or output.
4   The variables to be input or output in the order to be read or written.

The basic specifications of device and FORMAT statement can be extended by other specifications, two of which will be explained later in this chapter and the rest in Chapters 4, 6, and 7.

There are two basic input/output statements—one for reading (input) and one for writing (output):

READ (*u,fs*) list

WRITE (*u,fs*) list

where *u* refers to the unit number assigned to the input or output device and *fs* refers to the label of the FORMAT statement to be used. The four specifications are provided as follows:

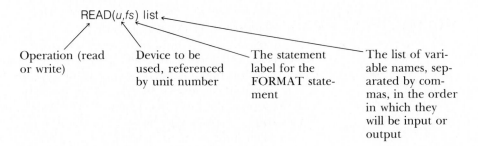

Operation (read or write)

Device to be used, referenced by unit number

The statement label for the FORMAT statement

The list of variable names, separated by commas, in the order in which they will be input or output

Examples

READ (5, 710)A, B, X	Read values for A, B, and X (in that order) using unit 5 and FORMAT statement 710.
WRITE (6, 720)X, A, B	Write values for X, A, B (in that order) using unit 6 and FORMAT statement 720.

Note that the space following each right parenthesis is optional. The text examples of FORMAT statements are numbered in the 700s. This is an arbitrary designation and has no special significance.

The unit specification in the input/output statement can be either an integer constant or an integer variable. Both of the following are correct forms:

READ (5, 705)A, B, C

READ (NREAD, 705)A, B, C

If an integer variable such as NREAD is used, then it must be defined in the program as having a value equal to the desired unit. For example, if the unit number to be used in the above example is 5, then NREAD may be defined by a statement such as:

NREAD = 5

The input or output statement requires a unit number to specify a card reader, printer, etc. But what unit number shall be used? There are no universally agreed-upon unit numbers, nor are any unit numbers specified in the FORTRAN standard. This means that a user of each implementation of FORTRAN must obtain the unit numbers assigned by that implementation. (There is a place to record these unit numbers for your computer on the inside of the back cover). Although there are no universally agreed-upon standard numbers, the most generally used unit numbers are 5 for card reader and 6 for printer. For terminal use, unit 5 commonly designates keyboard input and unit 6 writes to the terminal printer or display. These unit numbers are used by WATFOR, WATFIV, M77, and other versions of FORTRAN.

One of the desirable features of FORTRAN is its portability such that a program written and run on one computer can be run without significant change on another computer. The use of different unit numbers can inhibit portability, but there are fairly easy ways to handle the differences. One way is to write all READ and WRITE systems with variable names for the unit designation (such as NREAD) and merely to change the statement that assigns a value to NREAD. The other way is to assign the desired value to an input or output device by the use of a job control card. In other words, each installation will have assigned default values such as 5 or 6 for the card reader, printer, etc., but other values may be used by a simple job control instruction. These instructions to assign unit numbers are specific to each FORTRAN implementation, and thus must be obtained from the computer center being used.

An alternate form of the input and output statement that does not use the unit designation is included in both the full 1966 and 1977 FORTRAN standards and is provided in most implementations. In the name-description form, READ means read from the standard device (generally card reader), and PRINT means to output using the standard device (generally printer). Note that a comma must follow the FORMAT number in the name-designation form.

Unit-designation form	Name-designation form
READ (5, 705)A, B	READ 705, A, B
WRITE (6, 710)A, B	PRINT 710, A, B

The advantage of the name-designation form is that the card reader and printer (or other standard devices such as a terminal) can be specified when the programmer does not know the unit number. However, the name-designation form is not always available in restricted versions such as Subset FORTRAN. Since the unit-designation form is the more general form and always available, it is the preferred form and will be used in all examples in this text.

The unit-designation form can be used for list-directed input or output by writing an asterisk in place of a format statement number. For example, the following are equivalent:

```
READ (5, *) A, B, C
READ *, A, B, C
```

In summary, the basic input/output instructions for format-directed input and output require only four elements: the command word (READ, WRITE), the input/output unit designation, the FORMAT statement label number, and the list of variable names in the order they are to be read, printed, punched, etc.

> ## BASIC INPUT/OUTPUT INSTRUCTIONS
>
> *Symbols used in description*
>
> u = unit designation (integer variable or integer constant) for input/output unit. Unit designations for various devices differ among implementations. Common usage is 5 for card reader and 6 for printer.
>
> fs = statement label of FORMAT statement to be used with the input or output instruction. If an asterisk (*) is used in place of a statement number, the instruction is list-directed.
>
> list = list of variables, which are to be read, printed, punched, etc., in the order in which they are to be used. The variable names are separated by commas. There need be no spaces between items in the list, but spaces may be used for readability.
>
> *Form of instructions*
>
> READ (*u,fs*) list
>
> Reads from an input unit the quantities associated with the listed variable names and puts them into storage for use by the program.
>
> WRITE (*u,fs*) list
>
> Writes variables using an output unit. Form of output varies with output unit and FORMAT statement having label *fs*.
>
> *Alternate forms without unit designation (not part of subset)*
>
> READ *fs*,list
>
> Reads from a standard input device (such as card reader) the quantities associated with the listed variable names and puts them into memory.
>
> PRINT *fs*,list
>
> Prints a line of output using the quantities represented by list of variable names in the form specified by FORMAT statement *fs*.

Examples

READ (5, 705)A, B, C READ 705, A, B, C	Read data from the card reader to variable names A, B, and C. Read according to the format specified by statement 705.
WRITE (6, 710)I, BETA PRINT 710, I, BETA	Write on printer the quantities from variable names I and BETA. Use format specified by statement 710.

Self-testing exercise 3-1

1 Explain the meaning of the following input/output statements, assuming unit number 5 is card reader and unit number 6 is printer.
(*a*) READ (5, 700)A, B, C
(*b*) PRINT 710, X, Y, Z
(*c*) WRITE (NRITE, 720)L, N, O
(*d*) READ 730, Q, Z, T
(*e*) WRITE (6, *)X, Y, IX

2 A FORTRAN program has been written using unit numbers 1 for card reader and 3 for printer. The program is now to be run on a computer with default unit numbers 5 for card reader and 6 for printer. How is this change made?

The FORMAT statement

The purpose of the FORMAT statement is to describe the specific form of the data being read or written. The FORMAT statement uses a standard method of describing data that is the same for all input/output media. The same FORMAT statement can define data to be read from a card reader, to be punched into cards, or to be printed on the printer as long as the form of the data is the same in all cases. One FORMAT statement can be used by more than one input or output statement. The FORMAT statement does not have to appear next to the input/output statement using it. The statement label is sufficient identification, so that the FORMAT statement can be written before or after the input/output command using it. Some programmers put a FORMAT statement next to the first input/output statement referencing it; others group all FORMAT statements together at the beginning or end of the program. A convention used in this text is to place each FORMAT statement closely following the first input/output statement that references it and to use a statement label from the numbers in that block.

In order to describe the form of the data for input/output, three elements must be specified or implied:

1. *Type of editing*   This can specify real, integer, real with exponent editing, or character data. (Other less-common types will be explained in Chapter 7.)
2. *Field size*   This is the number of columns on punched cards or printer paper, or character positions on other storage media, that are available for reading, storing, or printing the quantity.
3. *Location of decimal point*   This is expressed as number of places from the right of the field. This element is eliminated from the FORMAT specification for integer quantities and character data (because it has no meaning).

The FORMAT statement consists of the statement label (columns 1–5), the word FORMAT (normally beginning in column 7), and then the sets of specifications separated by commas. The group of specifications is enclosed in parentheses. Spaces may be used freely to improve readability. Examples (to be explained later) are:

1	2	3	4	5	6	7	8	9	10	11	12	13	14	15	16	17	18	19	20	21	22	23	24	25	26	27	28	29	30	31	32	33	34	35	36	37	38	39	40
	1	0	9			F	O	R	M	A	T	(	F	1	0	.	2	,	F	5	.	1	)																
	2	0	9			F	O	R	M	A	T	(	F	7	.	0	,	I	/	2	)																	
	3	0	9			F	O	R	M	A	T	(	E	1	5	.	8	,	E	1	5	.	8	,	F	1	0	.	2	)								

As illustrated by the examples, each specification set consists of three elements: a single-letter edit descriptor, field size, and decimal location. The three elements in the specifiation F10.2 are useful in seeing how the three elements are contained in the specification.

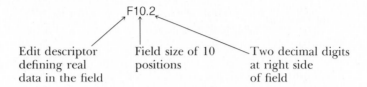

The first part of the specification is the single-letter edit descriptor. The four most commonly used edit descriptors are F, E, and I for numeric data and A for character data. The three numeric data edit descriptors will be explained in this section. The character-data descriptor is described in a later section. Additional descriptors for other data types are explained in Chapter 7.

FOUR COMMON EDIT DESCRIPTORS

Letter	Type of quantity	Form	Where
F	Real	Fw.d	w = field size
E	Exponent form of real	Ew.d	d = positions to right
I	Integer	Iw	of decimal
A	Character	Aw	

The next part of the FORMAT specification is the field size in numbers of spaces or columns. This is the maximum number of character spaces or columns the quantity can occupy. The data quantity need not use all of the field; the unused positions are left blank. The field size for numeric output should allow space for characters such as the sign and, for real output, a decimal point. For example, the field size for the following real and integer outputs are computed as follows (the E edit descriptor will be explained later):

Type of variable	Form of data		Sign	Integer digits	Decimal point	Digits in fraction	Total	Edit specification
				Minimum field size				
Real	±ddd.dd	=	1	3	1	2	7	F7.2
Real	±ddd.	=	1	3	1	0	5	F5.0
Integer	±dddd	=	1	4	0	0	5	I5

The third part of the FORMAT statement (not used with the I edit descriptor) is the location of the decimal point in the field. The field specification and decimal point specification are used in input in a slightly different way than in output. The use in output will be discussed first, and then the differences will be noted.

FORMAT editing for output

The handling of numeric data on output is quite simple in the normal case. However, there are special rules for a field size that is too large or too small for the data. Also, the first position on the printed line is not available but is used for vertical spacing control. It will be convenient to separately describe integer data, real data with F edit descriptor, and real data with E edit descriptor. The use of the first print position for vertical spacing will be explained later in the chapter.

For integer data, no decimal point is printed, the quantity is right-justified (number starts at right side of field), and unused positions to the left are blank. A minus sign will print for a negative quantity, but a plus sign will not print for a positive quantity. If the field size is too small for the quantity (for example, a field defined as I4 and a quantity to be output of 39764), there is an error condition called *overflow*. In cases of overflow, the output for the field consists of asterisks to indicate the the overflow error.

Examples

Specifica-tion	Data	Output (b indicates blank)
I6	−479	bb−479
I10	3	bbbbbbbbb3
I4	36754	****

Note that a field specification that is larger than needed is one method of leaving space between output items. Another method will be explained later. As an example of the uses of I specifications, the following statements will produce data and blanks in columns as illustrated.

```
    WRITE (6, 700) IX, JIX, KIX
700 FORMAT (I10, I5, I6)
```

where the value for IX is −37454; for JIX, 495; and for KIX, 1159.

For real output using the F edit descriptor, the computer right justifies in the field. The integer digits are positioned to the left of the decimal point, and the fractional digits are positioned to the right. As shown at the top of the next page, a printing specification of F10.3 will place the decimal point in the fourth position from the right.

When using the F specification for output, the following conditions can occur for the integer portion and fractional portions of the F specification field:

1 Digits in result to be output do not fill the field
   (*a*) Integer portion
   (*b*) Fractional portion

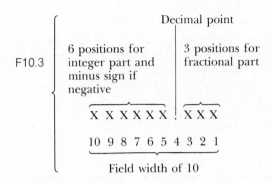

2 Digits in result to be output exceed positions in field
 (a) Integer portion
 (b) Fractional portion

These conditions will be explained and illustrated.

1 Digits do not fill field.
 (a) If digits in integer portion do not fill all positions, the unused positions to the left are filled with blanks. For example, 98.5 and F10.1 = bbbbbb98.5. The integer portion must be large enough to include a minus sign when the output quantity is negative. It is good programming practice in writing specifications to allow for a negative sign even when only positive values are expected.
 (b) If fractional digits do not fill the fractional portion of the field, the remaining positions to the right are filled with zeros. For example, 347.56 and F10.5 = b347.56000.
2 Digits exceed positions available.
 (a) When the number of integer digits exceeds the available field width to the left of the decimal, there will be overflow resulting in output of a field of asterisks. For example, 67943.2 to be printed with a FORMAT statement F8.4 will cause overflow, and the output will be a field of asterisks.

			Field positions
d = 4	Fractional digit position (d)	=	4
67 943.2000	Decimal point	=	1
Field size of 8	Remaining for integer position =		3
Overflow digits		Total =	8

 (b) If the number of fractional digits exceeds fractional field size (specified by d portion of specification), the excess digits will be truncated after rounding. No error indication occurs. For example, 7.6543 printed with F8.2 will print 7.65 and 3.9462 with F8.2 will print 3.95.

The E or exponent form of output editing is preferred in all cases where the result is very large, is very small, or has an unknown range of magnitude.

127

In output with the E format, the result is expressed as a decimal fraction plus an exponent that indicates the number of places the decimal point of the fraction should be moved to the right (for a positive exponent) or to the left (for a negative exponent). The E specification indicates the number of positions in the E result field and the number of positions (digits) in the fraction.

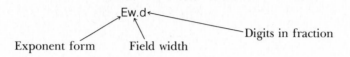

Exponent form   Field width   Digits in fraction

Specification	Quantity	Output
E15.8	375.76001	b0.37576001E+03
E15.8	−.0000037576001	−0.37576001E−05
E13.6	375.76082	b0.375761E+03

The zero to the left of the decimal point in the E form of output is optional, so some implementations of FORTRAN produce it; others do not. In the text explanations, we will use it, but keep in mind that it is not always implemented.

The following examples illustrate how data characters and blank spaces are positioned when integer data items are output with I edit specifications and real data items are output using F and E edit specifications.

```
      WRITE (6, 701)A, B, IX        ⎧ A = −493.122
                                    ⎨ B = 4.755
 701 FORMAT (F10.3, F8.2, I6)       ⎩ IX = 5628
```

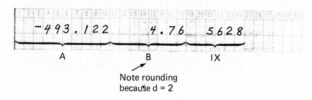

```
      WRITE (6, 702)X, JIX, Y       ⎧ X = 1976.43
                                    ⎨ JIX = 2
 702 FORMAT (E16.8, I7, E15.4)      ⎩ Y = 0.001
```

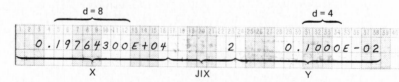

Assuming a leading zero, an E specification requires at least seven digit positions more than the size of the fraction to allow for the sign of the fraction, the zero, the decimal point, and the four positions for the exponent. If there is no leading zero, only six positions are required beyond the fraction size. (Assume seven for all problems.) If the field size for output is more than required, the result will be right-justified and blank spaces will be inserted at the left. If the number of digits in the specified fraction size is less than the number of digits stored in the computer, the quantity will be truncated after rounding, as in the third variable in the last example.

The form of the exponent can vary with different implementations of FOR-TRAN and different sizes of exponents. The following are all standard: E±nn or ±0nn for exponents of 99 or less, and ±nnn for exponents between 99 and 999, where the n's stand for the digits in the exponent. Note that all forms use four output positions. For illustration purposes, we will use E±nn.

FORMAT editing for input

FORMAT editing may be used for both input from punched cards and input from terminals. If input data items are being entered from a terminal, it is generally simpler to specify a free format input (READ *,list) with data items separated by commas or spaces. However, there may be cases when the terminal user wishes to enter data in a fixed-field formatted form, and a FORMAT statement is then required to specify the different input items. The explanation uses a punched card as the example, but fixed-field terminal input can be visualized as identical to a punched card input.

The FORMAT statement is treated differently with a READ punched-card statement than with a WRITE or PRINT statement in three cases. First, with data in punched cards, no provision need be made for an input sign or decimal point unless it occupies columns by being punched. If an input value is negative, the sign must be punched as a leading minus sign, but if the values to be input are positive, no sign is needed. Within a field, blanks may precede the negative sign, but zeros must not be punched to the left of the sign.

The second difference is in the meaning of the d portion of the specification. In input from punched cards, a decimal point in the data takes precedence over the decimal location specification of the FORMAT statement. If no decimal point is punched, the decimal point location is based on the edit specification in the FORMAT statement. If the quantity does not fill all positions in the field, leading blanks are not significant (assume they become leading zeros) and trailing blanks are ignored.

The third difference for input is in the form of input data for E format reading. The E is optional; if E is used, a plus sign is optional. However, clear input forms should be used to avoid mistakes. The following two sets of data are all valid, the items in the set showing different ways to represent the same quantity:

Examples

Set 1	Set 2
13795.2E12	.2684E01
13795.2+12	2684.−3
.137952+17	26.84E−1

Note that the exponent changed when the decimal point was moved. A number punched in an E format may also be read by an F specification.

The following examples illustrate the rules for input FORMAT specifications.

1   Several data items are punched on an input card without spaces between. Variable names are assigned as shown. No decimal points are punched, but the locations of the implied decimal points are shown by the carets; for example, X = 9.8, Y1 = 789.4, YJ = 1.094, YK = 86765.4, and KIX = 88.

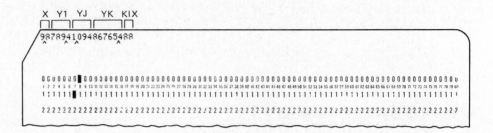

The statement to read these variables is the following. (Note that no allowance is made for a sign or a decimal point in the input field size because none appears in the data.)

```
READ (5, 201)X, Y1, YJ, YK, KIX
201 FORMAT (F2.1, F4.1, F4.3, F6.1, I2)
```

Note that spaces between specifications are optional and are used for readability only.

2   Applying the rules for reading input, a quantity in a punched card will be read as indicated using the given format:

Quantity in punched card	Format specifications to read data	Read as	Comments
3 2 5	I3	000	Because I3 reads only columns 1–3 and data is in columns 8 to 10.
3 2 5	I10	0000000325	Leading spaces = zeros.
3 2 5 4 5 7	I3, I4	325 and 0457	
3 2 5	I10	325	Trailing spaces are ignored.
3 7 5 . 5 6	F5.2, F5.2	000.03 and 75.56	Only first 5 columns read with first format specification.
3 7 5 . 5 6	F10.2	00000375.56	Leading spaces = zeros.
3 7 5 . 5 6	F10.0	0375.56	Punched decimal overrides format. Trailing spaces are ignored.

The basic approach to input and output has now been explained. The rules for the FORMAT statement for numeric data are summarized in the box.

FORMAT STATEMENT FOR NUMERIC DATA

General form

fs FORMAT (list of specifications separated by commas), where *fs* is a format statement label. Spaces before and after parentheses and between specifications are optional.

Form of specifications

Fw.d	Real variable	w stands for field size
Ew.d	Exponent form	d stands for number of decimal positions to right of
Iw	Integer variable	decimal

Fitting data to field size

1. Data is justified to the right in the field on output. On input, trailing blanks are ignored, but a field of all blanks is interpreted as zero. In the case of real data input, a punched decimal position overrides a FORMAT-specified decimal position.

2. If integer positions of an output are greater than the integer portion field size, an overflow error condition results and a field of asterisks is output.

3. If significant digits in the fractional portion exceed the number of positions in the fraction field to the right of the decimal point, the remaining quantity is rounded and the excess digits are truncated.

4. Using the E form can ensure maximum accuracy without overflow. The d portion should be the same as the number of significant digits, and the field width should be at least 7 higher.

Self-testing exercise 3-2

1. Read the following data from a punched card. The data items are referenced by the variable names ALPHA, BETA, IOTA, and JIX.

Note that the sizes of the fields, including blank spaces at the left, are:

Variable	Field size	Columns	Characters of data including sign position
ALPHA	10	1–10	10
BETA	9	11–19	9
IOTA	7	20–26	7
JIX	7	27–33	6

2 Print the above variables in reverse order. Use minimum space but allow for sign. Leave two spaces between ALPHA and BETA, not counting the sign position. Leave the first position on the line blank (not counting a space for a sign).

3 Print the variables IOTA and BETA. Do not print the fractional portion of BETA. Do not use a field size larger than absolutely necessary, but provide 10 spaces (not counting the space allowed for a sign) before the first quantity and between the actual quantities as printed.

4 What will be the result of the following set of WRITE and FORMAT statements if X = 1.0375 and IYEAR = 95

```
    WRITE (6, 701) IYEAR, X
701 FORMAT (I10, F10.2)
```

5 What is the minimum specification for printing the following variables? (Remember to allow for decimal point and one space for sign.) X's stand for nonzero integers.

Form of variable	To be printed as	FORTRAN FORMAT specification
(a) XXXXXXXX	XXXX.XX	
(b) XXXX0000	XXXX.0	
(c) −XXXXXXXX	−XX.XXXXXX	
(d) XXXXXXXX	.XXX	
(e) XXXX	XXXX	
(f) −XXXXXXX0000000	−0.XXXXXXX0E+14	

Repetition of FORMAT specifications

When several variables for input or output have the same specifications, a single specification can be repeated by placing an integer number in front of it. For example, 7F10.3 means that the F10.3 specification is to be used seven times.

By enclosing a set of specifications in parentheses and placing an integer number in front of the set, the set will be repeated the number of times indicated: 3(F10.0, I3) is the same as (F10.0, I3, F10.0, I3, F10.0, I3).

The following examples illustrate the repeat feature. The repeat stops when the list of variables to be used is exhausted. The program uses only as much of a FORMAT as is needed by the list of variables.

Examples of FORMAT repeat are:

FORMAT	Effect
FORMAT (I3, 7F10.0)	I3 and repeat F10.0 up to seven times.
FORMAT (5(I3, F10.0), F10.0)	Repeat (I3, F10.0) five times, then use F10.0.
FORMAT (I3, 5(F10.0, I2))	I3 and repeat (F10.0, I2) up to five times.
FORMAT (7I2, 3(F10.0, I3))	Repeat I2 up to seven times, and then repeat (F10.0, I3) up to three times.

Horizontal positioning specifications

Specifying excess positions in a field width causes blanks to be inserted in a line, but this is sometimes cumbersome. An alternative is the nX specification, which causes n positions to be skipped (and filled with blanks). For example, on output a FORMAT (1X, I3, 10X, I3) puts a blank in the first position, prints data in the next 3 positions, skips the next 10 (makes them blank), and prints in the following 3 positions.

A Tc specification is a tabulating specification that positions the input or output device at the cth character position. For example, writing a FORMAT (T50, F10.2) will output starting at position 50 on the line. Note that T50 means to start input or output at position 50, not to skip 50 and start 51.

The nX and Tc edit specifiers apply to input as well as to output. For example, the following read instructions read the data for Y in columns 51 to 60 and the data for IY in columns 71 to 75.

```
    READ (5, 100)Y, IY
100 FORMAT (T51, F10.0, 10X, I5)
```

HORIZONTAL POSITIONING

nX   Skip n positions to the right.

Tc   Tabulate to position c; that is, move to position c where next input or output will begin. Available only with full FORTRAN.

Self-testing exercise 3-3

What is the effect of each of the following FORMAT specifications?

1 FORMAT (5(F6.0), 3I4)
2 FORMAT (3I2, 4F10.0, 2E15.8)
3 FORMAT (4(I3, F10.0), I3)
4 FORMAT (I5, 10X, F10.2)
5 FORMAT (19X, F10.2, 20X, I3)
6 FORMAT (T20, F10.2, T50, I3)

Providing descriptive labels and headings on output

It is frequently desirable to provide descriptive labels and headings on output (primarily printed output). A program to compute the variance and standard deviation of an array of numbers might have an output such as the following:

```
THE VARIANCE IS                           XXXXXX.XX

THE STANDARD DEVIATION IS                    XXX.XX

THE NUMBER OF OBSERVATIONS IS                   XXX
```

The descriptive character output illustrated above is sometimes termed *Hollerith output.* FORMAT specifications permit any combination of letters, numbers, and special characters on a line of output. There are essentially four methods for providing headings and other character output.

1 Apostrophe edit descriptors in the FORMAT statement.
2 H edit descriptor in the FORMAT statement.
3 A set of characters in list-directed output enclosed in apostrophes.
4 Character data stored internally and referenced by variable names.

The first two methods, the apostrophe and H edit descriptors, are essentially identical in purpose and space. The H edit descriptor is the older method and tends to be error-prone. The apostrophe method is therefore preferred (but may not be available on older implementations of FORTRAN). The apostrophe and H edit descriptors are also used to control vertical spacing. The third method for descriptive labels and headings in list-directed output was explained in Chapter 1. The fourth method, explained in this section, involves input, storage, and output of character data.

Apostrophe edit descriptor

The apostrophe method encloses the characters to be output in apostrophes. If the field to be output contains an apostrophe, two consecutive apostrophes are used to specify an apostrophe in the printed output. The first position in the output is not printed, and thus should be left blank. Its use in vertical spacing control is explained later.

Examples

1	2│3│4│5	6	7│8│9│10│11│12│13│14│15│16│17│18│19│20│21│22│23│24│25│26│27│28│29│30│31│32│33│34│35│36│37│38│39│40
			WRITE(6,700)
	700		FORMAT(' NOW IS THE TIME.')
			WRITE(6,710)
	710		FORMAT(' I CAN''T DO IT.')

The apostrophe specification may be placed among a list of format edit specifications, or it may be the sole output of the WRITE (or PRINT) statement. For example, if the answer is the variable X, which has a specification of F10.2, the set of WRITE and FORMAT statements to print

THE ANSWER IS $\boxed{\pm\text{XXXXXX.XX}}$

will be:

1	2	3	4	5	6	7	8	9	10	11	12	13	14	15	16	17	18	19	20	21	22	23	24	25	26	27	28	29	30	31	32	33	34	35	36	37	38	39	40
						W	R	I	T	E	(	6	,	7	0	0	)		X																				
	7	0	0			F	O	R	M	A	T	(	'	'		T	H	E		A	N	S	W	E	R		I	S				'	,	F	1	0	.	2	)
						W	R	I	T	E	(	6	,	7	0	0	)		X																				
	7	0	0			F	O	R	M	A	T	(	'	'		T	H	E		A	N	S	W	E	R		I	S	'	,	F	1	2	.	2	)			

The first apostrophe specification provides for two spaces after the word IS. The second format shows how the blanks after the word IS can be provided by making the field size for the output of the variable X two spaces wider. Since the number on output is right-justified, the additional two spaces appear at the left. The Hollerith line starts at the left side with the first position kept blank. A heading such as ANALYSIS PROGRAM, to be centered on a page with 132 printing spaces, is written with a WRITE or PRINT statement having no variable list, as follows:

```
    WRITE (6, 700)
700 FORMAT (58X, 'ANALYSIS PROGRAM')
```

Note that it was simpler to skip the 58 spaces to the center than to include these in the apostrophe specifiation. The T specification could also have been used to start the heading in column 59 (same as skipping over 58 spaces).

```
700 FORMAT (T59, 'ANALYSIS PROGRAM')
```

H edit descriptor

The use of the H edit descriptor for character output is quite simple but is not recommended because it tends to be error-prone. It involves writing out the output exactly as it is to appear (including blanks) and then counting the number of character positions occupied. The number of character positions plus an H are written in front of the characters to indicate that the specified number of positions following is not to be translated, but is to be moved exactly as written to the output line. For example, to print THE ANSWER IS, which takes up 14 positions (if the first position is left blank), the H specification is:

```
700 FORMAT (14H THE ANSWER IS)
```

Programming errors often occur because the count of the positions is wrong. The separating comma in the FORMAT statement, necessary after an E, F, or I specification, is optional (but desirable) following the H and apostrophe edit specifications.

CHARACTER OUTPUT FROM FORMAT

Apostrophe edit   Enclose characters to be output in apostrophes. Two consecutive apostrophes are used to specify apostrophe in output.

H edit   Precede the characters to be output by nH, where n is the number of characters following H that are to be output.

Comma following apostrophe edit or H edit characters is optional.

Vertical spacing with control characters

On line printers running under FORTRAN, the first column on the line is not printed; that position is used for vertical spacing or carriage control of the printer. The output is written so that column 1 is blank unless vertical spacing control other than single spacing is desired. To implement vertical spacing control, a special character is assigned to the first position by an appropriate FORMAT statement. The usual method for including this in the FORMAT is to specify a one-character Hollerith field for output to column 1. The vertical spacing control characters are shown in the box:

VERTICAL SPACING WITH CONTROL CHARACTER

First position on output line is used for vertical spacing control. The character is usually placed in the first position by a character output using either apostrophe or H edit methods.

Character	Vertical spacing before output
Blank	One line (single space)
0 (zero)	Two lines (double space)
1	To first line of next page
+	No advance

Note: Some terminals do not use a carriage control character. In such a case, the character in the first position is displayed (except in list-directed output).

Either the apostrophe or the H edit descriptor form may be used to specify vertical spacing. The following pairs are identical:

1	2 3 4 5	6	7 8 9 10 11 12 13 14 15 16 17 18 19 20 21 22 23 24 25 26 27 28 29
	7 0 0		F O R M A T (' ' ' ')
	7 0 0		F O R M A T (1 H ')
	7 1 0		F O R M A T (' 0 ')
	7 1 0		F O R M A T (1 H 0)

The vertical spacing control character can be the only element in the FOR-MAT, or it may be included with other output on the same line. The following are equivalent:

```
700   FORMAT('1','THE ANSWERS')
700   FORMAT(1H1,11HTHE ANSWERS)
700   FORMAT(12H THE ANSWERS)
```

Space to top of page and print THE ANSWERS

Since a blank in the first position of any line of output is used for normal single spacing, single-spaced lines should have a format in which the first character is a space. The X edit descriptor can be used to skip the position (leaving it blank), or a blank can be established by apostrophe or H edit methods. Excess leading spaces in F or I edit descriptors may also leave a blank but are dangerous because large values may fill the first space. The following three examples all have the same effect of single spacing.

```
701   FORMAT(' THIS IS PAGE ',I2)
701   FORMAT(14H THIS IS PAGE ,I2)
701   FORMAT(1X,'THIS IS PAGE ',I2)
```

Self-testing exercise 3-4

Write a set of WRITE and FORMAT statements to provide the following lines of output. Write each using both the H and apostrophe edit descriptors to gain some experience (even though the apostrophe edit descriptor is recommended). A line is assumed to have 132 spaces.

1 ←—25—→ THE TOLERANCE IS bbXXX.XX

2 ←—10—→ AMOUNT OF SAVINGS IS $ XXX.XX

3 NUMBER IS XXXX

4 THE END. (with vertical spacing of 2 lines before printing.)

5 ←—5—→ ITEM ←—10—→ AMOUNT

6 PAYROLL REPORT centered at top of page.

Input, storage, and output of characters

There will be situations where characters cannot be placed in a FORMAT statement because the characters to be used are variable. In such cases, it may be desirable to input the characters and store them for later use.

Character data can be stored in the computer and therefore can be referenced by name. The character string GBD can be referred to by NAME just as the data 147.6 can be referred to as VALUE. Each character in the character string occupies one character storage unit. The length of a character data item is the number of character positions (including imbedded blanks) in the string. For example, 'I WILL' occupies six positions.

Variable names identified with a character string do not have a special first letter. In 1977 FORTRAN, the approach is to define variable names that reference character data as being of type CHARACTER. An alternate approach used in earlier versions of FORTRAN is explained later in the section. The CHARACTER type declaration was explained in Chapter 2. In this method, the declaration not only specifies a name as being a character variable name but also specifies the maximum number of characters that can be stored and referenced by the variable name. The maximum number of characters stored and referenced by a name can range from 1 to a very large number (limit set by the implementation of FORTRAN). As an example,

```
CHARACTER HEAD*15, SUBHED*8, MSGE01*20
```

defines the variable name HEAD as referencing locations that can store 15 characters, SUBHED as a variable that can reference 8 characters, and MSGE01 as a variable that can reference 20 characters.

Declaring variable names as referencing variable data does not put any characters in the storage locations to which the names are assigned. This must be done by other instructions. A common method for doing this is to read the character data from input (on punched cards or entered at a terminal). The reading of character data can use list-directed input, format-directed input with explicit character-type variables, and format-directed input with implied character-type variables.

When character data is read using a list-directed read statement (with no FORMAT statement), the variable list contains a variable name that has been declared as character. The character data input is enclosed in apostrophes. For example, to read 'HI THERE!' and store it in GREETN using list-directed input requires the following:

```
CHARACTER GREETN*9
READ *,GREETN
```

The data on the punched card or entered at the terminal would be in the form:

```
'HI THERE!'
```

If the greeting is to be printed, the list-directed method would include the character variable in a print statement:

```
PRINT *,GREETN
```

The output will be the characters stored under the variable name GREETN but not the apostrophes. The output will be arranged according to the rules for list-directed output. In this case, the characters will be printed in columns 2–10 (list-directed output always leaves column 1 blank).

If formatted input or output statements and explicit character-type variables are used, the variable names referencing character data must be declared as CHARACTER type. The FORMAT statement must be described by an A edit descriptor in the input/output fields that contain characters. The form is A followed by the length of the field designated for characters. If the length is not specified, the declared length in the character-type declaration applies. On input, if the length specified by the A edit descriptor is greater than the declared length for the variable, the rightmost characters will be taken from input until the storage declared for the variable is full; if the length specified by the A descriptor is less than the length of the variable storage, the data characters that are read are stored at the left side of the set of storage positions and the unused positions at the right are filled with blanks. On output, a field size larger than the number of characters stored will result in leading blanks to fill the field. An output field size smaller than the number of characters declared for the character variable will result in the characters stored in the leftmost positions being used. For example,

```
Declaration      CHARACTER LABEL1*10
Input statement  READ (5,700) LABEL1
Input data:      NOW IS THE TIME        (Note that this is 15 characters)
```

If the FORMAT statement is:

```
FORMAT (A10)   or (A)
FORMAT (A15)   (larger)
FORMAT (A6)    (smaller)
```

data will be stored in 10 positions of LABEL1 as:

```
NOW IS THE
S THE TIME     (take rightmost from input field)
NOW ISbbbb     (take leftmost and fill with blanks)
```

The output when NOW IS THE is stored in LABEL1 and statement WRITE (6,700)LABEL1 follows:

```
FORMAT (A10)   or (A)      NOW IS THE
FORMAT (A15)   (larger)    bbbbbNOW IS THE   (leading blanks to fill
                                             field)
FORMAT (A3)    (smaller)   NOW               (use stored characters
                                             starting at left)
```

The alternative approach to character data storage, used in previous versions of FORTRAN, is the implicit method. Because of its previous use, this method is provided as an extension of the standard in many implementations of 1977 FORTRAN. In the implicit method, there is no type declaration for variables storing character data. Character type is implied when input data is read and stored using an A format descriptor. Since the length of the character string is not specified in a CHARACTER type declaration, the length of character variable storage is predefined as a fixed number of characters. This can vary with implementations of FORTRAN, but common limits are 4, 6, or 10 characters.

A EDIT DESCRIPTOR

A*n* defines a character variable field on input or output containing *n* characters (including space characters). When no *n* is specified, the field size is made equal to the declared length for the variable name in the READ or WRITE statement.

When *n* is not equal to the length of the storage assigned to the variable name by the CHARACTER type declaration:

Input

n > length   Store rightmost characters of input to fill length.
n < length   Store *n* characters of input at left of variable storage and fill the remainder of storage with blanks.

Output

n > length   Use leading blanks to fill output field.
n < length   Use leftmost *n* characters.

When the older, implicit method of defining character variables is used, there is no type declaration. When a variable is used as a character variable by input or output using an A edit descriptor. *n* must be specified. Maximum values for *n* are machine-dependent.

Self-testing exercise 3-5

1   Read an input 'WE ARE ALL ENLISTED' using list-directed read. Declare the variable as CHARACTER type and print the character string using formatted output. Leave the first character on the line blank. Show the form of the input.

2   Repeat question 1 but use formatted input. Show the input.

3   Use the specifications in question 2 but use the following A edit descriptors. Indicate the content of storage on input and the content of the output line when printed.
    (*a*) Input using:
        (1) A19 but length declared as 10
        (2) A20
    (*b*) Output assuming A19 on input and using:
        (1) A20
        (2) A10
        (3) A

4   Using the specifications in question 2, print a line that says:
bbbbb WE ARE ALL ENLISTED, I THINK.

5   Assume the implicit method and the phrase 'WE ARE ALL ENLISTED' to be read, stored, and output using A edit decriptors. Assume a four-character maximum width for character data. Write all necessary instructions.

Checking for end of data and data error

If the number of data records (such as punched cards) to be input is variable, the program should test for the end of the data. An attempt to read a data record when there are no more input records causes the operating system that manages the computer to abort the job and provide a message indicating an abnormal termination. Rather than an abnormal termination, an explicit, programmed termination procedure is preferred. The two methods for explicit termination are:

1   Use a special end-of-data data item (explained in Chapter 2).
2   Use an END specification in the READ statement.

The END specification in the READ statement may not be available in some older FORTRANs. When available, it is very useful. The form of the item is END = s, where s is the label of the statement to which control should go when the data has been read completely. To identify the end of a set of input records in batch processing, it is normal practice to have a special end-of-data operating system control card following the last data card. When the computer reads this system control card, the END = s statement is executed. For terminal input, the END specification is executed when no data is entered and the operator performs an end-of-data operation as specified by the implementation manual. As an example, the READ statement below is executed until there are no more data cards, at which time control goes to the statement labeled 400.

```
READ (5, 700, END = 400)A, B, C
```

Spaces are optional and used only for readability.

END-OF-DATA SPECIFICATION IN INPUT STATEMENT

END = s

where s is the label of the statement to which control passes when all data has been read but a read command is attempted and no data record is available.

The specification is placed after the unit number and FORMAT statement label in the input statement.

If a data input, say on a card, is not readable with the specified format, such as, for example, alphabetic characters in an integer field, the operating system aborts the job with some data error message. To avoid this type of termination and to keep the control in the program, full 1977 FORTRAN provides a data-type error specification in the READ statement. The form is ERR = s where s is the label of the statement to which control is to transfer if a data error is encountered. This statement should probably print an error message and take appropriate action, such as returning to read the next record. For example, if the card shown at the top of the next page is read by the following statement, there will be a data-type error.

```
    READ (5, 701, END = 801, ERR = 901) NIX, X
701 FORMAT (I5, F5.0)
```

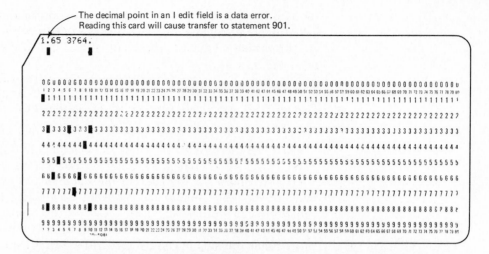

The decimal point in an I edit field is a data error.
Reading this card will cause transfer to statement 901.

DATA-TYPE ERROR SPECIFICATION IN INPUT STATEMENT

ERR = s

where s is the label of the statement to which control passes when a data-type error is encountered.

The specification is placed after the unit number and FORMAT statement label (and before or after the END specification if used) in the input statement. Available only in full FORTRAN.

Self-testing exercise 3-6

1 Write READ and IF statements to read all data cards, each card having variables ID, HOURS, and RATE in columns 1 to 5, 6 to 7, and 8 to 11. There is a trailer card after the last data card with 99999 in the ID field. At end, go to 500.

2 Write a READ statement to perform the same result as question 1, but use the END feature and omit the trailer card with 99999 for ID.

3 Write a READ statement to perform the same results as in question 2 but also with a data error specification transferring to 910 if a data error is encountered.

Handling physical records with slash editing

One FORMAT statement has thus far been assumed for each line of output, each card read, etc. FORTRAN allows considerably more versatility in input and output. Lines, cards, etc., may be skipped, and a single FORMAT statement may be used for more than one line of output.

The concepts of a physical record and a logical record are useful in understanding how to use FORMAT specifications effectively. A *physical record* is a separable element of a storage or recording medium from which data can be read or on which data can be written. Examples are a punched card, a line of terminal input, and a line on the printer paper. A *logical record* consists of items of data that logically belong together. They may occupy less than one physical record, exactly one physical record, or more than one physical record. For example, a logical record may require two punched cards. Punched cards will be used for the examples, but the same principles apply to lines of terminal input.

The slash (/) is used in a FORMAT statement to terminate the current physical record. The closing right parenthesis of the FORMAT statement also terminates the current physical record. Using more than one slash causes multiple records to be skipped. The slash can be written anywhere in the FORMAT statement. Examples are:

```
FORMAT (//, 3F10.0)
FORMAT (I2, /, F10.0)
FORMAT (I2, F10.0, /)
```

Since the closing parenthesis also terminates a physical record (and therefore can be thought of as a slash), rules can be formulated for the effect of slashes.

USE OF SLASHES IN FORMAT

1 The use of n slashes at the beginning or end of a FORMAT causes n physical records to be skipped.

2 A slash in the middle of a FORMAT causes the current record to be terminated, and a new physical record to be brought into use (starting at the beginning of the new record).

3 More than one slash in the middle of a FORMAT terminates the current record and causes $n - 1$ of the following records to be skipped.

4 Commas before and after the slashes in the FORMAT specifications are optional.

Examples of the use of slashes

FORMAT (with READ)	Effect
FORMAT (F10.0 / I3)	Reads two values from a set of two cards; the first card has a data item with specification of F10.0, and the second uses I3.
FORMAT (3F10.0 /)	Reads a card with three F10.0 values, then skips a card.
FORMAT (/// F6.3)	Skips three cards and uses F6.3 for variable on fourth.

FORMAT (with WRITE or PRINT)	Effect
FORMAT (1X, F10.0 /)	Prints one value on a line with specification of F10.0, and then skips one line.
FORMAT (1X, 3F10.0, /, 1X, I3)	Prints three values on a line using F10.0, skips to the next line, and prints a value using an I3 specification.
FORMAT (1X, F10.0, ///)	Prints using F10.0, then skips three lines

Have to be there Commas optional

Note the placement of a blank space as first character of line for vertical spacing control by use of 'b' or 1X specification.

143

Reuse of FORMAT specifications

At this point, it is appropriate to consider what happens if the number of variables in the input/output list is not equal to the number of specifications in the FORMAT statement. There can be:

1 Fewer variables in the input or output list than edit specifications (too many specifications).

2 More variables in the input or output list than edit specifications (not enough specifications).

In the case of too many specifications, the specifications required for the input or output list are used and all remaining edit specifications are ignored and not used. For example, the following statement (if I = 40, J = 12, and K = 19) will result in the output as shown:

```
    WRITE (6,700)I, J, K
700 FORMAT (1X, '*', 5I4, '*')
```

Output:

```
 * 40 12 19
```

There is no second asterisk on the line of output because only three of the five I4 specifications were used; the remaining edit specifications (two I4s and the '*') were ignored.

If there are not enough edit specifications to edit all variables in the input or output list, the edit specifications will be reused. However, reuse of specifications can affect use of physical records for input or output, because the rightmost parenthesis in the FORMAT statement is a specification to terminate the current physical record. When the end of the format specifications are reached without exhausting the list of variables, the current record is terminated, a new record is brought into use, and the format specifications are repeated. However, the program goes back only to the most recent unmodified left parenthesis in the format specifications (a specification in parentheses without a repeat number in front of it) and begins at that point for the repeating of the specifications. For example:

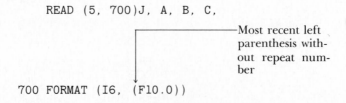

```
    READ (5, 700)J, A, B, C,
```

Most recent left parenthesis without repeat number

```
700 FORMAT (I6, (F10.0))
```

This will read J and A from the first card, but the list is not exhausted, so the specifications must be repeated with a new punched card. Because of the repeat at unmodified parenthesis rule, only F10.0 is repeated in the above example, not the entire specification. The list is still not exhausted, and F10.0 is again repeated with a new card. In other words, the example reads from three cards: J and A on card 1, B on card 2, and C on card 3. The following examples for FORMAT (and a WRITE statement) illustrate the repeat at unmodified parenthesis rule.

`(I3 / (F10.0))`	Prints I3 values on one line, goes to the next line, and prints an F10.0 value. If more variables, it continues printing one F10.0 to a line until the output list is exhausted.
`(I2 / (3F10.0))`	Prints I2 value on one line, then prints three values with F10.0s per line until the output list is exhausted.

```
I2
F10.0  F10.0  F10.0
F10.0  F10.0  F10.0
F10.0  F10.0  F10.0
```

The effects of too few or too many specifications can be summarized as:

Condition	Effect	Example

More specifications than variables in the list	Extra specifications are ignored.	`READ (5, 700)A, B, C`
		`700 FORMAT (5F10.0)`
		Uses only the first three specifications.

More variables than specifications	When specifications are exhausted (that is, the right parenthesis of the FORMAT is reached, which terminates the current record) a new record is brought into use, and the FORMAT specifications are repeated at the most recent unmodified left parenthesis	`WRITE (6, 700)A, B, C`
		`700 FORMAT (1X, 2F10.0)`
		Write output on two lines with A and B on first line and C on second line.

What happens if the FORMAT specifications call for a total of field widths (a logical record) greater than one physical record? The result is implementation-dependent. For some, the first physical record is used in its entirety, and another physical record is brought into use for the remainder. For others, the result may be a fatal error that aborts the job. It is poor practice to have logical records larger than physical records.

Self-testing exercise 3-7

Explain the effect of each of the following FORMAT specifications.

1 `(I5 / F10.0)`

2 `(F10.0 /// F10.0 /)`

3 `(/// F10.0)`

4 `(F10.0, /////)`

Rounding with FORMAT specifications

Before concluding the discussion of FORMAT editing, the impact of FOR-MAT rounding needs to be mentioned. It is especially important to be aware of rounding errors in business or accounting reports where totals often need to be the exact sum of individual items. For example, the gross pay amount for each individual listed in a payroll report should be rounded to the nearest penny and the total gross pay for the report should be equal to the sum of the individual pay amounts, yet this may not happen in some situations.

The FORMAT specifications result in rounding in cases where the underlying data contains more digits than are printed out. For example, if pay rate is 5.764 per hour and hours worked are 37, the gross pay is 213.268. If this amount is printed out as dollars and cents for a report, a format of F8.2 will result in an output of 213.27 because the result is rounded and the excess digit is then truncated and not printed. But if the original unrounded data items are used to prepare the sum, there could be small differences. This can be seen from three items.

Gross pay	Printed as F8.2
213.268	213.27
312.177	312.18
249.266	249.27
Total 774.711	774.72
Unrounded sum	Sum of rounded outputs
774.71	
Rounded sum	

In the majority of programming situations, the rounding of output under format control does not create any special problem. However, when situations arise such as the above example, it is important to understand the reason for it. It is, of course, possible to round and truncate the stored data so that it matches the output. In the example at the top of the next page, GRSPAY has an initial value of 213.268. Three statements are used to round the stored value to the nearest penny. The stored amount for summing is then identical to the amount printed. Even though these three statements could be combined, it is rather cumbersome and a different approach to handling the problem is shown in Chapter 5B in connection with the payroll program.

Expressions in output list

A feature of the 1977 full ANS FORTRAN not found in some older FOR-TRANs (but available in WATFOR/WATFIV and M77) is the use of expressions in the output list. The expression, a constant or an arithmetic expression, is evaluated and the resulting value is output as specified by the format.

	GRSPAY	
	213268	
GRSPAY = GRSPAY + .005	213273	Add rounding factor.
GRSPAY = REAL (INT (GRSPAY * 100.0))	21327,	Multiply by 100 to make the integer portion include cents, change to integer to truncate remainder, and then change back to real number.
GRSPAY = GRSPAY / 100.0	21327	Divide by 100 to restore to dollars and cents.

For example, to print the value of a variable called A, its square, and its square root, only an output statement need be used:
WRITE (6, 700)A, A**2, SQRT(A).

Additional testing, debugging, and quality-control suggestions

Testing and debugging a program to remove all errors is a significant part of the total programming time, taking perhaps one-fourth to one-third of the time required to produce a complete, tested, documented program. In addition to the test data explained in Chapter 2, the test should include data which violates the input format specifications (if ERR is used).

In general, a program should be written to reject erroneous inputs but to continue processing the rest of the input data. If rejected in validation, the contents of an input should usually be printed; when rejected because of data-type error, the erroneous record contents cannot be printed but are identified by an input record number. Error messages may be printed in place of a regular line of output or may be printed in an error message area (say to the right).

```
NORMAL OUTPUT 999.99

***ERROR MESSAGE***

NORMAL OUTPUT 999.99
```

```
NORMAL OUTPUT:
                    ERROR MESSAGE
NORMAL OUTPUT:

NORMAL OUTPUT:
```

Where the number of input items can be reasonably large (say over 10), it is good programming practice to count the records that are read and to print a message at the end of the output identifying the number of records that were processed, perhaps dividing the count into accepted and rejected records.

In debugging, it is often useful to insert temporary debugging statements in the program. These are generally print statements that print out intermediate results before and after important program processing or before IF statements. It is convenient to use list-directed PRINT statements for this purpose.

If there are a number of these PRINT statements, each statement should include a Hollerith output of the number assigned to the debugging statement. For example, debugging statement number 8 outputting results of J and X might be: PRINT *, '8', J, X. When the program is debugged, these PRINT statements are removed. To make removal easy, it is helpful to put an identifying statement label on each temporary statement that clearly marks it as one of the statements to be removed. For example, the statement PRINT *, '8', J, X might be labeled with a 9998:

```
9998 PRINT *, '8', J, X
```

Programming style suggestions

Style suggestions related to format-directed input and output are summarized below:

1 Place the FORMAT statement as nearly adjacent to the input/output statement as possible.

2 Use the apostrophe edit descriptor instead of the H descriptor.

3 Print headings as early as possible in the program (say in the initialization block). This output at the beginning provides evidence during debugging that the program began correctly.

4 Remember to leave column 1 blank on output. Either begin a line with an explicit one-blank-character specification or skip the first position by an X edit specification. Do not rely upon an extra width I, F, or E edit descriptor.

5 Use END specification and ERR specification (if available) in READ statements.

6 Use formatted output for more readable results.

7 Use list-directed output for temporary PRINT statements inserted to print out results during debugging.

8 For input, selection of format-directed or list-directed mode is dependent on the data. For example, list-directed data is much simpler to input from a terminal.

9 Where number of input records can be fairly large, keep a record count. Print the record count at the end of the program. The record count can also specify accepted and rejected records.

10 Print error messages that identify the record in error, the reason for the error, and whether or not the record is rejected. Consider a printout of the contents of the rejected input record.

Summary

The chapter has described the FORTRAN instructions to control input and output using the FORMAT statement. When a FORMAT statement is employed in a program, the READ or WRITE statement specifies the FORMAT statement to be used by a FORTRAN statement reference. The FORTRAN statement specifies the form of the data by a set of edit descriptors, which include the type of data (integer, real, or exponent form of real data), the number of record positions allowed for the data items, and the decimal point position for real data. Horizontal movement (skipping over record positions) is specified by an X edit descriptor or by a T-tabulating edit descriptor.

Providing descriptive labels and headings on output is done mainly with an apostrophe or H edit descriptor that defines the characters to be output. Vertical spacing while printing on a line printer is specified by a character in column 1 of a line. Input and output of characters that are assigned to a character variable name are specified by an A edit descriptor.

It is convenient to be able to operate on data where the number of input records is unspecified. The chapter has described the use of the END specification in the READ statement. Another specifier, ERR, is used for transfer of control when input data does not match format type specifications. As part of the FORMAT statement specifications, a slash (stroke) is used to terminate the use of the current physical record and to skip physical records. In addition to variables, the output statement list may contain expressions.

Answers to self-testing exercises

Exercise 3-1

1 (a) Read from a punched card using card reader (unit 5) values for the variable names A, B, and C. The format of the data is defined by FORMAT statement 700.

(b) Print output on the printer consisting of values stored in variable name locations X, Y, and Z. Use format described by FORMAT statement 710.

(c) Write values for variables L, N, and O according to FORMAT statement 720 using unit number NRITE. If the printer has a unit number of 6, a value of 6 for NRITE will result in the instruction using the printer.

(d) Read, using the card reader (since no unit designation), values to be assigned to variable names Q, Z, and T. The format of the data on the punched card is given by FORMAT statement 730.

(e) Write in list-directed form on unit 6 (the printer) the values for variables X, Y, and IX.

2 The input/output statements may be rewritten but this is not necessary. A better approach is to use a job control instruction to assign unit 1 as the card reader and unit 3 as the printer.

Exercise 3-2

1
```
    READ (5, 710) ALPHA, BETA, IOTA, JIX
710 FORMAT (F10.2, F9.2, I7, I7)
```

2
```
    WRITE (6, 720) JIX, IOTA, BETA, ALPHA
720 FORMAT (I7, I7, F9.2, F12.2)
```

3
```
    WRITE (6, 730) IOTA, BETA
730 FORMAT (I17, F17.0)
```

The result will be (IOTA = 6 for data, 1 for sign, and 10 leading blanks for field size of 17; BETA = 5 for data, 1 for decimal, 1 for sign, and 10 leading blanks for field size of 17)

bbbbbbbbbbb824341bbbbbbbbbbbbb53429.

4 The result will be:

bbbbbbbb95bbbbbb1.04   (X is rounded and truncated to two digits in fractional part.)

5 (a) F8.2   (c) F10.6   (e) I5
(b) F7.1   (d) F5.3   (f) E15.8

Exercise 3-3

1 Repeat F6.0 five times (parentheses are redundant) and then repeat I4 three times.

2 Uses 3 of I2, 4 of F10.0, and 2 of E15.8.

3 The set of I3, F10.0 is used four times followed by I3.

4 Use first five positions for integer output, skip next ten positions, and then use next ten positions as F10.2.

5 Skip 19 positions from the normal starting position of 1. Start at position 20 with F10.2 (20–29 and move to 30 for next field), skip 20 positions (30–49 and move to position 50 for next field), and then use three positions with I3.

6 Same effect as 5. Start at position 20 with 10.2 then do I3 starting at position 50.

Exercise 3-4

1
```
      WRITE (6, 721) TOLER
  721 FORMAT (25X, 16HTHE TOLERANCE IS, F8.2)
  721 FORMAT (25X 'THE TOLERANCE IS', F8.2)
```

2
```
      WRITE (6, 722) SAVIN
  722 FORMAT (10X, 'AMOUNT OF SAVINGS IS $',F7.2)
  722 FORMAT (10X, 22HAMOUNT OF SAVINGS IS $,F7.2)
```

3
```
      WRITE (6, 723) NMBER
  723 FORMAT (' NUMBER IS', I5)
  723 FORMAT (10H NUMBER IS, I5)
```

4
```
      WRITE (6, 724)
  724 FORMAT ('0', 'THE END.') or ('0THE END.')
  724 FORMAT (1H0, 8HTHE END.)
```

5
```
      WRITE (6, 725)
  725 FORMAT (5X, 'ITEM', 10X 'AMOUNT')
  725 FORMAT (5X, 4HITEM, 10X, 6HAMOUNT)
```

6
```
      WRITE (6, 726)
  726 FORMAT ('1', 58X, 'PAYROLL REPORT')
  726 FORMAT (1H1, 58X, 14HPAYROLL REPORT)
```

Exercise 3-5

1
```
      CHARACTER MESAGE*19
      READ *, MESAGE
      WRITE (6, 710) MESAGE
  710 FORMAT (A20)    (could also have been FORMAT (1X, A19)
```

Input in form 'WE ARE ALL ENLISTED'

2
```
      CHARACTER MESAGE*19
      READ (5, 700) MESAGE
700 FORMAT (A19)
      WRITE (6, 710) MESAGE
710 FORMAT (A20)
```

Input in form WE ARE ALL ENLISTED starting in column 1 of punched card or terminal input.

3 (*a*) Content of storage (b = blank)
   (1) L ENLISTED
   (2) WE ARE ALL ENLISTEDb
(*b*) Content of output line
   (1) bWE ARE ALL ENLISTED
   (2) WE ARE ALL   Note that the first character is not blank and
   (3) WE ARE ALL ENLISTED   may not actually print since the position is
                          used for carriage control.

4
```
      WRITE (5, 710) MESAGE
710 FORMAT (5X, A19,', I THINK.')
```

5
```
      READ (5, 700) MESAG1, MESAG2, MESAG3, MESAG4, MESAG5
700 FORMAT (4A4, A3)
      WRITE (6, 710) MESAG1, MESAG2, MESAG3, MESAG4, MESAG5
710 FORMAT (1X, 4A4, A3)
```

Exercise 3-6

1
```
      READ (5, 700) ID, HOURS, RATE
700 FORMAT (I5, F2.0, F4.3)
      IF (ID.EQ.99999) GO TO 500
```

2
```
      READ (5, 700, END = 500) ID, HOURS, RATE
700 FORMAT (I5, F2.0, F4.3)
      READ (5, 700, END = 500, ERR = 910) ID, HOURS, RATE
```

3
```
700 FORMAT (I5, F2.0, F4.3)
```

Exercise 3-7

1 I5 is used for value on first card or line, F10.0 for value on second. If list of variables is not exhausted, the next card or line will use I5, etc.

2 First card or line has one value F10.0; it is terminated and the next two cards or lines are skipped. Then F10.0 is used for the next unit record. If list is not exhausted, the next card or line is skipped and the FORMAT is repeated.

3 Skips three cards or lines and then uses F10.0. If repeated, it will skip three cards or lines again.

4 Uses F10.0 and then skips five lines or cards.

Questions and problems

1 Explain three methods of identifying which input or output unit is to be used with a READ or WRITE statement.

2 Differentiate between physical and logical records.

3 Explain two methods for testing end of data.

4 Complete the following table using minimum FORMAT specification:

Data as found on card	Format to read	Desired printing	Format for printing
(a) XXX.XXX		XXX.XXX	
(b) XXX		XXX.0	
(c) .XXXXE+17		0.XXXXE+17	
(d) −.XXXXE+5		−XXXX0.	
(e)	F5.2		F5.1

5 What is the effect of the following FORMAT specification sets?
(a) ('0') or (1H0)
(b) (3F10.0, 3/)
(c) (1F10.0)
(d) (I6, 2(I7))
(e) (3F10.0, 4(I3))
(f) (3F10.0, 5E15.8)
(g) (I6, F10.0)
(h) (I6 / F10.0)
(i) (5(F10.0, I7))
(j) (F10.4, F10.3, /// I6)
(k) (I10, 10X, F13.2)
(l) (50X, I3)
(m) (T50, I3)

6 Print a heading XYZ COMPANY centered at the top of a page. Double-space and center 12/31/82 below the heading. Do it two ways—with an apostrophe and with an H edit descriptor.

7 Write sets of WRITE and FORMAT statements to make the following outputs. Leave first position on line blank in all cases.
(a) 52 spaces ANALYSIS PROGRAM
$\longleftrightarrow$

(b) CHI SQUARE TEST IS XX.XX

(c) PART NO. 20 spaces QUANTITY 10 spaces AMOUNT
$\longleftrightarrow$ $\longleftrightarrow$

(d) PROGRAM DATA IS INCORRECT.

8 Write statements to read a 10-character heading from columns 36 to 45 on a punched card and to print it using the printer at columns 76 to 85.

9 Explain what happens if there are too many format specifications. Also explain what happens if there are more variables in the list than edit specifications in the FORMAT statement.

10 Write all necessary FORTRAN statements (including CHARACTER type declarations) to perform the following:
(a) Read a phrase 'WHAT IS TRUE?', store it, and print it in reverse order 'TRUE IS WHAT?'. *Hint:* Use four variables to store the four parts of the phrase that must be manipulated.
(b) Read the phrase 'HOW NOW, BROWN COW' and print on two lines as:
HOW NOW?

    BROWN COW!!

chapter **3B**

Example programs and programming exercises using format-directed input and output

The example programs and exercises in this chapter use the features presented in Chapters 1 and 2 as well as the format-directed input and output explained in Chapter 3A. The two examples—payroll reports and tables of ordinates of the normal curve—show the use of formatting in two different environments. Both examples are instructive, but the payroll report is particularly useful in showing the use of formatting features.

General notes on Chapter 3 examples

Examine the sample outputs for the two programs (Figures 3-7 and 3-12). The outputs were formatted to use only 72 spaces instead of the full width of the printer paper. The limit on output size made the output suitable for exhibits in the text without significant reduction in size. Also, many of the programs were written from terminals which had carriages of 72 to 80 spaces.

Use of input and output layouts

The use of input and output layouts is illustrated for the payroll report program but not for the table of ordinates program. In many FORTRAN programs, the input and output is simple enough that layout forms are not needed. As output becomes more complex, layouts are useful, especially output layouts.

The layouts (such as Figures 3-1 and 3-2) allow the placement of data on input and output media to be identified. On output, it helps line up headings and data amounts. A useful convention followed by many programmers is to mark the maximum field to be occupied by each data item by 9s or X's. The 9s are used to indicate numeric digits. Decimal points are written at the position occupied on output. The X's indicate alphanumeric character output such as labels and headings.

Four very important points to remember in regard to input data as illustrated in the example programs are:

1 Data items in FORMAT-directed input are not delineated by commas or blanks (as they were for the list-directed inputs of Chapters 1 and 2).

2 Data items are assigned by the FORMAT statement to a specific set of positions on each punched card used for input (or terminal line). The data items must be placed in the assigned set of positions.

3 For real data, if the decimal point is punched, it overrides the input format decimal specification. A data item may be placed anywhere in the set of positions assigned to it on the card. Unused positions may be left blank. However,

Figure 3-1
Input card layout for general example 3—payroll reports.

Input Card — General Example 3 — Payroll

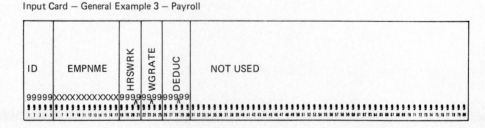

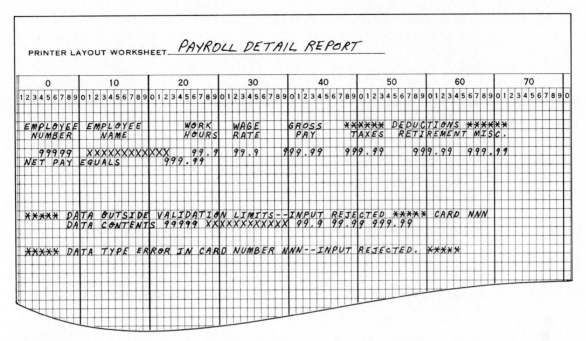

Figure 3-2
Layout for detail report for general example 3—payroll reports.

in some older FORTRANs, data items without decimal points must be right-justified (all unused positions at left). Right justification is therefore preferred for compatibility.

Error-control features

Both programs use the END and ERR specifications in the input statement. These specifications simplify programming (but may not be available on older compilers). With the END feature, an attempt to read input after the last data card transfers control to the statement number given by the END specification. This is a very clear and effective method for handling an unspecified number of inputs. The ERR feature is used because it allows the program to retain control when reading input that is incompatible with the format specifications. An error in keypunching or data entry will often cause such an error.

Both programs print a summary statement stating the number of input cards read. The payroll report program divides this figure into those accepted and those rejected.

Note the use of error messages that print out the card contents or identify the card number of an input data card that is in error. The error message for an input data item that does not meet the validation limit tests is instructive (see lines 17 to 19 in the payroll report program). Although the input data items are tested individually, only a single error output is used. The exact nature of the error is not specified. This approach is satisfactory for most fairly simple input validation. However, in more complex validation, it may be useful to have a separate error message for each error detected. The error message shows the output without any special formatting. The printing of the card contents (perhaps with spaces between data items) usually allows the error to be noted; an alternative is to label the parts of the input data being printed out.

General program example 3 — payroll reports

Problem description for general example 3

Compute employee pay information for an unspecified number of employees (but less than 15) and print formatted output for each individual and a summary. Input consists of an employee's ID number, the employee's name (up to 12 characters long), hours worked, wage rate, and miscellaneous deductions. Hours worked in excess of 40 are paid at 1.5 times the regular rate. In addition to miscellaneous deductions, there are deductions for pension (5 percent of gross pay) and taxes (15 percent of gross pay). The total for all employees —hours worked, gross pay, taxes, retirement contributions, deductions, and net pay—are printed on a separate page following the last employee printout. Input data is validated and error messages are printed when errors are detected.

Program documentation for general example 3

The documentation consists of an input layout (Figure 3-1), an output layout (Figure 3-2), a pseudocode description of the program (Figure 3-3), a program flowchart (Figure 3-4), a listing of the program (Figure 3-5), a list of input data used in testing the program (Figure 3-6), and a sample output (Figure 3-7) that includes program handling of error inputs.

The input layout (Figure 3-1) is designed for planning and documenting the placement of the input data on a punched card (or a terminal screen). Its use is optional because most FORTRAN programs have simple input. Note the use of the 9s and X's (as with output layout) to define the contents of the fields and the caret (∧) to indicate the decimal location (if not punched).

In the input layout, note that the employee's name, consisting of 12 characters, is declared as CHARACTER type. If the older implicit method were used, the employee's name might be given three separate data names, each referencing four characters.

The output layout (Figure 3-2) has already been mentioned. It is especially helpful in this case in laying out the headings and lining up the data under the headings. The two types of error messages are also shown on the layout. Layout forms usually have 132 to 140 positions horizontally; the layout form in Figure 3-2 has been trimmed to 80 positions because, as explained, the outputs in the text are all designed to fit on 72 positions.

The list of input data used to test the program is important documentation of the testing performed. At each change or correction in the program, the test data list provides a useful review of the prior testing, which can be expanded, if desired, and repeated with the changed program.

Test data items are designed to test each branch in a program. This requires three test data items for each branching instruction: the boundary value, the boundary value plus one, and the boundary value minus one. Nega-

Figure 3-3
Pseudocode description
of general example 3—
payroll reports.

```
WRITE heading for employee data
Initialize counters and constants
READ an employee card
     IF (END) go to Summary
     IF (ERR) WRITE message, increment total card counter, and go back to READ
Increment total card counter
Validate input data
     Hours worked > 0.0 and ≤ 60.0
     Wage rate > 0.0 and ≤ 10.0
     Misc deductions ≥ 0.0 and ≤ 35.0
     IF invalid, print data validation message and go back to READ employee card
     Else continue
Increment counter for valid records
Compute overtime hours
IF overtime hours
     Calculate gross pay with overtime at 1.5 times regular rate
ELSE
     Calculate gross pay at regular rate
Compute taxes and retirement contribution
Compute total deductions
Compute net pay
Update cumulative totals
WRITE detail for an employee
Test for negative net pay
     IF negative, print warning message
     Else continue
Go back to READ employee card
Summary
WRITE heading for summary
WRITE cumulative totals
Compute number of invalid records
WRITE number of valid and invalid records
STOP
```

tive and zero values should also be included in a test. Therefore, a complete set of test data items for program 3A will include the following:

1 Test for end of data. This will be done without additional coding by having an end-of-job card with the input data deck.

2 Test for data-type error. This will be performed by coding alphabetic characters as the employee number (ID).

3 Test for valid data:
   (a) Hours worked (HRSWRK) of:

   (1)   0.0 (invalid)   ⎫
   (2) − 0.1 (invalid)   ⎬ Zero and negative
   (3) 60.0 (valid)   ⎫
   (4) 59.9 (valid)   ⎬ Boundary value ± .1
   (5) 60.1 (invalid)   ⎭

Figure 3-4
Program flowchart for
general example 3—pay-
roll reports. (Numbers beside symbols refer to line
numbers on program list-
ing.)

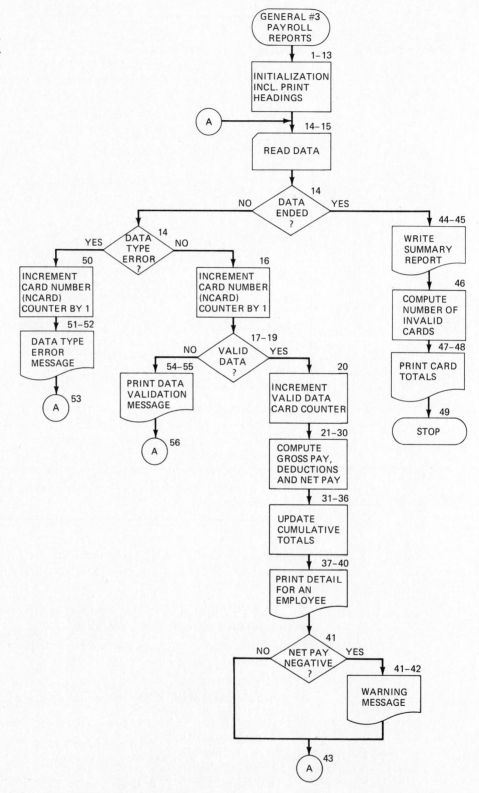

Figure 3-5
Listing of FORTRAN pro-
gram for general example
3—payroll reports.

```
*********          PROGRAM IDENTIFICATION                *********
*                                                                *
*     COMPUTE PAYCHECKS FOR EMPLOYEES AND PRINT FORMATTED        *
*     REPORTS FOR BOTH INDIVIDUALS AND THE COMPANY              *
*     WRITTEN BY T. HOFFMANN  4/22/77   REV. 1/06/82            *
*                                                                *
******************************************************************
*                                                                *
*********          VARIABLE IDENTIFICATION                *********
*                                                                *
*     ID      = EMPLOYEE IDENTIFICATION NUMBER                  *
*     HRSWRK  = TOTAL HOURS WORKED                               *
*     GRSPAY  = GROSS PAY: $                                     *
*     WGRATE  = WAGE RATE: $/HOUR                                *
*     PAYCHK  = NET PAYCHECK AMOUNT: $                           *
*     TAXES   = TAXES DUE: $                                     *
*     DEDUC   = MISCELANEOUS DEDUCTIONS                          *
*     EMPNME  = EMPLOYEE NAME                                    *
*     OTIME   = HOURS OF OVERTIME WORKED (EXCESS OVER 40.0)      *
*     TDEDUC  = TOTAL OF ALL DEDUCTIONS BY EMPLOYEE              *
*     RETIRE  = RETIREMENT CONTRIBUTION BY EMPLOYEE              *
*     TOTHRS  = TOTAL HOURS WORKED BY ALL EMPLOYEES              *
*     TOTRET  = TOTAL RETIREMENT CONTRIBUTION BY ALL EMPLOYEES   *
*     TOTPAY  = TOTAL GROSS PAY FOR COMPANY : $                  *
*     TOTTAX  = TOTAL TAXES FROM ALL EMPLOYEES :$                *
*     TOTCKS  = TOTAL OF ALL PAYCHECKS                           *
*     TOTDUC  = TOTAL OF ALL DEDUCTIONS                          *
*     NCARD   = NUMBER OF CARDS (RECORDS) READ                   *
*     NACEPT  = NUMBER OF ERROR FREE CARDS                       *
*     NOTACP  = NUMBER OF NOT ACCEPTABLE RECORDS                 *
*                                                                *
*****              CONSTANT IDENTIFICATION                   *****
*                                                                *
*     PNRATE  = PENSION CONTRIBUTION RATE = 0.05                 *
*     TAXRT   = TAX RATE = 0.15                                  *
*                                                                *
******************************************************************
*                                                                *
*********      TYPE DECLARATION AND STORAGE BLOCK         *********
*                                                                *
1.          CHARACTER EMPNME*12                                  *
*                                                                *
******************************************************************
*                                                                *
*********          INITIALIZATION BLOCK          BLOCK 0000
*                                                                *
*          PRINT HEADER/TITLE LINE                               *
*                                                                *
2.          WRITE(6,3)
3.        3 FORMAT('1',2('EMPLOYEE '),5X,'WORK   WAGE',4X,'GROSS',3X,6('*'),
          1  ' DEDUCTIONS ',6('*')/2X,'NUMBER',4X,'NAME',8X,'HOURS',
          2   ' RATE',5X,'PAY',4X,'TAXES  RETIREMENT  MISC.')
4.          PNRATE = 0.05
5.          TAXRT = 0.15
6.          NACEPT = 0
7.          TOTPAY = 0.0
8.          TOTTAX = 0.0
9.          NCARD = 0
10.         TOTHRS = 0.0
11.         TOTRET = 0.0
12.         TOTCKS = 0.0
13.         TOTDUC = 0.0
*                                                                *
******************************************************************
*                                                                *
*********      READ AND VALIDATE EMPLOYEE DATA    BLOCK 0100
*                                                                *
14.       101 READ(5,102,END=401,ERR=901) ID,EMPNME,HRSWRK,WGRATE,DEDUC
15.       102 FORMAT(I5,A12,F4.1,F4.2,F5.2)
16.           NCARD = NCARD + 1
*                                                                *
*              VALIDATE INPUT DATA                               *
*                                                                *
17.           IF(HRSWRK .LE. 0.0 .OR. HRSWRK .GT. 60.0) GOTO 910
18.           IF(WGRATE .LE. 0.0 .OR. WGRATE .GT. 10.0) GOTO 910
19.           IF(DEDUC .LT. 0.0 .OR. DEDUC .GT. 35.0) GOTO 910
*                                                                *
******************************************************************
*                                                                *
*********        COMPUTE GROSS AND NET PAY        BLOCK 0200
*                                                                *
20.           NACEPT = NACEPT + 1
```

Figure 3-5
Continued.

```
        *                                                                    *
        *             COMPUTE OVERTIME, IF ANY                                *
        *                                                                    *
21.         OTIME = HRSWRK - 40.0
22.         IF(OTIME .GT. 0.0) THEN
23.             GRSPAY = WGRATE*(40.0 + 1.5*OTIME)
24.         ELSE
25.             GRSPAY = HRSWRK*WGRATE
26.         ENDIF
        *                                                                    *
        *          COMPUTE EACH TYPE OF DEDUCTION AND NET PAY                 *
        *                                                                    *
27.         TAXES = TAXRT*GRSPAY
28.         RETIRE = PNRATE*GRSPAY
29.         TDEDUC = DEDUC + TAXES + RETIRE
30.         PAYCHK = GRSPAY - TDEDUC
31.         TOTPAY = TOTPAY + GRSPAY
32.         TOTTAX = TOTTAX + TAXES
33.         TOTHRS = TOTHRS + HRSWRK
34.         TOTRET = TOTRET + RETIRE
35.         TOTDUC = TOTDUC + TDEDUC
36.         TOTCKS = TOTCKS + PAYCHK
        *                                                                    *
        **********************************************************************
        *                                                                    *
        **********          PRINT DETAIL                     BLOCK 0300
        *                                                                    *
37.         WRITE(6,301) ID,EMPNME,HRSWRK,WGRATE,GRSPAY,TAXES,RETIRE,DEDUC
38.     301 FORMAT('0',2X,I5,2X,A12,F7.1,F6.2,1X,2F8.2,1X,2(3X,F6.2))
39.         WRITE(6,304) PAYCHK
40.     304 FORMAT(' NET PAY EQUALS',6X,F6.2)
        *                                                                    *
        *          CHECK FOR VALID PAYCHECK AMOUNT                            *
        *                                                                    *
41.         IF(PAYCHK .LE. 0.0) WRITE(6,303)
42.     303 FORMAT('+',28X,'NET PAY IS NOT POSITIVE.',
           1       ' DO NOT ISSUE CHECK')
        *                                                                    *
        *          GO BACK AND READ ANOTHER EMPLOYEE DATA CARD                *
        *                                                                    *
43.         GOTO 101
        *                                                                    *
        **********************************************************************
        *                                                                    *
        **********          PRINT SUMMARY AND TERMINATE      BLOCK 0400
        *                                                                    *
44.     401 WRITE(6,402) TOTHRS,TOTPAY,TOTTAX,TOTRET,TOTDUC,TOTCKS
45.     402 FORMAT('1','*****',18X,'SUMMARY TOTALS'17X,5('*')/
           1     ' HOURS',4X,'GROSS    TAXES    RETIREMENT   DEDUCTIONS',
           2     2X,'PAYCHECKS'/' WORKED',4X,'PAY',11X,'CONTRIBUTION'/
           3     '0',F6.2,2F8.2,5X,F5.2,2X,2(6X,F6.2))
46.         NOTACP = NCARD - NACEPT
47.         WRITE(6,403) NACEPT,NOTACP
48.     403 FORMAT(//10X,'RECORDS ACCEPTED',I3,5X,'RECORDS REJECTED',I3)
        *                                                                    *
        *          NORMAL TERMINATION                                        *
        *                                                                    *
49.         STOP
        *                                                                    *
        **********************************************************************
        *                                                                    *
        **********          ERROR MESSAGE BLOCK              BLOCK 0900
        *                                                                    *
50.     901 NCARD = NCARD + 1
51.         WRITE(6,902) NCARD
52.     902 FORMAT(//' ***** DATA TYPE ERROR IN CARD NUMBER',I3,
           1      '--INPUT REJECTED. *****')
        *                                                                    *
        *          GO BACK AND READ ANOTHER EMPLOYEE DATA CARD                *
        *                                                                    *
53.         GOTO 101
        *                                                                    *
54.     910 WRITE(6,911) NCARD,ID,EMPNME,HRSWRK,WGRATE,DEDUC
55.     911 FORMAT('0','***** DATA OUTSIDE VALIDATION LIMITS--INPUT ',
           1      'REJECTED ***** CARD',I3/7X,'DATA CONTENTS ',
           2      I5,1X,A12,1X,F4.1,F5.2,F6.2)
        *                                                                    *
        *          GO BACK AND READ ANOTHER EMPLOYEE DATA CARD                *
        *                                                                    *
56.         GOTO 101
        *                                                                    *
57.         END
```

Figure 3-6
Input test data with purposes noted for general example 3.

INPUT TEST DATA

ID	NAME	HOURS	WAGE RATE	MISC. DEDUCTIONS	PURPOSE OR EXPECTED OUTPUT
23456	T. HOFFMANN	40.0	3.57	27.95	NET PAY SHOULD BE 86.29
15786	RALPH JONES	39.9	6.28	24.68	GROSS PAY SHOULD BE 250.57
15968	W. RONG	14.4	2)KM	45.68	ERROR-NONNUMERIC DATA IN NUMERIC FIELD
36985	J. JOHNSON	22.0	0275	03598	FORMAT SETS DECIMAL POINT. ERROR-DEDUCTIONS EXCEED LIMITS
JKLUI	ONA				ERROR-NONNUMERIC DATA IN NUMERIC FIELD
69852	T. NAMAN	10.0	2.67	27.50	NET PAY NEGATIVE
35748	L. SMITH	40.1	9.94	30.68	GROSS PAY = 399.09
					4 RECORDS-ACCEPTED
					3 RECORDS-REJECTED

Figure 3-7
Sample output for general example 3—detail and summary payroll report.

DETAIL OUTPUT

```
EMPLOYEE EMPLOYEE         WORK   WAGE    GROSS     ****** DEDUCTIONS ******
 NUMBER    NAME           HOURS  RATE     PAY      TAXES  RETIREMENT  MISC.

  23456   T. HOFFMANN      40.0  3.57   142.80     21.42        7.14  27.95
NET PAY EQUALS          86.29

  15786   RALPH JONES      39.9  6.28   250.57     37.59       12.53  24.68
NET PAY EQUALS         175.78


***** DATA TYPE ERROR IN CARD NUMBER  3--INPUT REJECTED. *****

***** DATA OUTSIDE VALIDATION LIMITS--INPUT REJECTED ***** CARD  4
      DATA CONTENTS 36985 J. JOHNSON    22.0 2.75 35.98


***** DATA TYPE ERROR IN CARD NUMBER  5--INPUT REJECTED. *****

  69852   T. NAMAN         10.0  2.67    26.70      4.00        1.34  27.50
NET PAY EQUALS          -6.14  NET PAY IS NOT POSITIVE. DO NOT ISSUE CHECK

  35748   L. SMITH         40.1  9.94   399.09     59.86       19.95  30.68
NET PAY EQUALS         288.59
```

SUMMARY OUTPUT

```
*****                          SUMMARY TOTALS                      *****
HOURS     GROSS     TAXES     RETIREMENT    DEDUCTIONS   PAYCHECKS
WORKED     PAY                CONTRIBUTION

130.00   819.16   122.87        40.96          274.64      544.52


              RECORDS ACCEPTED  4      RECORDS REJECTED  3
```

(b) Wage rate (WGRATE) of:

(1)   0.0 (invalid) ⎫
(2) −0.1 (invalid) ⎬ Zero and negative
(3) 10.0 (valid) ⎫
(4)   9.99 (valid) ⎬ Boundary value ± .01
(5) 10.01 (invalid) ⎭

(c) Miscellaneous deductions (DEDUCT) of:

(1)   0.0 (valid) ⎫
(2) −0.1 (invalid) ⎬ Zero and negative
(3) 35.00 (valid) ⎫
(4) 34.99 (valid) ⎬ Boundary value ± .01
(5) 35.01 (invalid) ⎭

4   Test for overtime computation:

(a) Hours worked (HRSWRK) = 39.9 (no overtime) ⎫
(b) Hours worked = 40.0 (no overtime) ⎬ Boundary value ± .1
(c) Hours worked = 40.1 (overtime) ⎭

5   Test for zero and negative paycheck. Use hours worked, pay rate, and miscellaneous deductions that will provide a net paycheck amount (PAYCHK) of:
(a) 0.0
(b) Negative

In other words, a complete test of this very small program requires at least 21 different sets of input data. It is understandable why it is difficult to completely test very large programs. Even for small programs, a smaller set of test data may be used, focusing on the most significant error possibilities. The test data items in Figure 3-6 are not a complete set; they only illustrate how to set up a test data list with expected output defined for each.

Notes on general example 3

The usual identification blocks are present. The computational section has been divided into six logical blocks with block numbers. In the initialization section, printing the detail report heading is done first. This also has advantages for debugging, since it is useful to have some output from a program as early as possible to provide an indication that the program has compiled and begun execution.

The variable NCARD has been created to keep count of the cards read. This assists in locating erroneous data cards and in ensuring that all cards which were intended to be processed have been processed by comparing the final count to the intended value. The initial value and the locations of the increment instructions for the counter must be carefully considered. Note that this is done right after reading the card (line 14), but if there is a data error, the ERR specification causes a transfer and this line is never reached. Therefore, the counter is alternatively incremented with statement 901 at line

50 just before the data error printout. Separate counters are also kept for rejected and accepted records.

The block IF is used in the program (lines 22–26). As an alternative, the logic can be coded with a simple logical IF statement as follows:

```
    IF (OTIME.GT.0.0) GOTO 204
    GRSPAY = WGRATE * HRSWRK
    GOTO 205
204 GRSPAY = WGRATE * (40.0 + 1.5 * OTIME)
205 TAXES =
```

Updating the totals could be done before or after the printing of the pay information. However, grouping the computations in a block makes the program more readable and easier to debug.

Output formatting can be a very lengthy and tedious job. It is often useful to print lines of asterisks or other symbols as part of output, but writing out long lines of them in FORMAT statements can be time-consuming and error-prone. An alternative is the use of repetition counts. The following are equivalent methods for programming a set of five asterisks to be printed on an output line:

```
FORMAT (' ' '*****')
FORMAT (' ', 5('*'))      } Preferred apostrophe method

FORMAT (1H, 5H*****)
FORMAT (1H, 5(1H*))       } Alternative H specification
```

Vertical spacing is controlled in several ways in the program. In the FORMAT statement 3 at line number 3 the page is set to the top ('1'); in the FORMAT statement 303 at line 42, no spacing takes place before the print ('+'), so that the message is printed on the same line as the amount; in FORMAT statement 301 at line 38, double spacing takes place before printing ('0'); and in FORMAT statement 403 at line 48, double spacing is accomplished by issuing two line feeds before printing (//). Horizontal spacing is accomplished by having blanks in Hollerith fields (FORMAT statement 902 at line 52), using the nX field (FORMAT statement 304 at line 40), and by specifying a larger than necessary I or F field (FORMAT statement 301 at line 38).

Multiple print lines are contained in FORMAT statement 402 at line 45 by separating them with one or more slashes. Note also that column 1 is left blank in all cases where a spacing control character is not specified (for example, the 2X on the second line of FORMAT statement number 3 at line number 3 and the blank in the Hollerith field of statement number 902 at line 52).

The problem of rounding with the format on output is illustrated in this program. The payroll detail is printed out as dollars and cents using a format with two places to the right of the decimal point. The printed totals are the same as the sum of the individual outputs rounded at printing except for total taxes. The rounding difference is not corrected in this simple program. An approach to correcting this type of rounding error situation is described in Chapter 5. The sum of the individual taxes as printed is 128.96, whereas the total is shown as 128.97. The difference arises from rounding individual amounts but summing unrounded amounts for the total as follows:

Unrounded taxes (gross pay × 15)	Rounded output
21.42 00	21.42
34.85 40	34.85
4.00 50	4.00
68.68 95	68.69
Totals 128.96 85	128.96
Output 128.97	

Statistical program example 3 — tables of ordinates of the normal curve

Problem description for statistical example 3

Produce formatted tables of the ordinates of the normal curve based upon an initial value, an incremental value, and the number of entries desired. Validate input data for number of entries not zero, negative, or greater than 50. Use END and ERR specifications. Keep a record count and print this count at the end of the program.

Program documentation for statistical example 3

The documentation consists of a pseudocode description of the program (Figure 3-8), a program flowchart (Figure 3-9), a program listing (Figure 3-10), and a list of input data used in testing the program (Figure 3-11). Sample out-

Figure 3-8
Pseudocode description of statistical example 3— tables of ordinates of normal curve.

```
WRITE global heading
Initialize problem counter and constants
READ starting X value, X increment, number of values to compute (NVALUS)
        IF no more data then Terminate
        IF data-type error, increment record count, print error message, and GO back
           to READ
Increment record count by 1
Test for valid input data for number of values — not zero, negative, or >50
IF input data for number of values to compute not valid
        Print error message and GO back to READ
ELSE
        Continue
WRITE problem title
Initialize step counter to one
IF step counter greater than NVALUS
        Go back to READ
ELSE
        Compute ordinate Y
        WRITE X, Y
        Increment X by X increment and step counter by one
        GO back to IF step counter
Terminate with WRITE end of program and number of cards read
STOP
```

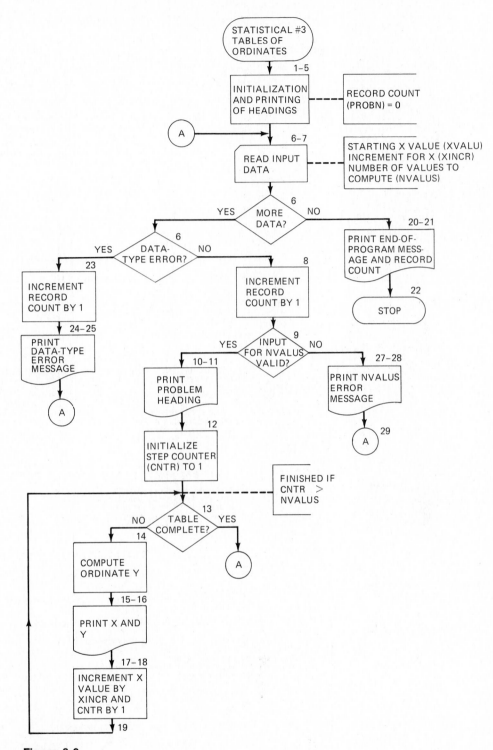

Figure 3-9
Program flowchart for statistical example 3—tables of ordinates of normal curve. (Numbers beside symbols refer to line numbers on program listing.)

```
**********              PROGRAM IDENTIFICATION               **********
*                                                                      *
*         CALCULATE TABLES OF ORDINATES OF THE NORMAL CURVE            *
*         WRITTEN BY T. HOFFMANN 05/03/77   REV.01/06/82               *
*                                                                      *
************************************************************************
*                                                                      *
**********               VARIABLE IDENTIFICATION             **********
*                                                                      *
*         NVALUS  = NUMBER OF VALUES TO COMPUTE                        *
*         CNTR    = COUNTER TO LIMIT AGAINST NVALUS                    *
*         PROBN   = PROBLEM NUMBER COUNTER                             *
*         XVALU   = VALUE OF X TO USE IN COMPUTATION OF YVALU          *
*         YVALU   = VALUE OF THE ORDINATE CORRESPONDING TO XVALU       *
*         XINCR   = INCREMENT OF X                                     *
*                                                                      *
*****                    CONSTANT IDENTIFICATION             *****
*                                                                      *
*         PIROOT  = RECIPROCAL OF THE SQUARE ROOT OF TWO PI            *
*                                                                      *
************************************************************************
*                                                                      *
**********          TYPE DECLARATION AND STORAGE BLOCK       **********
*                                                                      *
            INTEGER CNTR,PROBN
*                                                                      *
************************************************************************
*                                                                      *
**********               INITIALIZATION BLOCK        BLOCK 0000
*                                                                      *
            WRITE(6,1)
          1 FORMAT('1',7X,'TABLES OF ORDINATES OF THE NORMAL CURVE')
            PIROOT = 1.0/SQRT(6.2832)
            PROBN = 0
*                                                                      *
************************************************************************
*                                                                      *
**********          READ - COMPUTE - PRINT BLOCK      BLOCK 0100
*                                                                      *
        101 READ(5,102,END=200,ERR=901) XVALU,XINCR,NVALUS
        102 FORMAT(2F4.1,I2)
*                                                                      *
*              STEP PROBLEM COUNTER                                    *
*                                                                      *
            PROBN = PROBN + 1
            IF(NVALUS .LE. 0 .OR. NVALUS .GT. 50) GOTO 910
            WRITE(6,103) PROBN
        103 FORMAT('0',5X,'PROBLEM NUMBER',I3/5X,'X VALUE',4X,'Y VALUE')
            CNTR = 1
*                                                                      *
*              IF NVALUS NOT COMPUTED, CALCULATE NEXT ORDINATE.        *
*              IF THEY HAVE BEEN, THEN READ A NEW PROBLEM CARD.        *
*                                                                      *
        104 IF(CNTR .GT. NVALUS) GOTO 101
            YVALU = PIROOT*EXP(-XVALU*XVALU/2.0)
            WRITE(6,105) XVALU,YVALU
        105 FORMAT(6X,F6.2,5X,F6.4)
            XVALU =  XVALU + XINCR
            CNTR = CNTR + 1
            GOTO 104
*                                                                      *
************************************************************************
*                                                                      *
**********             NORMAL TERMINATION BLOCK       BLOCK 0200
*                                                                      *
        200 WRITE(6,201) PROBN
        201 FORMAT(///' END OF PROGRAM'/3X,I3,' CARDS READ')
            STOP
*                                                                      *
************************************************************************
*                                                                      *
**********               ERROR MESSAGE BLOCK          BLOCK 0900
*                                                                      *
        901 PROBN = PROBN + 1
            WRITE(6,902) PROBN
        902 FORMAT('0','***** DATA ERROR IN CARD NUMBER ',I3,' *****')
*                                                                      *
*              GO BACK AND READ NEXT PROBLEM                           *
*                                                                      *
            GOTO 101
*                                                                      *
        910 WRITE(6,911) PROBN,XVALU,XINCR,NVALUS
        911 FORMAT('0','***** DATA LIMIT ERROR FOR NUMBER OF VALUES *****'/
          1     7X,'CARD NUMBER ',I2,3X,'CONTENTS ',F4.1,2X,F4.1,2X,I2)
*                                                                      *
*              GO BACK AND READ NEXT PROBLEM                           *
*                                                                      *
            GOTO 101
*                                                                      *
            END
```

Line numbers (left margin): 1. through 30.

Figure 3-10
Listing of FORTRAN program for statistical example 3—tables of ordinates of normal curve.

Figure 3-11
Input test data with purpose noted for statistical example 3.

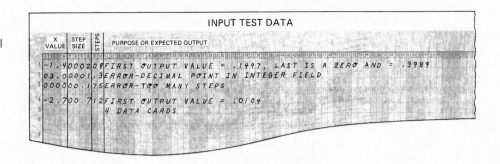

INPUT TEST DATA

X VALUE	STEP SIZE	STEPS	PURPOSE OR EXPECTED OUTPUT
-1.4	00020	8	FIRST OUTPUT VALUE = .1497, LAST IS A ZERO AND = .3989
03.	00001.	3	ERROR-DECIMAL POINT IN INTEGER FIELD
000000.	1	75	ERROR-TOO MANY STEPS
-2.7	00.7	12	FIRST OUTPUT VALUE = .0104
			4 DATA CARDS

put is given in Figure 3-12. For the simple formatted output of this program it was not considered useful to use a printer layout form.

Notes on statistical example 3

The constant PIROOT used in the formula was computed using the SQRT function. The value of 2π used in computing PIROOT (that is, 6.2832) is not used elsewhere in the program, so no variable name was assigned to it (see line 4). The overall report heading (global header) was printed as early as possible in the program execution (line 2). It is logical to do so and, as mentioned previously, it aids in debugging because the printout of the heading lets the au-

Figure 3-12
Sample output for statistical example 3—tables of ordinates of normal curve.

```
        TABLES OF ORDINATES OF THE NORMAL CURVE

        PROBLEM NUMBER  1
        X VALUE     Y VALUE
          -1.40       .1497
          -1.20       .1942
          -1.00       .2420
           -.80       .2897
           -.60       .3332
           -.40       .3683
           -.20       .3910
            .00       .3989

    ***** DATA ERROR IN CARD NUMBER    2 *****

    ***** DATA LIMIT ERROR FOR NUMBER OF VALUES *****
          CARD NUMBER  3    CONTENTS    0    .1  75

        PROBLEM NUMBER  4
        X VALUE     Y VALUE
          -2.70       .0104
          -2.00       .0540
          -1.30       .1714
           -.60       .3332
            .10       .3970
            .80       .2897
           1.50       .1295
           2.20       .0355
           2.90       .0060
           3.60       .0006
           4.30       .0000
           5.00       .0000


    END OF PROGRAM
         4 CARDS READ
```

thor know the program has been compiled and begun execution. Reading of cards is terminated by the END specification in the READ statement rather than by a termination value. Note how a single FORMAT statement with slash editing prints both heading lines for each problem.

Counters can be initialized to either 1 or 0 and checked at either the beginning or end of an execution loop. In this program, the choice is to set the record count to 0 and increment after reading. When a data error causes a transfer of control (ERR = 901), the record count following the READ is not executed, so another increment statement is needed at line 23. CNTR (the counter, declared as integer, for numbers of table entries) is set to 1 at the beginning of the instructions to do the table. As long as CNTR is less than or equal to NVALUS (the number of entries to be printed), the computation and printing is performed, the counter is incremented by 1, and control is returned to the beginning of the loop.

As an alternative to the simple block IF (lines 12 through 21), the section could be coded with a block IF as follows (note reversal of test to use LE instead of GT):

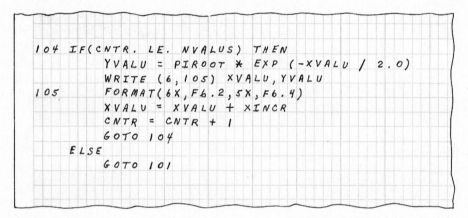

```
104   IF(CNTR. LE. NVALUS)  THEN
            YVALU = PIROOT * EXP (-XVALU / 2.0)
            WRITE (6,105) XVALU,YVALU
105         FORMAT(6X,F6.2,5X,F6.4)
            XVALU = XVALU + XINCR
            CNTR = CNTR + 1
            GOTO 104
      ELSE
            GOTO 101
```

Programming exercises

Description of assignment

Select one or more problems (or take the problems assigned to you by the instructor). Write the program including the following features.

1   A heading for the output.

2   Labels and/or headings on lines of output.

3   Use END, if available, to control program transfer at end of data.

4   Data validation with error message. Include some form of printout of input data. (Alternative: Rather than rejecting some data, you may wish to accept the data and give a warning message.)

5   Error message for data-type error. Include record number. If ERR is not available on your compiler, omit this step as well as the test data item with a data-type error.

6   Keep a record count. Print the count at the end of the program. If appropriate, print a separate count for accepted and rejected items.

7   Identify data values for a complete set of test data. Test the program using all test data items (or if large, using a subset that performs critical tests).

Mathematics and statistics

1 The natural logarithm (base *e*) of *X* can be approximated by the following series:

$$\log_e(X) = \frac{X-1}{X} + \frac{1}{2}\left(\frac{X-1}{X}\right)^2 + \frac{1}{3}\left(\frac{X-1}{X}\right)^3 + \cdots$$

Prepare a table for *X* = 0.5, 2.0, 6.0, and π that compares the computed series value for the first 20 items with the values from the ALOG intrinsic function. The table format should be as follows:

```
            SERIES VS. INTRINSIC FUNCTION
               FOR NATURAL LOGARITHM

X              SERIES      FUNCTION    DIFFERENCE
               VALUE       VALUE


 .50000


2.00000


6.00000


3.14159
```

2 The following formulas describe properties of portions of circles, with radius *r* and central angle θ in degrees.

$$\text{Area} = \pi r^2$$

$$\text{Length of arc} = \frac{\pi r \theta}{180}$$

$$\text{Length of chord} = 2r \sin \frac{1}{2}\theta$$

$$\text{Area of segment} = \frac{\pi r^2 \theta}{360} - \frac{r^2 \sin \theta}{2}$$

Prepare a table giving each of these properties for input data values for *r* and θ as follows:

r	θ
10.0	65
5.0	97
12.4	134
15.2	12

The table should have the following headings for the outputs:

```
                    PROPERTIES OF CIRCLES
                          LENGTH        LENGTH        AREA OF
     R      THETA    AREA  OF ARC       OF CHORD      SEGMENT
```

3 The sum of the first N numbers is $N(N + 1)/2$. The sum of the squares of the first N numbers is

$$\frac{N(N + 1)(2N+1)}{6}$$

The sum of the cubes of the first N numbers is

$$\frac{N^2(N + 1)^2}{4}$$

For values of N of 3, 7, 10, 12, and 13, prepare a table of these three sums in the following format:

```
N       SUM         SUM OF          SUM OF
                    SQUARES         CUBES
```

Business and economics

4 The annual payment p to repay a loan of b dollars for t years at an interest rate of i percent is given by:

$$p = b\frac{i(1 + i)^t}{(1 + i)^t - 1}$$

Prepare a repayment table of the following form showing the payment, interest, and loan balance for each of three loans:

```
            REPAYMENT SCHEDULE FOR LOAN OF $ XXXX
            AT A RATE OF  XX   PERCENT FOR  XX YEARS
                 ANNUAL PAYMENT IS $  XXXX.XX

PAYMENT         INTEREST        PRINCIPLE       BALANCE
NUMBER                                          DUE
```

The data items to be used are:

Loan amount	Interest rate (%)	Length of repayment period
$ 10,000	12	7
100,000	14	12
50,000	16.5	4

Note: The annual interest due is computed on the outstanding balance before the payment.

5 As transactions are received by a bank, they are entered as to transaction type (D for deposit and W for withdrawal), amount, and account number. The following four accounts exist:

Account number	Beginning balance
3201	$ 652.87
4331	127.95
1604	6043.80
1134	1097.81

The entry cards have the following format:

Card columns	
1	Transaction type
2–10	Amount
11–15	Account number

Read in the following input data:

W	250.17	3201
D	458.24	4331
W	1265.86	1604
W	27.18	3201
S	784.33	1134
D	685.32	3201
W	537.00	4331
D	16.84	1134
W	484.39	1604
W	127.45	1134

Prepare a report showing invalid transactions and summarizing for each account the ending balance and the number of each type of transaction. *Hint:* A character data item can be compared with a character constant, for example, IF(CODE .EQ. 'W') THEN. . . .

TRANSACTION SUMMARY

INVALID TRANSACTIONS   [If none, print a line saying so.]

ACCOUNT SUMMARY

ACCOUNT NUMBER	BEGINNING BALANCE	NUMBER OF TRANSACTIONS	ENDING BALANCE

6   Referring to problem 6 in Chapter 2, assume the input data is in the following format:

Input columns	Item
1–4	Sales person number
5–14	Sales person name
15–18	Sales goal
19–22	Actual sales
23–24	Blank
25–30	Bonus factor

Prepare a report in the following form:

```
            SALES COMMISSION REPORT

NAME OF            PERCENT OF      COMMISSION
SALES PERSON       GOAL ATTAINED
```

Note: Remember to print message "FAILED TO MEET GOAL" if a person fell short of the stated goal. Also check for invalid input.

Science and engineering

7   Air pressure p declines as altitude h increases. The approximate relationship is

$$p = 14.6 \times 10^{-0.0164h}$$

where p is expressed in pounds per square inch and h in thousands of feet. Prepare a table of this function for h values of 4, 10, 35, 70, and 100.

```
   HEIGHT            PRESSURE
(1000 OF FT.)     (LBS./SQ. FT.)

    4.0

   10.0

   35.0

   70.0

  100.0
```

8   A projectile fired at an angle θ given an initial velocity of v_0 will travel a distance r according to the following formula:

$$r = \frac{v_0^2 \sin 2\theta}{g}$$

where g is the acceleration constant of 32 ft/sec². It will be in motion for a time t given by

$$t = \frac{2v_0 \sin \theta}{g}$$

and reach a maximum height h of

$$h = \frac{v_0^2 \sin \theta}{g}$$

For all angles from 20 to 70 degrees in 10-degree increments and initial velocities of 200, 400, and 1000 ft/sec, produce tables of the following form:

```
            PROJECTILE CHARACTERISTICS

        (INITIAL VELOCITY EQUALS  200. FT/SEC)

     ANGLE        RANGE        TIME         HEIGHT
```

9 Produce a table showing the weight of cylindrical drums produced out of materials of various types and thicknesses. The area is obtained from the formula

$$Area = 2\pi r(r + h) \qquad r = radius; \; h = height$$

The drums are from 2.5 to 3.5 ft in diameter in half-foot increments and the height is 4.5 ft. The specifications for material are:

Material	Thickness	Weight, lb/ft²
Steel	.0908 in	3.70
Brass	.0908 in	3.884
Copper	.0908 in	4.110
Steel	.0201 in	.820
Brass	.0201 in	.860
Copper	.0201 in	.910

Assume input in the following format:

Column	Contents
1–15	Material
16–20	Blank
21–25	Weight

Produce output as shown below:

```
               WEIGHT OF CYLINDRICAL DRUMS
                    4.5 FEET HIGH

                    DIAMETER (FEET)
MATERIAL            2.5        3.0          3.5

STEEL   .0908"

BRASS   .0908"

COPPER .0908"

STEEL   .0201"

BRASS   .0201"

COPPER .0201"
```

Humanities and social sciences

10 Each degree of latitude represents approximately 68.84 miles. For each of the towns, given the input data, compute how far north of the equator it is and produce a tabular output:

```
DISTANCE FROM EQUATOR

FOR SELECTED CITIES

CITY                     MILES
```

Use the following data:

City	North latitude
London	51°30′
Minneapolis	44°58′
Honolulu	21°18′
Cairo	30°31′
Fairbanks	64°50′
New York City	40°40′

Assume input in the following format:

Column	Contents
1–22	City name
23–25	Blank
26–27	Latitude (degrees)
28	Blank
29–30	Latitude (minutes)

11 A transition matrix shows the percentage of people of each class who will switch to the other classes or remain in their own each year. An example is switching political parties.

Party	Republican	Democrat	Independent
Republican	.5	.1	.4
Democrat	.1	.6	.3
Independent	.2	.2	.6

Given that the system starts with 1000 Republicans, 1500 Democrats, and 2000 Independents, prepare a table for the next 10 years showing the number of each type. Assume an input format (one input per line of matrix):

Column	Contents
1–15	Party
16–20	Blank
21–23	Percentages (no decimal points)

Produce an output report:

```
                    PARTY MEMBERSHIP BY YEARS

       YEAR      REPUBLICANS     DEMOCRATS     INDEPENDENTS

        Ø           1ØØØ           15ØØ            2ØØØ

        1           1Ø5Ø           14ØØ            2Ø5Ø

        2

        3

        4

        5

        6

        7

        8

        9

       1Ø
```

12 Personalized letters are desired to increase participation in a political survey. The input consists of names and addresses, and the output is a personalized letter. Assume the following output:

```
   Mr. & Mrs. _____name_____

   _____street address_____

   _____city, state_____
   Dear Mr. & Mrs. _____name_____

        You have been selected as representative of the people in

   ___city___ to assist us in determining public sentiment toward

   the federal budget. The ___name___ family, we feel, as citizens

   of ___state___ will want to have a part in this important project.
```

Prepare a program to write such letters using the following input data:

Jones	1838 W. Vliet Street	Madison, Wisconsin
Smith	125 E. 75 Avenue	Kansas City, Kansas
Johnson	4501 S. Custar Road	St. Paul, Minnesota
Alvarez	3286 N. 125 Street	Seattle, Washington
Vilas	5101 E. Ontario Blvd.	Miami, Florida

Assume an input format:

Column	Contents
1–10	Name
11–15	Blank
16–40	Street address
41–45	Blank
46–57	City
58–68	State

General

13 A professor must prepare a grade report in the following format:

```
                         PROFESSOR:  your name

                         DATE:        today's date

              STUDENT GRADE REPORT

                         FINAL      FINAL       COURSE
STUDENT NAME             EXAM       SCORE       GRADE
```

Student grades are entered on cards or at a terminal in the following format:

Column	Entry
1–20	Name
21–25	Quiz 1 grade
26–30	Quiz 2 grade
31–35	Homework grade
36–40	Final exam grade

The final score = .2(quiz 1) + .2(quiz 2) + .3(homework) + .3(final exam). Letter course grades are assigned as follows:

Final score	Letter grade
0–49	F
50–59	D
60–79	C
80–89	B
90–100	A

For the following set of students and grades, prepare a common grade report.

Name	Quiz 1	Quiz 2	Homework	Final Exam
J. C. Johnson	90	85	95	93
L. W. Juergens	82	65	88	84
C. B. Smile	75	70	83	71
L. W. Thatcher	80	69	74	74

14 A company has a fleet of many different automobiles. It gathers data on the operating costs of each one to produce a report.

GASOLINE OPERATING EXPENSE REPORT

AUTO	ID	TOTAL MILES	MILES PER GALLON	COST PER MILE

Based on the following input data format and input data, prepare a report:

Column	Contents
1–10	Car type
11–15	Car ID number
16–20	Blank
21–25	Starting mileage
26–30	Ending mileage
31–32	Blank
33–35	Gallons put into tank
36–40	Cost of fill-up

Car	ID	Starting mileage	Ending mileage	Gallons	Cost
Ford Wagon	0123	6718	7204	21.2	28.62
Ford Sedan	1854	8179	8415	8.7	11.31
Chevy 2-door	7835	10012	10341	10.6	13.67
Chevy 2-door	6114	7315	7784	15.6	19.97
Ford Wagon	1005	5663	5902	9.6	12.76

15 If inventory on hand falls below the reorder point, a replenishment order is placed. The amount to be ordered (Q) is given by the following formula:

$$Q = \sqrt{\frac{2AS}{ci}}$$

where A is annual usage, S is setup cost, c is unit cost, and i is interest rate for carrying inventory. The reorder point R equals $L \times U$, where L is the lead time in weeks and U is the weekly usage. Print an output report that shows the reorder point and order quantity for each of the following items. (*Note:* The quantity to order at reorder point should be in whole units). Use the headings shown:

INVENTORY REPORT

ITEM NUMBER	DESCRIPTION	REORDER POINT	REORDER QUANTITY

Item Number	Description	Lead Time	Set-up Cost	Unit Cost	Interest Rate	Annual Usage
1124	Washer	1.6	1.25	0.001	.10	200
2106	Cone subassembly	2.4	35.00	125.00	.15	5000
4603	Socket	3.0	6.25	7.25	.10	12000
5119	Plug	1.8	4.37	1.39	.15	650
7732	Engine	4.2	45.50	650.78	.20	3050

The format for the input is:

Column	Contents
1–5	Item number
6–10	Blank
11–30	Description
31–35	Lead time
36–40	Blank
41–45	Setup cost
46–55	Unit cost
56–57	Blank
58–60	Interest rate
61–65	Usage

chapter **4** **A**

Repetition program structure, subscripted variables, and DO loops

A very important program design and coding element is the repetition structure used to program the repeated execution of a block of instructions. The repetition structure is implemented in FORTRAN by the DO loop. Many repetition problems are simplified by the use of subscripted variables, and thus the FORTRAN notation for subscripted variables will be explained before describing the DO loop.

Subscripted variables

Subscripts are frequently used in mathematical formulations, and therefore it is important to understand this method of identifying data items. The mathematical concept of subscripts can be directly applied to FORTRAN.

Arrays and matrices

A list of quantities that can be grouped together can be thought of as a one-dimensional array. A quantity in the list is identified by a name given to the entire list, as well as by a number that refers to the position in the list occupied by the quantity. Mathematical notation uses a lowered number, hence the term subscript. For example, sales by customers would form a single-dimension array as shown in Figure 4-1. If S is used to denote sales, the sales to customer 3 can be identified as an array element S_3, sales to customer 4 as S_4, etc.

A two-dimensional array, or rectangular array (often called a *matrix*), provides a twofold classification. For example, a classification of persons by height and weight would result in a rectangular array. A single name can be used to refer to the matrix, and when any particular element or classification in the array is referred to, the name is used with subscripts designating row and column. By convention, the row is always written first and the column second. For example, if F is used to refer to the twofold classification of females, $F_{3,4}$ refers to the number of those who are in weight class 3 and height class 4, as illustrated in Figure 4-2.

A threefold classification uses three subscripts. The first subscript refers to the row, the second to the column, and the third to the level. For example, a classification by weight, height, and age will result in the three-dimensional array shown in Figure 4-3. If the entire classification by weight, height, and

Figure 4-1
Single-dimension array.

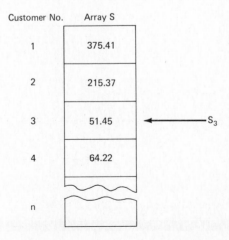

Customer No.	Array S	
1	375.41	
2	215.37	
3	51.45	← S_3
4	64.22	
n		

Figure 4-2
Two-dimensional array.

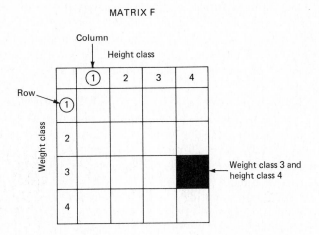

MATRIX F

Column

Height class

Row

Weight class

Weight class 3 and
height class 4

age is termed C, persons falling into weight class 2, height class 4, and age class 1 are identified as $C_{2,4,1}$. The classifications are listed as subscripts in order by row, column, and level.

In short, subscripts are used to identify one out of a related set of items. All items in an array have the same name because they are all in the same category. The subscript identifies a specific element within the array.

Form of FORTRAN subscripts

Standard mathematical notation for subscripts uses numbers or letters written below the level of the symbol to which they apply. But since neither the keypunch nor the printer in a computer system is usually equipped to handle lowered characters, subscripts are represented in FORTRAN as a set of numbers enclosed in parentheses that follow immediately after the name. The subscripts are separated by commas. The previous array examples would appear in FORTRAN as S(3), F(3,4), and C(2,4,1). The number of subscripts is limited to three in Subset FORTRAN and to seven in full FORTRAN.

Figure 4-3
Three-dimensional array.

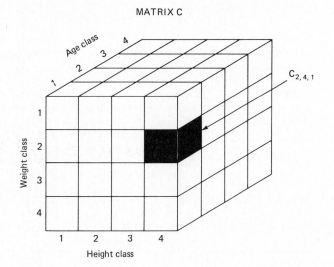

MATRIX C

Age class

$C_{2,4,1}$

Weight class

Height class

The name of an array consists of from one to six characters (same rules as for a simple variable name). The first letter of the array name identifies the data items in the array as being integer or real. Or array names may be declared in a TYPE statement as referencing storage locations holding integer-, real-, or character-type data items without regard to the first letter of the name.

When array names are used in FORTRAN statements, they are followed by subscripts to identify the specific data item or element in the array (except in special cases). The subscripts referring to elements in the array must have an integer value, since positions in an array can only be whole numbers. The integer values for subscripts can be specified by integer variables, integer constants, or integer expressions. In 1977 FORTRAN, the subscript expression can follow the general rules for arithmetic expressions; in older FORTRANs, the expressions were limited to multiplication, subtraction, and addition, in the following forms (where k is an integer constant and i is an integer variable):

Addition or subtraction	$i \pm k$
Multiplication	$k * i$
Combinations	$k * i \pm k$

GENERAL FORM OF SUBSCRIPTS

$A(iek_1)$
$A(iek_1, iek_2)$
$A(iek_1, iek_2, iek_3)$

A = any array name. First letter of array name identifies array variables as integer or real in same way as variable names, unless name is declared as different type. A character array must be declared as CHARACTER.

iek = integer variables, integer expressions, or integer constants as subscripts. Full FORTRAN also allows array element references as subscripts.

Subscripts are separated by commas. The number of subscripts is limited to three in Subset FORTRAN and to seven in full FORTRAN. Spaces are optional for readability.

Examples of allowable array references

Array reference	Comments
ALPHA (9)	References the 9*th* element in array ALPHA.
BETA (1,7)	References the element in row 1 and column 7 of array BETA.
IOTA (I,J,K)	References the element in I*th* row, J*th* column, and K*th* level of array IOTA. In order to locate the element, the program must have values for I, J, and K.
GAMMA (M,3)	References the M*th* row and 3*rd* column of array GAMMA. A value for GAMMA must be known before execution of statement.
Y(7 * KIX,8)	Value of KIX is multiplied by 7 to arrive at row number; column is 8*th*.
Z(NIX+3, JIX)	Add 3 to value of NIX to compute row number; number of column is the value of JIX.

Examples of array references not allowed

Variable	Why not allowed
ALPHA (X)	Cannot be a real subscript; code as ALPHA (INT(X))
X(NIX, YIX)	Cannot be a real subscript; code as X(NIX, INT(YIX))

Use of subscripts

Each time the compiler program translating the FORTRAN source statement to machine language encounters a variable name, it assigns a memory location to it. An array name presents a problem because the number of memory locations to be assigned to it is not always apparent from the program. In fact, the number may vary, depending on the problem being run. To allow the compiler to assign the correct number of memory locations for an array, the programmer must specify the maximum size of the array. The statement for doing this is the DIMENSION statement, which may appear any place in the program before the first use of the array name. However, it is usually good practice to put all DIMENSION statements at the beginning of the program in a type declaration and storage allocation block.

The basic form of the DIMENSION statement is the word DIMENSION followed by the dimension declarations for each array being described. The dimension declaration consists of the array name followed by parentheses that enclose the maximum values for each dimension of the array. For example, if there are three arrays A, B, and C, the first of which is a simple column of 15, the second is 4×5, and the third is $3 \times 4 \times 6$, the DIMENSION statement would appear as follows:

```
DIMENSION A(15), B(4, 5), C(3, 4, 6)
```

The three dimensions are the maximum number of rows, columns, and levels that will be needed by the program to store data elements under the array name. In 1977 subset FORTRAN and previous versions of the language, the array declarations in the DIMENSION statement can use only integer constants, and all array dimensions are assumed to start with 1 and end with the number specified as being the maximum dimension. In other words, A(15) declares an array with elements numbered from 1 to 15; B(4, 5) declares an array with elements numbered from 1 to 4 for the rows and from 1 to 5 for the columns.

The full 1977 FORTRAN allows the dimensions to be expressed as an upper and lower bound in the form L:U, where the value of either bound may be positive, negative, or zero. The value of the upper bound must be greater than the value of the lower bound. The lower-bound/upper-bound dimension is not necessary, since the program can always include instructions to convert to standard dimensions starting at 1, but the bounds are very convenient in some problem situations. For example, data (called D) for the years 1945 to 1959 can be referenced by subscripts as D(1) to D(15), but it is probably more meaningful to use D(1945) to D(1959). This is done by a DIMENSION D(1945:1959). Other situations arise in which subscripts would be more meaningful if started at zero or with a negative number. An interest problem over 10 periods might have computations for time zero. An experi-

183

ment might generate data to be identified as starting at -10 and going to $+20$. DIMENSION statements for these two cases would be:

```
DIMENSION PERIOD (0:10)
DIMENSION EXPRNT (-10:20)
```

The number of storage locations allocated by the dimension statement is only enough to meet the range specified. The computer translates from the subscripts used to the storage location. In the above examples, 11 locations would be provided for PERIOD and 31 for EXPRNT.

Another feature of full 1977 FORTRAN is the use of constant expressions (expressions using constants and plus or minus operators) and exponentiation in dimensions. For example, in full FORTRAN, H(5 + 30, 10), and K(10**2) are allowed.

Type declarations and DIMENSION statements are placed in the same program block for convenience. Also, the dimension for a variable can be incorporated in the type statement. For example, REAL X(10, 10) specifies X as a real array with dimensions 10×10. For clarity, we prefer to use separate DIMENSION and type statements rather than combination statements.

BASIC FORM FOR DIMENSION FOR ARRAYS

DIMENSION A(k), A(k_2,k_2), A(k_1,k_2,k_3), A(k_1,k_2, . . . ,k_n)

If more than one array is dimensioned, the variables are separated by commas.

A = any array name
k = an integer constant
k_1, k_2, k_3, . . . = the maximum number of rows, columns, levels, etc.

1977 Standard FORTRAN allows up to 7 dimensions; 1977 Subset FORTRAN allows up to 3 dimensions. 1977 full FORTRAN allows a dimension to be declared as an upper and lower bound:

k_L:k_U where k_L must be less than k_U

1977 full FORTRAN also allows an expression using integer constants as a dimension.

Care should be taken not to dimension larger than necessary for the maximum set of data. A DIMENSION X(100,100,100) calls for $100 \times 100 \times 100$ memory locations. Although valid in form, this requirement for 1 million memory locations exceeds the internal capacity allowed on most computers.

When an array name is used in an executable statement, it must always be used with a subscript to identify the desired location. The only exception to this rule is a specialized input/output situation in which an array name without a subscript references the entire array (to be explained later in the chapter). Two short sample problems illustrate two types of uses for arrays.

Array example 1

The first problem is a program to tally the number of students whose grade-point averages fall into each of five categories. The array called TALLY has five categories:

Category	Grade point
TALLY(1)	0.0–0.99
TALLY(2)	1.0–1.99
TALLY(3)	2.0–2.99
TALLY(4)	3.0–3.99
TALLY(5)	4.0

The program reads a card with the grade-point average for a student given on it. This variable, called GPA, is in the form X.XX. The END condition causes the tallies to be printed. After reading the input, the next step is to determine which category the student's grades are in and to add 1 to the tally for that category (Figure 4-4). Note that the data itself is used to provide the subscript category by which it is classified. The statement I = INT(GPA + 1.0) thus provides the proper integer for the tally statement. (The INT or IFIX function is redundant but clarifies the logic.)

Array example 2

The second problem is to sum 100 quantities stored in an array called X. The quantities have been read and placed in the array by instructions not shown. A simple IF loop is used to repeat the processing using a new value at each repetition, as shown in Figure 4-5. The test for termination of the loop is an IF statement, which is placed at the beginning of the loop. If subscripts were not available, the program to add 100 numbers would require statements listing all 100 variable names. In order to understand the logic of Figure 4-5, trace the value of JIX and SUM when data values for X(1), X(2), and X(3) are 9.0, 11.0, and 20.0.

Figure 4-4
Program segment for tally grade-point problem.

```
*********          STORAGE ALLOCATION                      *********
*                                                                  *
      DIMENSION TALLY(5)                                           *
*                                                                  *
*******************************************************************
*                                                                  *
*********          INITIALIZATION                      BLOCK 0000
*                                                                  *
      TALLY(1) = 0.0
      TALLY(2) = 0.0
      TALLY(3) = 0.0
      TALLY(4) = 0.0
      TALLY(5) = 0.0
*                                                                  *
*******************************************************************
*                                                                  *
*********          READ AND TALLY GPA CATEGORY         BLOCK 0100
*                  (VALIDATION OF INPUT DATA NOT SHOWN)            *
*                                                                  *
  100 READ(5,110,END=300) GPA
  110 FORMAT(F5.2)
      I = INT(GPA + 1.0)
      TALLY(I) = TALLY(I) + 1.0
*                                                                  *
*         GO BACK TO READ ANOTHER DATA CARD                        *
*                                                                  *
      GOTO 100
*                                                                  *
*******************************************************************
*                                                                  *
*********          OUTPUT (NOT SHOWN)                  BLOCK 0300
*                                                                  *
```

PROGRAM SEGMENT   FLOWCHART

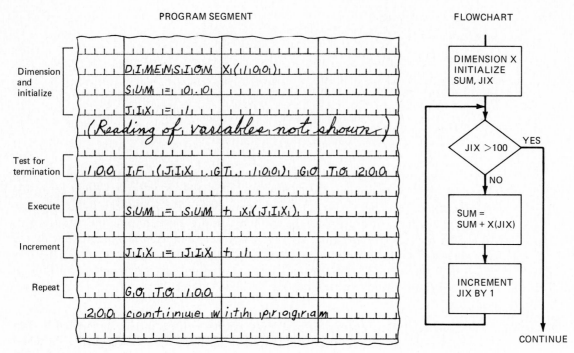

Figure 4-5
Program segment to sum quantities stored in a one-dimensional array.

Self-testing exercise 4-1

1 State whether the following statements or expressions are valid or invalid. If invalid for some FORTRANs, state why.

Statement or expression	Valid or invalid for full 1977 FORTRAN	Versions of FORTRAN for which invalid and why
(a) DIMENSION C(100), NIX (100)		
(b) A (14, NIX, X)		
(c) A (JIX * KIX)		
(d) ALPHA (10, 10, 5)		
(e) DIMENSION ALPHA (100), BETA (100, 10)		
(f) GAMMA (A + 5.0)		
(g) DELTAS (I*5)		
(h) Y (5, 10, 4, 3)		
(i) DIMENSION BETA (0:15, −5:10)		
(j) DIMENSION TBL (10**3, 5*5)		

2 Write the DIMENSION statements for the following arrays:
(a) An array of 100 sample observations
(b) A two-dimensional array to classify persons by sex and by one of 10 occupations

(c) An array to classify business firms by one of eight size groups, one of 15 types of business groups, and one of five location classes

(d) Four arrays A, B, C, and D, each having 15 entries

3 Give the subscripted variable names by which the following matrix array elements are identified.

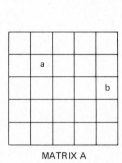

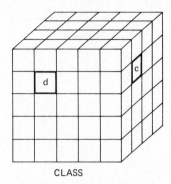

MATRIX A   CLASS

4 Give the DIMENSION statements for the arrays in question 3.

5 A variable NX to be used as an index to identify elements in an array A has values from 0 to 8. Array A is dimensioned by DIMENSION A(0:8). Assume that the lower-bound/upper-bound dimensions are not available and show an alternate DIMENSION statement and a reference to an element in the array based on NX.

6 Using logic similar to that in Figure 4-5, write program segments to initialize a loop counter, to dimension three arrays (A, B, and C) for five values, and then to read pairs of numbers from five input cards (F10.2,F10.2) into two arrays A and B. Multiply the arrays A and B to create an array C. The DO statement to be presented next is a simpler way to code these operations, but the exercise is a useful learning experience.

DO statement

The DO statement or DO loop is one of the most powerful features of FORTRAN. It greatly simplifies the writing of program repetition (also called program loops).

Concept of repetition or looping

Looping is repetition based on program modification. A set of one or more instructions is executed a number of times, each time altering one or more variables in the set, so that each execution is different from the preceding one. The effect of looping is to reduce substantially the number of instructions required for a program.

The repetition structure (looping) is implemented in FORTRAN by the DO statement. Loops can be written in FORTRAN without the DO statement by coding all the loop control statements (see Figure 4-5), but the DO loop form is generally preferred.

The DO loop repetition structure follows the DO WHILE logic explained in Chapter 1 (see Figure 4-6). The repetition is said to continue WHILE the condition governing the loop is true; when it is not true, the repetition ceases.

Figure 4-6
Flowchart of DO WHILE repetition structure.

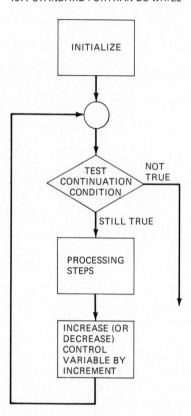

1977 STANDARD FORTRAN DO WHILE

The logic of a DO WHILE or DO loop includes the following procedures:

1   Initialize the loop control variable to the first value.
2   Test to see if the loop control variable is within the limit for continuation. If it is within the limit, continue with the loop; if it exceeds the limit, branch out of the loop.
3   Execute the set of statements in the loop.
4   Modify the loop control variable.
5   Go back to the beginning of the loop (step 2).

Form of the DO statement

The DO statement is a repetition command that simplifies the writing of loops. It automatically initializes the loop variable, tests to see if the variable is within the limit for continuation, passes control to the statements to be executed (or branches out of the loop), modifies the loop variable, and branches back to the start of the loop.

The DO loop structure begins with a DO statement, which identifies in order the following elements required for the loop execution:

1   The statement label of the last or terminal statement of the set of statements included in the loop. In other words, the DO statement is the statement at the

beginning of the loop; the terminal statement, with its statement label, is the last statement in the loop (it defines the range of the loop).

2 The variable controlling the loop (the DO variable).

3 The initial value of the DO control variable.

4 The limit-of-continuation value for the DO variable.

5 The increment by which the DO variable will be changed each time the loop is executed.

The terminal statement in a loop can be any executable statement except a transfer-of-control statement (GOTO, DO, and, in most cases, IF). To avoid ending a loop with a transfer-of-control statement, a CONTINUE statement is often written as the last loop statement. As a matter of style, we have chosen to write a CONTINUE statement as the terminal statement in every DO loop because it adds clarity to the program structure. Also, for clear style, the statements between the DO statement and the CONTINUE statement may be indented (say four spaces) to visually show the range of the loop. For example:

```
      DO 150 I = 1,10,2
          C(I) = A(I) * B(I)
          WRITE (6,700) A(I),B(I),C(I)
  150 CONTINUE
```

In the above example, the DO statement says that the statements from the DO statement through the statement labeled 150 should be executed repeatedly based on the DO variable I. The loop is repeated as long as I is not greater than 10. The DO variable I begins with a value of 1 and is incremented by 2 at the end of each execution of the loop. As in the above example, the DO variable can be used in statements within the loop, but it is not required. The general form of the DO statement is summarized in the box on the next page.

In most cases, the number of executions for a DO loop is clear; DO 100 I = 1,5 executes the loop five times. If the terminal value is less than the initial value, the loop is not executed. (Older FORTRAN compilers may execute the loop once.) The number of executions is computed from the integer value of

$$\frac{\text{Terminal value} - \text{initial value} + \text{increment}}{\text{Increment}}$$

Thus, the loop specified in DO 100 X = 5, 18,3 is executed five times:

$$\frac{18 - 5 + 3}{3} = 5$$

The basic form of the DO statement defined in older FORTRANs is continued in the 1977 standard, but there are some additional features. The basic form in older FORTRANs uses only positive integer variables and integer constants for the loop parameters and only an integer variable for the DO control variable. The subset of 1977 FORTRAN allows negative parameters. In addition to negative integer parameters, the full 1977 FORTRAN allows a real variable as the control variable and real variables as parameters; real or integer expressions may also be used as parameters. In older FORTRANs,

189

DO STATEMENT

DO statement in 1977 full FORTRAN

DO s v = vek_1, vek_2, vek_3 If vek_3 is 1, it may be omitted.

where s = statement label of the last statement in the loop (the terminal statement).
    v = DO control variable, which may be a real or integer variable.
  vek = parameters, which may be integer or real variables, constants, or real or integer expressions. Parameters may be negative.
  vek_1 = initial parameter, that is, the initial value of the loop variable.
  vek_2 = terminal parameter, that is, the maximum value the loop variable can be and have the loop processing continue.
  vek_3 = incrementation parameter, that is, the increment value by which the loop variable is to be modified. If vek_3 is not stated, it is assumed to be 1.

DO statement in Subset and older FORTRANs

DO s i = ik_1, ik_2, ik_3 If ik_3 = 1, it may be omitted.

 where i = integer variable as the DO control variable.
   ik = integer variable or integer constant for initial, terminal, and increment parameters.

In Subset FORTRAN but not in older FORTRAN, parameters may be negative. In older FORTRAN, a comma between s and i is an error; in the 1977 standard, a comma between s and i is optional; for example, DO s,i = . . . is allowed. For compatibility, do not use the comma.

placement of a comma after the statement label in the DO statement was an error, even though it seemed natural for many programmers to put one there. The 1977 FORTRAN allows the comma, thereby eliminating a potential coding error.

A repetition structure involving a DO loop can be described in the pseudocode of a program design language. A statement defining the nature of the loop is followed by the statements in the range of the loop, which are indented to aid visual definition of the range. The end of the loop is explicitly defined by an End of DO or End DO pseudocode statement. The pseudocode statements in the loop should explain clearly the processing to be performed. Words, mathematical expressions, or combinations may be used. These alternatives will be illustrated in the chapter.

In flowcharting a DO loop, the programmer can write the flow diagram in terms of the DO loop statement itself. The terminal statement label, control variable, initial value, terminal value, and incrementation value are specified within a special processing symbol. A dotted line may be used to visually define the range of the DO loop as shown in Figure 4-7.

A DO loop can contain DO loops within its range. This is termed *nesting*. When nesting one DO loop inside another, the inner DO loop must be entirely contained within the range of the outer DO loop. However, the loops may have the same terminal statement, but, as a matter of clear style, we use a

Figure 4-7
Flowcharting a DO loop.

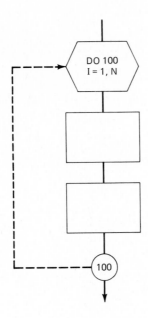

separate CONTINUE for each loop. There is no specified limit to the number of DO loops that can be nested. The inner loop is repeated the specified number of times each time the loop in which it is contained is incremented. For clear program design, the inner DO is indented to show the relationship and range of the inner DO loop to the outer DO loop. As an example, assume a program segment to sum the elements in an N × 5 matrix.

```
      SUM = 0.0
      DO  110  I = 1, N
          DO  100  J = 1, 5              ⎤
              SUM = SUM + A(I, J)        ⎥  Range of    ⎤
100           CONTINUE                   ⎦  inner DO    ⎥  Range of
110   CONTINUE                                          ⎦  outer DO
```

Each time the outer loop is executed, the inner loop is executed 5 times. Therefore, the outer loop is executed N times and the inner loop 5 * N times.

Use of the DO statement

The following examples illustrate and explain the way the DO statement is used in programming the repetition structure. The examples also illustrate the rules for DO loops and the style suggestions for clarity in programming.

DO example 1   Write a DO loop to sum the variables in an array DELTA with odd-numbered subscripts between 1 and 210 (Figure 4-8).

DO example 2   Multiply two arrays A and B, with N entries in each, to form a new array C (Figure 4-9).

Figure 4-8
DO example 1.

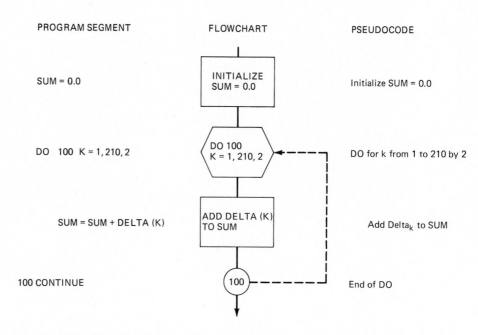

PROGRAM SEGMENT	FLOWCHART	PSEUDOCODE
SUM = 0.0	INITIALIZE SUM = 0.0	Initialize SUM = 0.0
DO 100 K = 1, 210, 2	DO 100 K = 1, 210, 2	DO for k from 1 to 210 by 2
SUM = SUM + DELTA (K)	ADD DELTA (K) TO SUM	Add Delta$_k$ to SUM
100 CONTINUE	100	End of DO

Note that SUM has to be set to zero before the loop is entered if it is to be used as the accumulator variable.

DO example 3

Read K punched cards with a variable X in each card in columns 1–10 in the form 99.99. Find the arithmetic mean (average) of the numbers (Figure 4-10).

DO example 4

Add two 4 × 6 matrices A and B to form matrix C; that is, C(1,1) = A(1,1) + B(1,1), etc. (Figure 4-11). The order in which the program will perform the computation is defined by the DOs. The J values go through a cycle from 1 to 6 each time I changes by 1. Thus, the order of computations in Example 4 will be:

```
C(1, 1) = A(1, 1) + B(1, 1)
C(1, 2) = A(1, 2) + B(1, 2)
C(1, 3) = A(1, 3) + B(1, 3)
C(1, 4) = A(1, 4) + B(1, 4)
C(1, 5) = A(1, 5) + B(1, 5)
C(1, 6) = A(1, 6) + B(1, 6)
```
I is set to 1 and J loops from 1 to 6.

```
C(2, 1) = A(2, 1) + B(2, 1)
C(2, 2) = A(2, 2) + B(2, 2)
etc.
```
I is set to 2 and J loops from 1 to 6 again.

(Not shown)

I is set to 2 and J loops from 1 to 6 for the third time.

⋮

```
C(4, 5) = A(4, 5) + B(4, 5)
C(4, 6) = A(4, 6) + B(4, 6)
```
I is set to 4 and J loops from 1 to 6 for the fourth time.

Figure 4-9
DO example 2.

Figure 4-10
DO example 3.

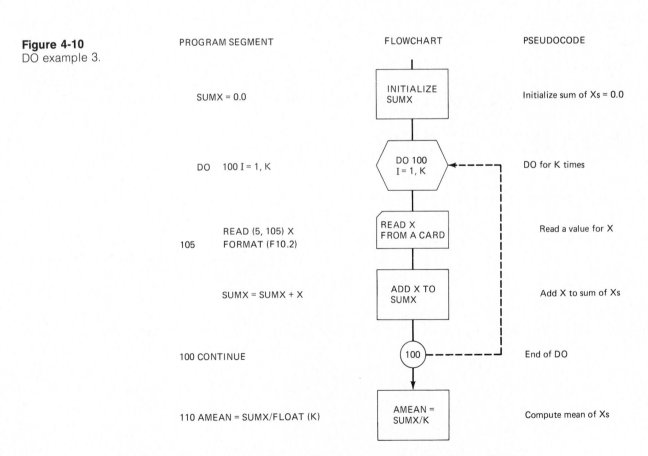

Note that the loop index I was not used in any loop statement but simply as a counter.

Figure 4-11
DO example 4.

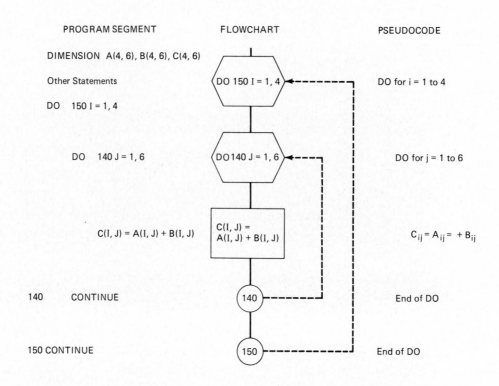

| PROGRAM SEGMENT | FLOWCHART | PSEUDOCODE |

DIMENSION A(4, 6), B(4, 6), C(4, 6)

Other Statements — DO 150 I = 1, 4 — DO for i = 1 to 4

DO   150 I = 1, 4

DO   140 J = 1, 6 — DO 140 J = 1, 6 — DO for j = 1 to 6

C(I, J) = A(I, J) + B(I, J) — C(I, J) = A(I, J) + B(I, J) — $C_{ij} = A_{ij} = + B_{ij}$

140   CONTINUE — 140 — End of DO

150 CONTINUE — 150 — End of DO

DO example 5

Compute how much $1000 invested today will return in 10 years if the interest rate is 10, 11, 12, 13, 14, or 15 percent and interest is compounded annually. The formula is $1000(1.0 + r)^{10}$, where r is the interest rate. Print out each rate and amount. The program, flowchart, and pseudocode are shown in Figure 4-12. This illustrates the use of real data for DO parameters.

Rules for using the DO statement

A few rules need to be observed in coding DO loops. A basic rule is to enter the DO loop through the DO statement and to end each execution with the

Figure 4-12
DO example 5.

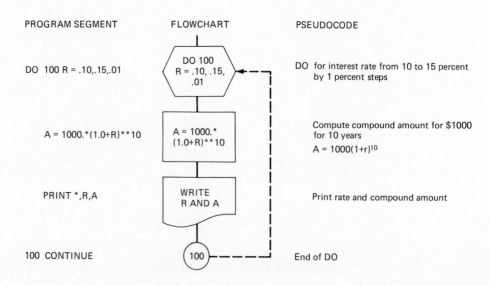

| PROGRAM SEGMENT | FLOWCHART | PSEUDOCODE |

DO 100 R = .10,.15,.01 — DO 100 R = .10, .15, .01 — DO for interest rate from 10 to 15 percent by 1 percent steps

A = 1000.*(1.0+R)**10 — A = 1000.* (1.0+R)**10 — Compute compound amount for $1000 for 10 years $A = 1000(1+r)^{10}$

PRINT *,R,A — WRITE R AND A — Print rate and compound amount

100 CONTINUE — 100 — End of DO

194

terminal statement. A DO loop is initialized by the execution of the DO statement, and the loop makes a normal exit after it has been executed the requisite number of times. The terminal statement (the CONTINUE statement if the pattern described here is followed) must be executed in order for the incrementation and return action of the loop mechanism to be activated.

RULES FOR DO LOOPS

1 The parameters of a DO statement should not be altered by statements within the range of the DO. This includes the values for the control variable, the initial value, the terminal value, and the increment.

2 The control variable can be used in statements inside the range of the DO loops or it may be used only as a repetition counter. When exit is made from the loop, the current value of the control variable is available for use outside the loop.

3 DO loops must be entered only through the DO statement because that execution establishes the loop controls. Never transfer from a statement outside the range of a DO to the inside of the range of a DO. An inner-nested DO can transfer into the range of an outer DO because the inner DO is already within the range of the outer DO.

4 The iteration count for number of times the loop will execute is established as the integer value from [(terminal value − initial value + increment) / increment]. If negative, the count is set to zero. A count of zero means the loop will not be executed at all. (Older FORTRANs may execute the loop once.) Note that the iteration count formula allows an initial value larger than a terminal value if there is a negative increment value. (Older FORTRANs do not allow a negative increment.)

In writing loops, there are efficiency considerations. A computation can often be performed outside the loop once and the result furnished to the loop, thereby reducing processing time. However, such efficient coding should be carefully used because it tends to make the program logic less clear.

Efficiency example A program is to produce a table of interest rates for \$1 using the formula $A = 1.0(1 + i)^n$, where i is the interest rate (called XI) and n is the number of periods. Since $1 + i$ is the same for each computation, it can be computed once outside the loop for efficiency. But unless the tables are very large, the efficiency is not significant enough to justify loss of clarity.

Clear coding of loop	More efficient coding of loop
| ```
      DO 150 I = 1, N
         A = (1.0 + XI)**I
         (other statements)
  159 CONTINUE
``` | ```
      FACTR = 1.0 + XI
      DO 150 I = 1, N
         A = FACTR**I
         (other statements)
  150 CONTINUE
``` |

Self-testing exercise 4-2

1 Complete the table:

DO statement	Valid or invalid for 1977 full FORTRAN	If invalid for Subset or for older FORTRANs, explain why
(a) DO NIX I = 1, 7		
(b) DO 120, I = 1, NIX		
(c) DO 230 MIX = 1, J, K		
(d) DO 350 JANE = JOE, + 7		
(e) DO 450 K = 10, 8		
(f) DO 560 LUCK = 7, 7		
(g) DO 670 ILL = 7, 15, 3		
(h) DO 780 I = 1, N − 1		
(i) DO 890 X = 1, 10, 2		

2 At the completion of the following program loops, what will be the value of K, L, and M?

```
      M = 0
      DO 150 I = 1, 10
         K = I
         DO 140 J = 1, 5
            L = J
            M = M + 1
140      CONTINUE
150 CONTINUE
```

3 How many times will the loops defined by the following DO statements be executed? Note where the answer for common pre-1977 FORTRAN versions may differ from the answer with the 1977 standard. Which statements are allowed by the 1977 standard FORTRAN but not allowed by 1977 Subset FORTRAN standard? Show computation for iteration count using the formula.

(a) DO 3 I = 5, 5

(b) DO 3 I = 5, 1

(c) DO 3 I = 1, 5

(d) DO 3 I = 1, 5, 3

(e) DO 3 A = 0.1, 0.5, 0.2

(f) DO 3 A = 0.03, 0.30, 0.05

(g) DO 3 I = 5, 1, − 2

4   In what order will the following program segment print out the subscripted variables from a three-dimensional array?

```
       DO 120 I = 1, 2
           DO 110 J = 1, 2
               DO 100 K = 1, 2
                   WRITE (3,900) ARRAY (I, J, K)
100            CONTINUE
110        CONTINUE
120 CONTINUE
```

5   What will the following program segment do?

```
       DO 150 I = 1, 30
           SUM = 0.0
           SUM = SUM + A(I) * B(I)
150 CONTINUE
```

6   Which of the DO loop nests in Figure 4-13 are valid?

7   Write a program segment to sum the products from multiplying the elements in array LIX by the corresponding elements in array MIX. There are N entries in each.

8   Write a program segment to create and print a table of Celsius (centigrade) temperatures corresponding to Fahrenheit temperatures from -10 to $+65$ degrees using intervals of 5 degrees. Centigrade = $^5/_9$(Fahrenheit -32).

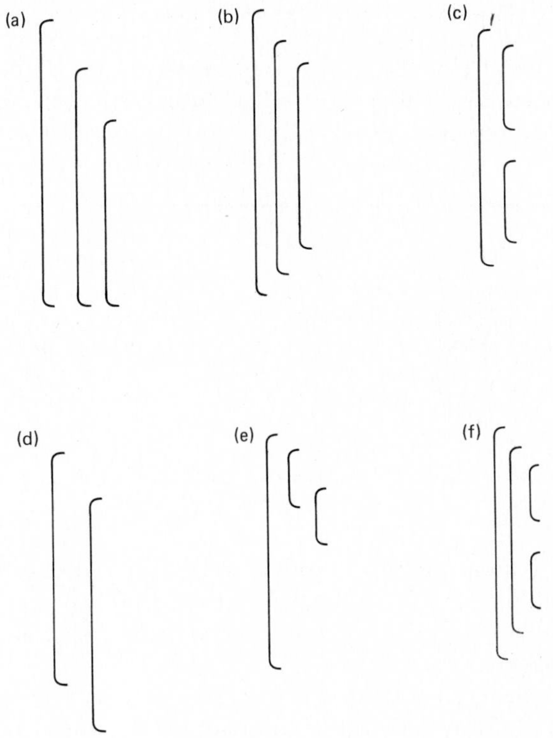

Figure 4-13
Loop nesting for question 6 in Self-testing exercise 4-2.

197

9 Write a program segment to print out every other entry in the K-entry array DAD, starting with the second entry.

10 Write a program segment to shift the values in an array A so that A(1) = A(2), A(2) = A(3), etc. A(N) should contain original value of A(1). Be careful with A(1).

11 Write a program segment to shift the values in the 25-entry array ALPHA so that A(2) = A(1), A(3) = A(2), etc., and A(1) = A(25). Be sure to check your logic carefully.

Implied DO loops in input/output

In reading or writing subscripted variables, each subscripted variable may be listed, but this is very cumbersome. Another method is to include the READ or WRITE statement inside a DO loop, but this method is limited by the fact that each loop initiates a repeat of the input/output command. A very useful FORTRAN feature that may simplify input and output of subscripted variables is a form of the input/output statement called an *implied* DO *loop*.

The form of the implied DO loop input or output statement is similar to that of the DO loop. In fact, as many as three implied loops may be nested. The form is shown by the following examples:

```
READ (5,700) (A(I), I = 1, N)
READ (5,700) ((A(I, J), J = 1, M), I = 1, N)
```

Note that each of the loop parameter specifications is enclosed in parentheses. Note also the placement of the commas, particularly after the parentheses.

In addition to the fact that it is a shorter form, the implied DO loop has an advantage over the regular DO loop in that the resulting variables are treated as a single list so that input or output from physical records is entirely under FORMAT control. For example, READ(5,700)(A(I),I = 1,100) will read the data items from 2 to 100 cards, depending on the format specifications. Keep in mind that the closing parenthesis of the FORMAT statement terminates the current physical record. If additional variables are still available in the list to be read or written and the format specifications have been exhausted, the format specifications are used again with a new record.

FORMAT	READ instruction READ(5,700)(A(I),I = 1,100)
700 FORMAT (F10.0)	One value per card (100 cards).
700 FORMAT (8F10.0)	Eight values per card (13 cards with only four values from the 13*th*).
700 FORMAT (2F10.0 / F10.0)	Two values from first card, one variable value from second card, two variable values from third card, etc., because slash terminates use of a record (skips to next record).

The above example applies equally well to output. A program statement of the form WRITE(6,700)(A(I),I = 1,100) will write 100 values as specified by the FORMAT statement, for example, one value per line, eight values per line, etc.

The implied DO loop can therefore be considered as a DO loop that creates a list of input or output variables to be input or output under FORMAT control. Nested loops can be used in implied input or output DO loops. The outer loop is written last, and the innermost DO (the one that changes most rapidly) is placed next to the variable. The loops should be listed to match the arrangement of data. Example implied DO loop statements and order in which variables are read follow:

```
READ (5, 700)(A(I), I = 1, N)
A(1), A(2), A(3), . . . . . . , A(N)

READ (5, 700)((A(I, J), I = 1, M), J = 1, N)
A(1, 1), A(2, 1), A(3, 1), . . . , A(M, N)

READ (5, 700)((A(I, J), J = 1, N), I = 1, M)
A(1, 1),A(1, 2), A(1, 3), . . . , A(M, N)

READ (5, 700)(((A(I, J, K), I = 1, M), J = 1, N), K = 1, L)
A(1, 1, 1), A(2, 1, 1), A(3, 1, 1), . . . , A(M, N, L)
```

(handwritten annotations: "VARIABLE", "CHANGE FASTEST", "SLOWEST")

A special form of the implied DO can be used when an entire array is to be read or printed. The array name is written without subscripts or implied DO loops. The DIMENSION statement will already have specified both the fact that it is an array name and the size of the entire array to be read or written. This input or output form can be used only when the entire array is to be read or written in natural order, that is, in the column order (row varies most rapidly). For example, array Y dimensioned as (2,2) will be processed by an implied DO in the order (1,1), (2,1), (1,2), (2,2)). This form, in essence, creates a list of the entire array in natural order, and it is input or output under FORMAT control. Reliance upon default procedures such as the array name without subscripts are quite error-prone and should be used with caution. The explicit specifications in the implied DO loop are preferred style.

There is no special method for flowcharting implied DO loops. Since the effect is entirely contained within the READ or WRITE statement, it is probably satisfactory to merely indicate that data is to be read or written by the normal input or output symbol. If additional detail is desired in the flowchart, the implied loop can be noted in the symbol, or an annotation symbol can be used.

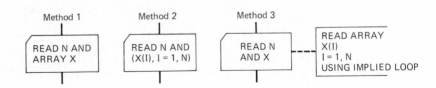

Self-testing exercise 4-3

Explain the effect of each of the following sets of statements. It may be helpful to review the section on "Reuse of FORMAT Specifications" in Chapter 3.

1
```
     DIMENSION A (10, 10)
     READ (5, 700) A
700 FORMAT (F10.0)
```

```
2        DIMENSION B (5, 5)
         READ (5, 710)  ((B(I, J) J = 1, 5), I = 1, 5)
   710 FORMAT (8F10.0)
3        DIMENSION C (6, 6)
         READ (5, 720) (C(1, J), J = 1, 6)
   720 FORMAT (6F10.0)
4        DO 130 K = 1, 3
             DO 120 J = 1, N
                 DO 110 I = 1, N
                     READ (5, 105) X (I, J, K)
   105               FORMAT (F10.0)
   110           CONTINUE
   120       CONTINUE
   130 CONTINUE
5        WRITE (6, 730) ((KIX (I, J), J = 1, 4), I = 1, 4)
   730 FORMAT (4I10, /)
```

Initializing data values with the DATA statement

In many programs, there are variables that should be set to an initial value. This may be accomplished by input of data as the first step in the program, by assignment statements, or by a DATA statement. The DATA statement provides initial values for variables, entire arrays, and array elements.

> DATA STATEMENT
>
> DATA nlist/clist/nlist/clist/   or   DATA nlist/clist/, nlist/clist/
>
> nlist is a list of variable names, array names, or array element names. clist is a list of the values to be assigned. A value can be repeated by using an integer plus an asterisk in front of the value, the integer specifying the number of repetitions of the value. The nlist (in 1977 full FORTRAN, but not in 1977 Subset FORTRAN) can be an implied DO statement.
>
> The DATA statement is placed in the program after specifications statements such as DIMENSION.

Essentially, the DATA statement lists variables to which data values are to be assigned and then lists the data values to be assigned. The first data value is assigned to the first variable, etc. If an array name is used, it must have been dimensioned previously. If an array name is listed without a subscript or an implied DO loop, the entire array is used.

Examples

DATA A, B, I / 5.0, 3.5, 4 /   Assigns 5.0 to A, 3.5 to B, and 4 to I.

DATA A, B, C(3) / 3 * 10.0 /   Assigns 10.0 to A, 10.0 to B, and 10.0 to C(3).

DATA ALPHA / 50 * 0.0 /   Places zeros in all 50 elements of array ALPHA.

DATA (BETA(I), I = 11, 20) / 10 * 5.0 /   Initializes (with value 5.0) elements 11–20 in array BETA. (Note implied DO loop.)

DATA ((IGAMMA(I, J), I = 6, 10), J = 1, 15) / 75 * 0 / Initializes to zero the last five rows of elements in 10×15 array.

The DATA statement must be placed after specification statements such as DIMENSION. In the style used in this text, the DATA statements will be placed after the type declarations and DIMENSION statements in a type declaration and storage allocation block. It is a useful statement, especially when an entire array or a number of variables used as accumulators are set to zero. For example, setting TALLY1, TALLY2, and a 100-element array GAMMA to 0 can be performed using assignment statements and a DO loop, but it is more efficient and very clear coding to use a DATA statement.

Without DATA statement

```
   TALLY1 = 0.0
   TALLY2 = 0.0
   DO  150 I = 1, 100
       GAMMA (I) = 0.0
150 CONTINUE
```

With DATA statement

```
DATA TALLY1, TALLY2 / 2 * 0.0 / GAMMA / 100 * 0.0 /
```

Note that the DATA statement could also have been written as:

```
DATA TALLY1, TALLY2, GAMMA / 102 * 0.0 /
```

Self-testing exercise 4-4

1   Use the DATA statement to initialize A to 40.1, B to 3.7, C and D to 1.0, and all elements in a 100-element array BETA to 0.

2   Use an implied loop in a DATA statement to initialize to 2.0 every other element between 15 and 49 in array ARRAY.

Style guidelines for arrays and DO loops

As in previous chapters, the style guidelines reflect one example of good practice. There are alternative styles that may also result in clear, disciplined program coding.

1   Do not dimension an array to be excessively large.

2   Subscript values used in a program at execution generally are not checked to ensure that they do not exceed the maximum value dimensioned for the array. If such values are used, they may cause serious errors. In reviewing the logic of a program, check for this error.

3   In the variable identification block, use a separate array name section to clearly identify array names (see examples in Chapter 4B).

4   Clearly specify the DIMENSIONs for all arrays in a separate type declaration and storage allocation block.

5   End each DO loop with a CONTINUE statement. It is not required except when the last statement in the range of the DO loop would be a transfer of control. However, as a matter of style, the CONTINUE clearly marks the range of a DO loop.

6   As a matter of style, statements may be indented between the DO statement and the CONTINUE statement to define visually the range of the DO loop.

7   For nested DO loops, each inner loop may be indented. Each nested loop may end with a separate CONTINUE. Example:

```
      DO 130 I = 1, N
         DO 120 J = 1, M
            DO 110 K = 1, 5
               SUM = SUM + A (I, J, K)
110         CONTINUE
120      CONTINUE
130 CONTINUE
```

Note: The statement labels are not indented for the indented CONTINUE statements, since statement labels must appear in columns 1–5.

8   Since the single letters I through N are often used as loop parameters, it is a practical matter of style to avoid using these single letters as simple variable or array names, and to reserve them for DO loop parameters. In following this suggestion, it is not necessary to define these index variables in the variable identification block.

9   Use the DATA statement to initialize data items. Place DATA statements in a type declaration and storage allocation block.

Summary

The repetition structure is very important in programming. In FORTRAN, it is implemented by the DO loop. Subscripted variables are frequently used in connection with loops to simplify the programming of processing of data items that can be grouped together and assigned a common name. Subscripts indicate data-item position in the array. The DIMENSION statement defines the maximum number of entries in an array.

The DO loop begins with the DO statement that specifies the range of the loop, the DO control variable, the initial value, the terminal value, and the increment. Good practice suggests that the terminal statement for a DO loop should be a CONTINUE statement and indentation should be used to define visually the statements inside the loop.

An implied DO loop may be contained within a READ or WRITE statement. This is very useful because it allows input and output to be completely under FORMAT control.

Data values, especially arrays, can be initialized to starting values by assignment statements, but a very useful alternative is the DATA statement.

Answers to self-testing exercises

Exercise 4-1

1

Valid or invalid	If invalid for some versions of FORTRAN, why
(a) Valid	
(b) Invalid	Real subscript (X) not allowed.
(c) Valid	Not an allowable subscript form in older FORTRANs.
(d) Valid	
(e) Valid	
(f) Invalid	Real subscript expression (A + 5.0) not allowed.
(g) Valid	Not allowable form in order FORTRANs; should be 5 ∗ I
(h) Valid	Subscripts limited to three in Subset FORTRAN and many older FORTRANs.
(i) Valid	Not valid for 1977 Subset FORTRAN or older FORTRANs.
(j) Valid	Not valid for 1977 Subset FORTRAN or older FORTRANs.

2 (a) DIMENSON ARRAY (100)

(b) DIMENSION PERSNS (2, 10)

(c) DIMENSION BUSNES (8, 15, 5)

(d) DIMENSION A(15), B(15), C(15), D(15)

3 (a) A (2, 2)

(b) A (3, 5)

(c) CLASS (2, 5, 2)

(d) CLASS (2, 2, 1)

4 DIMENSION A(5, 5), CLASS(5, 5, 4)

5 DIMENSION A(9)
A(NX + 1) Adding 1 to NX changes array references from 0–8 to 1–9.

6 Figure 4-14

Figure 4-14
Program segment using
loops to read and multiply
array values.

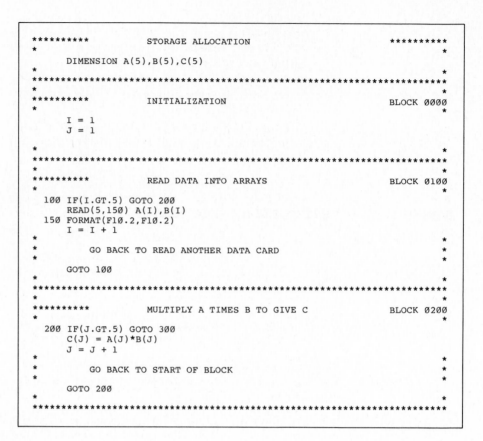

```
**********              STORAGE ALLOCATION                    **********
*                                                                     *
      DIMENSION A(5),B(5),C(5)
*                                                                     *
***********************************************************************
*                                                                     *
**********              INITIALIZATION                        BLOCK 0000
*                                                                     *
      I = 1
      J = 1

*                                                                     *
***********************************************************************
*                                                                     *
**********            READ DATA INTO ARRAYS                   BLOCK 0100
*                                                                     *
  100 IF(I.GT.5) GOTO 200
      READ(5,150) A(I),B(I)
  150 FORMAT(F10.2,F10.2)
      I = I + 1
*                                                                     *
*        GO BACK TO READ ANOTHER DATA CARD                            *
*                                                                     *
      GOTO 100
*                                                                     *
***********************************************************************
*                                                                     *
**********          MULTIPLY A TIMES B TO GIVE C              BLOCK 0200
*                                                                     *
  200 IF(J.GT.5) GOTO 300
      C(J) = A(J)*B(J)
      J = J + 1
*                                                                     *
*        GO BACK TO START OF BLOCK                                    *
*                                                                     *
      GOTO 200
*                                                                     *
***********************************************************************
```

Exercise 4-2

1

Full 1977 FORTRAN	If invalid for Subset or older FORTRANs, why
(a) Invalid	Because a variable may not be used as a statement label.
(b) Valid	Comma after statement label optional in 1977 Standard, but not allowed in older versions.
(c) Valid	
(d) Valid	Parameters may not be signed for older FORTRANs.
(e) Valid	But note that the terminal value is less than the initial value. The 1977 Standard says execute zero times. Some older versions will execute the loop once.
(f) Valid	The loop will be executed once; count = $(7 - 7 + 1)/1 = 1$.
(g) Valid	Note that the loop stops when the terminal value is exceeded. Therefore, this will be executed three times. Using the iteration count formula, the count = $(15 - 7 + 3)/3 = 11/3 = 3$.
(h) Valid	Arithmetic expression allowed only in 1977 full FORTRAN.
(i) Valid	DO control variable must be integer in 1977 Subset FORTRAN and in older FORTRANs.

2 K = 10, L = 5, M = 50

3   (a) $1 \; (5 - 5 + 1)/1 = 1$
     (b) $0 \; (1 - 5 + 1)/1 = -3 = 0$ Might execute once in older FORTRANs.
     (c) $5 \; (5 - 1 + 1)/1 = 5$
     (d) $2 \; (5 - 1 + 3)/3 = 2$
     (e) $3 \; (.5 - .1 + .2)/.2 = 3$ Not allowed by Subset or older FORTRANs.
     (f) $6 \; (.30 - .03 + .05)/.05 = 6$
     (g) $3 \; [1 - 5 + (-2)]/-2 = 3$ Not allowed by older FORTRANs.

4   ARRAY (1, 1, 1), (1, 1, 2), (1, 2, 1), (1, 2, 2), (2, 1, 1), (2, 1, 2), (2, 2, 1), (2, 2, 2)

5   The program will end with SUM = A(30) * B(30). The initializing of the accumulating variable must be done outside the loop in which it is used.

6   Valid: *a, b, c,* and *f.*
     Invalid: *d* and *e.* Inner DO must be entirely within range of outer.

7
```
      ISUM = 0.0
      DO  150 I = 1, N
          ISUM = ISUM + LIX (I) * MIX (I)
  150 CONTINUE
```

8
```
      DO 100 FTEMP = -10.65,5
          CTEMP = (5.0 / 9.0) * (FTEMP - 32.0)
          PRINT*, FTEMP, CTEMP
  100 CONTINUE
```

9
```
      DO  160 I = 2, K, 2
          WRITE (5, 700) DAD(I)
  160 CONTINUE
```

10
```
      TEMP = A(1)
      DO  100 I = 2, N
          A(I - 1) = A(I)
  100 CONTINUE
      A(N) = TEMP
```

11
```
      TEMP = A(25)
      DO  100 I = 1, 24
          K = 25 - I
          A(K + 1) = A(K)
  100 CONTINUE
      A(1) = TEMP
```

Possible alternative in 1977 full FORTRAN
```
          TEMP = A(25)
          DO 100 I = 24, 1, -1
              A(I + 1) = A(I)
      100 CONTINUE
          A(1) = TEMP
```

Exercise 4-3

1   One hundred values for A will be read from cards. One value will be read from each card, arranged in natural order by columns; the row subscript will vary most rapidly.
     A(1,1), A(2,1), A(3,1), . . .

2   Twenty-five values for B will be read, eight to a card, in row order:
     B(1,1), B(1,2), B(1,3), . . .

3 Six values will be read from a card. These will form the first row of a 6 × 6 matrix.

4 This will read an N × N × 3 array, punched one to a card and arranged in natural order. The row varies most rapidly, column next, and level last.

5 The 16-value array KIX will be printed out with four column values per line, double-spaced between lines (because the closing parenthesis does single spacing and the slash skips a line).

Exercise 4-4

1 `DATA A, B, C, D / 40.1, 3.7, 2 * 1.0 / , BETA / 100 * 0.0 /`

2 `DATA (ARRAY (I), I = 15, 49, 2) / 18 * 2.0 /`

Questions and problems

1 Define or explain:
(*a*) The purpose of the DIMENSION statement
(*b*) Array
(*c*) Matrix
(*d*) Subscript

2 Write the DIMENSION statements for the following:
(*a*) An array X with 59 entries
(*b*) An array YES with 39 rows and 10 columns
(*c*) An array to accept a threefold classification—by state, by 1 of 20 sizes of cities, and by one of two classes relating to growth in the past 10 years

3 A company wishes to classify SALES by salesmen (10 of them), by size of company (four size categories), and by product sold (eight of these). Set up the classification for SALES, and write a program segment to calculate totals by a salesman.

4 Complete the table below.

DO statement	Valid or invalid for 1977 full FORTRAN	If invalid for Subset or older FORTRANs, why
(*a*) DO 19 NIX = JIX, KIX, LIX		
(*b*) DO 100 FIX = 1, TRIX		
(*c*) DO 50 I = 1, N, L + 1		
(*d*) DO 30 I = 1, N, K		
(*e*) DO 17 I = 1, 4, 2		
(*f*) DO X J = 1, K		
(*g*) DO 150 Z = -10, 12		
(*h*) DO 200 Y = .15, .25, .05		

5 What is the purpose of the CONTINUE statement?

chapter **4^B**

Example programs and programming exercises using subscripted variables and DO loops

The example programs illustrate the use of data stored as arrays and referenced by subscripted variables, DO loops, and implied DO loops. The general example of payroll makes use of implied DO loops for input and output; the statistical program output does not require an implied DO, but the computational procedures make effective use of DO loops. Both example programs should be reviewed because they illustrate features in different ways.

General comments on the example programs

Both programs store data items in an array as they are computed. The stored array of data is then used for processing and output. Without the array, it is cumbersome to store lists, tables, or matrices of data.

The variable identification block has previously contained only variable names and constant identification. An array names block is added to identify array names clearly. The DIMENSION statements are placed in a *type declaration and storage allocation block*.

In the flowcharts (which require more than one page), note the use of off-page connector references.

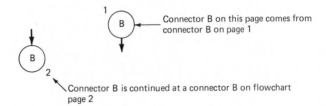

Some programmers use a special off-page connector symbol found on IBM

flowchart templates: and when the flowchart continues off the

page. Either method is satisfactory.

There is no special flowchart symbol or notation to indicate implied DO loops with input or output. The flowchart need not show all details of the program coding and, in these programs, implied DO loops were not significant for the flow of program logic.

General program example 4 — payroll reports

The program computes gross pay, deductions, and net pay as with the previous programs. However, new techniques are used, such as storing the valid input data in an array. This allows the program to delay the payroll reports until all data has been read. Also, the reports can list the employees in a different order than the order of the input.

Problem description for general example 4

The program is to read employee pay data and produce two reports: (1) Error and Control Report (see Figure 4-21, page 220) and (2) Report of Pay

Amounts (see Figure 4-16, page 211). There are two sets of input for the program. The first consists of five pairs of department numbers and names, one pair per card. The second set of input data consists of employee data, one card for each employee, giving ID number, name, department number where employed, hours worked, wage rate, and miscellaneous deductions. The program will process 14 or fewer valid employee input cards.

The Error and Control Report produced during input validation consists of three parts (see Figure 4-21, page 220):

1 An echoing of the table of department numbers and names for visual validation.

2 Error messages identifying errors detected during input validation.
   (*a*) For invalid data (invalid department number), the error message identifies the cause of the rejection and the card number of the rejected record.
   (*b*) For data-type errors, the message identifies the card number.
   (*c*) For array overflow caused by excess employee data cards, an excess data error message is printed and the program is terminated.

3 A record count of total records read and total records rejected.

The Report of Pay Amounts consists of a heading, a line of output for each employee, and a total line (see Figure 4-16, page 211). The employees are not listed in order of input; rather, they are listed by department. Because the report does not have space for an error message if net pay is zero, negative, or over $300, there is a column for notes and a code in the column is used to reference an error message at the bottom of the report.

Program documentation for general example 4

The documentation of program design is given by a pseudocode description (Figure 4-17) and a program flowchart (Figure 4-18). The program listing is given in Figure 4-19. Test data used for the sample output is listed in Figure 4-20. An example of an Error and Control Report is shown in Figure 4-21, and an example of a Report of Pay Amounts is given in Figure 4-16. The test data items merely illustrate the output, and are not a complete test of the program.

Notes on general example 4

The outputs from program example 4 are in much better form than previous reports. Error messages are removed from the detail report, headings are more meaningful, and the order of output is under program control. The variable identification block has been enlarged to include a section that names temporary variables. These are variable names that are used only in a short block of code and that are not needed either before or after that block is executed. Such variables may arise to function as temporary counters or, as in this case, to improve readability or efficiency. The reason for listing them is that if the program is later revised and modified, the same name should not be used as a variable name.

DIMENSION and DATA statements appear in the type declaration and storage allocation block. Some variables have been initialized by a DATA statement and others by arithmetic assignment statements. Although logically

Figure 4-16
Example of Report of Pay
Amounts from payroll re-
ports program.

```
  EMPLOYEE      ID    DEPT    GROSS     TOTAL      NET    NOTES
    NAME              NAME     PAY    DEDUCTIONS

R. M. NELSON  42753   FIN     298.00   117.24    180.76

T. NAMAN      69852   ENGR     26.70    32.84     -6.14     A

L. SMITH      35748   ENGR    399.09   110.50    288.59

Q. SIBLEY     62475   ENGR    309.00   127.14    181.86

J. JOHNSON    36985   MKTG     60.50    48.08     12.42

J. HOFFMANN   23456   PROD    142.80    56.51     86.29

A. PETERSON   74365   PROD    294.02   113.43    180.59

RALPH JONES   15786   ACCT    250.57    74.79    175.78


              TOTALS         1780.68   680.54   1100.15



NOTES
A - NET PAY IS OUT OF BOUNDS. DO NOT ISSUE CHECK.
```

equivalent, these are handled differently by the FORTRAN compiler. The DATA statement method is generally preferred, but there are some restrictions in special cases that will be explained in Chapter 5.

In the computation block, note that two counters are incremented (line 22 and line 40). The first (NCARD) keeps track of all cards read while the second (NUM) counts those accepted (error-free). These counters were initialized in lines 10 and 11.

Arrays are used to store data previously referenced by individual variable names. The arrays are both one- and two-dimensional. Conceptually, there are arrays for the department table, input data, and results.

1   The department table arrays consist of two one-dimensional arrays with five entries containing the numbers and names for departments.

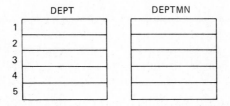

2   Arrays for input data consist of 15 rows to accommodate 14 valid employee records as well as a potential error case. The use of these arrays allows all input data to be stored so that the error report can be prepared separately and the output can be in a different order than the input.

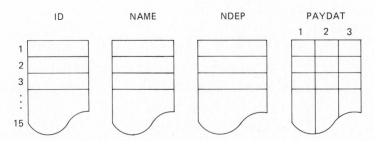

There is an array for identification numbers, an array for names, a number-of-department list, and a table for three different types of payroll data (previously called HRSWRK, WGRATE, and DEDUC). A reference to hours worked for the I*th* valid record is now PAYDAT(I, 1).

3   The arrays for results consist of 3 one-dimensional 15-element arrays for gross pay, total deductions, and net pay.

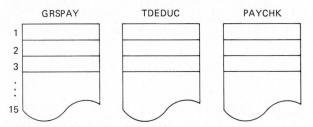

On input, data items are assigned to rows in the different arrays by using the value of the valid input counter (NUM). Invalid data is not stored in the arrays. If the current value of NUM is 3, then a statement that reads ID(NUM), NDEP(NUM), etc., will place the ID in element 3 of the ID array, and NDEP in the third element of the array for number of department where employee works. If the data on input turns out to be invalid, the counter NUM does not change and the next input card is stored in the same locations, replacing the invalid input.

   If a program attempts to store more data in arrays than has been allocated in the DIMENSION statement, there will be an error that may cause incorrect results or abnormal termination. Therefore, a program should be designed to prevent attempting to store too many data items in arrays. There are various methods for doing this. Note two cases in the sample program.

1   A specified number of data items to be stored. Since the program specifications define five departments, the department table arrays are dimensioned at five cells. The READ statement (line 12) reads and stores only five items by using NDEPTS as the termination value of the implied DO loop. NDEPTS is initialized at 5 (line 4).

2   An unspecified number of data items to be stored. Since the program description calls for an unspecified number of input cards but not to exceed 14 accepted records, a count is established for accepted records stored in the various arrays. This count is tested against a limiting value. If more records are available to be read after the limit has been reached, an error message is printed and the program is aborted. Because the records are read directly

Figure 4-17
Pseudocode description of logic of general program example 4—payroll reports.

Dimension arrays for 5 departments and 15 employee records (14 accepted records and 1 potential error case)
WRITE heading at top of page for Error and Control Report
Initialize counters, summing variables and rates
READ set of allowable department numbers and names
WRITE table of department numbers and names for visual validation
WRITE error message heading
READ an employee card and test for end of data and data-type error
    If no more cards, go to Print Detail Report, else continue
    If data-type error, increment record counter, print message, and go back to READ, else continue
Increment record counter
Test for invalid department number
    IF invalid department number, print message and go back to READ, else continue
Compute payroll data and store in arrays
    Compute overtime
    Compute gross pays, including overtime (if any)
    Compute taxes, pension contribution, all deductions
    Compute net pay
Add employee gross pay, total deductions, and net pay to totals
Increment accepted employee records counter by 1
Test number of accepted records
    If number exceeds limit of array storage, print excess records message and stop
    Else go back to READ an employee card
Print Detail Report
WRITE record counts at bottom of Error and Control Report
WRITE heading for Report of Pay Amounts at top of new page
DO for all departments
    Select department numbers in order
    For each employee PRINT detail (Name, ID, Dept. Name, Gross Pay, Deductions, Net Pay)
    IF net pay is outside limits (negative or >300), PRINT error code on same line
End of DO
WRITE summary totals and error code explanation
STOP

into storage arrays rather than into temporary input locations, one additional storage position must be allocated in each array for a possible excess record in process. This is the reason that the program has a limit of 14 accepted records and the arrays are dimensioned at 15.

The program makes use of implied DO loops for input and output. Review these:

	Lines
1 READ table of department names	12
2 PRINT table of department names	16
3 READ employee data	20

In the print detail block, note the use of the local variable MATCH. The value of MATCH (line 49) is a function of the "outside" loop index J; it does

213

Figure 4-18
Program flowchart for
general program example
4—payroll reports. (Num-
bers next to symbols are
line numbers from pro-
gram listing.)

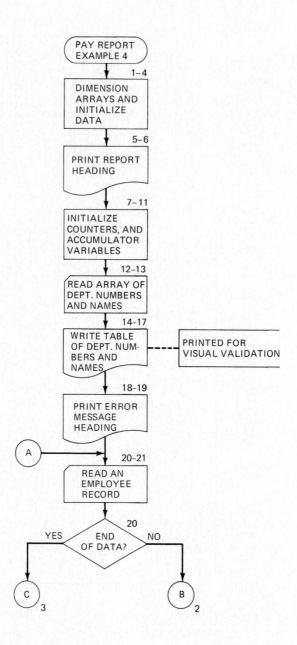

Figure 4-18
Continued

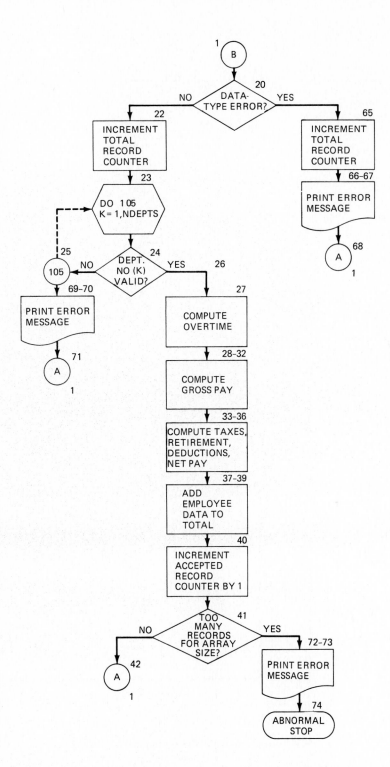

Figure 4-18
Continued

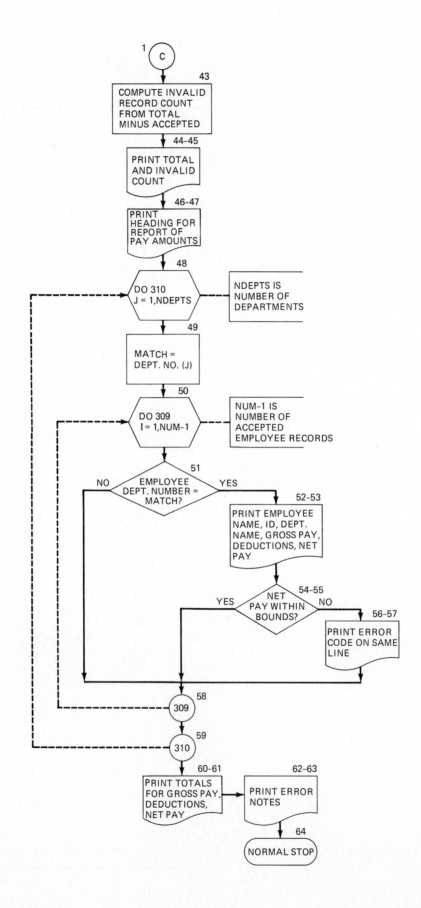

Figure 4-19
Listing of FORTRAN program for general program example 4—payroll reports.

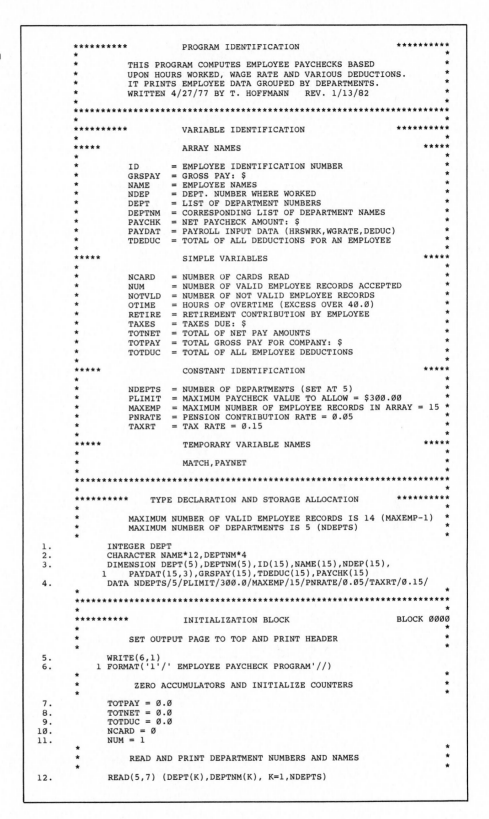

```
*********         PROGRAM IDENTIFICATION              *********
*                                                             *
*      THIS PROGRAM COMPUTES EMPLOYEE PAYCHECKS BASED         *
*      UPON HOURS WORKED, WAGE RATE AND VARIOUS DEDUCTIONS.   *
*      IT PRINTS EMPLOYEE DATA GROUPED BY DEPARTMENTS.        *
*      WRITTEN 4/27/77 BY T. HOFFMANN   REV. 1/13/82          *
*                                                             *
***************************************************************
*                                                             *
*********         VARIABLE IDENTIFICATION             *********
*                                                             *
*****                 ARRAY NAMES                         *****
*                                                             *
*      ID      = EMPLOYEE IDENTIFICATION NUMBER               *
*      GRSPAY  = GROSS PAY: $                                 *
*      NAME    = EMPLOYEE NAMES                               *
*      NDEP    = DEPT. NUMBER WHERE WORKED                    *
*      DEPT    = LIST OF DEPARTMENT NUMBERS                   *
*      DEPTNM  = CORRESPONDING LIST OF DEPARTMENT NAMES       *
*      PAYCHK  = NET PAYCHECK AMOUNT: $                       *
*      PAYDAT  = PAYROLL INPUT DATA (HRSWRK,WGRATE,DEDUC)     *
*      TDEDUC  = TOTAL OF ALL DEDUCTIONS FOR AN EMPLOYEE      *
*                                                             *
*****                SIMPLE VARIABLES                     *****
*                                                             *
*      NCARD   = NUMBER OF CARDS READ                         *
*      NUM     = NUMBER OF VALID EMPLOYEE RECORDS ACCEPTED    *
*      NOTVLD  = NUMBER OF NOT VALID EMPLOYEE RECORDS         *
*      OTIME   = HOURS OF OVERTIME (EXCESS OVER 40.0)         *
*      RETIRE  = RETIREMENT CONTRIBUTION BY EMPLOYEE          *
*      TAXES   = TAXES DUE: $                                 *
*      TOTNET  = TOTAL OF NET PAY AMOUNTS                     *
*      TOTPAY  = TOTAL GROSS PAY FOR COMPANY: $               *
*      TOTDUC  = TOTAL OF ALL EMPLOYEE DEDUCTIONS             *
*                                                             *
*****               CONSTANT IDENTIFICATION               *****
*                                                             *
*      NDEPTS  = NUMBER OF DEPARTMENTS (SET AT 5)             *
*      PLIMIT  = MAXIMUM PAYCHECK VALUE TO ALLOW = $300.00    *
*      MAXEMP  = MAXIMUM NUMBER OF EMPLOYEE RECORDS IN ARRAY = 15 *
*      PNRATE  = PENSION CONTRIBUTION RATE = 0.05             *
*      TAXRT   = TAX RATE = 0.15                              *
*                                                             *
*****              TEMPORARY VARIABLE NAMES               *****
*                                                             *
*                  MATCH,PAYNET                               *
*                                                             *
***************************************************************
*                                                             *
*********    TYPE DECLARATION AND STORAGE ALLOCATION  *********
*                                                             *
*      MAXIMUM NUMBER OF VALID EMPLOYEE RECORDS IS 14 (MAXEMP-1) *
*      MAXIMUM NUMBER OF DEPARTMENTS IS 5 (NDEPTS)            *
*                                                             *
1.          INTEGER DEPT
2.          CHARACTER NAME*12,DEPTNM*4
3.          DIMENSION DEPT(5),DEPTNM(5),ID(15),NAME(15),NDEP(15),
     1         PAYDAT(15,3),GRSPAY(15),TDEDUC(15),PAYCHK(15)
4.          DATA NDEPTS/5/PLIMIT/300.0/MAXEMP/15/PNRATE/0.05/TAXRT/0.15/
*                                                             *
***************************************************************
*                                                             *
*********         INITIALIZATION BLOCK          BLOCK 0000
*                                                             *
*         SET OUTPUT PAGE TO TOP AND PRINT HEADER             *
*                                                             *
5.          WRITE(6,1)
6.        1 FORMAT('1'/' EMPLOYEE PAYCHECK PROGRAM'//)
*                                                             *
*          ZERO ACCUMULATORS AND INITIALIZE COUNTERS          *
*                                                             *
7.          TOTPAY = 0.0
8.          TOTNET = 0.0
9.          TOTDUC = 0.0
10.         NCARD = 0
11.         NUM = 1
*                                                             *
*          READ AND PRINT DEPARTMENT NUMBERS AND NAMES        *
*                                                             *
12.         READ(5,7) (DEPT(K),DEPTNM(K), K=1,NDEPTS)
```

Figure 4-19
Continued

```
13.         7 FORMAT(I4,A4)
14.           WRITE(6,9)
15.         9 FORMAT('0','TABLE OF DEPARTMENTS'/' NUMBER    NAME')
16.           WRITE(6,11) (DEPT(K),DEPTNM(K),K=1,NDEPTS)
17.        11 FORMAT(2X,I4,4X,A4)
      *                                                              *
      *          PRINT ERROR MESSAGE HEADER                          *
      *                                                              *
18.           WRITE(6,13)
19.        13 FORMAT(///6X,'ERROR MESSAGES DURING DATA INPUT'//)
      *                                                              *
      ****************************************************************
      *                                                              *
      *********              READ EMPLOYEE DATA          BLOCK 0100
      *                                                              *
20.       101 READ(5,102,END=301,ERR=901) ID(NUM),NAME(NUM),
          1      NDEP(NUM),(PAYDAT(NUM,K),K=1,3)
21.       102 FORMAT(I5,A12,I4,F4.1,F4.2,F5.2)
22.           NCARD = NCARD + 1
      *                                                              *
      *          CHECK FOR VALID DEPARTMENT NUMBER IN EMPLOYEE CARD  *
      *          WHEN FOUND, PROCESS EMPLOYEE DATA                   *
      *                                                              *
23.           DO 105 K=1,NDEPTS
24.             IF(DEPT(K).EQ.NDEP(NUM)) GOTO 201
25.       105 CONTINUE
      *                                                              *
      *          ERROR -- NO MATCH FOUND FOR EMPLOYEE DEPT. NUMBER   *
      *                                                              *
26.           GOTO 903
      *                                                              *
      ****************************************************************
      *                                                              *
      *********              COMPUTATION BLOCK           BLOCK 0200
      *                                                              *
      *          COMPUTE PAY, INCLUDING OVERTIME, IF ANY.            *
      *                                                              *
27.       201 OTIME = PAYDAT(NUM,1) - 40.0
28.           IF(OTIME.GT.0.0) THEN
29.             GRSPAY(NUM) = (40.0 + 1.5*OTIME)*PAYDAT(NUM,2)
30.           ELSE
31.             GRSPAY(NUM) = PAYDAT(NUM,1)*PAYDAT(NUM,2)
32.           ENDIF
      *                                                              *
      *          COMPUTE EACH TYPE OF DEDUCTION AND NET PAY          *
      *                                                              *
33.           TAXES = GRSPAY(NUM)*TAXRT
34.           RETIRE = GRSPAY(NUM)*PNRATE
35.           TDEDUC(NUM) = PAYDAT(NUM,3) + TAXES + RETIRE
36.           PAYCHK(NUM) = GRSPAY(NUM) - TDEDUC(NUM)
37.           TOTPAY = TOTPAY + GRSPAY(NUM)
38.           TOTDUC = TOTDUC + TDEDUC(NUM)
39.           TOTNET = TOTNET + PAYCHK(NUM)
40.           NUM = NUM + 1
      *                                                              *
      *          TEST TO PREVENT ARRAY OVERFLOW. IF ARRAYS NOT FULL  *
      *          RETURN TO READ NEXT EMPLOYEE DATA CARD.             *
      *                                                              *
41.           IF(NUM.GT.MAXEMP) GOTO 906
      *                                                              *
      *          GO BACK TO READ ANOTHER DATA CARD                   *
      *                                                              *
42.           GOTO 101
      *                                                              *
      ****************************************************************
      *                                                              *
      *********          PRINT DETAIL BY DEPARTMENT GROUPING  BLOCK 0300
      *                                                              *
      *          PRINT SUMMARY OF DATA INPUT MESSAGES               *
      *                                                              *
43.       301 NOTVLD = NCARD - NUM + 1
44.           WRITE(6,302) NCARD,NOTVLD
45.       302 FORMAT('0',I4,' CARDS READ'/I5,' CARDS REJECTED')
      *                                                              *
      *          PRINT HEADER/TITLE LINE FOR EMPLOYEE DETAIL         *
      *                                                              *
46.           WRITE(6,303)
47.       303 FORMAT('1',4X,'EMPLOYEE',5X,'ID',3X,'DEPT'3X'GROSS',4X,
          1      'TOTAL',6X,'NET',4X,'NOTES'/7X,'NAME',12X,'NAME',4X,
          2      'PAY',3X,'DEDUCTIONS')
```

Figure 4-19
Continued

```
      *                                                                    *
      *              FOR EACH DEPARTMENT FIND EACH EMPLOYEE                 *
      *                                                                    *
48.          DO 310 J=1,NDEPTS
49.             MATCH = DEPT(J)
50.             DO 309 I=1,NUM-1
51.                IF(NDEP(I).NE.MATCH) GOTO 309
52.                WRITE(6,304) NAME(I),ID(I),DEPTNM(J),
     1                GRSPAY(I),TDEDUC(I),PAYCHK(I)
53.      304       FORMAT('0',2X,A12,I6,2X,A4,3X,F6.2,3X,F6.2,3X,F6.2)
54.                PAYNET = PAYCHK(I)
      *                                                                    *
      *              CHECK FOR VALID PAYCHECK AMOUNT                        *
      *                                                                    *
55.                IF(PAYNET.GT.0.0 .AND. PAYNET.LE.PLIMIT) GOTO 309
56.                WRITE(6,306)
57.      306       FORMAT('+',57X,'A')
58.      309    CONTINUE
59.      310 CONTINUE
      *                                                                    *
      ************************************************************************
      *                                                                    *
      **********         PRINT SUMMARY AND TERMINATE          BLOCK 0400
      *                                                                    *
60.          WRITE(6,402) TOTPAY,TOTDUC,TOTNET
61.      402 FORMAT(//20X,'TOTALS',3X,F7.2,2F9.2)
62.          WRITE(6,403)
63.      403 FORMAT(///5X,'NOTES'/5X'A - NET PAY IS OUT OF BOUNDS',
     1          '. DO NOT ISSUE CHECK.')
64.          STOP
      *                                                                    *
      ************************************************************************
      *                                                                    *
      **********              ERROR MESSAGE BLOCK             BLOCK 0900
      *                                                                    *
65.      901 NCARD = NCARD + 1
66.          WRITE(6,902) NCARD
67.      902 FORMAT(//' *****',' ERROR IN DATA CARD NUMBER ',I2,' *****')
      *                                                                    *
      *          GO BACK TO READ NEXT EMPLOYEE DATA CARD                    *
      *                                                                    *
68.          GOTO 101
      *****                                                          *****
69.      903 WRITE(6,904) NCARD
70.      904 FORMAT(//' ***** ERROR - DEPT. NO. NOT VALID. CARD NO.   ',I4,
     1       2X,'*****')
      *                                                                    *
      *          GO BACK TO READ NEXT EMPLOYEE DATA CARD                    *
      *                                                                    *
71.          GOTO 101
      *****                                                          *****
72.      906 WRITE(6,907)
73.      907 FORMAT(///' ***** ERROR. ATTEMPTED TO READ ',
     1       'MORE THAN 14 VALID DATA CARDS'/7X,'PROGRAM ABORTED. ')
74.          STOP
75.          END
```

not change with the "inner" loop I. To reduce execution time (to eliminate the necessity to reevaluate DEPT(J) for each change in I), a local temporary variable has been used. Similarly, PAYNET (line 55) has been set so that PAYCHK(I) need be referenced only once, not twice, in line 56. In this simple program, these temporary variables are not needed to reduce execution time, but are used to illustrate the technique of programming for efficiency.

The program uses input and output validation techniques similar to those used in previous programs; an additional technique is the printout of the table of department names. It is good style to print out tables such as these for visual validation. The validation of net pay (line 55) illustrates how to combat those classic $1,000,005.37 "computer errors" described in newspaper articles. It is always good style to test, if possible, critical output data to see if it is in a range of reasonable values.

Figure 4-20
Annotated input test data
for general problem 4.

INPUT TEST DATA

DEPT NO.	DEPT NAME	PURPOSE
1234	FIN	COLLECTIVELY THESE FORM A DATA SET OF DEPARTMENT
4275	ENGR	NUMBERS AND NAMES. NO ERROR MESSAGES ARE
7269	MKTG	GENERATED.
7531	PROD	
8551	ACCT	

ID	NAME	DEPT NO.	PAYROLL DATA	PURPOSE OR EXPECTED OUTPUT
234565	J. HOFFMANN	7531	40.03.5727.95	NET PAY = 86.29
15786	RALPH JONES	8551	39.96.2824.68	GROSS PAY = 250.57
369853	J. JOHNSON	7269	22.0027503598	GROSS PAY = 60.50
234560	T. HOFFMANN	1596	40.03.5727.95	ERROR-NOT VALID. CARD NO. 4
698527	T. NAMAN	4275	10.02.6727.50	NET PAY NEGATIVE
35748	L. SMITH	4275	40.19.9430.68	NET PAY = 288.59
15966	EN			ERROR-NONNUMERIC DATA IN NUMERIC FIELD. CARD NO. 7
42753	R. M. NELSON	1234	40.07.4557.64	NET PAY 180.76
74365	A. PETERSON	7531	64.04.8254.63	GROSS PAY = 294.02
624759	Q. SIBLEY	4275	37.58.2465.34	THIS PERSON IN ENGR DEPT SET
				10 DATA CARDS
				2 REJECTED ON INPUT
				2 ERROR NOTES

Figure 4-21
Example of Error and
Control Report from pay-
roll reports program.

```
EMPLOYEE PAYCHECK PROGRAM


    TABLE OF DEPARTMENTS
    NUMBER  NAME
     1234   FIN
     4275   ENGR
     7269   MKTG
     7531   PROD
     8551   ACCT



       ERROR MESSAGES DURING DATA INPUT



***** ERROR - DEPT. NO. NOT VALID. CARD NO.    4  *****


***** ERROR IN DATA CARD NUMBER  7 *****

    1Ø CARDS READ
     2 CARDS REJECTED
```

Statistical program example 4 — tables of cumulative normal probability

This example illustrates the use of a DO loop in a computational procedure. In this case, the computation is numerical integration. As a review of this procedure, recall that integration means computing the area under a curve within an interval of the function. One approach to this is to divide the interval into small segments, to define each segment as a rectangle, and to compute the areas of each of these using the formula Area = base × height. The areas for the segments are summed to give the area for the interval. For example,

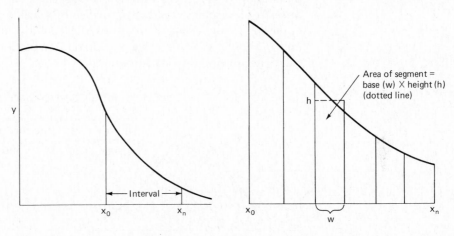

The difficulty with the approach is selecting an approximate height, since the heights of the two sides (given by the ordinates of the curve) are not the same. A simple method is to average the two heights. The area equation becomes

$$a_n = \frac{y_{n-1} + y_n}{2} w$$

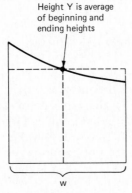

While this averaging of the beginning and ending ordinates is a good approximation, it can be improved. If the curve is approximated by a second-degree polynomial, Simpson's rule provides a better measure of the area. The interval is divided into n segments (n must be an even number).

$$\text{Area} = \frac{w}{3} (y_0 + 4y_1 + 2y_2 + 4y_3 + \cdots + 4y_{n-1} + y_n)$$

221

The n ordinates are multiplied by 1, 2, or 4 (first and last ordinates by 1, even-numbered ordinates by 2, and odd-numbered ones by 4). The sum of these products is divided by 3 and multiplied by interval width w. It is not necessary to understand the formula to read the program; just accept it as the formula for computing the area.

Problem description for statistical example 4

The program is to calculate and print a normal probability table of positive Z values and corresponding probability of Z or less. The positive Z values represent multiples of the standard deviation greater than the mean. The probability of Z or less represents the cumulative probability of an item being included in the range containing all items up to Z standard deviations greater than the mean. These Z values are vital in statistical hypothesis testing, and tables of Z values are included in statistics texts.

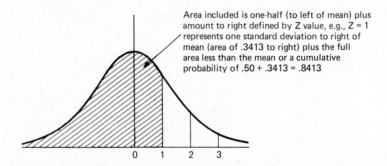

Area included is one-half (to left of mean) plus amount to right defined by Z value, e.g., Z = 1 represents one standard deviation to right of mean (area of .3413 to right) plus the full area less than the mean or a cumulative probability of .50 + .3413 = .8413

The program produces a new table with appropriate headings for each valid input. The input defines the beginning of the table, the end of the table, and the interval between table entries for Z. The input is checked for invalid values—negative values or initial value greater than ending value. An invalid value results in an error message with card number.

$$\text{Probability} = \int_{-\infty}^{Z^*} f(Z) = .5 + \int_{0}^{Z^*} \frac{1}{2\pi} e^{-(X^2/2)}$$

The area under $y = f(Z)$ in the interval 0 to Z^* is to be computed using Simpson's rule. The distance on the x axis between zero and the Z entry for which a probability is being computed is divided into 20 segments. The area is then computed using Simpson's rule with 20 values of y corresponding to the 20 values of x. Each ordinate (height) is computed as

$$\text{Ordinate} = \frac{1}{2\pi} e^{-(X^2/2)}$$

Program documentation for statistical example 4

The documentation consists of a pseudocode program description (Figure 4-22), a program flowchart (Figure 4-23), a program listing (Figure 4-24), and an example input (Figure 4-25) and output (Figure 4-26).

Figure 4-22
Pseudocode description of program for statistical example 4—normal probability tables.

```
Initialize problem counter (one problem per card)
READ start value, end value, and step size
    If out of data, go forward to Terminate
    If data-type error, increment problem counter, write error message and go
        back to READ
Increment problem counter
Validate data
    If invalid data, write error message, and go back to READ
WRITE table heading
Set ZSTAR (Z value being computed) to start value for first entry
Set X to zero
Compute size of 20 X increments from zero to ZSTAR
Initialize sums to zero
Compute 20 ordinates and save in array
Sum first and last ordinate
Sum even-numbered ordinates
Sum odd-numbered ordinates
Compute TOTSUM of first sum plus 2 times second sum plus 4 times third sum
Probability equals 0.5 + (increment * TOTSUM)/3
WRITE ZSTAR and probability
Increment ZSTAR by step size to set ZSTAR to next value of Z entry in table
Compare ZSTAR with end value for Z
    IF end value for Z not exceeded, go back to Set X
    ELSE go back to READ another data card
Terminate with message and card count
```

Notes on statistical example 4

In this case, the variable identification block has been augmented by a special section for listing array names. An algorithm block has been added to explain the methodology. Also a storage allocation block is used for the DIMENSION statement.

The initialization and input block sets counters, reads a data card, and checks it for several kinds of potential errors. In this program, most of the code in this block is executed once for each input card. The upper value of the table is initialized for each card read.

The computation block implements Simpson's rule by computing 20 equally spaced ordinates and saving them in an array. (The zeroth ordinate is known to be 0.3989 from setting Z to 0 in the normal equation.) Three partial sums are created: one for those ordinates multiplied by 1 (zeroth and last), a second for the even-numbered ordinates (those to be multiplied by 2), and the third for the odd-numbered ones (those to be multiplied by 4). Note the use of the DO loops and the values of the DO parameters in lines 15 and 20. The total sum is computed (line 26) by multiplying the partial sums by their appropriate values and adding. A less efficient way of doing this would have been to put a 2 multiplier and a 4 multiplier in front of ORD in lines 19 and 21, respectively. This would have caused 18 multiplications. (Why?)

223

Figure 4-23
Program flowchart for statistical program example 4—normal probability tables. (Numbers next to symbols are line numbers from program listing.)

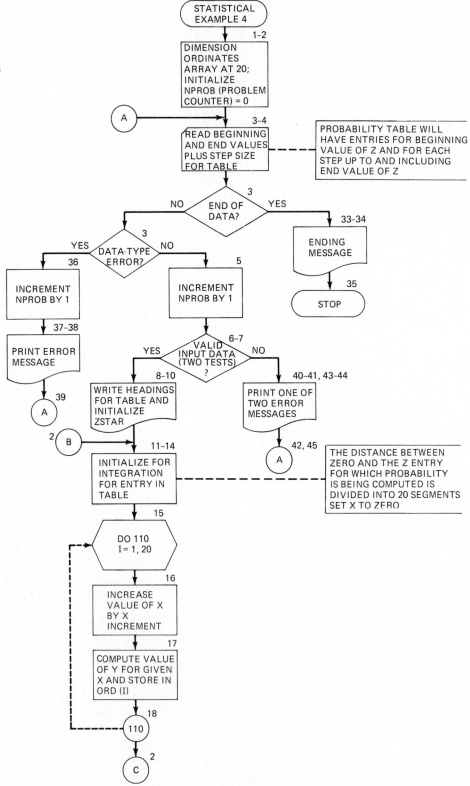

6 In what order will the first six subscripted variables be processed when N is 2 and M is 3?

```
DO   102 I = J, N
        DO   101 J = 1, N
                DO   100 K = 1, M
                        A (K, J, I) = . . .
100             CONTINUE
101     CONTINUE
102 CONTINUE
```

7 A matrix contains the number of A's, B's, etc., earned by each student in a class of 25. Each course is three credits. (See Figure 4-15.) Write a program segment to calculate the grade-point average for each student and for the class.

8 What is the effect of the following statements?

(*a*)   READ (5, 700) (((A(I,J,K), K =1,3), J =1,5), I =1,3)
   700 FORMAT (F10.0)

(*b*)   DIMENSION BETA (5, 5, 5)
      READ (5, 700) BETA
   700 FORMAT (F10.0 /)

(*c*)   DIMENSION IOTA (8, 8)
      WRITE (6,700) IOTA
   700 FORMAT (I10)

(*d*)   DO   750 J = 1, N
         WRITE (6, 700) J, A(J)
   700   FORMAT (I10, F10.2)
   750 CONTINUE

(*e*)   READ (5, 700) B(1, 1), B(3, 2), B(4, 1)
   700 FORMAT (F10.0)

Figure 4-15
Course-grade matrix for problem 7.

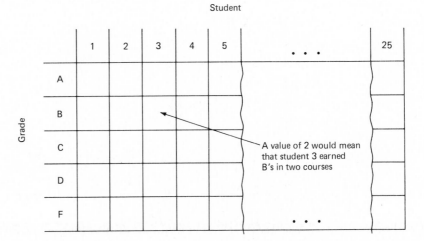

Figure 4-23
Continued

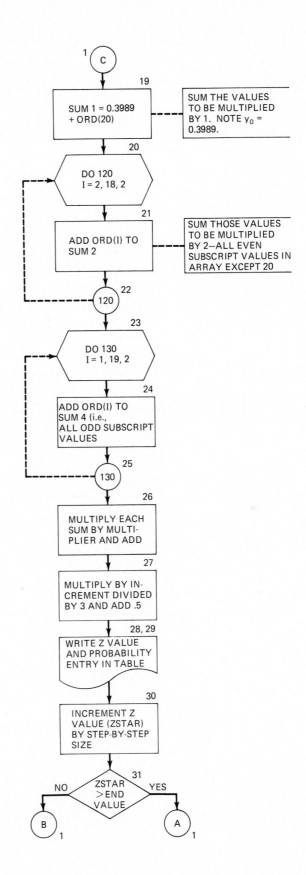

1
C

19
SUM 1 = 0.3989 + ORD(20)
··· SUM THE VALUES TO BE MULTIPLIED BY 1. NOTE y_0 = 0.3989.

20
DO 120
I = 2, 18, 2

21
ADD ORD(I) TO SUM 2
··· SUM THOSE VALUES TO BE MULTIPLIED BY 2—ALL EVEN SUBSCRIPT VALUES IN ARRAY EXCEPT 20

22
120

23
DO 130
I = 1, 19, 2

24
ADD ORD(I) TO SUM 4 (i.e., ALL ODD SUBSCRIPT VALUES

25
130

26
MULTIPLY EACH SUM BY MULTI-PLIER AND ADD

27
MULTIPLY BY IN-CREMENT DIVIDED BY 3 AND ADD .5

28, 29
WRITE Z VALUE AND PROBABILITY ENTRY IN TABLE

30
INCREMENT Z VALUE (ZSTAR) BY STEP-BY-STEP SIZE

31
ZSTAR > END VALUE
NO   YES

B
1

A
1

225

Figure 4-24
Listing of FORTRAN program for statistical program example 4—normal probability tables.

```
*********          PROGRAM IDENTIFICATION               **********
*                                                                *
*        PROBABILITIES OF VALUES LESS THAN Z (Z GT Ø) FOR        *
*        NORMAL PROBABILITY TABLES, BETWEEN LIMITS, ARE          *
*        GENERATED USING SIMPSON'S RULE FOR NUMERICAL INTEGRATION.*
*        WRITTEN Ø4/3Ø/77 BY T. HOFFMANN    REV. 1/13/82         *
*                                                                *
******************************************************************
*                                                                *
*********          VARIABLE IDENTIFICATION              **********
*                                                                *
*****                 ARRAY NAMES                       *****
*                                                                *
*        ORD     = ORDINATES OF THE NORMAL CURVE                 *
*                                                                *
*****                 SIMPLE VARIABLES                  *****
*                                                                *
*        NPROB   = PROBLEM COUNTER                               *
*        VALU1   = STARTING VALUE FOR TABLE                      *
*        VALU2   = ENDING VALUE FOR TABLE                        *
*        STPSIZ  = STEP SIZE (I.E. TABLE INCREMENT)              *
*        ZSTAR   = UPPER BOUND OF INTEGRATION INTERVAL           *
*        X       = ABCISSA VALUES IN SIMPSON'S RULE              *
*        XINCR   = INTEGRATION INTERVAL                          *
*        SUM1    = SUM OF FIRST AND LAST ORDINATE                *
*        SUM2    = SUM OF EVEN ORDINATES                         *
*        SUM4    = SUM OF ODD ORDINATES                          *
*        TOTSUM  = TOTAL OF SUMS                                 *
*        PROB    = NORMAL PROBABILITY VALUE                      *
*                                                                *
******************************************************************
*                                                                *
*********          ALGORITHM - SIMPSON'S RULE           **********
*                                                                *
*  PROB=.5+(XINCR/3)*(ORD(Ø)+4*ORD(1)+2*ORD(2)+...+4*ORD(N-1)+ORD(N))*
*                                                                *
******************************************************************
*                                                                *
*********          STORAGE ALLOCATION                   **********
*                                                                *
1.        DIMENSION ORD(2Ø)
*                                                                *
******************************************************************
*                                                                *
*********          INITIALIZATION AND INPUT BLOCK      BLOCK ØØØØ
*                                                                *
2.        NPROB = Ø
3.      6 READ(5,2,ERR=9Ø1,END=2Ø1) VALU1,VALU2,STPSIZ
4.      2 FORMAT(3F4.2)
*                                                                *
*          INCREMENT PROBLEM COUNTER                             *
*                                                                *
5.        NPROB = NPROB + 1
6.        IF(VALU1.LT.Ø.Ø) GOTO 92Ø
7.        IF(VALU1.GT.VALU2) GOTO 91Ø
8.        WRITE(6,11)
9.     11 FORMAT('1',5X,'NORMAL PROBABILITY TABLE'//6X,
       1     'Z VALUE    PROBABILITY OF'/,18X,'Z OR LESS'/)
1Ø.       ZSTAR = VALU1
*                                                                *
******************************************************************
*                                                                *
*********          COMPUTE PROBABILITY VALUES          BLOCK Ø1ØØ
*                                                                *
11.   1Ø1 X = Ø.Ø
12.       XINCR = ZSTAR/2Ø.Ø
13.       SUM2 = Ø.Ø
14.       SUM4 = Ø.Ø
*                                                                *
*          COMPUTE 2Ø ORDINATES IN TABLE INTERVAL                *
*                                                                *
15.       DO 11Ø I = 1,2Ø
16.         X = X + XINCR
17.         ORD(I) = Ø.3989*EXP(-X*X/2.Ø)
18.   11Ø CONTINUE
19.       SUM1 = Ø.3989 + ORD(2Ø)
2Ø.       DO 12Ø I= 2,18,2
21.         SUM2 = SUM2 + ORD(I)
22.   12Ø CONTINUE
23.       DO 13Ø I = 1,19,2
```

Figure 4-24
Continued

```
24.              SUM4 = SUM4 + ORD(I)
25.       130 CONTINUE
26.           TOTSUM = SUM1 + 2.0*SUM2 + 4.0*SUM4
27.           PROB = 0.5 + XINCR*TOTSUM/3.0
28.           WRITE(6,108) ZSTAR,PROB
29.       108 FORMAT(7X,F6.2,7X,F6.4)                                           *
    *                                                                          *
    *             INCREMENT TABLE VALUE AND REAPPLY RULE                       *
    *                                                                          *
30.           ZSTAR = ZSTAR + STPSIZ
31.           IF(ZSTAR.LE.VALU2) GOTO 101
    *                                                                          *
    *             GO BACK TO READ NEXT PROBLEM                                 *
    *                                                                          *
32.           GOTO 6
    *                                                                          *
    ****************************************************************************
    *                                                                          *
    *********     TERMINATION BLOCK                         BLOCK 0200
    *                                                                          *
33.       201 WRITE(6,202) NPROB
34.       202 FORMAT('1','PROBABILITY PROGRAM TERMINATED NORMALLY.'/
          1      5X,I3,' DATA CARDS READ.')
35.           STOP                                                             *
    *                                                                          *
    ****************************************************************************
    *                                                                          *
    *********     ERROR MESSAGE BLOCK                       BLOCK 0900
    *                                                                          *
36.       901 NPROB = NPROB + 1
37.           WRITE(6,914) NPROB
38.       914 FORMAT('0','***** ERROR. CANNOT UNDERSTAND DATA CARD NUMBER',I3)
    *                                                                          *
39.           GOTO 998                                                        *
    *                                                                          *
40.       910 WRITE(6,907) NPROB,VALU1,VALU2
41.       907 FORMAT('0','***** ERROR IN DATA. CARD NUMBER',I3/
          1      ' STARTING VALUE OF TABLE,',F6.2,
          2      ', MUST BE LESS THAN ENDING VALUE,',F6.2)
    *                                                                          *
42.           GOTO 998                                                        *
    *                                                                          *
43.       920 WRITE(6,905) NPROB,VALU1
44.       905 FORMAT('0','***** ERROR IN DATA CARD NUMBER',I3/
          1      ' STARTING VALUE SHOULD BE POSITIVE, NOT',F6.2)
    *                                                                          *
    *             GO BACK TO READ NEXT PROBLEM                                 *
    *                                                                          *
45.       998 GOTO 6                                                          *
    *                                                                          *
46.           END
```

Figure 4-25
Annotated input test data
for statistical problem 4.

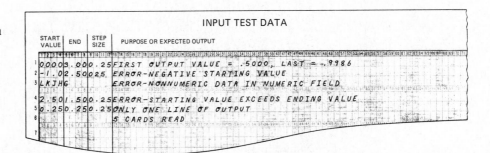

START VALUE	END	STEP SIZE	PURPOSE OR EXPECTED OUTPUT
1 0000	3.00	0.25	FIRST OUTPUT VALUE = .5000, LAST = .9986
2 -1.0	2.50	025	ERROR-NEGATIVE STARTING VALUE
3 LKJHG			ERROR-NONNUMERIC DATA IN NUMERIC FIELD
4 2.50	1.50	0.25	ERROR-STARTING VALUE EXCEEDS ENDING VALUE
5 0.25	0.25	0.25	ONLY ONE LINE OF OUTPUT
6			5 CARDS READ
7			

Figure 4-26
Example output from statistical program 4—normal probability tables.

```
       NORMAL PROBABILITY TABLE

       Z VALUE    PROBABILITY OF
                     Z OR LESS

            Ø           .5ØØØ
          .25           .5987
          .5Ø           .6914
          .75           .7733
         1.ØØ           .8413
         1.25           .8943
         1.5Ø           .9331
         1.75           .9599
         2.ØØ           .9772
         2.25           .9877
         2 5Ø           .9937
         2.75           .997Ø
         3.ØØ           .9986


***** ERROR IN DATA CARD NUMBER  2
STARTING VALUE SHOULD BE POSITIVE, NOT -1.ØØ

***** ERROR. CANNOT UNDERSTAND DATA CARD NUMBER  3

***** ERROR IN DATA. CARD NUMBER  4
STARTING VALUE OF TABLE,  2.5Ø, MUST BE LESS THAN ENDING VALUE,  1.5Ø
```

```
       NORMAL PROBABILITY TABLE

       Z VALUE    PROBABILITY OF
                     Z OR LESS

          .25           .5987
```

```
PROBABILITY PROGRAM TERMINATED NORMALLY.
       5 DATA CARDS READ.
```

Programming exercises

Description of assignment

Select one or more problems (or take the problems assigned by your instructor). Use DO loops in the program to process data and to perform input and output of subscripted variables. Use a DATA statement for initialization where appropriate. Follow the style guidelines and prepare the following:

1 Pseudocode description

2 Program flowchart

3 Program listing

4 List of test data and expected results, testing for both valid and invalid data where appropriate

5 Sample output including results of testing of all error conditions

Mathematics and statistics

1 For each of the following sets of n data points (X, Y), compute the correlation coefficients r.

$$r = \frac{n\Sigma XY - (\Sigma X)(\Sigma Y)}{\sqrt{[n\Sigma X^2 - (\Sigma X)^2][n\Sigma Y^2 - (\Sigma Y)^2]}}$$

Set 1		Set 2	
X	Y	X	Y
34.22	102.43	20	27.1
39.87	100.93	30	28.9
41.85	97.43	40	30.6
43.23	97.81	50	32.3
40.06	98.32	60	33.7
53.29	98.32	70	35.6
53.29	100.07	80	37.2
54.14	97.08		
49.12	91.59		
40.71	94.85		
55.15	94.65		

2 Pascal's triangle is a set of numbers having some very interesting properties. (Actually, Omar Khayyam wrote about them well before Pascal.) Arranged in the usual manner (as shown below), each number in the interior is the sum of the numbers on either side of it in the row above. Any row (labeling the top as row zero) contains the coefficients of the expansion $(a + b)^n$ or the ordered set of combinations of n things taken m (0, 1, 2, etc., from left to right) at a time. Write a program to compute and print the first 11 rows ($n = 0$ through 10) of Pascal's triangle. Printing need not be in the symmetric triangle form.

n							
0				1			
1			1		1		
2		1		2		1	
3	1		3		3		1
etc.			etc.				

3 Write a program using Simpson's rule to evaluate the gamma function (the generalization of the factorial) for the following set of values: $n = .05, 1.7, 2.0,$ and 1.5 *Hint:* Since log $1/x$ where $x = 0$ is undefined, use a very small number in place of zero, such as 1.0E-10.

$$\text{gamma} = \int_0^1 \left(\log \frac{1}{n}\right)^{n-1} \quad \text{for } n > 0$$

Business and economics

4   Prepare tables of the form given below showing the size of a loan that is possible from different monthly payments ($100 to $500 in $50 increments) for a given number of months m at annual interest rates of 7, 8, 9, 10, 11, and 12 percent. Assume the monthly rate is one-twelfth the yearly rate. Read in m as 240 and 300.

TERM IN MONTHS	NNN				
		Annual interest rate			
Monthly payments	.07	.08	.09	. . .	.12
$100	XXXXX.	XXXXX.			
150	XXXXX.				
200					
250					
300					
.					
.					
.					
500					

5   Prepare a table of the form shown below for given interest rates i and 1-year increments from 1 through 10 years showing the effect on an initial amount of $100 compounded annually, quarterly, monthly, weekly (assume exactly 52 weeks per year), daily (assume each year has 365 days), and continuously. Use i values of 7, 9, and 12 percent. (See problem 2-4 for formulas.)

NN INTEREST RATE						
	Frequency of compounding					
Year	1	4	12	52	365	Continuous
1	XXXX.XX	XXXX.XX				
2	XXXX.XX					
.						
.						
.						
10						

6   A business executive has the following portfolio of stocks at the start of a period and makes the given set of transactions during the period. Prepare a report showing her starting position, a summary of her transactions, and her final position. *Hint:* Reference the stocks by number rather than by name. You may wish to use current stock quotations.

STARTING PORTFOLIO

Stock number	Stock	Shares	Price/share
1	International Harvester	100	$33.50
2	White Consolidated	200	27.50
3	Texaco	100	29.25
4	Northern Natural Gas	300	44.00
5	National Distillers	500	24.25
6	Public Service of Colorado	200	19.75
7	Middle Southern Utilities	200	16.25

TRANSACTIONS

Number	Stock	Action	Shares	Price
3	Texaco	Buy	100	$28.75
8	Anheuser-Busch	Buy	200	23.00
4	Northern Natural Gas	Sell	200	45.25
7	Middle Southern Utilities	Buy	100	17.00
9	IBM	Buy	100	61.50
1	International Harvester	Sell	100	32.00
3	Texaco	Buy	100	29.50
6	Public Service of Colorado	Sell	200	20.25
10	Control Data	Buy	100	21.25

FINAL PRICES

Stock	Price	Stock	Price
International Harvester	$ 8.25	Public Service of Colorado	$13.75
White Consolidated	25.25	Middle Southern Utilities	12.75
Texaco	30.62	Control Data	31.38
Anheuser-Busch	22.25	IBM	61.50
Northern Natural Gas	47.50	National Distillers	22.37

Science and engineering

7 A frequently encountered computer science problem is to sort an array of numbers into descending order of magnitude. One procedure for doing this is called the *bubble-sort technique.* The steps in it are as follows:

(*a*) Compare the first and second number. If the second is larger, switch the order of the numbers.

(*b*) Take the next number in the array and compare it to its predecessor. If it is larger, switch positions and compare it to the next predecessor, making a switch if it is larger. Repeat until the selected number is not larger than a predecessor or it is in the first position.

(*c*) Take the next number after the previously selected one and repeat step 2 until the last number has been selected and compared.

For example, the original set is 8, 9, 5, 11, 7. The arrows show exchanges; the dotted lines show comparisons without exchanges.

Column	0	1	2	3	4	5	6
Array	8	9	9	9	9	11	11
	9	8	8	8	11	9	9
	5	5	5	11	8	8	8
	11	11	11	5	5	5	7
	7	7	7	7	7	7	5

Each column shows the array contents after the comparison and/or switch. The underlined number is the one that had been selected for comparison with its predecessor.

Write a program to perform a bubble sort on any set of less than 100 numbers. Use it to sort the following sets of data:

	Set number	
1	2	3
66	−6	.156
85	−87	.951
86	−56	.537
45	−34	.015
77	2	.126
74	6	.672
57	43	
49	18	
62	85	

8 Prime numbers are those divisible without a remainder only by themselves and 1. To find all the primes less than 1000, one can start with 2 and divide all higher numbers by it, eliminating all that have no remainder and then moving to the next largest that has not been eliminated and dividing by it in the same manner. This is a straightforward method based upon the definition. However, it is very time-consuming because division is lengthy. A quicker way is to use the *sieve of Eratosthenes* procedure. Fill an array with values from 1 to 1000. Starting with the second entry, set to zero all multiples of it in the array (all multiples of 2). Proceed to the next nonzero number and repeat the process, etc. At the conclusion of this all the nonzero entries will be prime numbers. Write a program to implement this procedure and print out a table of primes.

9 Data is often more meaningful if graphed. Write a program to both tabulate and graph the curve of damped vibration.

$$y = e^{-nx} \sin mx$$

for the following values:

n	m	x range
0.2	1	0 to 3π
0.2	2	$-\pi$ to 2π
0.3	3	0 to 2π

Hint: Create the graph sideways on the paper; that is, X is plotted vertically and Y horizontally on the page. Use an array of one-character variables set to blanks and insert an asterisk in the appropriate Y position for each X.

Humanities and social sciences

10 Data from a questionnaire has been punched into cards as follows:

Column	Data
1–2	Age: 0 = no response
3	Sex: 1 = female, 2 = male
4	Homeowner: 1 = yes, 2 = no, 0 = no response
5–7	Income (in thousands): 999 = none, 900 = no response
8	Political preference: 1 = Democrat, 2 = Republican, 3 = other, 0 = no response

DATA

Age	Sex	Homeowner	Income	Politics
35	1	1	25	1
19	2	0	18	3
17	1	2	999	3
39	2	1	35	2
54	2	1	17	1
73	2	2	900	1
27	2	1	27	2
72	1	2	8	0
0	2	2	40	2
43	1	1	25	1
55	2	1	27	1
39	2	2	43	3
32	1	0	11	3
23	1	2	900	0
66	1	1	7	1

Tally responses and nonresponses and prepare the following tables:

TABLE 1

Age, years	Income (in $000)				
	Less than $5	$5–$9	$10–$15	$15–$19	Over $19
Less than 20					
20–29					
30–39					
40–49					
50–59					
60–69					
Over 69					

TABLE 2

Age	Sex		Homeowner		Politics		
	F	M	Yes	No	Democrat	Republican	Other
Less than 20							
20–29							
30–39							
40–49							
50–59							
60–69							
Over 69							

TABLE 3

Nonresponses
    Age
    Homeowner
    Income
    Political preference

11   One step in preparing a concordance is to search the text for a selected phrase or word. Write a program that reads a paragraph, calculates the frequency of a selected word, and prints a summary. Paragraphs are limited to 800 characters, including spaces and punctuation, appearing on 10 cards. The paragraph is indented five spaces. *Caution:* Only individual words that match the key word are to be counted, not longer words that contain the key letters. *Hint:* Establish an array of 80 single character elements and read, process, and print the lines of the paragraph one at a time (using input/output format of A80). Read in the key word as single characters into another array including a beginning and ending blank as part of the key word. Test for the series of letters, for example, blank, T, H, E, blank, from the key word array. Also check for key word followed by period.

Key word: THE

Paragraph:
    Now is the time for all good men to come to the aid of their party. But let us not lose heart for there are 30 theocratic parties to console us.

Key word: LOVE

Paragraph:
    Love is patient and kind; it is not jealous or conceited or proud; love is not ill-mannered or selfish or irritable; love does not keep a record of wrongs.

12   Given the following data on population and immigration for the United States, produce a table showing, for each decade, initial population, total increase, net immigration, and percent of increase attributable to immigration.

Period	Initial population (000)	Net immigration (000)	Period	Initial population (000)	Net immigration (000)
1870–1880	39,818	2,274	1920–1930	105,711	3,089
1880–1890	50,156	4,490	1930–1940	122,775	1,067
1890–1900	62,948	2,531	1940–1950	131,669	875
1900–1910	75,995	5,289	1950–1960	151,326	2,660
1910–1920	91,972	3,201	1960–1970	179,323	3,282

General

13 A matrix contains the number of A's, B's, etc., earned by each student. Each course is four credits. Write a program to calculate the grade-point (A = 4, B = 3, etc.) average for each student and for all students.

Student name	Number of courses for each guide				
	A	B	C	D	E
George Thiel	0	8	2	2	1
Craig Ebert	3	4	9	1	0
Dean Greco	1	5	3	0	0
Paul Hogan	5	8	9	0	1
David Sellman	7	1	0	2	0
Bonnie Link	5	3	3	1	0
Susan Frye	9	6	4	4	0
Larry Maxwell	3	8	2	0	0
Kathy Adams	7	1	4	2	1
Jill Swift	3	3	4	2	0
Rebecca Young	7	5	2	0	1
Dan Johnson	1	1	1	0	0
Mark Snyder	1	3	0	2	0
Steve Fisher	2	4	0	2	0
Sally Crown	6	6	7	1	0

14 Given any amount of a restaurant check up to $25 and any amount tendered up to $40, find the quantity and denomination of paper money and coins to return as change. Print the result in order from smallest to largest denomination. Print an error message if the amount tendered is less than the check.

AMOUNTS

Check	Tendered
$ 2.13	$20.00
6.15	5.00
3.37	3.37
21.95	20.00
17.44	30.00

Hint: Results are obtained from largest to smallest, so save the results in an array for printing in small to large order.

15 Reprogram problem 13 of Chapter 3 and print the conversions in groups ordered by their codes as 3, 2, 1, −1, −2, −3.

chapter **5A**

FORTRAN subprograms and case program structure

A *subprogram* is a separate program unit used (called) by a main program or by other subprograms. Subprogram capability is a very important feature of the FORTRAN language. It is implemented in two different ways: the function subprogram and the subroutine subprogram, both of which are explained in this chapter.

The three basic programming structures (sequence, selection, and repetition) have been presented in previous chapters. The sequence structure of one statement following another was described in Chapter 1. The selection structure for choosing between two program paths as implemented by the FORTRAN IF was explained in Chapter 2. The repetition programming structure using the DO loop was presented in Chapter 4. Although all programming may be performed using only the three basic structures, it is convenient to use a fourth programming pattern, the case structure, to select among multiple alternatives. The FORTRAN implementation of the case structure using the computed GOTO is described in this chapter.

Characteristics of subprograms

As background for understanding the specific types of subprograms, the purpose and use of subprograms are explained and some general characteristics are described.

Purpose and use of subprograms

The purpose of subprograms is to simplify programming. Subprograms help to achieve this objective in two major ways:

1 *Reusable program elements* Processing functions that will be used more than once in the program (or used by more than one program) are written once and then used by programs needing the processing. Examples are subprograms to:
 (*a*) Generate random numbers
 (*b*) Calculate statistics (such as mean, variance, etc.)
 (*c*) Sort data into ascending or descending order
2 *Decomposition of programming tasks* Sections of the program are written as independent subprograms to reduce the complexity of the program design, to aid in testing the program, and to allow different programmers to work on different subprograms concurrently. For example, the instructions to print a report (which may be fairly complex) may be organized into a subprogram separate from the instructions to compute the data to be printed in the report.

The first objective of reusable program elements can be achieved through subprograms because each subprogram is treated as a separate program. This independence is reflected in the following features of a subprogram.

1 It can be compiled separately from the program using it.
2 The variable names in the subprogram refer to different storage locations (in other words, are different variables) than variables with the same names in programs that use the subprogram. If it is desired that these be the same, spe-

cial instructions are available to make the names refer to the same storage locations.

3   Use of a subprogram is achieved by a simple program statement in the using (calling) program.

4   Transfer of data between a program using a subprogram (a calling program) and the subprogram is specified by special instructions in the calling program and the subprogram.

The second objective of decomposing programming into smaller, simpler tasks is also possible because the subprograms can be written and tested separately. In this approach, a large program is written as a main control program (the main program) that uses (calls) subprograms. In other words, the main control program ties together the major segments of the program that are written and tested as separate programs. A subprogram may also use (call) other subprograms.

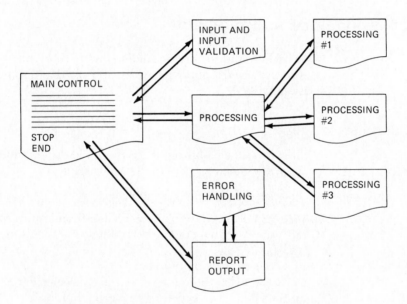

Three sources of FORTRAN subprogram are used by a main program or by subprograms.

1   *Intrinsic functions*   These are essentially internal subprograms that are part of the standard facilities of the language.

2   *User-written external subprograms*   These generally are unique to the program rather than being general subprograms.

3   *Library external subprograms*   These are part of a library of prewritten subroutines that may be made available.

If a program or subprogram invokes or calls a subprogram, the subprogram coding must be available to the calling program when it is executed. The ways in which this may be accomplished are:

1   *Intrinsic functions*   The compiler provides all necessary links to the internal intrinsic function subprograms. The programmer merely uses the intrinsic function name in a program statement in the calling program.

2   *User-written external subprograms*   These are included with the calling program, either by specifying their retrieval from storage or by including them with the job when it is input for compilation and execution. When subprograms are included in the compilation and execution job, each subprogram has an END statement, so that each will compile separately. The uniting of the subprograms and the calling program is done by job control instructions. For example, in a submission using a card deck, the structure is approximately as follows.

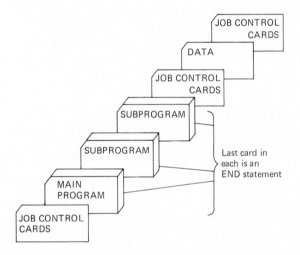

3   *Library external subprograms*   When a program calls for a subprogram that is part of a library of such programs, system control instructions are used to obtain the subprogram from the subprogram library and make it available to the program calling it.

When a large program uses a number of subprograms, it is good documentation practice to list in the comments at the beginning of each subprogram the program units that call upon the subprogram. This is especially helpful if the subprogram is altered, replaced, etc.

Checking on availability of prewritten subprograms

It is very important for the programmer to be aware of the extensive libraries of prewritten subprograms that are easily available for use as part of a program being written. These are in addition to the standard intrinsic FORTRAN functions. A university computer center will usually have several hundred such subprograms developed by the center or obtained from an outside supplier. For example, a well-known library of subroutines is the IMSL (International Mathematical and Statistical Libraries, Inc.) library of mathematics and statistics subroutines. There are over 400 prewritten subprograms classified as follows:

Analysis of Experimental Design Data

Basic Statistics

Categorized Data Analysis

Differential Equations: Quadrature; Differentiation

Eigensystem Analysis

Forecasting: Econometrics; Time Series

Generation and Testing of Random Numbers; Goodness of Fit

Interpolation; Approximations; Smoothing

Linear Algebraic Equations

Mathematical and Statistical Special Functions

Nonparametric Statistics

Observation Structure

Regression Analysis

Sampling

Utility Functions

Vector, Matrix Arithmetic

Zeros and Extrema; Linear Programming

It is always wise to check on the availability of a prewritten routine before designing, coding, and testing a new subprogram. Most computer centers maintain a directory of available subprograms as well as documentation manuals describing each and the exact procedure for calling them.

Function subprogram

The *function subprogram* is the method by which a programmer can write an external function to be invoked by other programs. Coded as a separate program unit, it is assigned a name by the programmer so that the function can be called using the name as a reference. A function subprogram is called into use by writing the name in a program statement followed by a list of values (variable names or constants) to be used by the function—the values separated by commas and enclosed in parentheses. The list of values are termed the arguments of the function. For example, a programmer may write a small program routine to find the largest value in a single-dimension array of n elements. The programmer decides to keep the routine as a separate program unit by defining it as a function subprogram and assigning it the name RAYMAX. Another program unit, such as a main program, may use the RAYMAX function by having a program statement that uses the function name RAYMAX followed by the arguments enclosed in parentheses. Assuming the RAYMAX function is to operate on array ALPHA with N entries, the function call would read RAYMAX(ALPHA,N). Two separate examples illustrate the way the example RAYMAX function subprogram is invoked by statements in the using (calling) program.

Example 1

Arguments of the function

```
X = RAYMAX(ALPHA,N)+6.0
```

This example calculates the maximum value from the N values in array ALPHA, adds 6.0 to it, and stores the result in X.

Example 2

```
IF (BIG.LE.RAYMAX(Y,10)) GOTO 120
```

This statement compares the value of BIG with the largest value in the 10 values in array Y. If BIG is less than or equal to that value, control goes to statement 120.

The process of using a user-written function can now be summarized. The statements that invoke the function are in the calling program. The function program unit that does the processing is a separate subprogram. The calling program statement identifies the function subprogram to be used and defines the data to be used (normally with the argument list). The function subprogram operates on the data in the argument list and transfers a single value back to the calling program in place of the function call.

The function subprogram begins with an identifying statement. This first statement consists of the word FUNCTION followed by the programmer-assigned name of the function and an argument list of variables required by the function, with the variables separated by commas and the list enclosed in parentheses. The initial letter of the function name indicates the type of the result to be returned from the function (integer or real). When the function is used, the value of the variables in the argument list in the calling statement of the using program are used in place of each corresponding variable in the argument list of the subprogram. For this reason, these variables in the function definition are termed *dummy variables;* they are replaced by the values of the actual variables in the argument list of the calling statement.

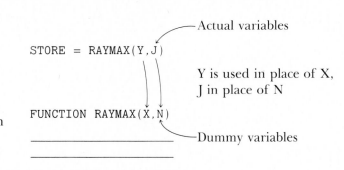

Calling statement — STORE = RAYMAX(Y,J) — Actual variables

Y is used in place of X, J in place of N

Function subprogram — FUNCTION RAYMAX(X,N) — Dummy variables

The actual argument list must correspond in number of values and type (real or integer) with the dummy argument list.

Program statements in a function subprogram follow the function-naming statement. One or more of the assignment statements in the subprogram must define the function name as the result variable, for example, function name = expression. An example of such a statement for the RAYMAX function is RAYMAX = BIG shown on the next page.

In the example RAYMAX function subprogram, there is an array named X and the number of entries in the array is N. Any array used in the subpro-

Outline	Example	
FUNCTION f(X₁,X₂,...,Xₙ)	FUNCTION RAYMAX(X,N)	
	DIMENSION X(100)	
	BIG = -9.99E - 10	
	DO 100 I = 1,N	Function
	BIG = AMAX1(X(I),BIG)	sub-
	100 CONTINUE	program
function name = expression	RAYMAX = BIG	
RETURN	RETURN	
END	END	

gram must be dimensioned in the subprogram itself; thus, array X is dimensioned in the example at a maximum of 100.

The RETURN statement is put at the logical end (or ends if there is more than one logical end) of the function subprogram. It signals that control is to return to the calling program from which the transfer to the subprogram was made. The END statement is required as the last statement or physical end of the subprogram. The END statement implies the RETURN statement, so the RETURN is optional if it would logically be the last statement before the END (except in older FORTRANs, which require RETURN before END).

Example 3

As a simple case to illustrate both the form of the calling program and the form of the function, a simple program to read two values from a card, sum them, and print the two inputs and the sum is written with a function subprogram to perform the summing operation.

Calling program	Function subprogram
READ*,A,B	FUNCTION ADDF(X,Y)
SUM = ADDF(A,B)	ADDF = X + Y
PRINT*,A,B,SUM	RETURN
STOP	END
END	

If the calling program reads a value of 4.0 for A and 3.5 for B, these values are provided as argument values to the function ADDF, which sums them (uses the value for A in place of X and the value for B in place of Y) and returns the sum of 7.5 to be stored in SUM by the calling program.

Example 4

Several programs may need to calculate the economic order quantity. This is therefore to be written as a function subprogram. The economic order quantity (EOQ) is calculated from the formula:

$$EOQ = \sqrt{\frac{24VS}{AC}}$$

where V = average monthly usage in units
     S = setup or order cost
     A = carrying cost expressed as a decimal
     C = variable cost per unit

The EOQ is the quantity calculated by the formula except that, for this program, it must not be less than 1 month's average usage nor more than 12 months' average usage. If it exceeds the 12 months' supply, the EOQ is set to 12 months' supply; if the EOQ is less than 1 months' supply, EOQ is set equal to 1 month's supply. The function subprogram is shown in Figure 5-1.

In order to make use of the EOQ formula function program in a statement, it is necessary only to write EOQ (a_1,a_2,a_3,a_4), where the a's stand for actual real arguments (variables or constants) used in place of the dummy real arguments V, S, A, and C of the subprogram. For example:

```
ORDER = SPECL + EOQ (USAGE, SETUP, CARRY, UNITC)
```

This statement will obtain the EOQ value using the values for USAGE, SETUP, CARRY, and UNITC as factors in the formula. The single value returned, the EOQ, is used in the replacement statement.

SUMMARY OF SPECIFICATIONS FOR FUNCTION SUBPROGRAM

Notation

f = function name
e = expression
$x_1,x_2, \ldots ,x_n$ = dummy arguments of the function
$a_1,a_2, \ldots ,a_n$ = actual calling arguments of the function

Where defined	Externally defined in a separately compiled independent subprogram.
How defined	FUNCTION $f(x_1,x_2, \ldots ,x_n)$ $f = e$ (at least one statement of this form in program) RETURN (at each logical exit from program) END
How named	Same as variable name—up to six characters, first letter determines type unless type declared. Type FUNCTION $f(x_1,x_2, \ldots ,x_n)$
How called into use	Appearance of name in an expression $v = f(a_1,a_2, \ldots ,a_n)$
Number of outputs	One
Restrictions on form of calling argument	Type, number, and order of calling arguments must agree with the dummy arguments of the definition; argument may be a variable name, subscripted variable, array name, expression, or subprogram name.

243

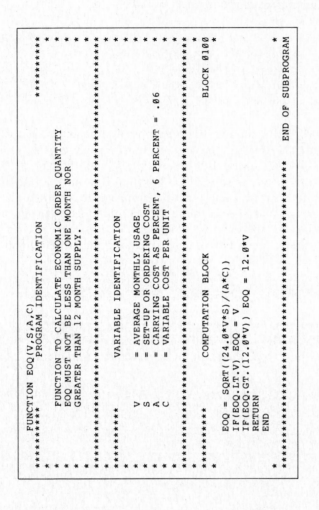

```
******************************************************
*                                                    *
*        FUNCTION EOQ(V,S,A,C)                        *
*        ******        PROGRAM IDENTIFICATION         *
*                                                     *
*        FUNCTION TO CALCULATE ECONOMIC ORDER QUANTITY *
*        EOQ MUST NOT BE LESS THAN ONE MONTH NOR       *
*        GREATER THAN 12 MONTH SUPPLY.                 *
*                                                      *
******************************************************
*        *********     VARIABLE IDENTIFICATION         *
*                                                      *
*        V    = AVERAGE MONTHLY USAGE                  *
*        S    = SET-UP OR ORDERING COST                *
*        A    = CARRYING COST AS PERCENT, 6 PERCENT = .06 *
*        C    = VARIABLE COST PER UNIT                 *
*                                                      *
******************************************************
*        *********     COMPUTATION BLOCK      BLOCK 0100 *
*                                                      *
*        EOQ = SQRT((24.0*V*S)/(A*C))                  *
*        IF(EOQ.LT.V) EOQ = V                          *
*        IF(EOQ.GT.(12.0*V)) EOQ = 12.0*V              *
*        RETURN                                        *
*        END                                           *
*                                                      *
*                              *      END OF SUBPROGRAM *
******************************************************
```

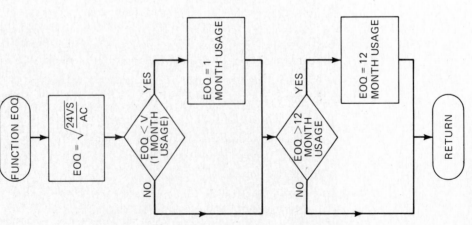

Figure 5-1
Function subprogram to calculate economic order quantity.

Self-testing exercise 5-1

1 What do the following programs do?

```
***** MAIN PROGRAM ******        FUNCTION SUM (X)
      DIMENSION A(100)           DIMENSION X(100)
      READ (5,700) A             SUM = 0.0
  700 FORMAT (10F8.0)            DO 100 I = 1, 100
      ANS = SQRT (SUM(A))           SUM = SUM + X (I)
      WRITE (6,700) ANS      100 CONTINUE
      STOP                       RETURN
      END                        END
```

2 A function is defined as IBOY(X,A,J). What is the type (interger or real) of the result returned by the function? What type are the variables in the calling argument list?

3 Write a function subprogram to find the positive, real root (if it exists) of a quadratic equation. The *a* term is always positive for this problem. The formula is:

$$\text{Root} = \frac{-b + \sqrt{b^2 - 4ac}}{2a}$$

If there are no real, positive roots ($b^2 - 4ac$ is negative), make the answer equal 0.

4 Write a main program statement that uses the function in problem 3.

5 Write a function subprogram to calculate the difference between yearly interest earned using two-interest rates for a given amount invested.

6 Write a main program statement to use the function in problem 5. Use variable names XINT1, XINT2, and AMOUNT for main program variables.

Subroutine

A function subprogram, as described previously, always has an argument list and returns a single value to the program statement where it is used. In contrast, the *subroutine* subprogram removes these restrictions. The subroutine may have arguments, but it does not require them. It does not automatically return a value to the main program; it may simply alter the value of a variable or print out the contents of various locations.

The subroutine is a separate program that is defined by the word SUBROUTINE followed by a name and dummy arguments (but no dummy arguments are required). The name, up to six characters, has no type (integer or real) significance.

```
SUBROUTINE f(x₁,x₂, . . . ,xₙ) or SUBROUTINE f
        _____
        _____
        _____
        _____
        _____
        _____

RETURN
END
```

The arguments of the subroutine definition may include dummy array names as well as single variable names. If a dummy array name is used, the dummy array name must be dimensioned in the subroutine.

The subroutine is used by writing a CALL statement. If an argument list is needed, the actual arguments to be used must be of the same type and be listed in the same order as the definition of dummy arguments. A subroutine can itself call other subroutines or functions, but cannot call itself.

$$\text{CALL } f(a_1, a_2, \ . \ . \ . \ , a_n)$$ for subroutine defined as having an argument list

or CALL f   for subroutine defined as without argument list

Example

To illustrate the form of both the calling program and the subroutine subprogram, the simple example will be used of a program that reads values for A and B, calls a subroutine to sum them, and prints the values for A, B, and the sum.

Calling program	Subroutine
READ *, A, B	SUBROUTINE SUMIT(X, Y, RESULT)
CALL SUMIT(A, B, SUM)	RESULT = X + Y
PRINT *, A, B, SUM	RETURN
STOP	END

When the calling program calls the subroutine, it provides the value of A and B to be used by the subroutine in place of X and Y. It also provides a variable name SUM that is equivalent to RESULT (both being third in the list). When the subroutine calculates X + Y and stores it in RESULT, it actually stores the sum in SUM. Compare this form with the previous example using a function.

Example

A program requires the ordering of several arrays in descending sequence by magnitude from the largest to the smallest value. The arrays are all one-dimensional, and the number of quantities in an array range from 10 to 100. The subroutine is written so that one of the arguments is the array name and the other is the number of entries. The subroutine program shown in Figure 5-2 is dimensioned to handle the largest array.

Note that the subroutine is general and will work for an array of 100 or less entries. The quantities are arranged by successive comparisons, shifting the larger values to the front until the array is ordered. A program needing to

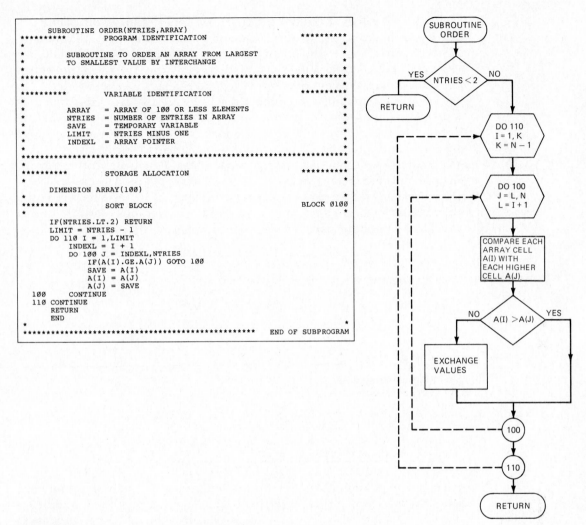

```
      SUBROUTINE ORDER(NTRIES,ARRAY)
**********          PROGRAM IDENTIFICATION          **********
*                                                            *
*       SUBROUTINE TO ORDER AN ARRAY FROM LARGEST            *
*       TO SMALLEST VALUE BY INTERCHANGE                     *
*                                                            *
**************************************************************
*                                                            *
**********          VARIABLE IDENTIFICATION         **********
*                                                            *
*       ARRAY   = ARRAY OF 100 OR LESS ELEMENTS              *
*       NTRIES  = NUMBER OF ENTRIES IN ARRAY                 *
*       SAVE    = TEMPORARY VARIABLE                         *
*       LIMIT   = NTRIES MINUS ONE                           *
*       INDEXL  = ARRAY POINTER                              *
*                                                            *
**************************************************************
*                                                            *
**********          STORAGE ALLOCATION              **********
*                                                            *
      DIMENSION ARRAY(100)
*                                                            *
**********          SORT BLOCK            BLOCK 0100         *
*                                                            *
      IF(NTRIES.LT.2) RETURN
      LIMIT = NTRIES - 1
      DO 110 I = 1,LIMIT
         INDEXL = I + 1
         DO 100 J = INDEXL,NTRIES
            IF(A(I).GE.A(J)) GOTO 100
            SAVE = A(I)
            A(I) = A(J)
            A(J) = SAVE
100      CONTINUE
110   CONTINUE
      RETURN
      END
*                                                            *
****************************************************** END OF SUBPROGRAM
```

Figure 5-2
Subroutine program to order an array from largest to smallest value.

order an N-element array called GRADES merely writes the following statement:

```
CALL ORDER (N, GRADES)
```

After the array GRADES is ordered, control is returned to the statement following the CALL.

In flowcharting programs with subroutines, the subroutine program or module symbol is used to indicate a subroutine CALL.

A subroutine does not automatically return a single value to the calling program as does a function. However, the subroutine must be able to communicate with the calling program and transmit the results of the subroutine processing. This communication occurs in two ways—through the arguments in the subroutine call or by common storage (to be explained later in the chapter). Communication of computation results by arguments in the calling list and corresponding dummy arguments in the subroutine declaration was illustrated by the first example. In that example, a single result was transferred through the argument list. This method is not limited to one result. For example, assume a subroutine that requires one value (Y) to be sent from the calling program and that provides two values (A1 and A2) returned as results. In the following program segment, the subprogram CALL causes the subroutine to use the storage locations for Y, A1 and A2 as the locations for B, C, and D. When the subroutine executes C = 50, it is actually executing A1 = 50.

Calling program	SUBROUTINE
CALL COMP (Y,A1,A2)	SUBROUTINE COMP (B, C, D)
	C =
A1 and A2 now contain quantities computed by subroutine (identified in subroutine as C and D).	D =
	END

This means that the subroutine is not limited in the number of values that may be communicated back to the calling program by this method. These values may include arrays.

The communication between the subroutine and the main program need not include any computed result. In the sorting example, the subroutine sequenced data that was specified by an argument in the call to the subroutine, but there was no computed value returned to the calling program.

Self-testing exercise 5-2

1 Why should a subroutine be used instead of a function?

2 Write the function problem 5 from Exercise 5-1 as a subroutine. The problem was to write a subprogram to calculate the difference between yearly interest earned using two interest rates for a given amount invested.

3 Write a statement to use (call) the subroutine in question 2 if the main program variables are XINT1, XINT2, AMOUNT, and D (for the difference).

4 Write a subroutine that will interchange rows and columns of square matrices. The subroutine should handle matrices of size 20 × 20. Name the routine MOVE (remember that the name of the subroutine does not indicate type).

5 If, with reference to problem 4, the matrix to be rearranged is called ALPHA, what is the statement to perform the interchange of rows and columns? ALPHA must be 20 × 20 in size.

SUMMARY OF SPECIFICATIONS FOR SUBROUTINE

Notation

f = function name
e = expression
$x_1, x_2, \ldots, x_n$ = dummy arguments in the function
$a_1, a_2, \ldots, a_n$ = actual calling arguments of the function

Where defined	Externally defined in a separately compiled independent program.
How defined	SUBROUTINE $f(x_1, x_2, \ldots, x_n)$ or SUBROUTINE f Program steps RETURN (at each logical exit from program) END
How named	Same as variable name (up to six characters, etc.) except that the name of subroutine has no type significance.
How called into use	CALL statement CALL $f(a_1, a_2, \ldots, a_n)$ or CALL f
Number of results	Any number
Restrictions on form of calling argument	Type, number, and order of actual calling arguments must agree with the dummy arguments of the definition. Argument may be a variable name, subscripted variable, array name, expression, or subprogram name; need not have an argument.

COMMON and EQUIVALENCE declarations

Use of COMMON storage

A variable name in a subprogram is not automatically related to a variable with the same name in the calling program. The two variables are assigned to different memory locations, and computations affecting one do not affect the other. The X's in the following example are completely independent (although they can be associated by the subroutine dummy argument list and subroutine call argument list).

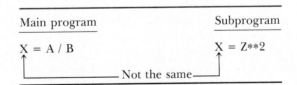

Main program	Subprogram
X = A / B	X = Z**2

Not the same

There are many instances in which it is convenient and desirable to have a variable name in both programs refer to the same memory location without having them appear in the argument lists. This is accomplished by the use of a special storage area designated as COMMON.

The use of common storage allows communication among independent program units. Instead of a list of variable names as arguments in the subroutine definition and subroutine CALL statement to specify data to be used and data names for results, the data required for processing and the results to be stored may be placed in common storage available to both calling program and subprogram.

Blank COMMON

The most frequently used common storage is also termed *blank* COMMON to distinguish it from a special form of common storage called *named* COMMON. A set or block of blank COMMON storage defines a blank COMMON declaration:

COMMON nlist

where nlist is a list of variable names or array names common to more than one program unit. An array name in a COMMON declaration defined the entire array as being in common storage. If any variable in a blank or named COMMON block is character type, all variables in that block must be character type. To declare both types of variables to be in COMMON, put the character variables in a named COMMON block (see next page).

The blank common storage sequence in all program units starts with the same storage location. The compiler assigns memory locations to the special blank common storage by sequentially assigning the variables listed in the COMMON declaration. The first variable in each list occupies the first position in common, the second (if an array of size 10) occupies the next 10 positions, etc. If there is more than one blank COMMON declaration, storage assignment for the next COMMON statement continues from the storage assignment of the previous statement. Because variables are associated by the order of appearance in the COMMON declaration, one or more COMMON declarations listing all variable or array names in the same order must be included in each subprogram having any (even one) of these common elements. One cannot list only those variables unique to a particular subprogram. Putting two variables in the same position in the COMMON declaration list of two different program units will result in their using the same memory location. If the variable and array names in all COMMON declarations are the same (the usual case), the COMMON declarations may be duplicated and a copy placed in each subroutine using any of the common variables.

Examples

Main program COMMON A,B,C Subprogram COMMON A,B,C	A,B,C in the main program reference same data as A,B,C in the subprogram.
Main program COMMON X,Y,Z Subprogram COMMON A,B,C	A,B,C in the subprogram reference the same data storage locations as X,Y,Z in the main program.
Main program COMMON D,G Subprogram 1 COMMON D,G,X Subprogram 2 COMMON D,G,X	If subprograms share X but it is not used by the main program, then the main program need not list X (since it is the last item, it is not required to keep other variables in same sequence), but recommended procedure is to have all COMMON declarations include the entire list.

An array included in a COMMON declaration must also be dimensioned in each program using the COMMON declaration. The dimensions must be the same for all using programs. Dimensioning may be done through DIMENSION statements or, alternatively, may be included in the COMMON declaration for the variable. This is recommended as being less error-prone. For example:

Single declaration (recommended)	Separate declarations
`COMMON X(100), Y(50)`	`DIMENSION X(100), Y(50)` `COMMON X, Y`

By following the style of including the dimension in the COMMON declaration, dimension statements are used only to dimension variables not in common storage. This style aids in keeping common variables and local variables (applying only to a single program unit) clearly identified. Also, an array variable name appearing in a COMMON-dimensioned declaration is clearly identified as being an array.

Named COMMON and block data subprogram

Blank COMMON is useful in that it applies to all program units declaring COMMON. Data stored in it is not affected by execution of RETURN or END statements of subprograms using blank COMMON. However, if data is shared only by some but not all of a number of subprograms, blank COMMON requires that the variables be accounted for in the COMMON declaration list of all subprograms with COMMON declarations. Also, variables in blank COMMON may not be initialized using the DATA statement.

An alternative common storage available in 1977 FORTRAN is the *named* COMMON. The form of the named COMMON declaration is to have a common block name enclosed in slashes preceding the list of variable names to be declared as common.

COMMON/common block name/nlist

If no name appears between the slashes, the variables that follow are blank COMMON; in other words, // is the same as blank COMMON. A named COMMON block has a unique storage sequence that starts at the same location for all COMMON blocks using the same name. Named COMMON blocks in different subprograms using the same name must be the same size.

Examples

`COMMON / A / X, Y, Z / B / M, N, F`	Named common block A contains X, Y, Z and named common block B contains M, N, F.
`COMMON // R, S, T(100)`	R, S, and array T are in blank COMMON.

If variables and array elements in common storage are to be initialized by the use of a DATA statement, these must be placed in named COMMON. The DATA statement is placed in a BLOCK DATA subprogram—a subprogram designed for this purpose. A BLOCK DATA subprogram is defined by the

BLOCK DATA statement:

BLOCK DATA [symbolic name for block data subprogram (optional)]

The BLOCK DATA statement is followed by statements that define the data specified in a named COMMON block. The BLOCK DATA subprogram contains storage specifications, but does not contain any executable statements. The DATA statement is used to initialize variables, and DIMENSION, COMMON, and EQUIVALENCE (to be explained below) statements, are used as appropriate. The last statement is END.

The reason for the BLOCK DATA subprogram is that named COMMON can be used by several program units, and thus no program unit can be relied upon to have the data initialization. The BLOCK DATA subprogram defines initialization at the global level of the entire set of programs and subprograms. An example of a BLOCK DATA subprogram is the following:

Example program unit using named COMMON	BLOCK DATA subprogram to initialize named COMMON

`SUBROUTINE CALCUL`
`COMMON /BD/ALPHA(50), BETA,A`
 	
`RETURN`
`END`
	`BLOCK DATA`
	`COMMON /BD/ALPHA(50), BETA,A`
	`DATA ALPHA/50*0/BETA/1.0/`
	`END`

Notice that in the 50-element array ALPHA, the variables BETA and A are defined in two or more program units as being in named COMMON (named BD). The BLOCK DATA subprogram initializes ALPHA as zeros and BETA as 1.0. All the variable names in a named common block must be named in the named COMMON statement even if they are not initialized in the DATA statement. More than one named COMMON block may be initialized by DATA statements in the same BLOCK DATA subprogram.

EQUIVALENCE declaration

The EQUIVALENCE declaration is used within a program unit to indicate that two variables are to use the same memory location. The reason for this statement may be that, due to an error, two different names have been written for the same item. Or the reason may be to conserve memory space. Two or more variables used at different points in the program may be assigned to the same memory location if the earlier variables' values do not have to be preserved. Using the same name for the variables would cause them to share the memory location, but this may not be consistent with the naming scheme, etc., being used. Other reasons may also arise in individual programs. Arrays may be equivalenced. An element from an array may be equivalenced to a nonsubscripted variable. Two arrays may be overlapped in whole or in part, but two individual array elements may not be equivalenced. However, it is error-

---

COMMON DECLARATIONS AND BLOCK DATA SUBPROGRAM

Blank COMMON block

COMMON nlist   or   COMMON // nlist

where nlist is a list of variable names, array names, and array declarators. Variables in blank COMMON list may not be initialized with DATA statements.

Named COMMON block

COMMON/named common block name/nlist

BLOCK DATA subprogram

BLOCK DATA [name for BLOCK DATA subprogram (name optional)]

Statements such as DIMENSION, COMMON, EQUIVALENCE type, or statements not yet explained (IMPLICIT, SAVE, PARAMETER). No executable statements.
DATA statement
END

BLOCK DATA is not included in Subset FORTRAN

The BLOCK DATA subprogram is used to provide initial values for variables and arrays in named COMMON. If any variables in a named COMMON block are initialized, all variables in the block must be specified in the named COMMON declaration in the BLOCK DATA subprogram.

---

prone to equivalence arrays, which are not of the same dimension. The form is:

EQUIVALANCE $(v_1, v_2, \ldots, v_n), (A_1, A_2, \ldots, A_n)$

where all the variable names or arrays listed inside each set of parentheses are to be assigned to the same memory location.

Example

EQUIVALENCE (X, Y)	X and Y are to be assigned to the same memory location.
EQUIVALENCE (A(3),X)	X and A(3) are to reference the same location.
EQUIVALENCE (I, J), (R, S)	I and J are the same, and R and S are the same.
Incorrect EQUIVALENCE (A(3), B(9))	This is incorrect because two array elements cannot be equivalenced.

The COMMON and EQUIVALENCE declarations should appear in the program ahead of any statements using the variables that they declare. A recommended order for these declarations (if any of the variables to be equivalenced are in COMMON) is:

1 DIMENSION   }   or, as recommended, include dimensioning in
2 COMMON   }   COMMON declaration.
3 EQUIVALENCE

The DATA statement follows these specifications.

Example

```
DIMENSION A(100),B(50) ⎫
COMMON A,B              ⎬      or COMMON A(100),B(50)
EQUIVALENCE (VALUE1,A(1)), (VALUE2,B(50))  ⎭
```

These three statements indicate that the two arrays, A and B, are to be located in the COMMON area. The variables A(1) and VALUE1 are different names for the same storage location, and VALUE2 and B(50) share common locations.

Self-testing exercise 5-3

1 Two subprograms and a main program all refer to the same set of three variables called X, IOTA, and CHI and to a 100-element array called SILLY by the two subprograms and DILLY by the main program. Write three statements for the three program units to declare these variables as COMMON (and dimension the arrays).

2 In a subroutine called SORT to sort an array, the array to be sorted is called X and dimensioned as 100. The main program also refers to the array as X and dimensions it as 100. Write statements to associate the two arrays X, (*a*) using the argument lists and (*b*) using COMMON declarations. Also, dimension the arrays.

3 Redo the answers to problem 2 assuming the name of the array is X in the subroutine and A in the main program.

4 Redo the answer to problem 1 putting the variables in named COMMON and initializing all variables to zero.

Case program structure

The case program coding structure is an extension of the IF and block IF selection structures. In the case structure, there are normally more than two program paths, one of which is selected (Figure 5-3). The case structure is useful because in many problems there are different processing actions to be performed on different classes or types of data. Each programming path may be termed a case. For example, the selection of a processing path for the different cases may be based on a code or other characteristic of the data. The multiple path selection can be programmed in FORTRAN by a set of IF statements or ELSEIF statements, but is usually more clearly programmed by the computed GOTO statement.

The computed GOTO transfers control to one of several program state-

Figure 5-3
Case structure.

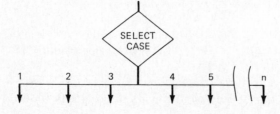

ments based on the value of an integer variable (or integer expression). The specifications are summarized in the box.

COMPUTED GOTO STATEMENT

GOTO $(s_1, s_2, s_3, \ldots, s_n)$[,]$i$

i = integer variable (or integer expression in 1977 full FORTRAN)
s_i = statement label

GOTO can also be written as GO TO. If the value of the integer variable (or the integer expression) is 1, control transfers to the first statement listed; if the value is 2, control goes to the second statement, etc. If the integer value is less than 1 or greater than n (number of statements listed), control goes to the statement following the computed GOTO (or may cause a fatal error in some older FORTRANs).

The maximum number of statement labels is not defined by the standard, but some compilers have limits. The comma following the right parenthesis, separating it from i, is required by many older compilers; it is optional in 1977 standard. Integer variable is required for i by many older compilers and by 1977 Subset FORTRAN; any integer expression is allowed by 1977 full standard.

A statement number can be repeated in the list so that, for example, both a value of 1 and a value of 3 will transfer control to the same statement. An integer value less than 1 or greater than the number of statements listed will cause the statement following to be executed; this is useful in error control. By always placing an error-control or error-message statement following a computed GOTO, the out-of-range condition is easily detected and reported. But since some older FORTRANs treat the out-of-range condition as a fatal error, it is preferable to explicitly test for out-of-range variable value before executing the computed GOTO. Some simple examples illustrate the form of the statement.

Computed GOTO example 1

A program will perform one of four types of statistical analysis based on a code of 1 to 4 input by the user. The input value is assigned to ICODE. The statement labels for the four cases are 201, 301, 401, and 501. The case statement to select the processing path is:

```
GOTO (201, 301, 401, 501), ICODE
```

Computed GOTO example 2

A program should transfer control to 410 if JVALUE is 1 or 2, to 450 if JVALUE is 3 or 4, and to 600 if JVALUE is 5. If JVALUE is zero, negative, or more than 5, print an error message.

```
GOTO (410, 410, 450, 450, 600), JVALUE
PRINT *,'JVALUE OUT OF RANGE', JVALUE
```

Computed GOTO example 3

A program to analyze the distribution of amount of sales by invoice may set up the following four categories (it is assumed that no sale exceeds $2999):

Less than $500
$500 to $999.99
$1000 to $1999.99
$2000 to $2999.99

If sales are negative, zero, or over \$2999.99, then control should go to an error statement (number 910). Sales are input in the form XXXX.XX. A partial program and flowchart are shown in Figure 5-4.

The computed GOTO in the example could have been written as a single statement:

```
GO TO ( . . . .), INT(1.0 + SALES / 500.0)
```

It was written in two steps for clarity in the example. In Figure 5-4, the INT (or IFIX) function that takes the integer portion of the result is redundant because there will be truncation across the equals sign to the integer variable K. However, use of an explicit function reduces the chance of error in under-

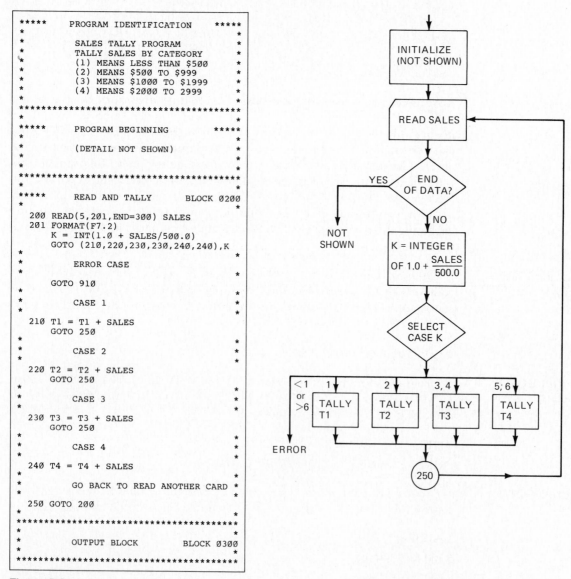

Figure 5-4
Partial program and flowchart for sales-tally program.

standing and maintaining the program. Note how the statement following the computed GOTO specifies transfer to an error-handling block.

To clarify the cases following a computed GOTO, it is useful to precede the beginning of each case (before each statement label specified in the computed GOTO) by a comment line that indicates the case to which the coding to follow applies. This is illustrated in Figure 5-4.

There must be GOTOs following each tally instruction. Note that all of the GOTOs are forward to a single statement at the end of the group (statement 250), which transfers back to begin with a new card. This is usually a clearer programming approach than frequent backward transfers.

Self-testing exercise 5-4

1 What happens if X = 4.51 in the execution of

```
GOTO (100, 200, 310, 450, 710) INT(X)
```

2 An input code (called ICODE) is either 2, 3, 4, or 5. Different processing is to be performed in each case (statement 200, 300, 400, and 500). If ICODE is one or less, or greater than 5, go to 900. Write a computed GOTO to perform this case selection.

3 Redo problem 2 with an ICODE of 0, 1, 2, and 3.

4 A programmer following the 1977 FORTRAN standard writes a computed GOTO as follows:

```
GOTO (100, 200, 400, 600), IX + 2
```

The statement is rejected. Rewrite in FORTRAN acceptable to both old and new versions.

5 Code problem 2 using IF statements. This illustrates the power and simplicity of the computed GOTO in a case situation.

6 A subroutine is used for all error messages. Before transferring to the error-message subroutine, the calling program defines a code from 1 to 6 for one of six messages as well as a value for a variable (call it XERR) that is to be printed with the error message. Write the statements to define the code, to call the subroutine, to define the subroutine, and to select from among the message cases.

Summary

Subprograms are an important programming technique useful for reducing the complexity of large programs, for separate writing and testing of parts of programs, for making use of prewritten routines, etc. The two types of subprograms are function subprograms and subroutines.

The function subprogram returns a single value to the main program. It is used for coding user-defined functions. It is invoked by using the function name, together with arguments, in an expression.

The subroutine subprogram is a separate program that is invoked by a CALL statement. The arguments of the CALL statement are variable names for data to be used by the subroutine and data names assigned to receive the results (if not in common storage). A subroutine may return no result, one result, or multiple results.

The COMMON declaration is an alternate method for two or more subprograms to communicate. Common storage assignments allow different subprograms to access the same storage locations, thereby using the same data.

The case structure is an extension of the selection structure in instances where multiple cases can be identified by integers between 1 and *n*. The case coding structure for selecting among multiple program paths for different cases is implemented in FORTRAN by the computed GOTO.

Answers to self-testing exercises
Exercise 5-1

1   The function subprogram SUM sums the elements of a 100-entry array. The main program reads the array A, takes the square root of the sum of A returned by the function, and prints the result.

2   The function IBOY returns an integer result; the variables in the calling argument list are real (X), real (A), and integer (J).

3
```
FUNCTION ROOT (A, B, C)
DESCR = B**2 - 4.0 * A * C
IF (DESCR .LE. 0.0) THEN
    ROOT = 0.0
ELSE
    ROOT = -B + SORT(DESCR) / (2.0 * A)
    IF (ROOT .LT. 0.0) ROOT = 0.0
ENDIF
RETURN
```

4   `X = A**2 + ROOT (X, Y, Z)`

5
```
FUNCTION DIFF (RATE1, RATE2, AMT)
DIFF = AMT * (RATE2 - RATE1)
RETURN  (optional)
END
```

6   `D = DIFF (XINT1, XINT2, AMOUNT)`

Exercise 5-2

1   The subroutine need not have arguments; the functions must have at least one argument. The subroutine returns any number of results; the function subprogram returns one result. The function is used in an assignment statement; the subroutine is called by a single, separate statement.

2
```
SUBROUTINE DIFF (RATE1, RATE2, AMT, RESULT)
RESULT = AMT * (RATE2 - RATE1)
RETURN  (optional)
END
```

3   `CALL DIFF (XINT1, XINT2, AMOUNT, D)`
The result of the call is to make D in the main program equal to the RESULT in the subroutine.

4
```
    SUBROUTINE MOVE (B)
    DIMENSION B(20, 20)
    DO  110 I = 1, 20
        L = I + 1
        DO 100 J = L, 20
```

```
              TEMP = B(I, J)
              B(I, J) = B(J, I)
              B(J, I) = TEMP
100      CONTINUE
110 CONTINUE
         RETURN  (optional)
         END
```

5   `CALL MOVE (ALPHA)`

Exercise 5-3

---

1   Main program   `COMMON X, IOTA, CHI, DILLY (100)`
Subprogram 1   `COMMON X, IOTA, CHI, SILLY (100)`
Subprogram 2   `COMMON X, IOTA, CHI, SILLY (100)`

---

2   (*a*) Argument list

Subroutine   `SUBROUTINE SORT (X)`
Main program   `CALL SORT (X)`

(*b*) Common

Subroutine   `SUBROUTINE SORT`

`DIMENSION X(100)` }
`COMMON X` }   or `COMMON X(100)`

Main program   `DIMENSION X(100)` }
`COMMON X` }   or `COMMON X(100)`

`CALL SORT`

---

3   (*a*) Subroutine   `SUBROUTINE SORT(X)`

Main program   `CALL SORT(A)`

(*b*) Subroutine   `SUBROUTINE SORT`

`DIMENSION X(100)` }
`COMMON X` }   or `COMMON X(100)`

Main program   `DIMENSION A(100)` }
`COMMON A` }   or `COMMON A(100)`

`CALL SORT`

Note that since A and X were both the first item in COMMON, they will occupy the same storage and therefore be equivalent.

4   Main program `COMMON / G1 / X, IOTA, CHI, DILLY (100)`
Subprogram 1 `COMMON / G1 / X, IOTA, CHI, SILLY (100)`
Subprogram 2 `COMMON / G1 / X, IOTA, CHI, SILLY (100)`
`BLOCK DATA`
`COMMON / G1 / X, IOTA, CHI, DILLY (100)`
`DATA X, IOTA, CHI, DILLY / 103 * 0.0 /`
`END`

Exercise 5-4

1 It will go to statement 450 because X will be truncated to 4. It could also have been coded in two steps.

```
JX = INT (X)
GOTO (100, 200, 310, 450, 710), JX
```

2 Subtract 1 from ICODE to make it within limits of 1, 2, 3, and 4.

```
    GOTO (200, 300, 400, 500), ICODE - 1
900 for out of limits
or  ICODE = ICODE - 1
    GOTO (200, 300, 400, 500), ICODE
900 for out of limits
```

3 Add 1 to ICODE to make it fit the form of 1, 2, 3, or 4.

```
    GOTO (200, 300, 400, 500), ICODE + 1
900 for out of limits
or  ICODE = ICODE + 1
    GOTO (200, 300, 400, 500), ICODE
900 for out of limits
```

4
```
I = IX + 2
GOTO (100, 200, 400, 600), I
```

5
```
IF (ICODE.LT.2.OR.ICODE.GT.5) GOTO  900
IF (ICODE.EQ.2) GOTO 200
IF (ICODE.EQ.3) GOTO 300
IF (ICODE.EQ.4) GOTO 400
IF (ICODE.EQ.5) GOTO 500
```

6 Main program
```
JCODE =
XERR =
CALL (JCODE, XERR)
Subprogram
SUBROUTINE (KODE, XMSSG)
GOTO (100, 200, 300, 400, 500, 600),KODE
```

Questions and problems

1 What is the difference between the function subprogram and subroutine?

2 What is the difference between the COMMON and the EQUIVALENCE statement?

3 What is the effect of each of the following statements or declarations?
(*a*) CALL WILMA
(*b*) CALL MOM (DAD, KIDS, SIS)
(*c*) EQUIVALENCE (TEEN, SILLY, CRAZY)
(*d*) FUNCTION NICE (I, J, K)
(*e*) SUBROUTINE COME (X, Y, Z, B)
(*f*) X = TALLY (GAMMA1, GAMMA2)

4 Make X in a main program equal to $\sqrt[3]{A^2 + B^2}$. Do this step using two different methods: a function subprogram and a subroutine (using two methods for transferring the answer). Write complete subprograms but show only the necessary segment of the main program.

5 Write a main program segment to read n (say 10) data items in F10.2 fields and print the input. Write a subroutine to order the data items from smallest to largest. Code statements for the main program to call this subroutine and then print out the ordered array. For a small array, interchange sorting is satisfactory. In interchange sorting, the first variable is compared with each of the other variables. If the value being compared is smaller, the two are interchanged. This continues through the array. The result is the smallest value in cell 1. The same procedure is followed for cell 2, etc. See Figure 5-2 for large-to-small sort logic.

chapter **5 B**

Example programs and programming exercises using subprograms and case structure

General notes on chapter 5 examples

The example programs illustrate the use of subroutines and function subprograms, COMMON and EQUIVALENCE statements, and the case structure. The program for general example 5, payroll report, makes use of two function subprograms and a subroutine. It includes the case structure as well as named and blank COMMON, EQUIVALENCE, DIMENSION, and DATA statements. The programs for statistical example 5, numerical integration, uses those same features, except for the case structure. We used the optional double slashes without a name for the blank COMMON declaration. This technique more clearly shows the difference between blank and named COMMON declarations. An additional section, *subroutine and function identification*, has been added to the variable identification block.

General program example 5 — payroll reports

The program produces the same sort of reports as its predecessor in Chapter 4 for gross pay, total deductions, and net pay. The report-printing logic is the same except that several other error conditions are checked and hence the "notes" section of the payroll report is altered. Retirement and tax computations are more complex and make use of additional input data. Tax is calculated by a function and retirement is calculated by a subroutine. The case structure is used in the pension subroutine. A rounding function is used to adjust all dollar and cents values to the nearest penny.

Problem description for general example 5

The program is to read employee pay data and produce two reports: (1) Error and Control Report and (2) Report of Pay Amounts. The latter report is to contain a line for each employee and a line of totals at the end of the report. The employees are to be grouped by department in the report. In the Report of Pay Amounts, net pay that is negative or over $300.00 is accompanied by a warning note. Also, errors in input code for union/management employees are to be noted.

The first input for the program consists of a set of five records with department numbers and names, one pair per card or input line. Input validation for this input consists of visual verification output that echoes the table. Subsequent input data consists of one record (card or input line) for each employee, giving ID number, name, department number where employed, hours worked, wage rate, miscellaneous deductions, number of dependents, and union/management code. During reading of this employee input data, error messages reflecting the detection of data-type errors or invalid data are printed immediately, and the error record is not processed further for the subsequent Report of Pay Amounts. After all records are read and validated for input errors, a total record count and number of rejected records are printed.

Program documentation for general example 5

The documentation of program design is given by a pseudocode description (Figure 5-5) and a program flowchart (Figure 5-6). The program listing is shown in Figure 5-7. Test data is documented in Figure 5-8, the corresponding Error and Control Report is given in Figure 5-9, and the Report of Pay Amounts is shown in Figure 5-10.

Notes on general example 5

The variable identification block has been enlarged to include a section to identify any subroutine and function subprograms by name and to provide a brief description. Note that throughout this entire block, each name must be unique.

Figure 5-5
Pseudocode description of general program example 5—payroll reports.

Main program

```
Establish storage common with other program units
Dimension arrays for 5 departments and 15 employees (14 plus 1 potential error
    case)
Initialize data for departments, net pay limits, and maximum number of employees
PRINT heading at top of page for Error and Control Report
Zero accumulators and initialize counters and constants
READ and echo department numbers and names for visual validation
PRINT error message heading
READ an employee data card and test for end of data and data-type errors
    If no more cards, go to Print Detail Report, else continue
    If data-type error, increment record counter, print message, and go back to
        READ an employee data card, else continue
Increment record counter
Check for valid department number
    If invalid, print message and go back to READ an employee data card
    Else continue
Compute overtime and gross pay
Compute taxes with tax rate function
Compute retirement contribution with pension subroutine
Compute total deductions
Compute net pay
Add employee gross pay, total deduction, and net pay to totals
Increment accepted employee records counter by 1
Test number of accepted records
    If number exceeds limit of array storage, print excess records message
    Else go back to READ an employee data card
Print Detail Report
Compute invalid record count
Print record counts at bottom of Error and Control Report
PRINT column headings for Report of Pay Amounts at top of new page
DO for all department numbers in order
    Select all employees in that department by matching departmental number
        with department number in employee record
    For each matching employee check for net pay outside limits. If invalid pay, set
        error note, else continue
    PRINT detail for matching employee
End of DO
Print summary totals and error-code explanations
STOP
```

Figure 5-5
Continued.

Function rate

Establish storage common with other program units
Test dependents code
    IF one dependent use standard rate;
    IF more than one dependent

$$RATE = \left(1 - \frac{N}{N+6}\right) * \text{standard rate}$$

    [N = number of dependents]
RETURN

Subroutine pnsion

Establish storage common with other program units
Test for legal employee type code
    If out of bounds, set error note to 2 and set type code to 1 as default option
    Else continue
Select case for employee type
    Case 1 (Union employee)
      Pension contribution = 6 percent of GRSPAY
    Case 2 (Management employee)
      Pension contribution is 5 percent of $200 base pay plus 7.5 percent of pay
      over base
RETURN

Function pnyrnd

Round a value to nearest penny
RETURN

Block data

Declare named COMMON storage
Initialize variables in named COMMON with DATA statement

    Since COMMON, DIMENSION, and DATA statements all control storage (memory) allocation, they are grouped at the beginning, before any executable code, in a single storage allocation block. However, data locations in common storage cannot be initialized using a DATA statement. The variables to be initialized are specified as being in named COMMON, and the DATA statement to initialize them is placed in a separate BLOCK DATA subprogram.

    Many of the features of this program are identical to general program example 4. However, the computation block has been altered somewhat to reflect more complex formulas (called RATE) of the number of dependents. While this relationship could have been inserted directly in the program in

Figure 5-6
Program flowchart for
general example 5—pay-
roll reports. (Numbers
next to symbols are line
numbers from program
listing.)

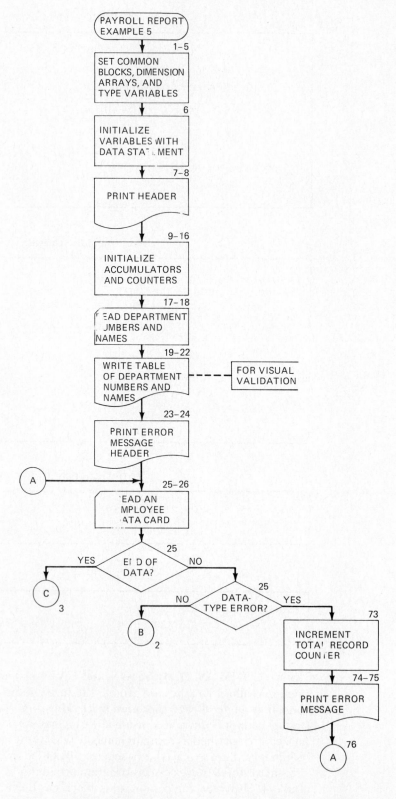

Figure 5-6
Continued.

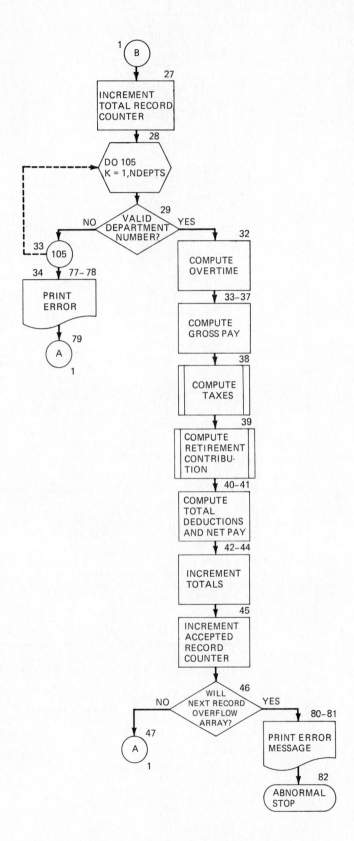

Figure 5-6
Continued.

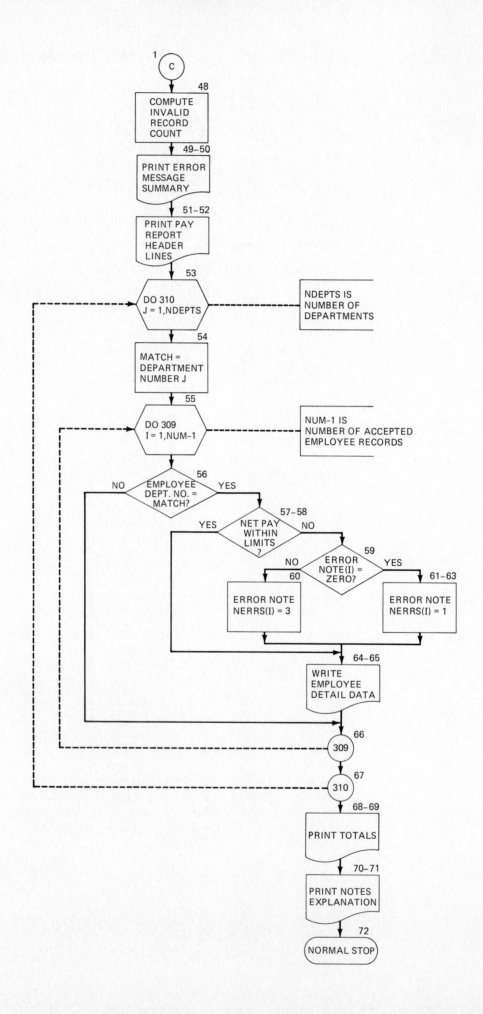

Figure 5-6
Continued.

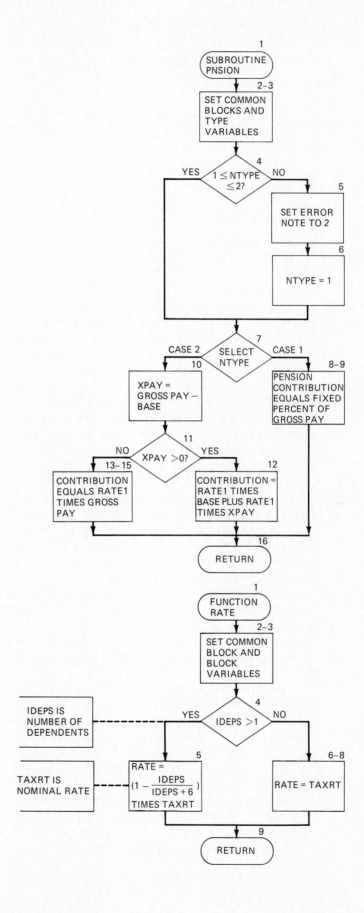

Figure 5-6
Continued.

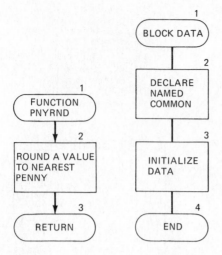

place of code line 38, it was preferable to code it as a function subprogram so that the specific formula could be isolated from the general program flow. If the formula changes, it is easily identified for changes to be made. Similarly, a subroutine called PNSION has been used to implement the specific procedure for computing pension contributions. The latter makes use of the computed GOTO and the case structure. The FORTRAN 1977 standard says that if the selection variable for a computed GOTO is less than 1 or greater than the number of cases cited, control is to go to the following statement, but many earlier compilers consider such a condition to be a fatal error causing abnormal program termination. Therefore, a specific test was made in the PNSION subroutine line 4 so that the program will work for earlier FORTRAN as well.

The test for error in the union/management code has been placed in the PNSION subroutine. The default option in the case of a code that is neither 1 nor 2 is to assume it is 1 (union) and set up an error code for the line being processed. This is an example of the use of default options to allow processing to continue. The most likely value is inserted and a warning message is output to alert the user to check that item.

As a matter of style to clarify program units, the last line of the main program has the comment END OF MAIN PROGRAM embedded in the last (comment) line of asterisks. An END OF SUBPROGRAM message is in the last line of each subprogram. Note that the identification blocks also appear at the beginning of each subprogram and block structuring is used as appropriate.

In Chapters 3A and 3B, the problem was discussed of format rounding in business-type reports that show all figures to the nearest cent and contain totals based on footing (adding down columns), and crossfooting (adding across rows). The result in the report footing and crossfooting totals may differ slightly if rounded data is used for one and unrounded data for the other. One solution is to round all data internally in the same form as it is to be printed out (nearest penny) and use the rounded data in all footing and crossfooting. It is cumbersome to write the rounding computations as part of every statement where applicable. An alternative method is to use a rounding function. Such a function, called PNYRND, is part of the pay report program. Note how it consists of only one assignment statement, a RETURN statement, and an

Figure 5-7
Listing of FORTRAN program for general example 5—payroll report

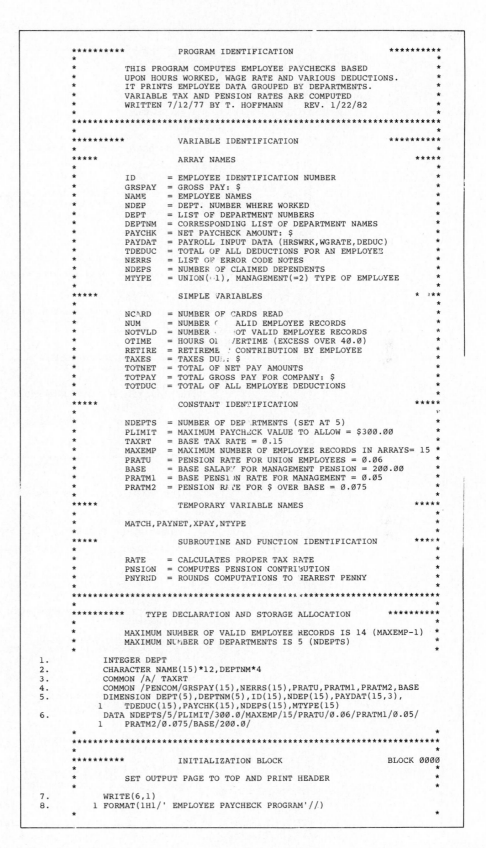

```
*********          PROGRAM IDENTIFICATION                *********
*                                                                *
*        THIS PROGRAM COMPUTES EMPLOYEE PAYCHECKS BASED          *
*        UPON HOURS WORKED, WAGE RATE AND VARIOUS DEDUCTIONS.     *
*        IT PRINTS EMPLOYEE DATA GROUPED BY DEPARTMENTS.          *
*        VARIABLE TAX AND PENSION RATES ARE COMPUTED             *
*        WRITTEN 7/12/77 BY T. HOFFMANN    REV. 1/22/82          *
*                                                                *
******************************************************************
*                                                                *
*********          VARIABLE IDENTIFICATION               *********
*                                                                *
*****            ARRAY NAMES                             *****
*                                                                *
*        ID      = EMPLOYEE IDENTIFICATION NUMBER               *
*        GRSPAY  = GROSS PAY: $                                 *
*        NAME    = EMPLOYEE NAMES                               *
*        NDEP    = DEPT. NUMBER WHERE WORKED                    *
*        DEPT    = LIST OF DEPARTMENT NUMBERS                   *
*        DEPTNM  = CORRESPONDING LIST OF DEPARTMENT NAMES       *
*        PAYCHK  = NET PAYCHECK AMOUNT: $                       *
*        PAYDAT  = PAYROLL INPUT DATA (HRSWRK,WGRATE,DEDUC)     *
*        TDEDUC  = TOTAL OF ALL DEDUCTIONS FOR AN EMPLOYEE      *
*        NERRS   = LIST OF ERROR CODE NOTES                     *
*        NDEPS   = NUMBER OF CLAIMED DEPENDENTS                 *
*        MTYPE   = UNION(=1), MANAGEMENT(=2) TYPE OF EMPLOYEE   *
*                                                                *
*****            SIMPLE VARIABLES                        *****
*                                                                *
*        NCARD   = NUMBER OF CARDS READ                         *
*        NUM     = NUMBER OF VALID EMPLOYEE RECORDS            *
*        NOTVLD  = NUMBER OF NOT VALID EMPLOYEE RECORDS        *
*        OTIME   = HOURS OF OVERTIME (EXCESS OVER 40.0)         *
*        RETIRE  = RETIREMENT CONTRIBUTION BY EMPLOYEE          *
*        TAXES   = TAXES DUE: $                                 *
*        TOTNET  = TOTAL OF NET PAY AMOUNTS                     *
*        TOTPAY  = TOTAL GROSS PAY FOR COMPANY: $              *
*        TOTDUC  = TOTAL OF ALL EMPLOYEE DEDUCTIONS            *
*                                                                *
*****            CONSTANT IDENTIFICATION                 *****
*                                                                *
*        NDEPTS  = NUMBER OF DEPARTMENTS (SET AT 5)            *
*        PLIMIT  = MAXIMUM PAYCHECK VALUE TO ALLOW = $300.00    *
*        TAXRT   = BASE TAX RATE = 0.15                         *
*        MAXEMP  = MAXIMUM NUMBER OF EMPLOYEE RECORDS IN ARRAYS= 15 *
*        PRATU   = PENSION RATE FOR UNION EMPLOYEES = 0.06      *
*        BASE    = BASE SALARY FOR MANAGEMENT PENSION = 200.00  *
*        PRATM1  = BASE PENSION RATE FOR MANAGEMENT = 0.05      *
*        PRATM2  = PENSION RATE FOR $ OVER BASE = 0.075         *
*                                                                *
*****            TEMPORARY VARIABLE NAMES                *****
*                                                                *
*        MATCH,PAYNET,XPAY,NTYPE                               *
*                                                                *
*****            SUBROUTINE AND FUNCTION IDENTIFICATION  *****
*                                                                *
*        RATE    = CALCULATES PROPER TAX RATE                  *
*        PNSION  = COMPUTES PENSION CONTRIBUTION               *
*        PNYRND  = ROUNDS COMPUTATIONS TO NEAREST PENNY        *
*                                                                *
******************************************************************
*                                                                *
*********   TYPE DECLARATION AND STORAGE ALLOCATION      *********
*                                                                *
*        MAXIMUM NUMBER OF VALID EMPLOYEE RECORDS IS 14 (MAXEMP-1) *
*        MAXIMUM NUMBER OF DEPARTMENTS IS 5 (NDEPTS)           *
*                                                                *
1.        INTEGER DEPT
2.        CHARACTER NAME(15)*12,DEPTNM*4
3.        COMMON /A/ TAXRT
4.        COMMON /PENCOM/GRSPAY(15),NERRS(15),PRATU,PRATM1,PRATM2,BASE
5.        DIMENSION DEPT(5),DEPTNM(5),ID(15),NDEP(15),PAYDAT(15,3),
         1    TDEDUC(15),PAYCHK(15),NDEPS(15),MTYPE(15)
6.        DATA NDEPTS/5/PLIMIT/300.0/MAXEMP/15/PRATU/0.06/PRATM1/0.05/
         1    PRATM2/0.075/BASE/200.0/
*                                                                *
******************************************************************
*                                                                *
*********          INITIALIZATION BLOCK              BLOCK 0000
*                                                                *
*        SET OUTPUT PAGE TO TOP AND PRINT HEADER               *
*                                                                *
7.        WRITE(6,1)
8.      1 FORMAT(1H1/' EMPLOYEE PAYCHECK PROGRAM'//)
*                                                                *
```

Figure 5-7
Continued.

```
          *        ZERO ACCUMULATORS AND INITIALIZE COUNTERS         *
          *                                                          *
  9.            TOTPAY = Ø.Ø
 1Ø.            TOTNET = Ø.Ø
 11.            TOTDUC = Ø.Ø
 12.            NCARD = Ø
 13.            NUM = 1
 14.            DO 6 I = 1,MAXEMP
 15.              NERRS(I) = Ø
 16.        6 CONTINUE
          *                                                          *
          *        READ AND PRINT DEPARTMENT NUMBERS AND NAMES        *
          *                                                          *
 17.            READ(5,7) (DEPT(K),DEPTNM(K), K=1,NDEPTS)
 18.          7 FORMAT(I4,A4)
 19.            WRITE(6,9)
 2Ø.          9 FORMAT('Ø','TABLE OF DEPARTMENTS'/' NUMBER    NAME')
 21.            WRITE(6,11) (DEPT(K),DEPTNM(K),K=1,NDEPTS)
 22.         11 FORMAT(2X,I4,4X,A4)
          *                                                          *
          *        PRINT ERROR MESSAGE HEADER                        *
          *                                                          *
 23.            WRITE(6,13)
 24.         13 FORMAT(///6X,'ERROR MESSAGES DURING DATA INPUT'//)
          *************************************************************
          *                                                          *
          *********        READ EMPLOYEE DATA            BLOCK Ø1ØØ
          *                                                          *
 25.      1Ø1 READ(5,1Ø2,END=3Ø1,ERR=9Ø1) ID(NUM),NAME(NUM),
          1     NDEP(NUM),(PAYDAT(NUM,K),K=1,3),NDEPS(NUM),MTYPE(NUM)
 26.      1Ø2 FORMAT(I5,A12,I4,F4.1,F4.2,F5.2,I2,I1)
 27.            NCARD = NCARD + 1
          *                                                          *
          *        CHECK FOR VALID DEPARTMENT NUMBER IN EMPLOYEE CARD *
          *        WHEN FOUND, PROCESS EMPLOYEE DATA                  *
          *                                                          *
 28.            DO 1Ø5 K=1,NDEPTS
 29.              IF(DEPT(K).EQ.NDEP(NUM)) GOTO 2Ø1
 3Ø.      1Ø5 CONTINUE
          *                                                          *
          *        ERROR -- NO MATCH FOUND FOR EMPLOYEE DEPT. NUMBER  *
          *                                                          *
 31.            GOTO 9Ø3
          *                                                          *
          *************************************************************
          *                                                          *
          *********        COMPUTATION BLOCK             BLOCK Ø2ØØ
          *                                                          *
          *        COMPUTE PAY, INCLUDING OVERTIME, IF ANY.          *
          *                                                          *
 32.      2Ø1 OTIME = PAYDAT(NUM,1) - 4Ø.Ø
 33.            IF(OTIME.GT.Ø.Ø) THEN
 34.              GRSPAY(NUM) = PNYRND((4Ø.Ø + 1.5*OTIME)*PAYDAT(NUM,2))
 35.            ELSE
 36.              GRSPAY(NUM) = PNYRND(PAYDAT(NUM,1)*PAYDAT(NUM,2))
 37.            ENDIF
          *                                                          *
          *        COMPUTE TAXES USING RATE FUNCTION                 *
          *                                                          *
 38.            TAXES = PNYRND(GRSPAY(NUM)*RATE(NDEPS(NUM)))
          *                                                          *
          *        COMPUTE RETIREMENT CONTRIBUTION BASED UPON         *
          *        UNION/MANAGEMENT TYPE                             *
          *                                                          *
 39.            CALL PNSION(MTYPE(NUM),RETIRE,NUM)
 4Ø.            TDEDUC(NUM) = PAYDAT(NUM,3) + TAXES + RETIRE
 41.            PAYCHK(NUM) = GRSPAY(NUM) - TDEDUC(NUM)
          *                                                          *
          *        INCREMENT TOTALS AND COUNTER                      *
          *                                                          *
 42.            TOTPAY = TOTPAY + GRSPAY(NUM)
 43.            TOTDUC = TOTDUC + TDEDUC(NUM)
 44.            TOTNET = TOTNET + PAYCHK(NUM)
 45.            NUM = NUM + 1
          *                                                          *
          *        TEST TO PREVENT ARRAY OVERFLOW. IF ARRAYS NOT FULL *
          *        RETURN TO READ NEXT EMPLOYEE DATA CARD.           *
          *                                                          *
 46.            IF(NUM.GT.MAXEMP) GOTO 9Ø6
          *                                                          *
          *        GO BACK TO READ ANOTHER DATA CARD                 *
          *                                                          *
 47.            GOTO 1Ø1
          *                                                          *
```

Figure 5-7
Continued.

```
        ***************************************************************
        *                                                             *
        *********          PRINT DETAIL BY DEPARTMENT GROUPING   BLOCK Ø3ØØ
        *                                                             *
        *          PRINT SUMMARY OF DATA INPUT MESSAGES              *
        *                                                             *
48.     3Ø1 NOTVLD = NCARD - NUM + 1
49.         WRITE(6,3Ø2) NCARD,NOTVLD
5Ø.     3Ø2 FORMAT('Ø',I4,' CARDS READ'/I5,' CARDS REJECTED')
        *                                                             *
        *          PRINT HEADER/TITLE LINE FOR EMPLOYEE DETAIL       *
        *                                                             *
51.         WRITE(6,3Ø3)
52.     3Ø3 FORMAT('1'/5X,'EMPLOYEE',5X,'ID',3X,'DEPT',3X,'GROSS',4X,
       1        'TOTAL',6X,'NET',4X,'NOTES'/7X,'NAME',12X,'NAME',4X,
       2        'PAY',3X,'DEDUCTIONS',3X,'PAY')
        *                                                             *
        *          FOR EACH DEPARTMENT FIND EACH EMPLOYEE            *
        *                                                             *
53.         DO 31Ø J=1,NDEPTS
54.             MATCH = DEPT(J)
55.             DO 3Ø9 I=1,NUM-1
56.                 IF(NDEP(I).NE.MATCH) GOTO 3Ø9
57.                 PAYNET = PAYCHK(I)
        *                                                             *
        *          CHECK FOR VALID PAYCHECK AMOUNT                   *
        *                                                             *
58.                 IF(PAYNET.GT.Ø.Ø .AND. PAYNET.LE.PLIMIT) GOTO 3Ø7
59.                 IF(NERRS(I) .NE. Ø) THEN
6Ø.                     NERRS(I) = 3
61.                 ELSE
62.                     NERRS(I) = 1
63.                 ENDIF
64.     3Ø7         WRITE(6,3Ø4) NAME(I),ID(I),DEPTNM(J),
       1                GRSPAY(I),TDEDUC(I),PAYCHK(I),NERRS(I)
65.     3Ø4         FORMAT('Ø',2X,A12,I6,2X,A4,3X,F6.2,3X,F6.2,3X,F6.2,I6)
66.     3Ø9     CONTINUE
67.     31Ø CONTINUE
        *                                                             *
        ***************************************************************
        *                                                             *
        *********          PRINT SUMMARY AND TERMINATE          BLOCK Ø4ØØ
        *                                                             *
68.         WRITE(6,4Ø2) TOTPAY,TOTDUC,TOTNET
69.     4Ø2 FORMAT(//2ØX,'TOTALS',3X,F7.2,2F9.2)
7Ø.         WRITE(6,4Ø3)
71.     4Ø3 FORMAT(///5X,'NOTES'
       1        /5X,'Ø - NO ERRORS'
       2        /5X,'1 - NET PAY IS OUT OF BOUNDS. DO NOT ISSUE CHECK.'
       3        /5X,'2 - UNION/MANAGEMENT CODE ERROR. UNION ASSUMED.'
       4        /5X,'3 - BOTH TYPE 1 AND 2 ERRORS.')
72.         STOP
        *                                                             *
        ***************************************************************
        *                                                             *
        *********          ERROR MESSAGE BLOCK                  BLOCK Ø9ØØ
        *                                                             *
73.     9Ø1 NCARD = NCARD + 1
74.         WRITE(6,9Ø2) NCARD
75.     9Ø2 FORMAT(//' *****',' ERROR IN DATA CARD NUMBER ',I2,' *****')
76.         GOTO 9Ø8
        *****                                                     *****
77.     9Ø3 WRITE(6,9Ø4) NCARD
78.     9Ø4 FORMAT(//' ***** ERROR - DEPT. NO. NOT VALID. CARD NO.  ',I4,
       1        2X,'*****')
        *                                                             *
        *          GO BACK TO READ NEXT EMPLOYEE DATA CARD          *
        *                                                             *
79.     9Ø8 GOTO 1Ø1
        *****                                                     *****
8Ø.     9Ø6 WRITE(6,9Ø7) MAXEMP-1
81.     9Ø7 FORMAT(///' ***** ERROR. ATTEMPTED TO READ ',
       1        'MORE THAN',I3,'VALID DATA CARDS'/7X,'PROGRAM ABORTED. ')
82.         STOP
83.         END
        *                                                             *
        ********************************************************* END OF MAIN PROGRAM
```

```
1.          FUNCTION RATE(DEPS)
        *                                                             *
        *********          PROGRAM IDENTIFICATION               *********
        *                                                             *
        *          COMPUTE PROPER TAX RATE BASED UPON NUMBER OF DEPENDENTS *
        *                                                             *
```

Figure 5-7
Continued.

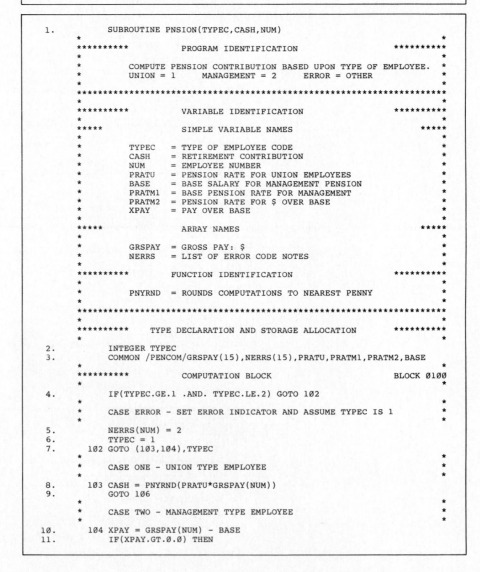

```
        *****************************************************************
        *                                                               *
        *********            VARIABLE IDENTIFICATION           *********
        *                                                               *
        *       DEPS    = NUMBER OF CLAIMED DEPENDENTS                   *
        *       TAXRT   = BASE TAX RATE                                  *
        *                                                               *
        *****************************************************************
        *                                                               *
        *********     TYPE DECLARATION AND STORAGE ALLOCATION  *********
        *                                                               *
  2.            INTEGER DEPS
  3.            COMMON /A/ TAXRT
        *                                                               *
        *********            COMPUTATION BLOCK           BLOCK Ø1ØØ
        *                                                               *
  4.            IF(DEPS .GT. 1) THEN
  5.                   RATE = (1.Ø - (FLOAT(DEPS)/FLOAT(DEPS+6)))*TAXRT
  6.            ELSE
  7.                   RATE = TAXRT
  8.            ENDIF
  9.            RETURN
 1Ø.            END
        *                                                               *
        ***************************************************  END OF SUBPROGRAM
```

```
  1.            SUBROUTINE PNSION(TYPEC,CASH,NUM)
        *                                                               *
        *********            PROGRAM IDENTIFICATION            *********
        *                                                               *
        *       COMPUTE PENSION CONTRIBUTION BASED UPON TYPE OF EMPLOYEE. *
        *       UNION = 1     MANAGEMENT = 2      ERROR = OTHER          *
        *                                                               *
        *****************************************************************
        *                                                               *
        *********            VARIABLE IDENTIFICATION           *********
        *                                                               *
        *****                SIMPLE VARIABLE NAMES                  *****
        *                                                               *
        *       TYPEC   = TYPE OF EMPLOYEE CODE                         *
        *       CASH    = RETIREMENT CONTRIBUTION                       *
        *       NUM     = EMPLOYEE NUMBER                               *
        *       PRATU   = PENSION RATE FOR UNION EMPLOYEES              *
        *       BASE    = BASE SALARY FOR MANAGEMENT PENSION            *
        *       PRATM1  = BASE PENSION RATE FOR MANAGEMENT              *
        *       PRATM2  = PENSION RATE FOR $ OVER BASE                  *
        *       XPAY    = PAY OVER BASE                                 *
        *                                                               *
        *****                    ARRAY NAMES                        *****
        *                                                               *
        *       GRSPAY  = GROSS PAY: $                                  *
        *       NERRS   = LIST OF ERROR CODE NOTES                      *
        *                                                               *
        *********            FUNCTION IDENTIFICATION           *********
        *                                                               *
        *       PNYRND  = ROUNDS COMPUTATIONS TO NEAREST PENNY          *
        *                                                               *
        *****************************************************************
        *                                                               *
        *********     TYPE DECLARATION AND STORAGE ALLOCATION  *********
        *                                                               *
  2.            INTEGER TYPEC
  3.            COMMON /PENCOM/GRSPAY(15),NERRS(15),PRATU,PRATM1,PRATM2,BASE
        *                                                               *
        *********            COMPUTATION BLOCK           BLOCK Ø1ØØ
        *                                                               *
  4.            IF(TYPEC.GE.1 .AND. TYPEC.LE.2) GOTO 1Ø2
        *                                                               *
        *       CASE ERROR - SET ERROR INDICATOR AND ASSUME TYPEC IS 1  *
        *                                                               *
  5.            NERRS(NUM) = 2
  6.            TYPEC = 1
  7.       1Ø2 GOTO (1Ø3,1Ø4),TYPEC
        *                                                               *
        *       CASE ONE - UNION TYPE EMPLOYEE                          *
        *                                                               *
  8.       1Ø3 CASH = PNYRND(PRATU*GRSPAY(NUM))
  9.            GOTO 1Ø6
        *                                                               *
        *       CASE TWO - MANAGEMENT TYPE EMPLOYEE                     *
        *                                                               *
 1Ø.       1Ø4 XPAY = GRSPAY(NUM) - BASE
 11.            IF(XPAY.GT.Ø.Ø) THEN
```

274

Figure 5-7
Continued.

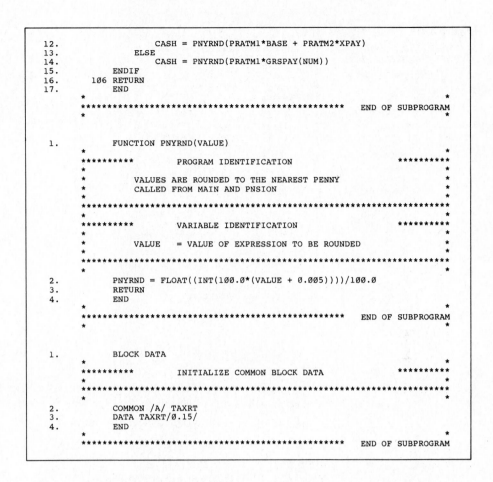

```
12.                    CASH = PNYRND(PRATM1*BASE + PRATM2*XPAY)
13.              ELSE
14.                    CASH = PNYRND(PRATM1*GRSPAY(NUM))
15.           ENDIF
16.      106 RETURN
17.          END
   *                                                                    *
   ****************************************************  END OF SUBPROGRAM
   *                                                                    *


1.            FUNCTION PNYRND(VALUE)
   *                                                                    *
   *********           PROGRAM IDENTIFICATION                  *********
   *                                                                    *
   *          VALUES ARE ROUNDED TO THE NEAREST PENNY                   *
   *          CALLED FROM MAIN AND PNSION                               *
   *                                                                    *
   **********************************************************************
   *                                                                    *
   *********           VARIABLE IDENTIFICATION                 *********
   *                                                                    *
   *          VALUE   = VALUE OF EXPRESSION TO BE ROUNDED               *
   *                                                                    *
   **********************************************************************
   *                                                                    *
2.            PNYRND = FLOAT((INT(100.0*(VALUE + 0.005))))/100.0
3.            RETURN
4.            END
   *                                                                    *
   ****************************************************  END OF SUBPROGRAM
   *                                                                    *


1.            BLOCK DATA
   *                                                                    *
   *********           INITIALIZE COMMON BLOCK DATA            *********
   *                                                                    *
   **********************************************************************
   *                                                                    *
2.            COMMON /A/ TAXRT
3.            DATA TAXRT/0.15/
4.            END
   *                                                                    *
   ****************************************************  END OF SUBPROGRAM
```

END statement. The function is used in statements in the main program. One example is line 36:

GRSPAY(NUM) = PNYRND(PAYDAT(NUM, 1)*(PAYDAT (NUM, 2))

See also lines 34 and 38.
In summary, review the following features of this pay report program.

Figure 5-8
Annotated input test data for general program example 5—payroll reports.

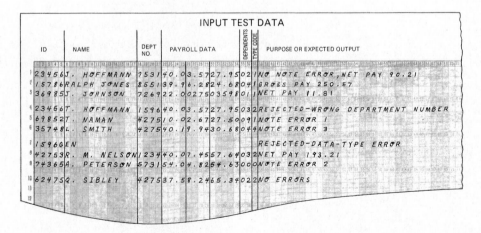

275

Figure 5-9
Example of Error and Control Report from payroll reports program.

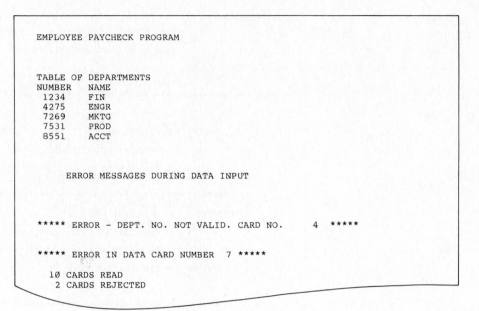

```
EMPLOYEE PAYCHECK PROGRAM


   TABLE OF DEPARTMENTS
   NUMBER   NAME
    1234    FIN
    4275    ENGR
    7269    MKTG
    7531    PROD
    8551    ACCT



       ERROR MESSAGES DURING DATA INPUT



***** ERROR - DEPT. NO. NOT VALID. CARD NO.     4  *****


***** ERROR IN DATA CARD NUMBER  7 *****

    10 CARDS READ
     2 CARDS REJECTED
```

1 The use of a function and a subroutine to isolate key computations that may need to change.

2 The identification list in the main program of all functions and subroutines called by the main program.

3 The use of named COMMON (lines 3 and 4).

4 The style of dimensioning all common arrays in the COMMON declaration and only local arrays in a DIMENSION statement (lines 4 and 5).

5 Use of a PNYRND rounding function.

Figure 5-10
Example of Report of Pay Amounts from payroll reports program.

EMPLOYEE NAME	ID	DEPT NAME	GROSS PAY	TOTAL DEDUCTIONS	NET PAY	NOTES
R. M. NELSON	42753	FIN	298.00	104.79	193.21	0
T. NAMAN	69852	ENGR	26.70	30.70	-4.00	1
L. SMITH	35748	ENGR	399.09	90.55	308.54	3
Q. SIBLEY	62475	ENGR	309.00	118.28	190.72	0
J. JOHNSON	36985	MKTG	60.50	48.69	11.81	0
J. HOFFMANN	23456	PROD	142.80	52.59	90.21	0
A. PETERSON	74365	PROD	294.02	116.37	177.65	2
RALPH JONES	15786	ACCT	250.57	62.26	188.31	0
		TOTALS	1780.68	624.23	1156.45	

```
NOTES
0 - NO ERRORS
1 - NET PAY IS OUT OF BOUNDS. DO NOT ISSUE CHECK.
2 - UNION/MANAGEMENT CODE ERROR. UNION ASSUMED.
3 - BOTH TYPE 1 AND 2 ERRORS.
```

EXAMPLE PROGRAMS AND PROGRAMMING EXERCISES

6 The use of the case structure in the pension subroutine.

7 The use of a default value and warning message as shown in the pension subroutine.

8 The use of a BLOCK DATA subprogram to initialize an array in named COMMON using a DATA statement.

Statistical program example 5 — numerical integration

Problem description for statistical example 5

The program compares different methods of numerical integration. The basic concept of computing small areas defined by the function to be integrated is still followed, but the area segments are approximated by three different methods and the results compared. The three methods are a simple rectangle method, a trapezoid method, and Simpson's rule. Each of the three methods is a separate subroutine; the function to be integrated is defined in a function subprogram.

Program documentation for statistical example 5

The documentation consists of a pseudocode program description (Figure 5-11), a program flowchart (Figure 5-12), a program listing (Figure 5-13), sample test data (Figure 5-14), and sample output (Figure 5-15).

Main program

Figure 5-11
Pseudocode description of statistical example program 5—numerical integration.

```
Dimension and initialize at zero array to hold error card sequence numbers
Establish storage common with other program units
PRINT heading at top of page
Initialize card counter, error card counter, and array to hold ordinates
READ a data card with beginning and ending x values and number of intervals for
     integration
     If no more cards, go to Termination, else continue
     If data-type error, increment card counter and bad record count, set number of
          error card in error array, and go to READ, else continue
Increment card counter
Test for even number of intervals (steps)
     IF number of segments is not even, print error message, add 1 to steps, and
          continue
     Else continue
Set initial abscissa to initial x value
Compute interval size based on beginning and ending value of x and number of
     intervals in range
Compute ordinates in range
Call Subroutines RECT, TRAP, and SIMP in order
PRINT results of three methods of integration
Go back to READ a data card
Termination
Print card counts and card numbers with data-type error
STOP
```

277

Figure 5-11
Continued.

Subroutine rect

Establish storage common with other program units
Set initial sum to value of ordinate zero
Add sum of ordinates for second through next to last one to initial sum
Area = interval size times sum of all ordinates
RETURN

Subroutine trap

Establish storage common with other program units
Set initial sum to average of zeroth and last ordinate
Add sum of balance of ordinates to initial sum
Area = interval size times sum of all ordinates
RETURN

Subroutine simp

Establish storage common with other program units
Set SUM1 to sum of zeroth and last ordinate
Initialize SUM2 and SUM4 to zero
Compute SUM2 as sum of even ordinates
Compute SUM4 as sum of odd ordinates
Area = (SUM1 + 2 * SUM2 + 4 * SUM4) * (interval width/3)
RETURN

Function anyf(x)

Any function of x may be used here
ANYF = $\sin x - \log x + e^x$
RETURN

Notes on statistical example 5

The variable identification block has been augmented with a section listing subroutine and function names. Note that all names in this block are unique. The storage allocation block now contains DIMENSION, blank and named COMMON, and DATA statements because these all affect memory (storage) allocation. Following the style suggestions in Chapter 5A, arrays used only in a particular program unit are defined in a DIMENSION statement. Arrays that are common to several program units are dimensioned in a COMMON statement. The named COMMON (line 2) is used to group variables that are logically associated.

The initialization block sets constants, zeros storage, and prints the output header. The block containing the main program's computation is quite short and explicit. The loop in lines 19–22 sets up the necessary ordinate values in the array ORD, which are then used by the several subroutines. This separa-

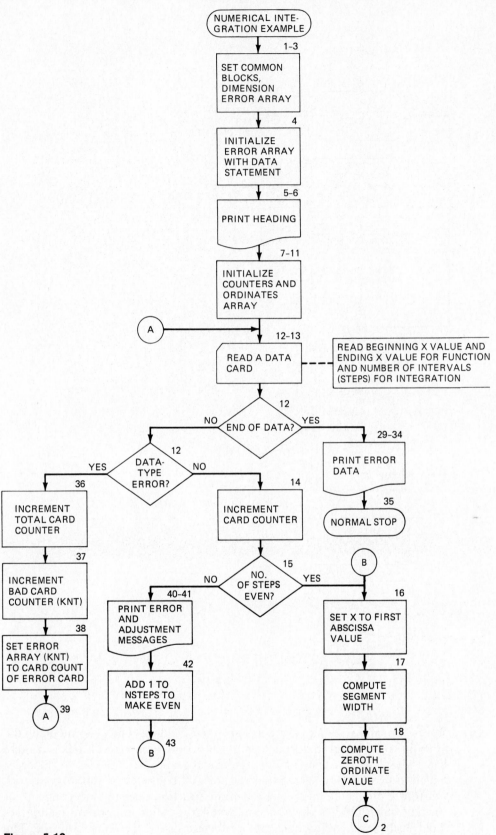

Figure 5-12
Program flowchart for statistical example 5—numerical integration. (Numbers next to symbols are line numbers from program listing.)

279

Figure 5-12
Continued.

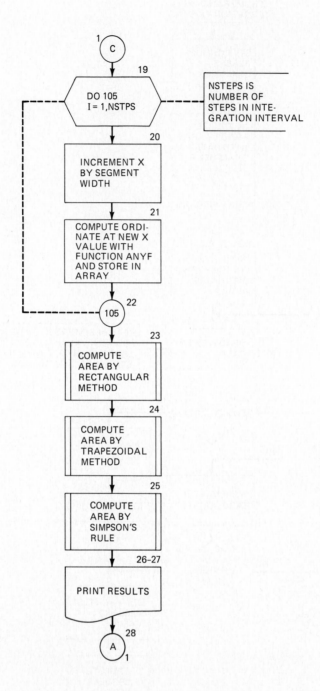

tion of functions allows easy program modification. The placement of the function to be integrated in a separate function subprogram makes it quite easy to test the efficiency of the several integration techniques on different functions by simply replacing the function-to-be-integrated subprogram with a different one. Note that a change in the function does not affect line 18 or line 21, which process the function. Similarly, other integration techniques could easily be added by replacing or substituting a different subroutine. The connection with the main program is through the CALL statement (lines 23–25).

Figure 5-12
Continued.

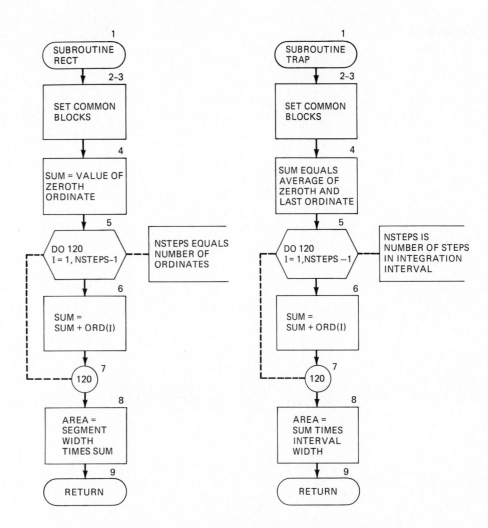

The variable identification and storage allocation blocks are similar in form in both the main program and the subprograms. As a matter of style, each program unit has a suitable END OF PROGRAM UNIT comment embedded in the last line of the program unit.

In order that error messages for cards with data-type errors will not clutter the principal output table, the card numbers for the unreadable cards are saved in an error array and printed at the end of the program. Line 12 is the READ statement with an ERR = 901, which tests for data-type errors. Lines 36–38 store the card numbers in an error array (NERRS), and lines 29–34 in the termination block print out the card numbers having type errors.

The handling of an uneven number of steps illustrates error correction techniques. Error correction should be used with caution but should be considered, especially when reasonable corrections can be specified. An uneven number of intervals is an error, but a "reasonable" correction is to add 1 to make the number even. This attempt at a reasonable correction must, of course, be clearly labeled. See lines 40–43 for error message and correction. In the output list of line 40, the last item to be printed is NSTEPS+1. This uses the feature of full 1977 FORTRAN (see Chapter 3A) that allows expressions in output lists.

Figure 5-12
Continued.

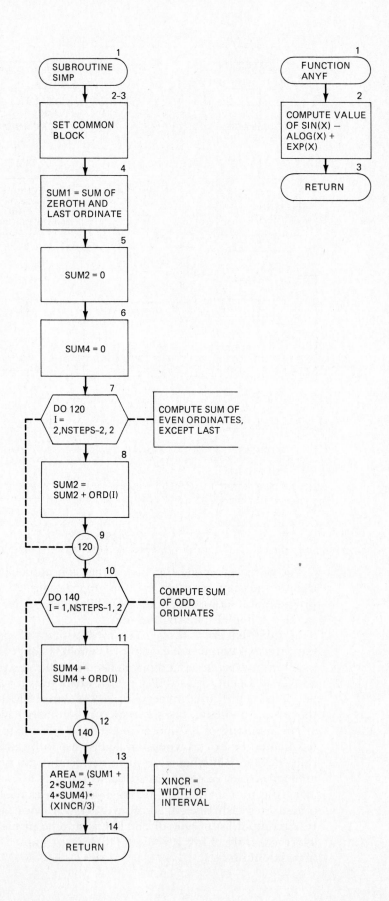

Figure 5-13
Listing of FORTRAN program for statistical example 5—numerical integration.

```
*********          PROGRAM IDENTIFICATION              *********
*                                                               *
*        PROGRAM TO COMPARE NUMERICAL INTEGRATION TECHNIQUES    *
*        RECTANGULAR, TRAPEZOIDAL, AND SIMPSON'S RULE --        *
*        BY USING ALL THREE FOR THE SAME FUNCTION OVER          *
*        VARIOUS INTERVALS AND WITH DIFFERENT NUMBERS OF        *
*        SEGMENTS. THE NUMBER OF SEGMENTS MUST BE EVEN.         *
*        WRITTEN BY T. HOFFMANN  Ø7/11/77   REV. 1/22/82        *
*                                                               *
***************************************************************
*                                                               *
*********          VARIABLE IDENTIFICATION             *********
*                                                               *
*        NSTEPS    = NUMBER OF SEGMENTS IN INTEGRATION INTERVAL *
*        XINCR     = WIDTH OF SEGMENT                           *
*        ORDØ      = VALUE OF ZERO'TH ORDINATE                  *
*        VALU1     = VALUE OF LEFT BOUNDARY OF INTEGRATION INTERVAL *
*        VALU2     = VALUE OF RIGHT BOUNDARY OF INTEGRATION INTERVAL *
*        X         = X VALUES (ABCISSAS) OF INTERVALS           *
*        NCARD     = NUMBER OF CARDS READ                       *
*        RAREA     = AREA USING RECTANGULAR TECHNIQUE           *
*        TAREA     = AREA USING TRAPEZOIDAL RULE                *
*        SAREA     = AREA USING SIMPSON'S RULE                  *
*        KNT       = NUMBER OF DATA ERROR CARDS                 *
*                                                               *
*****              ARRAY IDENTIFICATION                *****
*                                                               *
*        ORD       = ORDINATES OF THE FUNCTION                  *
*        NERRS     = STORES CARD NUMBER OF UNREADABLE CARDS     *
*                                                               *
*****          SUBROUTINE AND FUNCTION NAMES           *****
*                                                               *
*        RECT      = COMPUTES AREA USING RECTANGULAR PROCEDURE  *
*        TRAP      = COMPUTES AREA USING TRAPEZOIDAL PROCEDURE  *
*        SIMP      = COMPUTES AREA USING SIMPSON'S RULE         *
*        ANYF      = FUNCTION TO BE INTEGRATED                  *
*                                                               *
***************************************************************
*                                                               *
*********          STORAGE ALLOCATION                  *********
*                                                               *
1.          DIMENSION NERRS(10)
2.          COMMON /YBLOCK/ ORD(1000),ORDØ
3.          COMMON // NSTEPS,XINCR
4.          DATA NERRS/10*Ø/
*                                                               *
***************************************************************
*                                                               *
*********          INITIALIZATION BLOCK            BLOCK ØØØØ
*                                                               *
5.          WRITE(6,3)
6.        3 FORMAT('1',12X,'COMPARISON OF NUMERICAL INTEGRATION TECHNIQUES'/
           1   'Ø','    INTEGRATION OF SIN(X) - ALOG(X) + EXP(X)'//
           2   1X,'  FROM    TO  STEPS  STEP ',3X,6('*'),11X,'METHOD',
           3   10X,'******'/22X,'SIZE',5X,'RECTANGLE',7X,
           4   'TRAPEZOID',7X,'SIMPSON'//)
7.          NCARD = Ø
8.          KNT = Ø
9.          DO 9 I = 1,1000
10.           ORD(I) = 0.0
11.       9 CONTINUE
*                                                               *
***************************************************************
*                                                               *
*********          INPUT AND COMPUTATION BLOCK     BLOCK Ø100
*                                                               *
12.      101 READ(5,103,ERR=901,END=301) VALU1,VALU2,NSTEPS
13.      103 FORMAT(2F4.2,I3)
14.          NCARD = NCARD + 1
15.          IF(MOD(NSTEPS,2).NE.Ø) GOTO 905
16.      104 X = VALU1
17.          XINCR = (VALU2 - VALU1)/FLOAT(NSTEPS)
18.          ORDØ = ANYF(X)
19.          DO 105 I = 1,NSTEPS
20.            X = X + XINCR
21.            ORD(I) = ANYF(X)
22.      105 CONTINUE
23.          CALL RECT(RAREA)
24.          CALL TRAP(TAREA)
25.          CALL SIMP(SAREA)
*                                                               *
***************************************************************
*                                                               *
*********          DETAIL PRINT BLOCK              BLOCK Ø200
*                                                               *
```

Figure 5-13
Continued.

```
26.            WRITE(6,203) VALU1,VALU2,NSTEPS,XINCR,RAREA,TAREA,SAREA
27.       203 FORMAT(1X,F7.4,F7.2,I5,F5.3,2X,3E15.8)                          *
      *                                                                       *
      *            GO BACK TO READ ANOTHER DATA CARD                          *
      *                                                                       *
28.            GOTO 101
      *                                                                       *
      *************************************************************************
      *                                                                       *
      *********            TERMINATION BLOCK                     BLOCK 0300
      *                                                                       *
29.       301 WRITE(6,305) KNT
30.       305 FORMAT('0','THERE WERE',I3,' UNREADABLE DATA CARDS.'/
          1     ' THE FOLLOWING WERE NOT PROCESSED:')
31.            DO 303 I = 1,KNT
32.               WRITE(6,302) NERRS(I)
33.       302     FORMAT(5X,'CARD NUMBER ',I2)
34.       303 CONTINUE
35.            STOP
      *                                                                       *
      *************************************************************************
      *                                                                       *
      *********            ERROR MESSAGE BLOCK                   BLOCK 0900
      *                                                                       *
36.       901 NCARD = NCARD + 1
37.            KNT = KNT + 1
38.            NERRS(KNT) = NCARD
      *                                                                       *
      *            GO BACK TO PROCESS NEXT CARD                               *
      *                                                                       *
39.            GOTO 101
      *                                                                       *
40.       905 WRITE(6,906) NSTEPS,NCARD,NSTEPS+1
41.       906 FORMAT('0ERROR -- NUMBER OF STEPS MUST BE EVEN, NOT',
          1    I3,' AS IN CARD',I3/1X,'ADJUSTED TO ',I3,
          2    ' AND EXECUTION CONTINUED.')
42.            NSTEPS = NSTEPS + 1
      *                                                                       *
      *            GO BACK TO EXECUTE USING NSTEPS + 1                        *
      *                                                                       *
43.            GOTO 104
      *                                                                       *
44.            END
      *                                                                       *
      ***********************************************  END OF MAIN PROGRAM
```

```
1.             SUBROUTINE RECT(AREA)
      *                                                                       *
      *********            PROGRAM IDENTIFICATION               *********
      *                                                                       *
      *            THIS SUBROUTINE INTEGRATES THE AREA UNDER A CURVE          *
      *            USING THE METHOD OF RECTANGLES.  ORDINATES OF THE          *
      *            CURVE MUST HAVE BEEN PREVIOUSLY STORED IN THE              *
      *            ARRAY ORD.                                                 *
      *                                                                       *
      *************************************************************************
      *                                                                       *
      *********            VARIABLE IDENTIFICATION              *********
      *                                                                       *
      *            AREA      = AREA UNDER CURVE                               *
      *            SUM       = SUM OF ORDINATES OF CURVE                      *
      *            ORD       = ORDINATES OF CURVE                             *
      *            NSTEPS    = NUMBER OF SEGMENTS IN INTEGRATION INTERVAL     *
      *            XINCR     = WIDTH OF SEGMENT                               *
      *            ORD0      = VALUE OF THE ZERO'TH ORDINATE                  *
      *                                                                       *
      *****            ARRAY IDENTIFICATION                     *****
      *                                                                       *
      *            ORD       = ORDINATES OF THE FUNCTION                      *
      *                                                                       *
      *************************************************************************
      *                                                                       *
      *********            STORAGE ALLOCATION                   *********
      *                                                                       *
2.             COMMON /YBLOCK/ ORD(1000),ORD0
3.             COMMON // NSTEPS,XINCR
      *                                                                       *
      *************************************************************************
      *                                                                       *
      *********            COMPUTATION BLOCK                     BLOCK 0100
      *                                                                       *
4.             SUM = ORD0
5.             DO 120 I = 1,NSTEPS-1
```

Figure 5-13
Continued.

```
  6.              SUM = SUM + ORD(I)
  7.        120 CONTINUE
  8.              AREA = XINCR*SUM
  9.              RETURN
 10.              END
      *                                                              *
      ************************************************  END OF SUBPROGRAM
```

```
  1.          SUBROUTINE TRAP(AREA)
      *                                                              *
      **********          PROGRAM IDENTIFICATION          **********
      *                                                              *
      *          THIS SUBROUTINE INTEGRATES THE AREA UNDER A CURVE   *
      *          USING THE METHOD OF TRAPEZOIDS.  ORDINATES OF THE   *
      *          CURVE MUST HAVE BEEN PREVIOUSLY STORED IN THE       *
      *          ARRAY ORD.                                          *
      *                                                              *
      ****************************************************************
      *                                                              *
      **********          VARIABLE IDENTIFICATION          **********
      *                                                              *
      *          AREA      = AREA UNDER CURVE                        *
      *          SUM       = SUM OF ORDINATES OF CURVE               *
      *          ORD       = ORDINATES OF CURVE                      *
      *          NSTEPS    = NUMBER OF SEGMENTS IN INTEGRATION INTERVAL *
      *          XINCR     = WIDTH OF SEGMENT                        *
      *          ORD0      = VALUE OF THE ZERO'TH ORDINATE           *
      *                                                              *
      *****                ARRAY IDENTIFICATION                *****
      *                                                              *
      *          ORD       = ORDINATES OF THE FUNCTION              *
      *                                                              *
      ****************************************************************
      *                                                              *
      **********          STORAGE ALLOCATION          **********
      *                                                              *
  2.          COMMON /YBLOCK/ ORD(1000),ORD0
  3.          COMMON // NSTEPS,XINCR
      *                                                              *
      ****************************************************************
      *                                                              *
      **********          COMPUTATION BLOCK          BLOCK 0100
      *                  .                                          *
  4.          SUM = (ORD0 + ORD(NSTEPS))/2.0
  5.          DO 120 I = 1,NSTEPS-1
  6.              SUM = SUM + ORD(I)
  7.        120 CONTINUE
  8.          AREA = SUM*XINCR
  9.          RETURN
 10.          END
      *                                                              *
      ************************************************  END OF SUBPROGRAM
```

```
  1.          SUBROUTINE SIMP(AREA)
      *                                                              *
      **********          PROGRAM IDENTIFICATION          **********
      *                                                              *
      *          THIS SUBROUTINE INTEGRATES THE AREA UNDER A CURVE   *
      *          USING SIMPSON'S RULE.  ORDINATES OF THE            *
      *          CURVE MUST HAVE BEEN PREVIOUSLY STORED IN THE       *
      *          ARRAY ORD.                                          *
      *                                                              *
      ****************************************************************
      *                                                              *
      **********          VARIABLE IDENTIFICATION          **********
      *                                                              *
      *          AREA      = AREA UNDER CURVE                        *
      *          SUM       = SUM OF ORDINATES OF CURVE               *
      *          ORD       = ORDINATES OF CURVE                      *
      *          NSTEPS    = NUMBER OF SEGMENTS IN INTEGRATION INTERVAL *
      *          XINCR     = WIDTH OF SEGMENT                        *
      *          ORD0      = VALUE OF THE ZERO'TH ORDINATE           *
      *                                                              *
      *****                ARRAY IDENTIFICATION                *****
      *                                                              *
      *          ORD       = ORDINATES OF THE FUNCTION              *
      *                                                              *
      ****************************************************************
      *                                                              *
      **********          STORAGE ALLOCATION          **********
      *                                                              *
  2.          COMMON /YBLOCK/ ORD(1000),ORD0
  3.          COMMON // NSTEPS,XINCR
```

Figure 5-13
Continued.

```
 *                                                                          *
 ****************************************************************************
 *                                                                          *
 *********          COMPUTATION BLOCK                        BLOCK 0100
 *                                                                          *
 4.        SUM1 = ORD0 + ORD(NSTEPS)
 5.        SUM2 = 0.0
 6.        SUM4 = 0.0
 7.        DO 120 I = 2,NSTEPS-2,2
 8.            SUM2 = SUM2 + ORD(I)
 9.   120 CONTINUE
10.        DO 140 I = 1,NSTEPS-1,2
11.            SUM4 = SUM4 + ORD(I)
12.   140 CONTINUE
13.        AREA = (SUM1 + 2.0*SUM2 + 4.0*SUM4)*XINCR/3.0
14.        RETURN
15.        END
 *                                                                          *
 ****************************************************        END OF SUBPROGRAM
 *                                                                          *


 1.        FUNCTION ANYF(X)
 *                                                                          *
 *********          ANYF CAN BE EQUATED TO ANY FUNCTION      *********
 *                                                                          *
 2.        ANYF = SIN(X) - ALOG(X) + EXP(X)
 3.        RETURN
 4.        END
 *                                                                          *
 ****************************************************        END OF SUBPROGRAM
```

The program is written for batch input and illustrates the handling of errors, so that the job is executed using all good data and reasonable corrections of bad data. The problem fits the characteristics of interactive terminal execution better than batch because of its testing-of-values approach. If written for interactive mode, changes would need to be made as follows:

1   The card input would be replaced by terminal line input. List-directed input would then be preferred. The END = clause (see READ statement labeled 101) might be replaced by an explicit test-of-termination value.

2   Errors in data type and uneven intervals would be rejected with error message. The correction would be entered immediately. In the interactive mode, there is little reason to accept errors or to try to correct them, since the correction can be made at the terminal without significant delay of execution.

Figure 5-14
Annotated input test data
for statistical example 5—
numerical integration.

START VALUE	END	STEPS	PURPOSE OR EXPECTED OUTPUT
00.20	01.40	20	VALUE OF ABOUT 4.05096
00.20	01.40	998	IMPROVEMENT IN PRECISION
00.20	01.40	06	POORER ESTIMATE
JKL			ERROR-REJECT CARD (NONNUMERIC DATA)
0001	1.00	050	VALUE OF ABOUT 3.11186
0001	1.00	100	IMPROVED ESTIMATE
0001	1.00	010	POORER ESTIMATE
0001	1.00	.01	ERROR-REJECT CARD (DECIMAL POINT IN INTEGER FIELD)
1.40	1.90	031	ERROR-NUMBER OF STEPS NOT EVEN
1.40	1.90	060	VALUE OF ABOUT 2.87549
			10 DATA CARDS
			2 REJECTED FOR DATA-TYPE ERROR
			1 ERROR MESSAGE FOR INVALID DATA

Figure 5-15
Example of statistical output from numerical integration program.

```
              COMPARISON OF NUMERICAL INTEGRATION TECHNIQUES

          INTEGRATION OF SIN(X) - ALOG(X) + EXP(X)

          FROM   TO   STEPS  STEP     ******        METHOD        ******
                              SIZE    RECTANGLE     TRAPEZOID     SIMPSON


          .2000  1.40   20  .060   .40025963E+01  .40528363E+01  .40509643E+01
          .2000  1.40  998  .001   .40499419E+01  .40509487E+01  .40509479E+01
          .2000  1.40    6  .200   .39040517E+01  .40715184E+01  .40521335E+01
          .0100  1.00   50  .020   .31352949E+01  .31148468E+01  .31122731E+01
          .0100  1.00  100  .010   .31228486E+01  .31126245E+01  .31118838E+01
          .0100  1.00   10  .099   .32647225E+01  .31624819E+01  .31297218E+01

        ERROR -- NUMBER OF STEPS MUST BE EVEN, NOT 31 AS IN CARD  9
        ADJUSTED TO  32 AND EXECUTION CONTINUED.
         1.4000  1.90   32  .016   .28576766E+01  .28755372E+01  .28754899E+01
         1.4000  1.90   60  .008   .28659777E+01  .28755034E+01  .28754899E+01

        THERE WERE  2 UNREADABLE DATA CARDS.
        THE FOLLOWING WERE NOT PROCESSED:
             CARD NUMBER  4
             CARD NUMBER  8
```

In summary, the program has certain style characteristics that should be noted in reviewing it:

1 The list of subroutine and function names in the main program identifies the purpose of each subroutine and function used by the main program.

2 The DIMENSION statement is used only for arrays but not for named or blank COMMON. Arrays in COMMON are dimensioned in the COMMON declaration (lines 1–3).

3 Data in common storage cannot be initialized by a DATA statement. However, data in named COMMON could have been initialized by a DATA statement in a BLOCK DATA subprogram, but we chose to initialize by assignment statements in the main program (lines 9–11).

4 Input validation is performed to make sure the number of steps is even. Line 15 uses the MOD instrinsic function. MOD(NSTEPS,2) provides the remainder from division by 2. If the remainder is not zero, the number was an odd number. This could, of course, have been programmed without the MOD function as:

```
IF(NSTEPS - ((NSTEPS/2) * 2) .NE. 0) GOTO 905
```

5 There is a programmed attempt to correct an input error, report the correction, and execute the corrected data.

6 The block structure of the program follows a structured style:

Storage allocation

Initialization

Input and computation

Detail print

Termination

Error message

7 The subroutines have identical COMMON declarations.

8 The function to be integrated is put in a function subprogram ANYF(X) for ease of change. It is used by only two main program statements, and the function could easily have been coded in the main program at lines 18 and 21.

9 A single FORMAT statement is used to print a multiple-line heading. Note the use of slashes and the indentation of the continuation lines (line 6).

Programming exercises

Description of assignment

Select one or more problems (or take the problems assigned by your instructor). Write each of the computational procedures in the problem as a function and/or subroutine subprogram. Use the case structure where applicable. Follow the style guidelines and prepare the following.

1 Pseudocode description
2 Program flowchart
3 Program listing
4 List of test data and expected results, testing for both valid and invalid data
5 Output including output from error conditions

Mathematics and statistics

1 For each of the following sets of data, compute the mean and variance of each subset X and Y and the correlation coefficient of the sets. See problem 4-1 for the correlation coefficient formula. The variance for X can be calculated as:

$$\text{Var} = \frac{\Sigma X^2 - ((\Sigma X)^2)/n}{n - 1}$$

Set 1		Set 2	
X	Y	X	Y
34.22	102.43	20	27.1
39.87	100.93	30	28.9
41.85	97.43	40	30.6
43.23	97.81	50	32.3
40.06	98.32	60	33.7
53.29	98.32	70	35.6
53.29	100.07	80	37.2
54.14	97.08		
49.12	91.59		
40.71	94.85		
55.15	94.65		

2 There are many ways to prepare sequences of random numbers; two of these are the inner product or squaring method and the power residue procedure. The inner product method takes a number of digits, say four, squares it, and picks out the central four digits of the product as a random number. The four-digit random number is squared, etc. For example: starting with

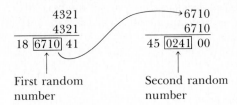

First random number   Second random number

4321 produces the sequence 6710,0241, etc. The power residue method chooses a starting value, neither even nor ending in a 5, and a special constant multiplier (91 is a good choice to obtain a sequence of four-digit random numbers). Form the product of the starting value and the constant and save the low-order four digits as the random number and the base to use for the next multiplication. For example, a starting value of 1907 and a constant of 91 produces the sequence 3537, 1867, etc.

$$
\begin{array}{c}
1907 \\
\underline{91} \\
17\ \boxed{3537}
\end{array}
\qquad
\begin{array}{c}
{\to}3537 \\
\underline{91} \\
32\ \boxed{1867}
\end{array}
$$

Write a program to generate random numbers by each of these procedures and compute the average value of each sequence. Use the following values as test cases:

Length of sequence	Initial value	Constant multiplier (method 2 only)
100	4321	91
1000	4321	91
10000	4321	91
500	5023	3219
5000	7023	3219

3 The Newton-Raphson technique can be used effectively to find the real roots of a function by successive approximations. Given a function of x, the following relationship is used:

$$x_{i+1} = x_i - \frac{f(x_i)}{f'(x_i)}$$

where x_i = the current estimated value

    x_{i+1} = the next estimated value

    $f(x_i)$ = the function evaluated at x_i

    $f'(x_i)$ = the first derivative of the function evaluated at x_i

An initial estimate x_0 is required as input to the process, and it must terminate when $|x_{i+1} - x_i| <$ some epsilon value. Write a program to compute a root of $f(x) = x^3 - 3x^2 + 5$ to an accuracy of .001 or better. Print out the number of iterations and root. Write the program so that it can be easily modified for other functions and epsilons. Use the following initial estimates: 1.0, -1.0, 0.0, 3.0, -30.0

289

Business and economics

4 Various techniques are used to depreciate capital assets; most common are the straight line, double-declining balance, and sum-of-the-years digits. Assuming an initial cost c, a salvage value s, and a useful life of N years, the relationships for depreciation D_n in year n are as follows:

Straight line:

$$D_n = \frac{C - S}{N}$$

Sum-of-the-years digits:

$$D_n = (C - S)\frac{N - n + 1}{\text{sum}}$$

where n is a particular year and

$$\text{sum} = \sum_{i=1}^{N} i = \frac{N(N + 1)}{2}$$

Double-declining balance:

$$D_n = \frac{2}{N}\left(C - \sum_{i=1}^{n-1} D_i\right)$$

until $C - \sum_{i=1}^{n} D_i = S$

Write a program to depreciate each of the following assets over their useful lives, showing the annual depreciation by each technique.

Asset number	Initial cost	Salvage value	Useful life
1	$ 10,000.00	$ 3,000.00	6 years
2	37,006.00	4,127.37	8
3	6,000.00	327.00	8
4	75,745.00	8,165.00	7
5	365,000.00	27,500.00	10

5 Modify problems 5 of Chapter 4 by making the interest computations as subprograms.

6 Various forecasting techniques can be applied to time series data. Among the simplest of these are exponential smoothing, weighted moving averages, and simple moving averages. These equations are as follows:

Three-period simple moving average:

$$f_{n+1} = \frac{d_n + d_{n-1} + d_{n-2}}{3}$$

where d_i is the ith actual demand and f_j is the forecast for the jth period.

Three-period weighted moving average:

$$f_{n+1} = \frac{3d_n + 2d_{n-1} + d_{n-2}}{6}$$

Exponential smoothing:

$$f_{n+1} = ad_n + (1 - a)f_n$$

where a is a decimal between 0 and 1. (Read in 0.2 for this problem.) Write a program to compute forecasts by each of these techniques: Start with period 4 and assume f_3 for exponential smoothing equals the mean of the first two values.

Period	Demand series 1	Demand series 2
1	31.8	100
2	33.7	300
3	32.1	450
4	29.3	570
5	33.9	750
6	37.0	820
8	42.5	915
9	36.7	945
10	31.0	975
11	35.8	1000

Science and engineering

7 Frequently an experiment results in a set of empirical data that arise because of a functional relationship. Fitting a straight line or curve to the data is often done in order to better understand the relationship. The method of least squares, which minimizes the squares of the differences between actual and fitted function values, is the most common mathematical technique used to do this. The general equation for a straight line is:

$$y = a + bx$$

From a set of x and y paired observations, the desired coefficients can be computed as:

$$b = \frac{n\Sigma xy - (\Sigma x)(\Sigma y)}{n\Sigma x^2 - (\Sigma x)^2}$$

$$a = \bar{y} - b\bar{x}$$

where $\bar{y}$ and $\bar{x}$ are the means of their respective data sets. Similarly, an equation of the form $y = ax^b$ can be rewritten as:

$$\log y = \log a + b \log x$$

Letting $Y = \log y$, $X = \log x$, and $A = \log a$, one can see that this is similar to a straight line equation as before:

$$Y = A + bX$$

and thus b and a can be derived with the same equations modified for logarithms. The following data was derived from the pull characteristics of an alternating current magnet. Write a program to compute coefficients for both types of equations.

Pounts pull, Y	Ampere-turns, X
3.0	1.5
4.5	2.0
5.5	3.5
6.0	5.0
7.5	6.0
8.5	7.5
8.0	9.0
9.0	10.5
9.5	12.0
10.0	14.0

8 Referring to problem 8 of Chapter 3, make the degree to radian conversion a function.

9 Referring to problem 9 of Chapter 4, place the graphing routine as a subroutine and the function to be plotted as a function subprogram.

Humanities and social sciences

10 Modify problem 10 of Chapter 4 so that alternate printouts are available at the user's choice. That is, the user can request only Table 1, only Table 2, both Table 1 and Table 2, a Table of Income versus Politics, or a Table of Income versus Sex.

11 The binomial probability distribution is often applicable to sampling situations. For example, among two candidates for office, there does not appear to be a clear winner. A poll is taken of 900 people and 540 prefer candidate A. How likely is this result if indeed the entire population of voters are evenly split? The equation for this is:

$$P\binom{n}{x} = \frac{n!}{x!(n-x)!} p^x(1-p)^{n-x}$$

where $p = 0.5$ for this problem.

Write a program to compute the probabilities for the following situations. If n is less than 10, compute factorials by multiplying, that is,

$$n! = 1 \times 2 \times 3 \times \cdots \times n$$

If n is 10 or greater, use Stirling's approximation for factorials:

$$n! = e^{-n}n^n\sqrt{2\pi n}$$

Situation number	Sample size	Yes answers
1	9	5
2	90	50
3	90	54
4	10	5
5	100	52

12 The combined effect of wind and temperature on the human body is quite severe, particularly in cold climates. The relative effect of their combination is referred to as the *wind-chill factor*. Prepare a wind-chill chart for Fahrenheit temperatures from -50 to $+10$ degrees (in 10-degree increments) and windspeeds of 5 to 30 miles per hour. The relevant formulas are:

V1 = .477 times windspeed
V2 = $(10.45 + 10\sqrt{V1} - V1) * (33.0 - TEMP_C)$
Wind-Chill $TEMP_C = 33.0 - (V2/22.034)$

Note that the temperatures are Celsius and the table is to be in Fahrenheit. (Use a function subprogram for conversion.)

General

13 Refer to problem 13 of Chapter 4 and replace inline code for computing averages with a function subprogram.

14 Write a program to deal three sets of four poker hands of five cards each. Shuffle the deck between each deal. Write the shuffling procedure as a subroutine and use either a random number generator available as a system library subprogram or one of the procedures described in problem 2 of this chapter.

15 Reprogram problem 13 of Chapter 13 to make use of the case structure for currency conversion.

chapter **6A**

Use of files on external storage

The FORTRAN problems and programs in the first five chapters assumed that data would be input from punched cards or at a terminal and output would be immediately printed or displayed. Data to be saved was placed in arrays in internal storage. These procedures are generally satisfactory for computational problems with relatively little data, but there are situations where large amounts of data need to be input, processed, and saved for later use. The method for storing the data in such cases is *external storage*. Also called *secondary* or *auxiliary storage*, the external storage generally uses magnetic disks or magnetic tape. This chapter will explain how to program the use of files on external storage.

Files in FORTRAN

As background for the input/output instructions, this section will review records and files and explain external storage file-access methods.

Records and files

A *data item* is a set of numeric (or alphanumeric) characters treated as a unit for processing. In FORTRAN, each data item is uniquely identified by a variable name. Examples are a pay rate, an identification number, a measurement, etc. A collection of related data items constitutes a *record*. Examples of a record are data items from a research questionnaire, all data items related to the payroll for one employee, or all data describing a chemical process. A collection of records constitutes a *file*. For example, the research questionnaire records make up the research record file, the payroll records make up the payroll file, and the chemical process records compose the chemical process data file. This relationship is shown in Figure 6-1.

The records in a file are stored on some medium such as punched cards, magnetic tape, or magnetic disks. Records occupy storage space on the storage medium and each item within the record takes up part of this space. The storage space (described conceptually in numbers of character storage positions) for an item is the *field* for the item. −3.758 takes a field of six characters; 3758 requires a field of four characters. The actual physical storage space used is implementation-dependent.

In FORTRAN, any set of input or output records constitute a file, but the term is most commonly used to refer to files on external storage. The user of

Figure 6-1
Relationship of character, item, record, and file.
Field

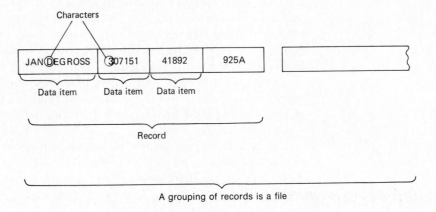

FORTRAN need not understand the technical characteristics of secondary storage because the language handles file storage in a standard manner rather than requiring the programmer to furnish all of the specifications. However, one storage characteristic that the programmer may specify is formatted versus unformatted representation.

Unformatted input and output

Two methods for input and output have been used in previous chapters: list-directed input and output and format-directed input and output. Both list-directed and format-directed input and output require considerable computer processing because at input the external representation of data must be converted to the internal representation suitable for processing. For output the internal representation must be converted back to external representation. If data is to be written onto a file for subsequent use but there is no human-readable output required, then it is more efficient to write the data record without any conversion to output format. When the records are subsequently read, no conversion to internal representation is required. The writing and reading of data in internal representation without formatting is termed an unformatted write or read. It is specified by a READ or WRITE with a unit number but no FORMAT statement number or asterisk. The files are sometimes referred to as binary files. If unformatted records containing X, Y, M are to be written onto a file on unit 8, the statement is:

WRITE (8)X, Y, M

A subsequent READ statement from this file must use the unformatted form because the records are not formatted:

READ (8)X, Y, M

Because unformatted records are more efficient in terms of processing time, they should be considered for all external FORTRAN files on magnetic tape or magnetic disk.

Storage media and file-access methods

The two most common external storage media—magnetic tape and disks—differ in their operation. The magnetic tape is read or written in serial fashion from beginning to end. The first record on the tape is read first, the second record is read second, etc. The second record cannot be accessed without reading the first. It operates very much like a reel of magnetic tape or a tape cassette used for home recording. Records on tape are stored in physical blocks separated by interblock gaps. The gaps allow the tape unit to start and stop between the reading and writing of blocks. The FORTRAN programmer need not be concerned with the physical record on tape because FORTRAN requires only that the programmer define a program record; the compiler arranges physical record storage.

The disk file can access any part of the storage by an access arm (or arms) that moves to the set of storage positions (on a track) where a record is stored. These storage positions have a physical location called an *address*. Records on disk storage may be written and read serially, or records may be accessed directly by taking advantage of the direct-access capabilities of the disk. The direct access method requires each record to have an identifier that specifies its location in the file. The identifier is not an actual disk address. The connection between the record address identifier and a disk address is performed automatically by the operating system.

In files to be read serially, it is common to have some method for noting the end of a set (file) of records. This is frequently accomplished by a special record containing an end-of-file character (or characters), but other methods may be used such as a record counter maintained by the system.

The file-access methods available in standard FORTRAN are sequential access and direct access. A file must be defined as either one or the other and may be used only in the defined access mode. However, a file on disk storage can be defined as sequential for one use and defined as direct-access for a different use, assuming the records are stored so that both methods are feasible.

1 *Sequential access* Records are read in serial fashion in the same order they were written. The data records in a file must be completely formatted or unformatted. An end-of-file record may be used to mark the end of the file. Sequential-access files can be implemented on either tape or disk storage.

2 *Direct access* This can be implemented only on direct-access storage such as disks. Direct-access input/output statements must be used to write or read, and records may be read or written in any order. Each record must have a unique positive integer identifier called a *record number,* specified when the record is first written. The records must have the same length and must be all formatted or all unformatted. List-directed input or output cannot be used. End-of-file records are not used.

Sequential files and direct-access files differ in the procedure for changing or updating a single record in the file. In general, to alter the contents of any record in a sequential file on magnetic tape, the entire file is read and rewritten, making the required change (delete a record, add a record, or change part of the record). In a direct-access file, the contents of a single record may be altered without rewriting the file. A complete discussion of file updating procedure is available in data processing references.

Self-testing exercise 6-1

1 Classify the following as probably a record or a file.
(*a*) Height and weight observations for 100 men from an experiment.
(*b*) Height and weight for one man.
(*c*) Income, age, children, and occupation for one family.
(*d*) Income, age, etc., for all families in a study.

2 True or false.
(*a*) A formatted file is generally more efficient for processing.
(*b*) Both tape and disk storage can be used for sequential access.
(*c*) Tape storage can be used for direct access.
(*d*) A record number is required for direct access.
(*e*) Secondary storage and auxiliary storage are the same.

3 Complete the table:

Access method	Order records read	File medium	Use of list-directed I/O	Use of end-of-file record
Sequential	Same order as written	Tape or disk	Allowed	Yes
Direct				

Sequential-access processing

READ and WRITE statements for sequential access

In simple sequential access, the READ or WRITE statement is the same as those used in previous chapters, but the unit number identifies the auxiliary storage device. The unit number to be used for tapes or disks may be preassigned by the installation, be specifically assigned by the job control cards placed with the program, or assigned by an OPEN statement to be explained later.

Example 1

Read a record from magnetic tape unit 10 based on the FORMAT statement 700.

READ (10, 700) A, B, X

This instruction specifies a formatted, sequential-access processing and assumes the records were written using a formatted WRITE statement.

Example 2

Read the three items in list-directed sequential access (that were written using a list-directed output statement).

READ (10, *) A, B, X

Note the use of the asterisk in place of the format to specify list-directed input.

The general form of the READ and WRITE statements is the same as presented in Chapter 3, with square brackets indicating an optional element.

READ (control list) [I/O variables list]
WRITE (control list) [I/O variables list]

The control list presented in earlier chapters consisted of the unit number for the input/output device, the FORMAT statement number, ERR, and END; additional specifiers may be used with files.

Each element in the control list consists of an alphabetic identifier, for example, UNIT, FMT, etc., followed by an equals sign and a specifier that may be a number identifying a unit, a statement label, or a variable name. Five specifications useful for sequential access are shown in the box on the next page. The alphabetic identifier is optional with the unit number and the format number specifications, but if the alphabetic identifier is not used, the unit number must be first in the list and the FORMAT statement label second. The

SPECIFIERS FOR SEQUENTIAL-ACCESS CONTROL LIST

[ ] mean optional part of specifier

[UNIT =] unit number of device

[FMT =] FORMAT statement label for specific formatting and * for list-directed formatting

ERR = statement label to which control goes if there is an I/O error

END = statement label to go to if end-of-file

IOSTAT = integer variable to hold error code. 0 = no error, negative = end-of-file, and positive = error code.

following are identical in their effect:

READ (5, 700) ALPHA

READ (UNIT = 5, FMT = 700) ALPHA

READ (5, FMT = 700) ALPHA

The ERR and END specifications have been explained in Chapter 3; the new specification is IOSTAT. The IOSTAT defines an integer variable to which the program will assign an error code in the event of an error. A zero value means no error, a positive error code identifies different errors, and a negative integer value signifies an end-of-file condition. The positive and negative integer values to be used as codes are defined by the FORTRAN implementor and will usually vary for different compilers.

The IOSTAT specifier is normally used in conjunction with the ERR specifier. An input or output error will send control to the statement number specified by ERR = s. If IOSTAT is also used, the processing statements specified by the transfer on ERR can be executed to analyze the error code of IOSTAT to determine the exact reason for the I/O error. Thus, a combination of ERR and IOSTAT can provide for more information and diagnostic messages than the use of ERR alone.

The END statement has been used in previous chapters to signal the end of input data. This condition has initiated a transfer of control to cause the printing of totals, end-of-program messages, etc. In the case of a sequential file to which records are going to be added, the END statement signals the end of the existing file (an endfile record is detected); new records may then be added.

File-positioning statements

In a sequential file, reading or writing is performed serially. In order to start over at the beginning of the file, the file is rewound. The term *rewind*, when applied to a file on magnetic tape, is physically implemented; that is, the tape is rewound. In the case of a disk file, rewind means to position the read/write arms at the first record in the file. To go back only to a previous record, the file must be backspaced. The last logical record of a sequential file may be an end-of-file record to activate the END feature with the READ statement. The logical end-of-file record is not always a separate physical end-of-file record since the system may implement end-of-file detection in other ways.

File-positioning statements are used to backspace one record, write an end-of-file record, or rewind back to the beginning. These statements, given in the box, apply to both tape and disk files. They cannot be used with input/output files on cards or lines entered or printed at a terminal.

> **FILE-POSITIONING STATEMENTS**
>
> BACKSPACE unit   or   BACKSPACE (alist)
> ENDFILE unit   or   ENDFILE (alist)
> REWIND unit   or   REWIND (alist)
>
> where alist contains:
>
> [UNIT =] unit (UNIT = is optional)
> ERR = statement label

Backspace example

```
    READ (10, 700, ERR = 800) JIM
700 FORMAT (I5)
    BACKSPACE 10
    READ (10, 700, ERR = 800) JON
```

The preceding program segment reads from unit 10 into a variable named JIM. The backspace and subsequent read does a re-read of the same value that was read into JIM, placing it into JON. (It is, of course, not efficient to do it this way, since JON = JIM will accomplish the same effects.) The ERR = 800 specification in the READ statement sends control to statement label number 800 if a data-type error is present. Statement 800 should probably begin a set of instructions to backspace and read the record using a character edit specification. This allows the data record to be read and to be output with an error message. For example, statements in connection with the above example might read as follows (assuming TEMP is declared as CHARACTER type):

```
800 BACKSPACE 10
    READ (10, 810) TEMP
810 format (A)
    WRITE (6, 820) TEMP
820 format (' THE DATA SHOULD BE ALL DIGITS INSTEAD OF', A)
```

Endfile example

```
ENDFILE 8   or   ENDFILE (UNIT = 8)
```

This statement writes an end-of-file record at the end of a sequential file on unit 8.

The rewind instruction positions a file at the beginning. There are occasions where the programmer may wish to read the data more than once (perhaps doing searching or using the data differently each time). It is often a good practice to rewind sequential files on auxiliary storage at the beginning of the program to ensure proper positioning. If the file is already rewound, no action is taken. It is generally a desirable procedure to rewind all files before terminating the program.

Self-testing exercise 6-2

1 Write statements to read the variables X, Y, Z from punched cards and write them onto a magnetic tape (use unit 8) in a list-directed, sequential input and output method.

2 Rewrite the list-directed statements from problem 1 to write onto a sequential file on a disk (unit 10), using the UNIT and FMT specifiers.

3 Rewind the file written in problem 1 and reread the data.

4 Repeat problems 1 and 2 using format-directed input and output and FORMAT statement 700.

5 Backspace the file(s) in problem 1 and then read the data.

6 Would using rewind in place of backspace in problem 5 have the same effect? Expain.

Direct-access processing

A direct-access file in FORTRAN consists of a set of storage locations; each location is capable of storing one record and each location has an identifying number. The storage locations are numbered from 1 to N (where N is the maximum number of records in the file). If, for example, the direct-access file is to hold a maximum of 100 records, the record locations are numbered 1 to 100. A numbered location can be empty—with no record currently being stored.

1	Storage for 1 record
2	Storage for 1 record
3	Storage for 1 record
n	Storage for 1 record

Storage and retrieval of records is based on the record location numbers. Using the record number, the records can be read or written in any order. For example, in building a file, the records could be written in the order 3, 7, 2, 1, 5, 9,. . . . Direct-access files are sometimes called *random-access files* (in contrast to serial-access sequential files).

The records in a direct-access file must all be the same length. The direct-access records can be formatted or unformatted, but not both in the same file. List-directed input and output is not allowed. An endfile record is not used because it has no purpose.

A direct-access file may be established and defined by job control cards or by OPEN statements (to be explained later in the chapter). The instructions for the direct-access file READ and WRITE are the same as for sequential file READ and WRITE except for one new control list specification and the omission of the END control specifier, as shown on the next page.

The ERR and IOSTAT are optional; their use is the same as with sequential files. The REC specifier is required because the program must have a variable name where the record number of the record storage location to be accessed

SPECIFIERS FOR DIRECT-ACCESS CONTROL LIST

[   ] means optional part of specifier

[UNIT =]   unit number of direct-access storage device

 [FMT =]   FORMAT statement label for formatted input or output

      REC = variable holding record number of record storage location to be accessed (this is required)

IOSTAT = integer variable to hold error code: 0 = no error, positive = type of error code

      ERR = statement number to go to if I/O error

will be stored. For example,

```
   READ (5, 10) IR, VAL
10 FORMAT (I3, F3.2)
   WRITE (7, REC = IR) VAL
```

The preceding reads two values, IR and VAL, from the card reader or input terminal and then writes VAL in unformatted form onto unit 7 (a disk file) at the record location specified by IR.

Once an individual record storage location in a direct-access file has been occupied by storing a record there, the location may be referenced to read the record or a new record may be stored there, replacing the existing record. Of course, a record may not be read before it has been written. Backspace and rewind are not meaningful in the context of direct-access processing.

Self-testing exercise 6-3

1 Read 12 records with the variables ID, NAME, and PAY in a format of (I2, A10, F6.2). Write them unformatted onto a direct-access file (unit 10) using a DO loop. Use IOSTAT and ERR, but the statements referenced need not be written.

2 Read record number 5 from the file created in problem 1.

3 Read every other record from the file in question 1 and print them with identifying labels.

OPEN, CLOSE, and INQUIRE statements

The previous file-handling statements have all assumed devices that were prespecified as having file space available (probably based on default specifications by the operating system or specified by job control instructions). The OPEN and CLOSE statements are provided by the new standard FORTRAN as facilities for the program to specify files, associate files with devices, disconnect files, etc. The INQUIRE statement allows the program to obtain characteristics and status of a file. The effects of these statements are often dependent on the specific FORTRAN compiler. Hence, they should be used only after reading the appropriate implementor reference manual(s). Because of the implementor-dependent status and advanced nature of the instructions, the discussion will survey the capabilities of the OPEN, CLOSE, and INQUIRE statements, but will not describe them in detail.

Opening and closing a file

The OPEN statement is used to associate (connect) an existing file to an input/output unit or create a new file on a unit. If an option is not specified, the compiler selects the most common or default option. The CLOSE statement terminates the connection. A character string as specifier (example OLD) can be a character constant enclosed in single quotes or a character variable having that value.

> **OPEN STATEMENT**
>
> OPEN(olist)
>
> The olist is a list of specifiers for the features of the file, the unit number always being required, others being optional except record length, which is required for a direct-access file:
>
> [UNIT =]   unit number (UNIT = is optional)
> IOSTAT = integer variable for input/output status
>   FILE = name of the file (character string); if absent, implementor-dependent
>   ERR = statement label for transfer if error
> STATUS = 'OLD,' 'NEW,' 'SCRATCH,' or 'UNKNOWN'; NEW is default.
> ACCESS = 'SEQUENTIAL' or 'DIRECT'; SEQUENTIAL is default option
>   FORM = 'FORMATTED' or 'UNFORMATTED'; default is FORMAT-
>   TED for sequential file and UNFORMATTED for direct-access file
>   RECL = record length for a direct-access file (required)
> BLANK = 'NULL' or 'ZERO' to specify handling of blanks; ZERO is default

A new direct-access unformatted file on unit 12 might be opened by:

```
OPEN (12, IOSTAT = INDIK, ERR = 600, FILE = 'SAMPLE.'
       STATUS = 'NEW,' ACCESS = 'DIRECT,' RECL = 200)
```

where the specifications indicate that the file is named SAMPLE, it is a new file, it is direct-access, and the length of each record is 200 characters. If an error is encountered in opening the file, control transfers to statement 600 and the variable INDIK receives an error code.

> **CLOSE STATEMENT**
>
> CLOSE(clist)
>
> where the clist is a list of specifiers, unit number being the only one required:
>
> [UNIT =]   unit number (UNIT = is optional)
> IOSTAT = input/output status specifier variable
>   ERR = statement label
> STATUS = 'KEEP' or 'DELETE': KEEP is default option

If a file on unit 8 is to be released for other use (it will no longer be available), the CLOSE might read:

```
CLOSE (8, STATUS = 'DELETE')
```

Obtaining information about a file

All the specifiers for an existing file are stored with the file, and thus information about a file can be obtained by using the INQUIRE statement.

INQUIRE STATEMENT

There are two forms of the INQUIRE statement: file and unit. The form of the file inquiry is:

INQUIRE(FILE = file name and other specifiers)

This returns specifications for the named file. The form of the unit inquiry is:

INQUIRE(UNIT = unit number, and other specifiers)

The list of specifiers is used by the programmer to assign a value such as a variable name of the correct type to be used to store each specifier that is included in the list.

Specifier	Assignment	Values returned or result
IOSTAT	Integer variable	0, negative or positive
ERR	Statement label	Transfer if error
EXIST	Logical variable (See Chapter 7)	True (exists) or false (does not exist)
OPENED	Logical variable	True (opened) or false (not open)
NUMBER	Integer variable	Number of unit connected to file
NAMED	Logical variable	True (named) or false (no name)
NAME	Character variable	Name of file
ACCESS	Character variable	"SEQUENTIAL" or "DIRECT"
DIRECT	Character variable	"YES", "NO," or "UNKNOWN"
FORM	Character variable	"FORMATTED," "UNFORMAT-TED," or "UNKNOWN"
FORMATTED	Character variable	"YES", "NO," or "UNKNOWN"
UNFORMATTED	Character variable	"YES", "NO," or "UNKNOWN"
RECL	Integer variable	Record length of records in file
NEXTREC	Integer variable	Number of next record in direct-access file
BLANK	Character variable	"NULL" or "ZERO" (zero blank control)

Example

INQUIRE (UNIT = 16, FORM = FRM, RECL = LENGTH)

After execution, FRM will contain the characters FORMATTED, UNFOR-MATTED, or UNKNOWN, and LENGTH will contain the length of the records in the file connected to unit 16. The variables to hold characters must be declared as CHARACTER.

Self-testing exercise 6-4

1 Write the statements to OPEN and to WRITE a record containing PAYNO and PAYRTE onto a new direct-access file called PAY on unit 8. The record number is IRNO, the error routine label is 900, and the record length is 250. The record is formatted.

2 Inquire what the next record number is after the one just written in question 1.

3 Write the statements to OPEN a formatted sequential file on disk unit 9 and to write a record composed of COURSE and GRADES. Backspace and read the record just written and print it. Close the file. The name of the file is STUDNT.

Summary

FORTRAN programs do not need auxiliary storage if card or terminal input is processed as entered and the results are then displayed or printed. The need for files on external storage arises when input data is to be stored for later use or data is to be used repeatedly by the same program or different programs or the data exceeds the storage space available for arrays. Under these conditions, storing the data as a file on external storage is a desirable approach.

A record in FORTRAN consists of a set of data items that is read or written by a READ or WRITE statement. All records of a given type (same data items) constitute a file. The file may be sequential-access or direct-access. The common storage media of magnetic tape and magnetic disks both support sequential access; direct access requires a direct-access device such as a disk.

In the simplest case of sequential access, reading or writing from the file is the same as for card reader or printer except for a different unit number. It is possible to add additional specifications by the control list. The file may be positioned (rewound or backspaced) by file-positioning statements.

A direct-access file consists conceptually of a numbered set of fixed-length storage locations numbered from 1 to N. The file may be predefined by the operating system, defined by job control statements, or defined by an OPEN statement. Direct-access READ and WRITE statements require a record number specification in the control list. Other specifications may be included.

The 1977 FORTRAN standard provides additional, very flexible facilities for specifying files, connecting files to devices, disconnecting files, inquiring about the status of a file, etc. These will be useful in situations requiring extensive file handling. Their use requires access to the implementor manual for the compiler being employed.

Answers to self-testing exercises

Exercise 6-1

1 (a) File (b) Record (c) Record (d) File

2 (a) False (b) True (c) False (d) True (e) True

3

Access method	Order records read	File medium	Use of list-directed I/O	Use of endfile record
Sequential	Same order as written	Tape or disk	Allowed	Yes
Direct	Random order	Disk	Not allowed	No

Exercise 6-2

1
```
READ (5, * )X, Y, Z
WRITE (8, * )X, Y, Z
```

2
```
READ (5, * )X, Y, Z
WRITE (UNIT = 10, FMT = *)X, Y, Z
```

3
```
REWIND 8
READ (8, * )X, Y, Z
```

```
4  (1)      READ(5, 700)X, Y, Z
            WRITE (8, FMT = 700)X, Y, Z
       700 FORMAT (3F2.0)
   (2)      READ (5, 700)X, Y, Z
            WRITE (10, 700)X, Y, Z
       700 FORMAT (3F2.0)

5  BACKSPACE 8
   READ (8, * )X, Y, Z
```

6 Yes, it would be the same, but only if there is only one record on file. If there were two physical records, rewind would always position to read the first, while backspace would position to read the second.

Exercise 6-3

```
1      DO  100 J = 1, 12
            READ (5, 20, ERR = 30, IOSTAT = ENCODE) ID, NAME, PAY
       20   FORMAT (I2, A10, F6.2)
            WRITE (10, REC = ID) NAME, PAY
   100 CONTINUE

2  READ (10, REC = 5) NAME, PAY

3      DO  10 I = 1, 10, 2
            READ (10, REC = I) N, P
            PRINT 30, I, N, P or WRITE (6, 30) I, N, P
       30   FORMAT (' ID = '12,' NAME = ',A10,' PAY = ',F6.2)
   10 CONTINUE
```

Exercise 6-4

```
1  OPEN (8, ERR = 900, FILE = 'PAY', STATUS = 'NEW',
        ACCESS = 'DIRECT', RECL = 250)
   WRITE (8, 700, REC = IRNO, ERR = 900) PAYNO, PAYRTE

2  INQUIRE (UNIT = 8, NEXTREC = INEXT)
```

where record number of next record will be placed in INEXT.

```
3  OPEN (9, ERR = 900, FILE = STUDNT, FORM = 'FORMATTED',
        STATUS = 'NEW', ACCESS = 'SEQUENTIAL')
```

Note that form, status, and access are not required because these specifications are default options.

```
       WRITE (9, 700, ERR = 900) COURSE, GRADES
   700 FORMAT (2F10.2)
       BACKSPACE 9
       READ (9, 700, ERR = 900) COURSE, GRADES
       WRITE (6, 700) COURSE, GRADES
       CLOSE (9)
```

Questions and problems

1 Define the following terms:
(a) Character
(b) Data item
(c) Direct-access storage
(d) End-of-file record
(e) Field
(f) File
(g) Record
(h) Sequential-access storage

2 Differentiate between (a) use of magnetic tapes and disks for FORTRAN files and (b) formatted and unformatted records and the impact on FORTRAN file use.

3 A researcher has 1000 sets of data that will be processed by a number of different programs over a period of 7 months. The data consists of sets of research observations (call them X's) with observations in each set (X_1 through X_9). Each card has an integer number from 1 to 1000 that identifies the set. The data is now in punched cards with each set on a separate card (as I4,9F8.2).
(a) Write statements to create a sequential file on device 10 (say a magnetic tape).
(b) Write statements to read half of the data, rewind, and repeat the reading of the first 500 sets of observations.

4 Assume a file as in problem 3.
(a) Create a direct-access file. Use the set number as the direct-access file record number.
(b) Read the sets of data having record numbers equal to the number created by a sampling function. The function is ISAMPL(SEED), where SEED has already been defined.

5 Assume a file as in problem 4, but create an unformatted file and then read the second 10 records.

6 Assume a file as in problem 3 but use list-directed data on cards (separated by commas). Read the data, create a file, rewind, and then read the first five records.

chapter **6**^B

Example programs and programming exercises using external files

The example programs illustrate typical use of external files. The program for general example 6, payroll reports, uses an external file to hold reference data, which is matched with variable data read in on cards; the program for statistical example 6, research measurements, uses both a direct-access and a sequential-access file. It is also written for terminal input and output of data. The second program example illustrates features not used in the first, so that both should be reviewed.

General notes on Chapter 6 examples

External data files are used in several ways. In one sense, these files are just a different form of an array. If the array must be saved between runs of the program, its contents can be written to a file and read in the next time the program is run. Such a run may simply extract data from the file, update it, or perform a combination of these procedures. In some cases, storing all data to be available for use by the program creates an array that is too large for storage in the main memory, and thus the data sets that would have been stored in an array for a small problem are now written as records on an external file.

General program example 6 — payroll reports

The program produces the same reports as its predecessor in Chapter 5. The report-printing logic and the computational procedures are identical to those in Chapter 5. The difference is that only the variable data (departments to be included in these reports and the hours worked by each employee) are read from cards. The reference data on each employee is kept on an external file.

In other words, the program illustrates one of the uses for files: retention of reference data. The reference file (also called *master file*) is a sequential-access file sequenced on the employee identification numbers (Figure 6-4). To avoid having to search the file from the beginning each time an employee data card is read, the data cards (Figure 6-4) also have been presorted on the ID numbers.

Problem description for general example 6

The program is to read employee pay data and produce two reports: (1) Error and Control Report and (2) Report of Pay Amounts. The Report of Pay Amounts is to contain a line for each employee and a total line at the end of the report. The employees are to be grouped by department in the report. In the Report of Pay Amounts, net pay that is negative or over $300.00 is accompanied by a warning note. Also, errors in input code for union/management employees are to be noted.

The first input to the program consists of a set of five department numbers and names, one pair per card. Input validation for this data consists of an output table that echoes the values for visual verification. Subsequent input data consists of one card for each employee, giving ID number, department where worked, and hours worked. These cards are arranged in ascending order on employee ID number. Errors detected on input are noted immediately with a suitable message. Following the reading of each employee card, one or more records are read from the reference file until reference data concerning the particular employee is found, or until it is established that the matching record is missing or a data error is present. When a matching record is found, it is retained in an array for use in computation and output. The reference file records consist of employee ID number, name, department number, pay rate, miscellaneous deductions, number of dependents, and type of employee (union/management). After all employee input cards have been read, a total record count and count of rejected cards are printed.

Program documentation for general example 6

Since there are very few differences between this program and general example 5, only a portion of the flowchart (Figure 6-5) and two blocks with code segments that are changed will be shown here (Figures 6-2 and 6-3). No pseudocode is given. New test data is documented in Figure 6-4. The Error and Control Report is shown in Figure 6-6. The Report of Pay Amounts, identical to Figure 5-10, is not shown here.

Notes on general example 6

The principal difference between this program and general example 5 is in block 100 where the employee data is read. Lines 25–27 of general example 5 have been replaced by lines 29–36 of general example 6 (Figure 6-2). Three new variable names have been added to name the employee data read from cards. These have been added to the list of variables at the beginning of the program (not shown). The reference master file is on unit 7; it was written by another program not shown.

Three additional error messages have been added in block 900 (Figure 6-3) to reflect possible file errors. Data-type errors and invalid input data errors print on the Error and Control Report (Figure 6-6); errors that cause the program to be terminated are not shown on the sample output. Since each employee number is supposed to be on the reference file and both the reference file and data cards have been sorted in ascending order, an error is indicated

Figure 6-2
Program block 100 as changed from general example 5 to general example 6 for payroll reports program.

```
          **********          READ EMPLOYEE DATA                    BLOCK 0100
        *                                                                     *
 29.      101 READ(5,103,END=301,ERR=901) IDNUM,NDEPT,HOURS
 30.      103 FORMAT(I5,I4,F4.1)
 31.          NCARD = NCARD + 1
 32.      102 READ(7,104,END=920,ERR=930) ID(NUM),NAME(NUM),
         1      NDEP(NUM),PAYDAT(NUM,2),PAYDAT(NUM,3),NDEPS(NUM),MTYPE(NUM)
 33.      104 FORMAT(I5,A12,I4,F4.2,F5.2,I2,I1)
 34.          IF(ID(NUM).LT.IDNUM) GOTO 102
 35.          IF(ID(NUM).GT.IDNUM) GOTO 910
 36.          PAYDAT(NUM,1) = HOURS
        *                                                                     *
        *          CHECK FOR VALID DEPARTMENT NUMBER IN EMPLOYEE CARD         *
        *          WHEN FOUND, PROCESS EMPLOYEE DATA                          *
        *                                                                     *
 37.          DO 105 K=1,NDEPTS
 38.              IF(DEPT(K).EQ.NDEP(NUM)) GOTO 201
 39.      105 CONTINUE
        *                                                                     *
        *          ERROR -- NO MATCH FOUND FOR EMPLOYEE DEPT. NUMBER          *
        *                                                                     *
 40.          GOTO 903
        *                                                                     *
        ***********************************************************************
```

Figure 6-3
Program block 900 as changed from general example 5 to general example 6 for payroll reports program.

```
          **********                    ERROR MESSAGE BLOCK                    BLOCK 0900
          *                                                                              *
  82.      901 NCARD = NCARD + 1
  83.          WRITE(6,902) NCARD
  84.      902 FORMAT(//' ***** ERROR IN DATA CARD NUMBER ',I2,' *****')
  85.          GOTO 908
          *****                                                                    *****
  86.      903 WRITE(6,904) NCARD
  87.      904 FORMAT(//' ***** ERROR - DEPT. NO. NOT VALID. CARD NO.  ',I4,
               1    2X,'*****')
          *                                                                              *
          *          GO BACK TO READ NEXT EMPLOYEE DATA CARD                             *
          *                                                                              *
  88.      908 GOTO 101
          *****                                                                    *****
  89.      906 WRITE(6,907) MAXEMP - 1
  90.      907 FORMAT(///' ***** ERROR. ATTEMPTED TO READ ',
               1    'MORE THAN',I3,' DATA CARDS'/7X,'PROGRAM ABORTED. *****')
  91.          GOTO 939
          *****                                                                    *****
  92.      910 WRITE(6,911) IDNUM,NDEPT,HOURS
  93.      911 FORMAT(//5X,'***** DATA CARD OUT OF ORDER OR NOT ON '/
               1    10X,'PERMANENT FILE.'/10X,2I5,F5.1,' IN DATA CARD.'/
               2    10X,'RUN ABORTED.')
  94.          GOTO 939
          *****                                                                    *****
  95.      920 WRITE(6,921) NCARD
  96.      921 FORMAT(//5X,'***** ATTEMPTED TO READ PAST END OF FILE 7.'
               1    /10X,I4,' CARDS READ. RUN ABORTED.')
  97.          GOTO 939
          *****                                                                    *****
  98.      930 WRITE(6,931)
  99.      931 FORMAT(//5X,'***** BAD DATA ON PERMANENT FILE. RUN ABORTED.')
          *                                                                              *
          *          ABNORMAL ERROR STOP                                                 *
          *                                                                              *
 100.      939 STOP
 101.          END
          *                                                                              *
          ****************************************************** END OF MAIN PROGRAM
```

Figure 6-4
Test data from card input and external file for general example 6 program. See also Figure 5-10.

INPUT DATA FROM CARDS

```
1234FIN      ⎫
4275ENGR     ⎪
7269MKTG     ⎬ Department numbers and names
7531PROD     ⎪
8551ACCT     ⎭
15786855139.9
23456753140.0
23457159640.0   Department number not valid
35748427540.1
36985726922.0
42753123440.0
4592.427537.5   Invalid. Data-type error
62475427537.5
69852427510.0
74365753154.0
```

DATA RECORDS ON EXTERNAL STORAGE FILE

```
15786RALPH JONES  85516.2824.68041
19834JOHN SMITH   24673.5730.93022
23456J. HOFFMANN  75313.5727.95021
23457T. HOFFMANN  15963.5727.95032
35748L. SMITH     42759.9430.68044
36985J. JOHNSON   7269027503598011
40865OSCAR JAMES  75314.5744.74042
42753R. M. NELSON12347.4557.64032
54309B. GRUENZEL  15964.85707.9021
62475Q. SIBLEY    42758.2465.34022
69852T. NAMAN     42752.6727.50091
74365A. PETERSON  75314.8254.63000
```

Figure 6-5
Flowchart showing file
processing in block 100
of general example 6 pro-
gram and associated
error messages in block
900.

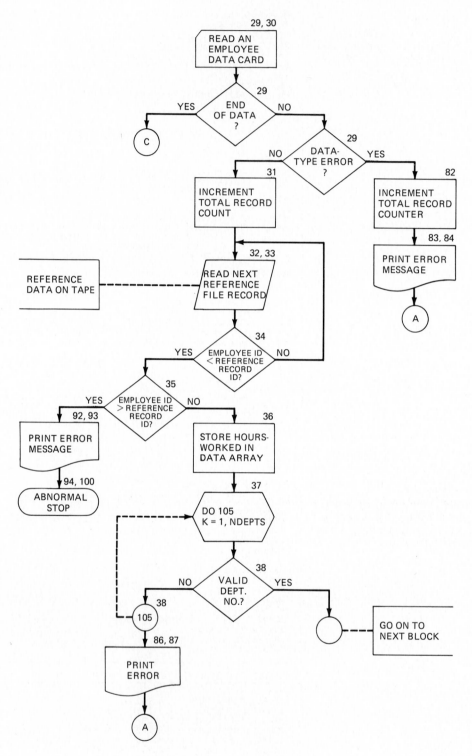

Figure 6-6
Error and Control Report
for general example 6
program using external
storage.

```
EMPLOYEE PAYCHECK PROGRAM


TABLE OF DEPARTMENTS
NUMBER   NAME
 1234    FIN
 4275    ENGR
 7269    MKTG
 7531    PROD
 8551    ACCT



    ERROR MESSAGES DURING DATA INPUT



***** ERROR - DEPT. NO. NOT VALID. CARD NO.      3  *****


***** ERROR IN DATA CARD NUMBER  7 *****

    1Ø CARDS READ
     2 CARDS REJECTED
```

if a higher ID number is found in the reference file than on the current input card. Also an error occurs if the reference file comes to an end without finding the ID number for the current input record. If the error were an improper sort or a mispunched data card rather than a missing employee record, more elaborate coding could be done to repeat the search of the file. For the sake of simplicity, the example program makes an abnormal stop after printing a suitable message and attempts no recovery or diagnostic procedure.

Statistical program example 6 — processing and filing research data with interactive input and output

This example illustrates the use of both a sequential file and a direct-access file. It also illustrates interactive terminal input and output, the use of a function for obtaining random numbers, the use of a subroutine for correction procedures, and the use of a log file for accumulating raw data and "backing up" analysis data. The problem has been deliberately kept simple to focus on these features.

Problem description for statistical example 6

A researcher takes temperature and humidity measurements from 12 sites selected randomly each day from 132 possible measurement locations. This will be done every day for 365 days. The data-recording procedure is the following:

1   Take measurements from 12 randomly selected locations (see step 4).

2   Add the measurements to the cumulative analysis record for each of the 12 sites. Use a random-access file with records numbered from 1 to 132, so that

record numbers correspond to site numbers; for example, the cumulative record for site 18 will be record number 18.

3 Add the 12 measurements to a log file of measurements. This sequential file is essentially a cumulative file of all measurements taken. It is a backup file of raw data in case there is a problem with the cumulative analysis file. It also provides raw data for further analysis at the end of the experiment.

4 Make random selection of the 12 sites from which to obtain measurements the following day.

The researcher sends the 12 data collection records to the computer through a terminal and receives back a report at the terminal consisting of four parts:

1 List of input data entered.
2 List of cumulative analysis results for the 12 sites affected by the input data.
3 Randomly selected list of 12 sites for measurement the next day.
4 Random start seed for use the next day.

The FORTRAN program processes data entered from a terminal and maintains the files at a computer center. This requires the program to do the following:

1 Establish an unformatted sequential file to act as the log file. This file will be opened each day and read until end of file, and will add records. Note that this may be a tape or a disk file used sequentially.

2 The unformatted direct-access analysis file is opened and, using the site number on the input as a record number, the analysis record to be processed is read. The input is used to update the analysis record and the updated result for the analysis record is printed. After all 12 inputs are processed and printed, the analysis file is closed.

3 The 12 sites are selected using a random number generator. The researcher enters a seed from the previous day. The terminal prints the 12 measurement sites as well as the random seed for the next day.

The data inputs, external file record contents, and outputs are as follows:

Data inputs at terminal
Date YYMMDD (characters for year, month, and day).

Measurements for 12 sites: site number, Fahrenheit temperature, humidity in percent.

Seed for random selection of sites for next measurement.

Record contents
Sequential log file: date, site, temperature, and humidity in each record.

Direct-access file for cumulative analysis: site (record number), number of observations to date, average temperature, and average humidity.

Outputs at terminal
Various messages to prompt input, verify data validation, and make corrections.

List of cumulative analysis for sites being processed.

List of sites for next measurements.

Seed for next use of random number generator.

List of input data.

Program documentation for statistical example 6

The documentation consists of a pseudocode program description (Figure 6-7), a program flowchart (Figure 6-8), a program listing (Figure 6-9), and a sample of results from processing a set of data (Figure 6-10). Note the three parts of the program—the main program, the correction subroutine, and the function to generate a random number.

Random number generation using a computer

When obtaining random numbers, it should not be possible to predict the next random number from the current random number, so true random numbers must be generated by some completely random process. When using a computer, numbers that appear to be random are generated by a deterministic process; if repeated, the computations yield the same sequence of numbers. For this reason, random numbers generated by computer are termed *pseudorandom numbers*. Overall, these numbers exhibit the characteristics of random numbers even though they are generated by a completely determined process.

If a random number computational process on a computer begins with the same initial value, it produces the same set of random numbers. This is very useful because a researcher may wish to repeat the same sequence of random numbers. However, in successive use of random numbers, it is important that the random number sequence continue rather than start over so that the random numbers used tomorrow do not repeat the random numbers used today. To continue the random number sequence, we carry forward from one session to the next a seed value that starts the random number computational process. For example, the seed at the end of one day can be saved and used as the seed at the beginning of the next day. (There are other possibilities for introducing randomness each day, but these are beyond the scope of this discussion.)

Random numbers typically are a string of digits in the range of values from 0 to 1 (decimal fractions) or in integer form. In the sample problem, the random numbers are in the range from 0 to 1. The user of the random number must process it to achieve a number within the desired range. For example, in the sample program (line 51), the program takes the integer value after multiplying the random number by 131 to yield a value between 0 and 131, and then adds 1 to provide a random number in the range 1–132.

In any set of random numbers, the same number can appear more than once. For example, if one is doing a random selection of numbers between 1 and 132, it is possible that 10 will appear twice, simply because of the random character of the sampling. This is the concept of *sampling with replacement*. What is desired in this particular case is sampling without replacement, so that a number will not be repeated within the sample once it has been chosen. This must be handled by the program. Each value is tested to determine if the number has already been obtained. This simple comparison is coded in the sample program in lines 52–54.

A random number can be obtained in two ways. One way is to write a ran-

Figure 6-7
Pseudocode description
of logic for statistical example 6—processing and
filing research data with
interactive input and
output.

Main program

```
OPEN log file (sequential access)
OPEN data file (direct access)
Position log file at its end
Input date of data readings from terminal
PRINT prompt of data
READ set of sites, temperatures, and humidities; store in arrays
PRINT input set (item number, sites, temperature, humidity)
PRINT 'ANY CHANGES OR CORRECTIONS'
READ answer
IF answer is Y (yes), then CALL data correction subroutine
WRITE report headings
For set of entries in arrays
     WRITE entry group to log file
     READ corresponding cumulative record from data file
     Compute new averages or establish initial values
     WRITE revised record to cumulative record data file
     PRINT revised record
End of loop
Prompt and READ new random number input seed
PRINT header
Compute 12 unique site numbers (1 ≤ site ≤ 132)
PRINT sites
PRINT new seed
REWIND log file
CLOSE data cumulative record file
END
```

Subroutine corect

```
Prompt and READ item number to be changed (on end-of-file, RETURN)
READ new site, temperature, humidity from terminal
Go back to Prompt
END
```

Function random

```
Initialize variables
Compute large random digit number
Compute high-order digits with MOD function
Compute low-order digits by subtraction of high-order digits
Scale random digits to between 0 and 1 (or bias interval)
RETURN
```

dom number function, as was done in this particular case. The second way is to use an external function, which is normally available from the computer center where one is running problems. Specifications must be obtained from the computer center to use such a function. It is not necessary to understand the details of random number computations to understand this problem. For more information, see the description of the procedure in programming exercise 2 of Chapter 5.

Figure 6-8
Program flowchart of statistical example 6 program processing and filing research data with interactive input and output.

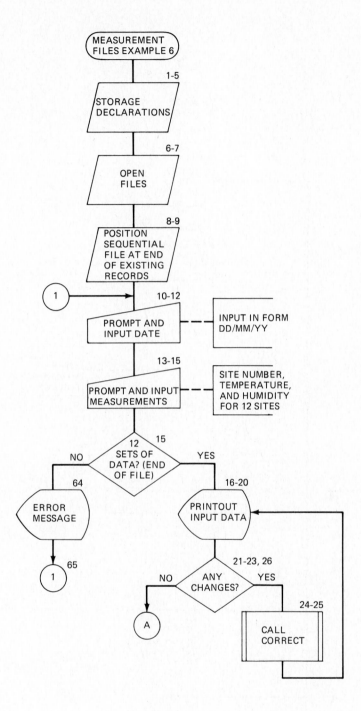

Figure 6-8
Continued.

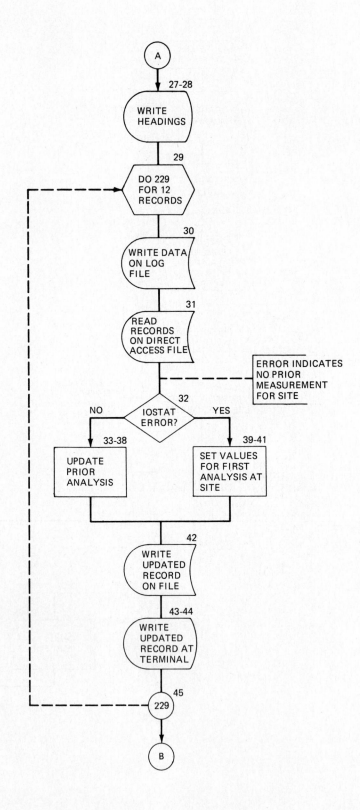

Figure 6-8
Continued.

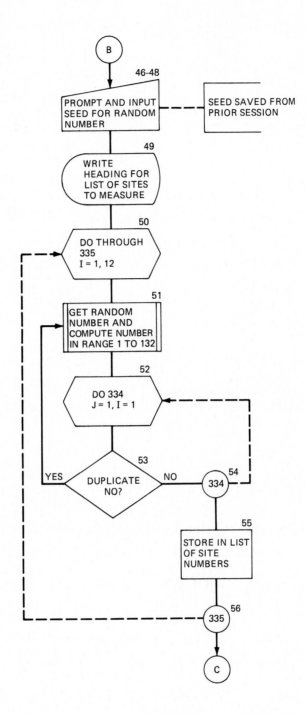

Figure 6-8
Continued.

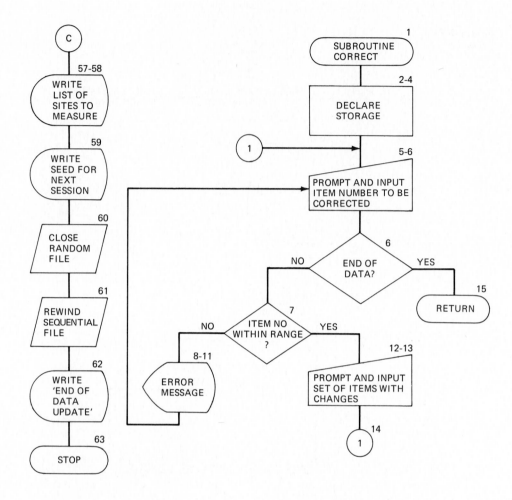

Flowcharting use of files and interactive input/output

The flowcharting of the file processing example with direct-access and sequential files and input/output at an online terminal uses symbols that do not appear in previous flowcharts.

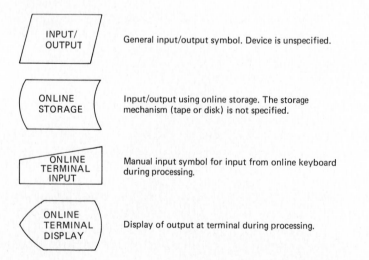

INPUT/OUTPUT — General input/output symbol. Device is unspecified.

ONLINE STORAGE — Input/output using online storage. The storage mechanism (tape or disk) is not specified.

ONLINE TERMINAL INPUT — Manual input symbol for input from online keyboard during processing.

ONLINE TERMINAL DISPLAY — Display of output at terminal during processing.

Figure 6-8
Continued.

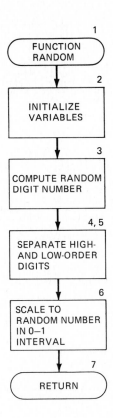

The first general symbol can be used instead of the three more specific symbols. The online file storage symbol can be used if the storage device or medium is unspecified. If it were known that magnetic tape or magnetic disk were being used for file storage, specific device symbols can be drawn:

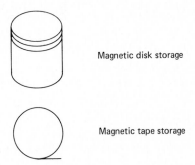

Magnetic disk storage

Magnetic tape storage

In the sample problem flowchart, the programmer specifies online storage. For the random-access file, this must be disk storage; for the sequential file, it can be either form of storage. Therefore, we chose to flowchart both files at the more general online storage symbol. General input/output preparation operations, such as opening and closing files, were diagrammed with the most general input/output symbol because these involve both operating system and device directory operations.

The flowcharting of input/output from the terminal could have always been done with a pair of symbols—the first for displaying the prompting message for entering input and the second for input from the terminal. If prompting

Figure 6-9
Program listing for statistical example 6—processing and filing research data with interactive input and output.

```
*********          PROGRAM IDENTIFICATION              *********
 *                                                               *
 *        RESRCH MAINTAINS A DIRECT ACCESS FILE OF AVERAGE TEMPS *
 *        AND HUMIDITIES AT 132 SITES. FOR FURTHER ANAYSIS AT THE*
 *        COMPLETION OF AN EXPERIMENT, A SEQUENTIAL LOG FILE IS   *
 *        MAINTAINED.  SITES FOR RANDOM SAMPLING ARE GENERATED.   *
 *        WRITTEN BY T.R. HOFFMANN 01/29/82                      *
 *                                                               *
 ****************************************************************
 *                                                               *
 *********          VARIABLE IDENTIFICATION             *********
 *                                                               *
 *        ANS    = RESPONSE TO INTERACTIVE INQUIRY               *
 *        DATE   = DATE OF UPDATE                                *
 *        HUMID  = AVERAGE HUMIDITY                              *
 *        IOS    = I/O STATUS: 0 = NO ERROR OR EOF               *
 *        MEASUR = NEW TEMP. AND HUMIDITY (ARRAY)                *
 *        NSITE  = NEW SITE CANDIDATE                            *
 *        OBS    = CUMULATIVE NUMBER OF OBSERVATIONS             *
 *        SEED   = SEED FOR RANDOM NUMBER GENERATOR              *
 *        SITE   = LIST OF SITES (ARRAY)                         *
 *        TEMP   = AVERAGE TEMPERATURE                           *
 *                                                               *
 *********     SUBROUTINE AND FUNCTION IDENTIFICATION   *********
 *                                                               *
 *        CORECT = CORRECTS INPUT DATA                           *
 *        RANDOM = RANDOM NUMBER GENERATOR                       *
 *                                                               *
 ****************************************************************
 *                                                               *
 *********     TYPE DECLARATION AND STORAGE ALLOCATION  *********
 *                                                               *
 1.          CHARACTER DATE*8,ANS*1
 2.          INTEGER SITE(12)
 3.          REAL MEASUR(12,2),HUMID
 4.          COMMON /IN/SITE,MEASUR
 5.          COMMON /RAN/SEED
 *                                                               *
 ****************************************************************
 *                                                               *
 *********          INITIALIZE FILES               BLOCK 0000
 *                                                               *
 6.          OPEN(7,FORM='UNFORMATTED')
 7.          OPEN(21,ACCESS='DIRECT',RECL=19)
 8.          DO 2 I= 1,4380
 9.        2 READ(7,END=101)
 *                                                               *
 ****************************************************************
 *                                                               *
 *********          READ INPUT DATA                BLOCK 0100
 *                                                               *
10.      101 WRITE(6,*) 'FOR WHAT DATE ARE THE FOLLOWING READINGS (DD/MM/YY)'
11.          READ(5,103) DATE
12.      103 FORMAT (A)
13.          WRITE(6,*) 'WHAT ARE THE 12 SITES, TEMPERATURES, AND HUMIDITIES'
14.          DO 112 I = 1,12
15.      112 READ(5,*,END=901) SITE(I),MEASUR(I,1),MEASUR(I,2)
16.      113 WRITE(6,114)
17.      114 FORMAT(1X,'ITEM',3X,'SITE',2X,'TEMP.',4X,'HUMIDITY')
18.          DO 115 I = 1,12
19.      115 WRITE(6,117) I,SITE(I),MEASUR(I,1),MEASUR(I,2)
20.      117 FORMAT(1X,I4,3X,I4,F7.1,F9.1)
21.          WRITE(6,*) 'ANY CHANGES OR CORRECTIONS (Y/N)'
22.          READ (5,103,END=201) ANS
23.          IF (ANS .EQ. 'Y') THEN
24.              CALL CORECT
 *                                                               *
 *****        GO BACK AND PRINT CORRECTED DATA INPUTS       *****
 *                                                               *
25.              GOTO 113
26.          ENDIF
 *                                                               *
 ****************************************************************
 *                                                               *
 *********     COMPUTE AVERAGES, UPDATE FILES, AND PRINT    BLOCK 0200
 *                                                               *
27.      201 WRITE(6,221) DATE
28.      221 FORMAT(///1X,'CUMMULATIVE ANALYSIS FOR SITES MEASURED ON',1X,
         1    A8//1X,'SITE',3X,'NUMBER OF',7X,'AVERAGE',5X,'AVERAGE'/
         2    8X,'OBSERVATIONS',2X,'TEMPERATURE',3X,'HUMIDITY'//)
29.          DO 229 I = 1,12
30.              WRITE(7) SITE(I),MEASUR(I,1),MEASUR(I,2)
31.              READ(21,REC = SITE(I),IOSTAT=IOS) OBS,TEMP,HUMID
32.              IF(IOS .NE. 0) GOTO 225
```

Figure 6-9
Continued.

```
33.                     TEMP = TEMP*OBS + MEASUR(I,1)
34.                     HUMID = HUMID*OBS + MEASUR(I,2)
35.                     OBS = OBS + 1.0
36.                     TEMP = TEMP/OBS
37.                     HUMID = HUMID/OBS
38.                     GOTO 227                                                 *
        *                                                                       *
        *               FIRST TIME PROCESSING                                   *
        *                                                                       *
39.         225         OBS = 1.0
40.                     TEMP = MEASUR(I,1)
41.                     HUMID = MEASUR(I,2)
42.         227         WRITE(21,REC = SITE(I)) OBS,TEMP,HUMID
43.                     WRITE(6,228) SITE(I),OBS,TEMP,HUMID
44.         228         FORMAT(1X,I3,6X,F5.0,8X,F7.1,5X,F7.1)
45.         229 CONTINUE
        *                                                                       *
        *************************************************************************
        *                                                                       *
        **********          GENERATE FUTURE SITE SAMPLE           BLOCK 0300
        *                                                                       *
46.             WRITE(6,331)
47.         331 FORMAT(///1X,'WHAT IS SEED FOR NEXT RANDOM SELECTION')
48.             READ(5,*) SEED
49.             WRITE(6,*) 'SITES FOR NEXT SET OF OBSERVATIONS'
50.             DO 335 I = 1,12
51.         333     NSITE = INT(RANDOM(0.0)*132.0) + 1
52.                 DO 334 J = 1,I-1
        *                   CHECK FOR UNIQUENESS - IF ALREADY SELECTED, CHOOSE ANOTHER
53.                         IF(NSITE .EQ. SITE(J)) GOTO 333
54.         334         CONTINUE
55.                 SITE(I) = NSITE
56.         335 CONTINUE
57.             WRITE(6,337) (SITE(I),I=1,12)
58.         337 FORMAT(1X,6(I5,2X))
59.             WRITE(6,*) 'NEW SEED IS ',INT(SEED)
60.             CLOSE(21)
61.             REWIND 7
62.             WRITE(6,*) 'END OF DATA UPDATE'
63.             STOP                                                            *
        *                                                                       *
        *************************************************************************
        *                                                                       *
        **********          ERROR MESSAGE BLOCK                   BLOCK 0900
        *                                                                       *
64.         901 WRITE(6,*) 'ERROR - INSUFFICIENT DATA. RE-ENTER FROM BEGINNING.'
65.             GOTO 101
66.             END                                                             *
        *                                                                       *
        ************************************************** END OF MAIN PROGRAM
```

```
1.      *       SUBROUTINE CORECT                                               *
        *                                                                       *
        **********          PROGRAM IDENTIFICATION               **********
        *                                                                       *
        *               CORRECT OR CHANGE INPUT DATA                            *
        *                                                                       *
        *************************************************************************
        *                                                                       *
        **********          VARIABLE IDENTIFICATION              **********
        *                                                                       *
        *       ITEM    = ITEM NUMBER OF SET TO BE CHANGED                      *
        *       MEASUR  = NEW TEMP. AND HUMIDTY (ARRAY)                         *
        *       SITE    = LIST OF SITES (ARRAY)                                 *
        *                                                                       *
        *************************************************************************
        *                                                                       *
        **********          TYPE DECLARATION AND STORAGE ALLOCATION   **********
        *                                                                       *
2.              REAL MEASUR(12,2)
3.              INTEGER SITE(12)
4.              COMMON /IN/ SITE,MEASUR
        *                                                                       *
        *************************************************************************
        *                                                                       *
        **********          CORRECT A DATA SET                    BLOCK 0100
        *                                                                       *
5.              WRITE(6,*) 'WHICH ITEM NUMBER DO YOU WANT TO CHANGE'
6.          103 READ(5,*,END=111) ITEM
7.              IF(ITEM .LT. 1 .OR. ITEM .GE. 12) THEN
8.                  WRITE(6,*) 'ERROR -- ITEM NUMBER MUST BE BETWEEN 1 AND 12.'
9.                  WRITE(6,*) 'RE-ENTER ITEM NUMBER.'
```

Figure 6-9
Continued.

```
10.                GOTO 103
11.          ENDIF
12.          WRITE(6,*) 'TO WHAT SITE, TEMPERATURE, AND HUMIDITY'
13.          READ(5,*) SITE(ITEM),MEASUR(ITEM,1),MEASUR(ITEM,2)
14.                GOTO 103
15.      111 RETURN
16.          END
      *                                                          *
      ****************************************************  END OF SUBPROGRAM
```

```
 1.          FUNCTION RANDOM(DUM)
      *                                                                *
      **********              PROGRAM IDENTIFICATION              **********
      *                                                                *
      *        RANDOM NUMBER GENERATOR                                 *
      *        CALLED FROM MAIN PROGRAM                                *
      *                                                                *
      ****************************************************************************
      *                                                                *
      **********              VARIABLE IDENTIFICATION              **********
      *                                                                *
      *        B       = CONSTANT MULTIPLIER = 3213.0                  *
      *        C       = HIGH ORDER DIGITS OF PRODUCT                  *
      *        SEED    = LOW ORDER DIGITS OF PRODUCT                   *
      *        F       = CONSTANT SCALE FACTOR = 1.0E7                 *
      *        S       = CONSTANT SCALE FACTOR = 10000.0               *
      *        DUM     = DUMMY ARGUMENT OR BIAS FACTOR                 *
      *        R       = RANDOM DIGITS                                 *
      *                                                                *
      ****************************************************************************
      *                                                                *
      **********      TYPE DECLARATION AND STORAGE ALLOCATION      **********
      *                                                                *
 2.          COMMON /RAN/SEED
 3.          DATA S/10000./,F/1.0E7/,B/3213.0/,C/1230000./
      *                                                          *
      ****************************************************************************
      *                                                                *
      **********              GENERATE RANDOM NUMBER              BLOCK 0100
      *                                                                *
 4.          R = AMOD((AMOD(B*C,F) + AMOD(B*SEED,F)),F)
 5.          SEED = AMOD(R,S)
 6.          C = R - SEED
 7.          RANDOM = R/F + DUM
 8.          RETURN
      *                                                          *
      ****************************************************  END OF SUBPROGRAM
 9.          END
```

is followed by input, we have used only one symbol and have included the prompt as part of the input symbol, as shown below:

Notes on statistical example 6

Although all of the problems presented in the text can be written and executed on a terminal using timesharing FORTRAN, this is the only regular problem that was written specifically to illustrate features of timesharing. Input is in list-directed input so that the user at the terminal does not need to spend time formatting and ensuring that the data appears in the correct columns (lines 15 and 48). Errors detected through input validation are immediately relayed to the terminal, and correct input is requested.

Figure 6-10
Output from interactive
execution of statistical
program 6—processing
and filing research data
with interactive input
and output.

```
 FOR WHAT DATE ARE THE FOLLOWING READINGS (DD/MM/YY)
? 02/09/82
 WHAT ARE THE 12 SITES, TEMPERATURES, AND HUMIDITIES
? 21,60,73
? 28,44,24
? 35,5,37
? 51,70,55
? 56,48,77
? 63,73,45
? 64,47,23
? 74,49,75
? 77,40,85
? 96,83,22
? 107,75,48
? 83,60,35
 ITEM   SITE   TEMP.    HUMIDITY
   1     21    60.0      73.0
   2     28    44.0      24.0
   3     35     5.0      37.0
   4     51    70.0      55.0
   5     56    48.0      77.0
   6     63    73.0      45.0
   7     64    47.0      23.0
   8     74    49.0      75.0
   9     77    40.0      85 0
  10     96    83.0      22.0
  11    107    75.0      48.0
  12     83    60.0      35.0
 ANY CHANGES OR CORRECTIONS (Y/N)
? N
```

```
 CUMMULATIVE ANALYSIS FOR SITES MEASURED ON 02/09/82

 SITE   NUMBER OF      AVERAGE       AVERAGE
        OBSERVATIONS   TEMPERATURE   HUMIDITY


  21       7.            59.9          72.7
  28      36.            45.1          20.2
  35       7.             4.4          32.7
  51      20.            68.0          56.7
  56      20.            44.6          76.3
  63      22.            71.6          43.9
  64      37.            45.9          14.4
  74      28.            48.4          80.4
  77      11.            39.4          88.1
  96      37.            80.8          17.3
 107      10.            74.7          47.4
  83       1.            60.0          35.0
```

```
 WHAT IS SEED FOR NEXT RANDOM SELECTION
? 4567
 SITES FOR NEXT SET OF OBSERVATIONS
    88     10     92     41     91    116
    26    122    131    113    121     43
 NEW SEED IS 7663
 END OF DATA UPDATE
```

The program has a number of interesting features and uses relative to files and interactive terminal input/output.

1   The files to be used are opened. The sequential file on unit 7 is declared to be unformatted (line 6), and the file on unit 21 is declared to be direct and have a record length of 19 units, which allows for expansion (line 7). The direct-access file is, by default, unformatted. The record length depends on the design of the computer being used, and thus the specific manual must be consulted.

2   The numbers for the files (7 and 21) are established by a job control statement before this program. Units 5 and 6 for reader and printer do not require definition if they are also default units for terminal input and output.

3   Since data items are to be added to the previous contents of the sequential file, the file must be positioned at this point. Lines 8 and 9 read until END; then, the file is positioned for addition of new records.

4   The prompting question for input of the date specifies the desired form since data could be in different forms (line 10).

5   The program asks for 12 sets of measurements. If the data sets end before 12 sets are received (ended by a terminal RETURN without data), the END condition is processed (line 15) and the program prints an error message and asks for re-entry of data from the beginning (line 64). The request for complete re-entry is reasonable for a small amount of input; if there were a large amount of input, some correction might be attempted.

6   The program prints the input data and specifically requests verification that there are no errors (line 21). Perhaps more validation could also be programmed, but a request for visual validation is a good control procedure. Note that file alteration does not occur until after data validation.

7   Error correction is an error-prone activity. In the example, prompting of error correction inputs is handled by a separate subroutine (CORECT) that is called if errors are identified (line 24). In CORECT, the line number to be changed is requested and the item number is validated as being within the range of 12 input items. The corrected set of data is then entered. Note that after the return from CORECT, control goes back to print the set of inputs with corrections (line 25).

8   The logic of the program is to read the previous analysis data on a site from the direct-access file, to add the current measurements, and to increment the count of measurements. The difficulty is the first measurement for a site. Until it is recorded, the record contents are undefined. In the sample program, this is handled by an IOSTAT specification in the READ statement (line 31). If the program attempts to read where no data has been stored, IOS is set to a nonzero value. IOS is tested and control is transferred appropriately. If there is no error, the record is updated; if an error is present, the three lines of code (lines 39–41) establish the initial contents using the first measurement. The program then continues with the analysis printout and writing of the updated (or initial) data on the direct-access file (lines 42, 43).

9   The program uses a seed saved from the previous time to start the random number generator. The first time the program is used, an initial seed is specified. A prime number is generally used for this purpose, but any odd number will do.

In reviewing the program, notice the way the characteristics of interactive input/output change the program from the way it might have been written for batch processing. Consider if additional input data validation might be useful.

Programming exercises

Description of assignment

Select one or more problems (or take the problems assigned by your instructor). Write each of the programs in such a manner as to make use of an external file. Follow the style guidelines and prepare the following:

1 Pseudocode description
2 Program flowchart
3 Program listing
4 List of test data and expected results; provide validity checks
5 Output including error detection

Mathematics and statistics

1 Sometimes data sets may be quite large and hence they are stored on external files. Modify the program for problem 1 of Chapter 5 to read the data sets from a file, each record of which contains a number pair.

2 When forming the product of two square matrices, it may be desirable to store the product in the location of one of the original matrices. An easy way to accomplish this is to form the product a vector at a time on a file and then to read the completed product back into the location of one of the original matrices. (For small matrices an array could be used, but that would not be practical for large matrices because of storage limitations.) Write a program that accomplishes this procedure. Print out the final matrix. As demonstration data use the following two pairs of matrices and form A × B and B × A (if defined).

A						B				
	2	7	11			1	5	7	11	
1	3	9	−3			−2	9	−3	4	
	4	−1	4			6	5	−2	1	
	−6	3	8			0	6	9	2	
	17	24	1	8	15	2	3	9	−10	−4
	23	5	7	14	16	−5	1	7	8	−11
2	4	6	13	20	22	−12	−6	0	6	12
	10	12	19	21	3	11	−8	−7	−1	5
	11	18	25	2	9	4	10	−9	−3	−2

3 Random number generators can be tested in a variety of ways to ensure that they are not biased. One way is the χ^2 (chi-square) test for uniform distribution of the numbers. In theory, if N random numbers distributed between 0 and 1 are generated and divided into n classes of equal size, there should be N/n values in each class. For example, if 20 classes were established they would be as follows:

Class number	Interval boundaries
1	0.00–0.04999 . . .
2	0.05–0.09999 . . .
3	0.10–0.14999 . . .
.	.
.	.
.	.
20	0.95–0.99999 . . .

Assuming 2000 numbers were used, they should be distributed with 100 values in each class. The conformance of actual (A_i for the ith class) to theoretical can be tested by computation of the following:

$$X^2 = \sum_{i=1}^{n} \frac{[A_i - (N/n)]^2}{N/n} = \sum_{i=1}^{20} \frac{(A_i - 100)^2}{100} \qquad \text{for the example}$$

This value can be compared to the appropriate χ^2 value for $n - 1$ degrees of freedom and a 5 or 10 percent significance level. If X^2 is greater than the appropriate χ^2 value, the random number generator is faulty.

Write a program to test three random number generators: the mid-square method described in problem 2 in Chapter 5, the power residue method shown as part of statistical example 6, and the function provided as a system or local library function. Write the program so that the number of values generated is from 100 to 10,000 and the number of cells from 10 to 30. The program should contain the capability of printing the computed X^2 and χ^2 values for 5 and 10 percent significance levels. Prepare a file containing a table of χ^2 values that might be needed and read the appropriate values from it.

Business and economics

4 Write a program designed to maintain the personnel data file of general example 6. It should be capable of correcting data errors (such as the incorrect union/management codes), deleting entire records, or adding new records in their appropriate place. A report should accompany each such update run that tells what alterations were made and accounts for the cards read, records changed, and new and old file sizes (in numbers of records).

5 Refer to problem 6 in Chapter 4. Write the program so that the portfolio is maintained as a direct-access file and only the transactions are from cards. Program it in such a way that both a summary report of the transactions and a final position statement are printed.

6 Do problem 5 above using a sequential file.

Science and engineering

7 A common utility package available at each computer installation is an external file sorting program. The sorting program, frequently used by many other programs, is called a *system utility*. Various techniques exist for sorting; one of these is the following. Assume first that two strings of presorted data exist and that they are to be merged into one long, sorted string. This can be accomplished by comparing just two records at a time as illustrated in Figure 6-11. If there were two such pairs of strings initially, each pair could be merged into a long string and then those long strings could be merged

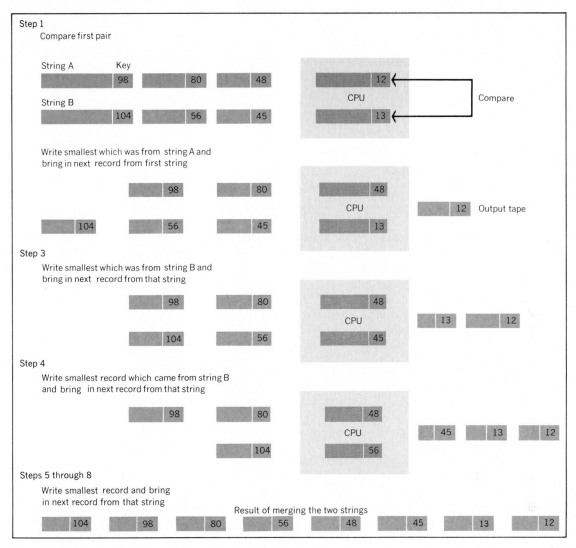

Step 1
Compare first pair

String A   Key

String B

Write smallest which was from string A and
bring in next record from first string

Step 3
Write smallest which was from string B and
bring in next record from that string

Step 4
Write smallest record which came from string B
and bring in next record from that string

Steps 5 through 8
Write smallest record and bring
in next record from that string

Result of merging the two strings

Figure 6-11 Logic of merge sorting of presorted strings.

into a final sorted string. The initial strings can be established by taking a relatively small set of records and sorting them internally by a method such as the bubble sort described in problem 7 in Chapter 4. Write a program that will take a file of unsorted four-digit numbers and sort it as described above. For sample data use either 80 randomly generated numbers or numbers taken from a phone directory. Internally sort groups of 10 numbers to generate the initial strings. Print out the initial unsorted data and the final sorted data.

8   Editing of data files is a common task, and many installations have text editors. As a very rudimentary form of text editing, write a program that will operate upon your program deck from Chapter 5 and separate all comment lines from the rest of the program. Print out three listings: full deck, comments only, and balance of program. Use external files so this can be accomplished in only one run.

9   External files are often established when data sets are expected to become very large. Write a program that can take as input hourly temperatures and add them to a data file on a daily basis. The program should also prepare periodic summary reports on daily maximum, minimum, and average temperatures.

In addition, it should print out the cumulative number of heating or cooling degree days for the period. These are defined as:

$$\bar{t} = \text{mean temperature} = \frac{\text{maximum temperature} - \text{minimum temperature}}{2}$$

degree day (cooling) $= t - 65$

degree day (heating) $= 65 - t$ (Fahrenheit temperatures used here)

Humanities and social science

10 Since the number of respondents to a survey is initially unknown and responses may come in over time, it is often useful to store the data on an external file. Create the file and reprogram problem 10 of Chapter 5 to read response data from such a file.

11 Concordances are usually not done on short texts such as given in problem 11 of Chapter 4. In fact the volume of data may be quite large. Create a text file and reprogram that problem to read the source text from an external file one line at a time.

12 A study is to be made of the eating habits of a target population. Create two programs: one that will add, correct, and maintain the data file and another that will summarize its contents. The file contains a record for each meal eaten by an individual. The record simply indicates whether or not something from each of the following food groups was eaten at a particular meal.

Dairy products

Cereals

Fruit

Meat

Vegetables

The survey data should indicate the percent for each major meal, that each category was consumed. The summary should be for all subjects or, alternatively, for a selected subject.

General

13 Student grades are a function of homework scores and grades on quizzes and a final exam. Write a program that creates, corrects, and adds to a file of student grades. Consider each of the following columns of data to be update information for the file that must be handled by separate runs of the program.

Name	HW1	Q1	Q2	F
Anderson, Alan	95	67	70	74
Brown, Stewart	95	87	70	80
Carr, David	100	60	80	70
Daly, William	60	65	65	68
Erickson, Jane	45	79	90	87
Gruenzel, Lorna	90	93	87	95
Kohler, Wayne	95	82	80	78
Nelson, Joyce	75	73	75	84
Ray, Ruth	100	85	65	87
Taylor, Alice	50	73	60	75

In addition, the following corrections had to be made after the original grade was recorded.

Name	Action
Carr, David	HW1 from 100 to 90
Kohler, Wayne	Q1 from 82 to 87
Ray, Ruth	Q2 from 65 to 73

14 External data files are often maintained because new data is being added over an extended period of time. Write a program that will create and maintain a file of batting statistics for a baseball team. Include times at bat, runs batted in, and hits. Print out updated totals with each change of a record. Employ a direct-access file and use each player's number as an index to the player's record.

15 A personalized dictionary of words or names can be quite useful. In the forthcoming age of personal computers, such files will be quite common. Write a program that will create, correct, and maintain such a file. It should be capable of adding or deleting definitions, and, of course, searching for words already in it and printing out the definition. As minimum test data select 15 FORTRAN words or commands from this text and create your own definition of them.

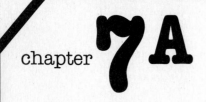

chapter **7A**

Additional Features

This chapter explains elements of FORTRAN not previously described—additional data types and character string processing, additional FORMAT specifiers, some additional statements and features having relatively little use, additional instructions for subprograms, and handling of internal files. Some statements are also summarized that should normally not be used because they impair clear, well-understood programming.

Additional data types

The concept of data type was presented in Chapter 2A, where the difference between integer and real types was explained and the first letter convention (I-N for integer-type data) was described. In addition to integer and real types, the character type was explained. The type statements to declare INTEGER, REAL, or CHARACTER were introduced and used in problems.

Three additional types of data are allowed in FORTRAN. The section will explain the three types, their representation, and the way a variable is specified as being one of these types. The three additional data types are double precision, complex, and logical. These additional types are not part of Subset FORTRAN.

1   Double-precision data items are real data items that provide greater precision (usually double) than single-precision real variables, which are normally used. This requires two storage spaces for each double-precision data item. A single variable name defined as a double-precision type is used to reference the double-length representation. A double-precision constant is written in the same form as a constant with an exponent, except that it is written with a D instead of an E. Examples are $0.317657695D - 15$ and $134565D + 50$. The reason for double precision is to improve the precision of computation and output. Some compilers use a high precision for single-precision variables, and thus double precision is rarely needed; but some compilers use fairly limited precision, thus making double precision useful when, a greater number of digits are required.

2   Complex data items are represented by an ordered pair of real data items: one representing the real part and one the imaginary part of a complex number. A complex data constant is written as an ordered pair inside parentheses; for example, (3.5,4.1) where 3.5 is the real part and 4.1 is the imaginary part.

3   Logical data variables assume only values for true or false. Values to input to a logical variable are T (or .TRUE.) or F (or .FALSE.); output of a logical variable is T or F. Logical constants consist of .TRUE. or .FALSE.. For example, if X is defined as a logical variable, X = .TRUE. will set X to the value for true.

Type declaration for other data types

As explained earlier, integer and real data types may be defined by the first-letter convention, but that convention may be overridden by a type declaration. Character data must be declared as CHARACTER in a type declaration. The additional data types (DOUBLE PRECISION, COMPLEX, and LOGICAL) may use any symbolic name (up to six characters) with any first letter. The name chosen for these data types is designated as referring to a given type by a type declaration. The type declaration must appear before the first use of any variable it defines. We recommend that it be placed in the type declaration and storage allocation block at the beginning of the program in which it is used.

TYPE DECLARATION FOR TYPES OTHER THAN CHARACTER

type $v_1, v_2, \ldots, v_n$

where *type* may be:

INTEGER
REAL
DOUBLE PRECISION
COMPLEX
LOGICAL

v_1 refers to a variable name, array name, array declarator, or function name to be defined as of the stated type.

Note that the type declaration can be used for a single variable, an array, or a function name. The array can be dimensioned as part of the type statement. Some examples illustrate these type declarations.

COMPLEX ALPHA makes ALPHA refer to a complex type variable.

DOUBLE PRECISION X,Y,Z makes X, Y, and Z the names of double-precision variables.

DOUBLE PRECISION GOOD (100) declares the array GOOD to be double precision and size 100.

LOGICAL FLAG makes FLAG refer to logical data.

The FORTRAN language has an implicit type for integer and real variables based on the first letter of the variable name (I–N for integer variables, A–H and O–Z for real variables). It is possible to alter the first-letter convention by making all variables with a given first letter a declared type. In other words, not only may the integer and real first-letter convention be altered, but first-letter typing may be defined for other types. This is done with the IMPLICIT declaration. It must appear before any other specification statements. Be careful when declaring variable names integer. One useful application of IMPLICIT INTEGER is to make all variables in a program of integer type.

IMPLICIT DECLARATION

IMPLICIT type $(C_1, C_2, \ldots, C_n)$

makes any variable name starting with the letter C_i of the declared type.

IMPLICIT type $(C_m - C_n)$

makes all variables names beginning with C_m to C_n of the declared type.

If type is CHARACTER, it defines a one-character length unless a length is specified as part of the IMPLICIT declaration or by individual CHARACTER declarations.

Example

```
IMPLICIT INTEGER (A, B), REAL (L-N)
COMPLEX ABLE, BAKER
IMPLICIT CHARACTER*6(O-R)
```

The first statement defines variables with names starting with A or B as integer and variable names starting with L, M, or N as real. Variable names ABLE and BAKER refer to COMPLEX variables even though they begin with A and B, because the explicit type declaration overrides the IMPLICIT declaration. The last statement defines all variable names beginning with the letter O–R as referencing character variables of six-character length.

Additional intrinsic functions for other data types

There are intrinsic functions to handle arithmetic involving the double-precision and complex data types. The generic name or the specific name may be used. In general, the specific name is the same one used for real variables but with a D prefixing double-precision functions and a C prefixing complex functions (where complex functions make sense). For example, the SQRT real function is DSQRT for double precision and CSQRT for complex data types. The complete list of functions is given on the inside of the front cover.

Self-testing exercise 7-1

1 Declare variables YEARS and PERIOD as integer variables and MONTH as a real variable.

2 Declare ALPHA, M, and Y as double-precision variables.

3 If ALPHA is declared as a double-precision variable, what does this mean in terms of (a) storage required and (b) precision (explain)?

4 Assume X is defined as the type specified and write statements to store the constant value in X.

Type	Constant to be stored
(a) COMPLEX	Real value of 4 and imaginary value of 2.1
(b) DOUBLE PRECISION	91.05676500007482
(c) LOGICAL	Value for false condition

5 Take the square root of a double-precision variable DRATE. Store the result in DX.

Additional character string instructions
Defining and manipulating a character string or substring

It may be useful to summarize handling of character data. The string of characters is assigned a variable name. Variable names assigned to character strings do not have any special first letter. A variable name is explicitly defined as character type by a CHARACTER type declaration. The CHARACTER type declaration can be used for individual variable names, for character arrays, and for functions that are to be declared as character type. Variables declared to be CHARACTER can be any length because the length is specified by the type statement. Also, variables declared to be CHARACTER can be initialized in a DATA statement.

A new 1977 FORTRAN feature is the substring. A character substring is a continuous portion of a character string. It has a name and may be assigned values and referenced. The substring name is followed by the character identification for the first and last characters to be included, separated by a colon. For example, the characters stored in positions 8 to 10 of character variable ALPHA are assigned a substring name BETA by the following:

```
BETA = ALPHA (8:10)
```

Integer expressions can also be used to specify the limits of the substring. For example,

```
BETA = ALPHA (3 * JIX:20)
```

where the beginning of the substring is the integer value of 3 * JIX and the end is 20.

Character strings or substrings can be combined by the concatenation operator //. For example, if A, B, and X are defined as a character type of length 3, 3, and 6 and A and B contain 'NOW' and ' IS', the statement

```
X = A//B
```

will produce a string X with the value 'NOW IS'. Character constants may be used. For example,

```
X = 'NOW'//B
```

will also yield a stored value in the character variable X of 'NOW IS'.

Intrinsic functions for character data

There are a number of intrinsic functions designed especially to process character data. Four functions are provided to locate the position and length of character data:

Intrinsic function	Argument	Result
LEN (c)	Character variable name	Length of the character string stored in the character variable
INDEX (c_1, c_2)	Character variable, expression, or constant for string c_1 and substring c_2	Integer giving starting position of first occurrence of substring in string
The n characters in the processor collating sequence of the computer being used are numbered from 0 to n − 1. For example, if G is 39, R will be 50.		
CHAR (ie)	Integer or integer expression	The character in the integer position of collating sequence
ICHAR (c)	A character variable containing one character	An integer identifiying position in the collating sequence of the character defined by the argument

Examples   Assume (for illustration purposes) collating sequence with A = 0, B = 1, etc.

IDL = ICHAR (UNKNON) will yield a value of 6 for IDL if UNKNON stores 'G'.

IDN = CHAR (NCARA) will provide a value of 'F' if NCARA contains 5.

ISTR = INDEX (STR1, STR2) will provide a value of 3 for ISTR if STR1 contains AWFUL and STR2 contains FU.

There are four intrinsic functions for comparing standard lexical relationships of two character strings.

Intrinsic function	Result returns value of true if
LGE (a_1,a_2)	The character string a_1 is equal to or follows a_2 in the collating sequence.
LGT (a_1,a_2)	The character string a_1 follows a_2 in the collating sequence.
LLE (a_1,a_2)	The character string a_1 is equal to or precedes a_2 in the collating sequence.
LLT (a_1,a_2)	The character string a_1 precedes a_2 in the collating sequence.

The collating sequence in all cases is defined as the ASCII, American National Standard Code for Information Interchange, which includes a standard collating sequence. Programs using these functions will therefore produce identical results without regard to the collating sequence designed into the computer being used. As an example of the lexical intrinsic functions, assume two character strings named NAME1 and NAME2 containing JENNIFER and CLARK. The instruction

IF (LGT (NAME1, NAME2)) GOTO 200

will transfer control to statement 200 because JENNIFER follows CLARK in the standard collating sequence. The importance of the LGE, etc., functions is apparent in comparisons with special characters. Is 'AB$' less than or greater than 'ABC'? When using standard .GT., etc., functions, it depends on the collating sequence built into the computer. The LXX comparison functions are based on an agreed-upon standard; thus, for all compilers, the results will be that 'AB$' is less than 'ABC'.

Self-testing exercise 7-2

1 Define a substring MISS (call it STR1) out of MISSISSIPPI that is stored in STATEM.

2 If I = 1, concatenate MISS in STR1 with STR2 containing OURI.

3 Compare a character variable LNAME with the constant CLARK. If equal, go to 600.

4 Define a substring ABREV as characters 1 to 3 of LNAME.

5 Concatenate the contents of ABREV and the constant 'ABC' to form CBREV.

6 Initialize a character variable FNAME with AARON.

7 An 11-character field MISSISSIPPI is to be printed using a specification of A6. What will be printed?

8 Find the length in characters of a heading (HEAD) to be centered. Store it in HEADLN.

337

Advanced **FORMAT** features

The basic FORMAT features were explained in Chapter 3. However, the additional data types explained in this chapter require special FORMAT edit descriptors. Also, there are additional FORMAT descriptors that are not commonly used, but they may be useful in special situations. It is also possible to be more flexible in FORMAT specification use by storing and referencing them as character variables or character arrays or by writing them in the input or output statement.

Additional **FORMAT** edit descriptors

Before presenting the added edit descriptors, it may be helpful to review the basic edit descriptors already explained (w = field length in characters, d = number of positions to right of decimal, n = integer constant, and h = Hollerith character).

Descriptor	Meaning
Iw	Integer input/output
Fw.d	Real input/output
Ew.d	Exponent form of real input/output
Aw	Character input/output
'h . . .'	Apostrophe form of character output
nHhhh . . .	H form of character output
/	Terminate record
Tc	Tabulate to position c for next output or input
nX	Skip over n positions

These basic edit descriptors are all included in Subset FORTRAN except for Tc. Of the additional edit descriptors, only Lw, BN, BZ, and nP are included in Subset FORTRAN.

A useful alternative to F or E when data values have a wide range is:

Gw.d	Same as F editing for input. Compiler chooses E or F editing for output based on data values.

The FORMAT edit descriptors for the double-precision and logical data types are:

Data type	Descriptor	Meaning
Double precision	Dw.d	To define input or output editing for double-precision data. The output will be similar to F format, but a larger number of digits may be available for use.
Logical	Lw	Logical field containing a T (or .TRUE.) for true or F (or .FALSE.) on input and a T or F on output.
Complex		Complex data (in two parts) is read by two F, E, D, or G edit descriptors.

There are also added FORMAT edit descriptors to alter the normal editing for input or output.

FOR INPUT

BN   BN specifies blank characters are to be ignored (the default case in 1977 FOR-TRAN).

BZ   BZ specifies blanks are zeros.

Specifies all subsequent handling of blanks in editing of numeric data by the input or output unit.

As an example of BN and BZ edit specifications, assume integer data called JCOUNT is defined as being in columns 1–5. Using three cards to illustrate, the data will be interpreted by an I5 specification and BZ or BN as follows:

Card	Data	Interpreted by I5 and BZ as	Interpreted by I5 and BN as
1	3 7	00370	37
2	1 2	01200	12
3	1 3	00013	13

Use of a BZ specification causes the input system to make blanks into zeros:

701 FORMAT (BZ, I5, BN, . . .)

The BZ refers to all subsequent data from the unit, and thus BN is used in the above example to restore the normal case of blanks being ignored.

These two instructions may be valuable in reading data prepared for some older FORTRAN compilers that may have relied upon BZ editing. BN editing removes the requirement that all integer data be right-adjusted within a field.

FOR INPUT AND/OR OUTPUT

nP   Scale factor. Used with F, E, D, and G fields. The scale factor is an integer constant or an integer constant signed with a minus. The scale factor of n on an input field without an exponent or on an F field for output increases the size of the number by 10^n. On input with an exponent, there is no effect; on output, the decimal point is shifted n places and the exponent adjusted accordingly so that the value is unchanged. Once the scale factor is written, it applies to all succeeding real field descriptors in the FORMAT statement. If normal scaling is to be reinstated, a zero scale factor is written.

       The scale factor is most commonly used with an E field to shift the decimal point in the output. For example, if E17.8 causes an answer to be printed out as 0.34769334E+05, then 2PE17.8 will cause an output of 34.76933425E + 03.

TLc The next character is input or output c positions backward from (to the left of) the current position. Essentially, this is a backward positioning.

TRc The next character is input or output c positions forward (to the right) from the current position—a forward positioning.

Ew.dEe Used for an exponent form in which the exponent may be more than three digits. The e represents an integer that specifies the number of digits in the exponent. For example, a FORMAT of E22.12E5 allows a 12-digit fraction and a 5-digit exponent. An edited output might be: −0.371945673256E + 19050.

: (colon)   Terminates format control if there are no more items in the input/output list. Used to suppress trailing characters in output.

FOR OUTPUT

SP	Print + for positive data for all subsequent data.
SS	Do not print + for positive data (the most common default conditions).
S	Restore + convention used by compiler.
Iw.m	m defines minimum number of digits for integer output. Leading zeros may be necessary. For example, at least a three-digit output may be desired even if result is less than three digits. The specification I5.3, if data is 7456, will print as 7456; but if data is 2, it will print three digits or 002.

FORMAT specifications in input/output statement or character storage

The FORMAT specification is normally included in a separate FORMAT statement, but 1977 full FORTRAN allows the FORMAT specification to be placed in a READ or WRITE statement. This can be done in two ways:

1 A character constant containing the characters in the FORMAT specifications is used in a READ or WRITE statement in place of the FORMAT statement label reference.

2 A character string containing the FORMAT specifications is stored as a character variable or a character array. The name of the character string is placed in a WRITE or READ statement in place of the FORMAT statement label reference.

In the character constant approach, the FORMAT specifications that follow the word FORMAT (including the parentheses) are placed in a READ or WRITE statement in place of the FORTRAN statement reference. This means that the character constant can follow the input/output unit without using FMT =, or it can appear elsewhere in the list of specifications by using FMT = constant. The following are equivalent:

```
    WRITE (6, 700)A, B, C
700 FORMAT (3F10.2)

    WRITE (6, '(3F10.2)')A, B, C
    WRITE (6, FMT = '(3F10.2)')
```

If character output is to be included in the format constant, each part of the specification before and after the characters must be enclosed by apostrophes.

```
WRITE (6, '("ANSWERS"3F10.2)')A, B, C
```

In some situations, it is useful to store format specifications in a character variable or character array. This allows the program to alter the format specifications themselves as a function of program computations. As an example, suppose the array IFORM contains the following character string (including the parentheses):

```
('1',T9,6F7.2)
```

and each character is stored in a separate cell in IFORM, that is,

IFORM(6) = T and IFORM(14) =). It would then be possible to do the following:

```
IF (LINE .EQ.1) THEN
    IFORM (3) = '1'
ELSE
    IFORM (3) = '0'
ENDIF
WRITE (6, IFORM) list
```

IFORM would be used as the format specification and if LINE, a counter, equals 1, the page would be set to the top before printing by the '1' in the format. Otherwise, double spacing would occur since IFORM would contain:

```
('0',T9,6F7.2)
```

Variable horizontal positioning could be achieved by altering IFORM(7).

Older FORTRAN versions may have similar character capabilities for referencing formats, but with slightly different rules. It is wise to check the implementor manual before attempting to use this feature.

Self-testing exercise 7-3

1　Write FORMAT statements to print the variables X, Y, Z under each of the following specifications:
(a) Make output as normal decimal form or as exponent form, depending on the size of output (eight significant digits).
(b) The varaible X is complex type data (field size of 12 with 6 fractional digits for each part of X); field size of 10 with 2 fractional digits for Y and Z.
(c) The output of Y is double precision (16 significant digits).
(d) The output of Z is a logical field (field size of 5).
(e) The plus sign is to be printed for X (field size of 10 with 2 fractional digits) but not for Y or Z.

2　Write FORMAT statements for input of A and B when blank characters should be treated as zeros.

3　Print the value for X but make it exponent form with an exponent that can be six digits.

4　Summarize the edit descriptors that are included in Subset FORTRAN (and therefore will be generally available on all sizes of computers). Make a separate list of specifiers included only in full FORTRAN.

5　Define an 80-character array called FARRAY that will be used to hold a FORMAT specification. Write an output statement to write X and Y using FORMAT specification in FARRAY.

6　Write the following READ and FORMAT statements as one statement.

```
READ (5, 100)X,Y,J
100 FORMAT (2F10.0, I6)
```

Additional statements and features

There are a number of additional, useful features that will be described in this section. In general, they are either new with the 1977 FORTRAN or have not received substantial use.

PARAMETER statement

The PARAMETER statement is used in full 1977 FORTRAN to give a constant a symbolic name. The form of the PARAMETER statement and an example are:

```
PARAMETER (name = constant, . . . . )
PARAMETER (FIVE = 5.0, RATE = 4.3, HEADING = 'PAYROLL REPORT')
```

The constant name can be used in any statement to refer to the constant, for example, IF (X.GT.FIVE). . . . But the value of the name cannot be altered by an assignment statement, that is, a symbolic constant name cannot appear to the left of the equals sign. The statement FIVE = FIVE + 1.0 is not allowed.

Constant expression in dimensions

An added dimension feature of full 1977 FORTRAN allows constant expressions (expressions using constants and + or − operators) and also exponentiation in dimensions. For example, 5 + 30 and 10**2 are allowed as dimensions.

Logical equivalence or nonequivalence

Two additional logical operators were added to the 1977 FORTRAN:

.EQV.   Logical equivalence (expression is true if both expressions connected by .EQV. have same truth value—both are true or both are false)

.NEQV.   Logical nonequivalence (opposite of .EQV.)

The precedence of EQV and NEQV is the lowest logical operator (performed last). For example,

```
   IF (A.GT.B.EQV.C.LT.D) GOTO 301
or IF ((A.GT.B).EQV.(C.LT.D)) GOTO 301
```

In this example, for the IF to be true so that control goes to statement 301, A must be greater than B and C must be less than D (both are true) or A is not greater than B and C is less than D (both are false).

Main PROGRAM statement

FORTRAN does not need or require a main program to have a name, but it does allow it. Some operating systems make use of the name, so that it may be required by some computer centers. The naming is performed by a PRO-GRAM statement, which is the first statement of the main program. It consists of the word PROGRAM followed by the symbolic name. For example, a program to be called DAVIS will use the statement PROGRAM DAVIS.

Self-testing exercise 7-4

1 Write a statement to define SIXTY as always referring to the constant 60.0.

2 A statement in a FORTRAN program reads:

```
IF (A .EQ. 100.0 .EQV. A .EQ. 1.0) GOTO 301
```

For what values of A will the program transfer to statement 301?

Additional subprogram features

As explained in Chapter 5, subprograms are a useful and versatile feature of FORTRAN. The fundamental features of subprograms were presented in that chapter; this section describes additional features. In general, these features receive less use than the basic features described in Chapter 5.

SAVE variables for subprograms

It was noted in Chapter 5 that variables in a subprogram that are not in blank COMMON or in the argument list are lost when control is returned to the calling program. It is possible to save all data from the subprogram by the SAVE statement.

SAVE STATEMENT	
SAVE	Saves all variables in the subprogram
SAVE variable or array names or named COMMON block name (written within slashes)	Save named items, for example: SAVE X, Y, /NBLOCK/
The SAVE statement is placed in the subprogram as the last statement in the type declaration and storage allocation block.	

Alternate entry to subprogram and alternate return points for the calling program

The ENTRY statement (in full FORTRAN but not Subset) allows a call to a function subprogram or subroutine subprogram to begin at a point other than the beginning. In essence, ENTRY defines a subprogram within a subprogram. There may be more than one such entry point in a subprogram. At each alternate entry point, the statement is written as ENTRY *en* or ENTRY *en* (dummy argument list), where *en* is the name assigned to the entry point. The call to the alternate entry point uses the name (and appropriate argument list) for the entry point. Program execution begins at the entry and proceeds until a RETURN or END statement is encountered.

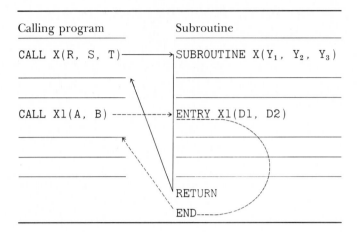

In Chapter 5, the subroutine return was always to the statement following the calling statement. In 1977 full FORTRAN, facilities were added to allow alternate return points in the calling program. The several return statements are defined by n statement numbers in the argument list of the CALL statement, each preceded by an asterisk. For example,

```
CALL SUBX (X, Y, * 101, * 210, * 215)
```

This specifies that the first return point (the first in the list) is 101, the second is statement 210, and the third is 215. The RETURN statements in the subroutine must then be numbered 1, 2, and 3. The subroutine dummy argument list contains asterisks to mark the existence of arguments that are alternate returns. If the RETURN statement is not numbered, control returns to the statements following the CALL.

The subroutine is written so that the numbered RETURN statements will be executed only if the return is to be to the alternate return associated with that statement. This approach might be useful for cases in which the results of processing by the subroutine should be followed by alternate calling program processing.

Variable dimensions

DIMENSION has been previously defined as requiring an integer constant or integer constant expression to define the maximum dimension requirements of an array. The main program must always completely specify the size of its array in order for storage to be allocated. However, a subprogram using the same array as the main program does not cause extra storage to be allocated, and thus subprogram array specifications can be variable and depend on the array defined by the main program. The array specifications in the subprogram (for an array that is defined by the main program) define a dummy array. The dummy array in the subprogram and the array in the main program are associated when the subprogram is called by the main program. In previous chapters, the size of the dummy array in the subprogram and the size of the array in the main program have been assumed to be the same. But what if they are not? Suppose the subprogram array is size 100 and the other is

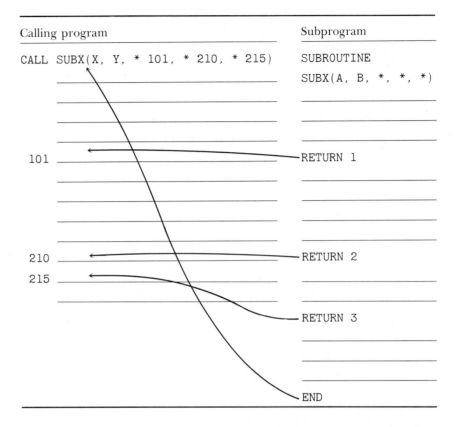

Calling program	Subprogram
CALL SUBX(X, Y, * 101, * 210, * 215)	SUBROUTINE SUBX(A, B, *, *, *)

101 — RETURN 1

210 — RETURN 2
215 — RETURN 3

END

size 50? This can be handled by making the dummy array equal to the maximum size and sending the actual size to the subprogram as an argument in the calling statement. This works only for one-dimensional arrays. Another approach that works with all arrays is the use of variable dimensions within the array specifications in the subprograms.

There are two forms of variable dimensions in subprograms:

1 *Assumed size array* The array size (or upper boundary if lower and upper boundary are used) is specified by an asterisk. This means that the subprogram array will be defined at execution as equal in size to the calling program array. If the calling statement contains an array name with a subscript (instead of simply the array name), this is interpreted as defining the subprogram array as the size of the remaining part of the calling array.

2 *Adjustable array* The array size is specified by an integer variable. The variable must be given a value before subprogram execution by including a value in the calling arguments or storing a value in COMMON.

These methods allow subprograms to be more general and to be specified fully at execution. The following examples illustrate the features.

1 Assumed size array declarations in subprograms:

```
DIMENSION A (*)
DIMENSION BETA (10,*)
```

2   Adjustable array declarations in subprograms:

Subprogram
```
SUBROUTINE SAMP (I, XDATA)

DIMENSION XDATA (I)
```

Main program
```
DIMENSION ZDATA (100)
CALL SAMP (100, ZDATA)
```

where ZDATA will be equated to XDATA and XDATA will be specified as size 100 during execution.

Subprogram and intrinsic function names in an argument list

There may be programs in which an intrinsic function name, an external function name (that is, the name of function subprogram that is not intrinsic), or a subroutine needs to be used in an actual argument list of a function or subroutine call. The difficulty is that because of their similar form, the compiler cannot distinguish between variable names and function or subroutine names. In order to specify that an intrinsic function name in an actual argument list is to be interpreted as the name of an intrinsic function, the program must contain an INTRINSIC statement. An EXTERNAL statement is used in the same way for names of external procedures (functions or subroutines). The form is the word INTRINSIC or EXTERNAL followed by the name to be declared. As an example, a CALL statement may wish to specify which function (SIN or COS) the subroutine is to use (in place of a function called TRIG). The name SIN or COS is therefore part of the actual argument list. This requires an INTRINSIC statement in the main program to declare SIN and COS as intrinsic function names.

Main program	Subroutine
INTRINSIC SIN, COS	SUBROUTINE DOIT(A, B, TRIG)
CALL DOIT(X, Y, SIN)	
	X = TRIG (〰〰〰〰〰〰)
	END

Self-testing exercise 7-5

1   Write a subroutine subprogram called XD0 having dummy variables X, Y, and I (with values of 0, 1, 2) with entry points at XD01 and XD02. Provide for alternate returns following XD01 and XD02. Code assignment statements for XD0, XD01, and XD02, setting X = Y**2+1.0 for XD0, X = Y**2+2.0 for XD01, and X = Y**2+3.0 for XD02. Based on the value of I, a call to XD0 will execute the first, second, or third of these statements (value of I is 0 for first, 1 for second, and 2 for third).

2 Code a call to XD0 with alternate return to 150 and 160 and actual variables A, B, and J.

3 Code a call to XD01 with actual variables A and B.

4 Save variables A, B, and J used locally in subroutine XDONE.

5 Write subroutine statements for an array ABX with variable dimension JIX. Show the main program statements required (array X in actual argument). Transfer dimension through common storage.

Internal files

Because of the difference between internal computational speeds and external data input or transfer speeds, the computer operating system always reads data into a temporary holding area called a *buffer*. This action is transparent to the user and usually requires no attention. However, FORTRAN also provides buffer capability under user control, and this may be useful in certain instances. This capability is provided through internal files. These are not really files in the sense of the external files discussed in Chapter 6; rather, these are character variables or arrays that are "written" to or "read" from with formatted WRITE or READ statements using a character variable name as unit specifier.

As an example of creating an internal file, consider a program segment:

```
    INTEGER A, B
    CHARACTER *12 C
    A = 17
    B = 269
    WRITE (UNIT = C, FMT = 15)A, B
 15 FORMAT (2I5)
```

Instead of writing to an input or output device, the statement writes to the character variable C. After executing this code, the 12 character positions of variable C contain

bbb17bb269bb

where b stands for blank. Note that UNIT = and FMT = are required in the WRITE statement. What has been accomplished is the conversion of the number 17 in A to the character 1 and 7 in C. Using a field of five positions (based on a FORMAT of I5), the values are right-adjusted and blanks are filled within each field. Any undefined characters in C (the two rightmost positions in the example) are filled with blanks.

As a visual aid, the character variable or array sometimes can be thought of as a punched card or set of cards that are being punched (WRITE) and read (READ). The external file statements OPEN, CLOSE, and INQUIRE are not allowed for internal files. After each READ or WRITE, the internal file is repositioned at its first location, and thus REWIND, BACKSPACE, and END-FILE are also prohibited. In addition, list-directed I/O is forbidden.

As an example of the way internal files might be used, consider a problem in which an external file consists of sets or blocks of 72-character records.

Each block consists of a header record followed by a variable number of detail records. As each READ is performed, there is no way to know in advance whether the record being read is a header or detail type. Assume that the header record contains a zero in position 1 and the rest of the card is alphabetic (for example, department names), while detail records contain a 1 in position 1 and mixed numeric or alphabetic data in the balance of the record (for example, employee numbers, names, hours worked, etc.). Since a different format is needed to read these different types of records, there is a problem: until the card has been read, there is no way to know which format to use to read it. To solve this, define an internal file and read each record into it as characters. After reading a card into the internal file, test the first position for card type and then read from the internal file into the appropriate variable locations as follows:

```
      INTEGER EMPNO
      CHARACTER COL1*1, BUFF*71, DEPTNM*15, EMPNM*20
      READ (5, 16, END = 101, ERR = 901) COL1, BUFF
   16 FORMAT (A1, A)
      IF (COL1 .EQ. '1') THEN
          READ (UNIT=BUFF, FMT=17, END=801, ERR=904) DEPTNM
      ELSE
          READ (UNIT = BUFF, FMT = 18, END = 803, ERR = 909)
     1       EMPNM, EMPNO, HRSWK
      ENDIF
      CONTINUE
   17 FORMAT (8X, A15)
   18 FORMAT (A20, I5, F4.1)
```

Another illustration of an application for internal files is to print out a real array with blanks in all locations having missing or zero values. Use of an F or G conversion will cause zeros to appear in the printout. To overcome this, an internal file can be created as a character array and blanks inserted whenever data is missing. This example illustrates the way in which the character array is treated as both an internal file and a normal character array. A simple program and its output are shown in Figure 7-1.

Statements and features recommended to be used with care

There are some FORTRAN features that are part of the language, but experience has shown them to be error-prone or inconsistent with a disciplined, clear programming style. The arithmetic IF [IF (condition) s_1,s_2,s_3] was explained in Chapter 2 with the recommendation that it not be used. Other features that generally should be avoided are the PAUSE statement, the assigned GOTO, and the statement function.

Figure 7-1
Simple program and its output to illustrate internal files.

```
**********          PROGRAM IDENTIFICATION                **********
*                                                                  *
*        ILLUSTRATION OF THE USE OF INTERNAL FILES                 *
*        WRITTEN BY T. HOFFMANN 02/08/82                           *
*                                                                  *
********************************************************************
*                                                                  *
**********          VARIABLE IDENTIFICATION                **********
*                                                                  *
*        MATRIX  = ARRAY CONTAINING MISSING VALUES                 *
*        ROW     = ROW OF CHARACTER VALUES                         *
*                                                                  *
********************************************************************
*                                                                  *
**********      TYPE DECLARATION AND STORAGE BLOCK        **********
*                                                                  *
 1.           REAL MATRIX(3,3)
 2.           CHARACTER*10 ROW(3)
*                                                                  *
********************************************************************
*                                                                  *
**********          INITIALIZE REAL ARRAY              BLOCK 0000
*                                                                  *
 3.           DO 4 I=1,3
 4.             DO 3 J=1,3
 5.               MATRIX(I,J)=0.0
 6.      3      CONTINUE
 7.      4    CONTINUE
 8.           MATRIX(1,1) = 7.57
 9.           MATRIX(1,3) = 12.23
10.           MATRIX(2,2) = 17.74
11.           MATRIX(3,1) = 10.98
12.           MATRIX(3,2) = 0.67
*                                                                  *
********************************************************************
*                                                                  *
**********   CONVERT REAL ARRAY TO CHARACTER ARRAY     BLOCK 0100
*                                                                  *
13.           DO 119 I = 1,3
14.             WRITE(UNIT=ROW,FMT=110) (MATRIX(I,J),J=1,3)
15.      110    FORMAT(F10.2)
*                                                                  *
*        SET ZEROS (MISSING DATA) IN REAL TO BLANKS IN CHARACTER ARRAY  *
*                                                                  *
16.             DO 115 J = 1,3
17.               IF(MATRIX(I,J) .LE. 0.0) ROW(J) = ' '
18.      115    CONTINUE
19.             WRITE(6,118) (ROW(J),J=1,3)
20.      118    FORMAT(3A10)
21.      119 CONTINUE
*                                                                  *
********************************************************************
*                                                                  *
**********          NORMAL TERMINATION BLOCK          BLOCK 0200
*                                                                  *
22.           STOP
23.           END
```

OUTPUT

```
     7.57           12.23
            17.74
10.98        .67
```

PAUSE statement

The PAUSE or PAUSE n statements are the same as the STOP and STOP n statements in that they cause the program to halt. In the case of PAUSE or PAUSE n, the halt is to be temporary; pressing RUN on the computer console or RETURN on a terminal allows the program to continue. PAUSE was useful in computing situations where results at a given point were to be examined before proceeding with the program. It is generally inconsistent with present computer center operations and will usually be treated the same as a STOP.

Assigned GOTO

Since the assigned GOTO is part of the language, it will be explained, but good programming practice suggests that it should not be used. The reason for advising against its use is that it makes the logic of a program difficult to follow. The assigned GOTO feature is essentially a variable GOTO. There are two statements: the ASSIGN and the assigned GOTO. The ASSIGN statement assigns an integer statement label to an integer variable.

```
ASSIGN s TO i
```

where s = a statement label
     i = an integer variable

Example

```
ASSIGN 23 TO KIX
```

The assigned GOTO list contains statement labels to which the program may go and specifies the variable that contains the value for the transfer of control. Both ASSIGN and GOTO must be in the same program unit.

```
GOTO i(s₁,s₂, . . . ,sₙ)
```

where s_i = statement labels to which control may transfer; list is optional
     i = integer variable containing the value of one of the statement labels
         to which control is to be transferred

As an example, suppose that the program might transfer to statements 13, 21, or 45 and that a variable KIX would specify which of these statements would be used. Then, the pair of statements to transfer control to 21 would be

```
ASSIGN 21 TO KIX
GOTO KIX (13, 21, 45)
```

The ASSIGN statement can also be used to assign a FORMAT statement label to an integer variable, which is used as the format reference in an input or output statement. For example, if there are three possible FORMAT statements labeled with statement numbers 360, 370, and 380 that can be selected by an output statement, the selection of 370 can be programmed by the ASSIGN statement as follows:

```
ASSIGN 370 to IFMAT
WRITE (6, IFMAT)A, B, JIX
```

Statement function

If the same one-statement computation appears several times in a program, FORTRAN allows a statement function to be defined in the program itself instead of using a separate function subprogram. The statement function is used in a program in the same manner as an intrinsic function. The statement function is defined by writing a statement in which the name chosen for the function is set equal to an expression that uses the dummy variables in it. The list of dummy arguments are separated by commas and enclosed in parentheses. The name is formed in the same way as a variable name (begins with I–N for integer, etc.). This statement only defines the function; it is not executed. The definition statement must precede its first use as a function.

In order to use the function that has been defined, the name of the function is written in an expression with the actual variable names to be employed written in place of the dummy variables. The actual variables are listed in the same order and have the same type as the dummy variables. The program will make the computation defined by the function using the values of the actual variables in the argument list. The resulting value will be put into the statement being executed as the value of the function. For example:

Defining statement `DESCF (B, A, C) = (B**2 - 4.0 * A * C)`

Using the function `X = BETA + DESCF (ALPHA, Y, Z)`

The effect of the function is the insertion of the function into the statement using the calling variables in place of the dummy variables. In the example, this means that the statement to be executed will perform the following computation:

`X = BETA + (ALPHA**2 - 4.0 * Y * Z)`

If it is appropriate to use this feature, confusion can be avoided by placing the statement function definition in a separate block preceding any executable statements.

Order of statements

The order of program statements is as follows:

1 PROGRAM (if used), FUNCTION, SUBROUTINE, or BLOCK DATA. In the block structure style in the text, this statement is the first in the program preceding the identification block.
2 IMPLICIT
3 Type statements
4 PARAMETER
5 Other specifications (DIMENSION, COMMON, EQUIVALENCE, EXTERNAL, INTRINSIC)
6 DATA

In the type declaration and storage allocation block

7 Statement function definition statement (if used, place in separate block)
8 Executable statements

Comments may appear anywhere in the program. FORMAT statements may appear anywhere after the first group of statements listed above (PROGRAM, FUNCTION, etc.) but, as a matter of style, we have chosen to place them immediately after the first input or output statement in which they are used.

Summary

Items explained in the chapter include additional data types, character string processing, and advanced format features. Also summarized but not explained in detail were advanced features and features of limited use.

Three additional data types—complex, double precision, and logical—were explained. The type statement is used to declare explicitly variables of these types. The first-letter conventions for integer and real can be changed by an IMPLICIT statement.

Useful new features for manipulation of character strings are defined by 1977 ANS FORTRAN. Putting together or concatenation of character strings is performed with a concatenation operator. Strings can also be compared.

A number of additional format edit descriptors were presented in the chapter. In addition, a method in FORTRAN for referencing the list of format descriptors stored as character data was explained. This stored character data reference approach allows flexible formatting and input of format editing lists as variable data.

Additional statements and features presented were the PARAMETER statement for naming a constant, logical equivalence, and the main PROGRAM statement.

Some additional features for subprograms were summarized. These provide for saving of subprogram variables, using intrinsic function and external procedure names in an actual argument list, alternate entry to subprograms, alternate return points, and variable dimensions for a subprogram.

There are situations in which it is desirable to be able to read data into an internal file or buffer for examination or processing and to read from the buffer using formatting based on the data. This is performed by internal file procedures.

The PAUSE, assigned GOTO, and the statement function were explained. Since these are error-prone, they generally should not be used.

Answers to self-testing exercises

Exercise 7-1

1
```
INTEGER YEARS, PERIOD
REAL MONTH
```

2 `DOUBLE PRECISION ALPHA, M, Y`

3 The computer uses a double storage area for a double-precision variable. The precision is the number of significant digits that are represented; for double-precision variables, this is approximately double the precision of a single-precision variable.

4 (a) X = (4.0, 2.1)
    (b) X = 91.05676500007842D+00 or
      X = 9.105676500007842D+01
    (c) X = .FALSE.

5 `DX = DSQRT (DRATE)`

Exercise 7-2

1
```
TEMP = INDEX (STATEM, 'MISS')
STR1 = STATEM (TEMP:TEMP + 4)
```

2 `IF (I.EQ.1) X = STR1 // STR2`

3 `IF (LNAME .EQ. 'CLARK') GOTO 600`

4 `ABREV = LNAME (1:3)`

5 `CBREV = ABREV // 'ABC'`

6 `DATA FNAME /'AARON'/`

7 `MISSIS`

8 `HEADLN = LEN (HEAD)`

Exercise 7-3

1 (a) `FORMAT (3G16.8)`
(b) `FORMAT (2F12.6, 2F10.2)`
(The complex data item requires two FORMAT specifications for the real and imaginary parts.)
(c) `FORMAT (F10.2, D23.16, F10.2)`
(d) `FORMAT (2F10.2, L5)`
(e) `FORMAT (SPF10.2, S2F10.2)`

2 `FORMAT (BZ, F10.2, F10.2, BN)`. BN is used to restore the blanks convention.

3 `FORMAT (E19.8E6)`

4 See the list of 1977 ANS standard FORTRAN statements (following the index).

In Subset FORTRAN	Only in full FORTRAN
Iw	Tc
Fw.d	Gw.d
Ew.d	Dw.d
Aw	Complex
'h . . .'	TLc
nHh . . .	TRc
/	Ew.dEe
nX	Gw.dEe
Lw	SP
BN	SS
BZ	S
nP	Iw.m

5 `CHARACTER FARRAY (80)`
`WRITE (6, FARRAY)X, Y`

6 `READ (5, FMT ='(2F10.0, I6)')X, Y,J`

Exercise 7-4

1 `PARAMETER (SIXTY = 60.0)`

2 Both expressions can never be true. If A = 100, it cannot also equal 1.0. However, both expressions can be false and control goes to 301. Thus, control goes to 301 as long as A is neither 100 nor 1.0.

Exercise 7-5

```
1      SUBROUTINE XD0 (X, Y, I, *, *)
       GOTO (50, 100, 200), I + 1
       GOTO 250
50  X = Y**2 + 1.0
    RETURN
    ENTRY XD01 (X, Y)
100 X = Y**2 + 2.0
    RETURN 1
    ENTRY XD02 (X, Y)
200 X = Y**2 + 3.0
    RETURN 2
250 PRINT *, 'ERROR WITH I', I
    END

2   CALL XD0 (A, B, J, * 150, * 160)

3   CALL XD01 (A, B)

4   SAVE A, B, J

5   SUBROUTINE EXAMPL (ABX)
    COMMON JIX
    DIMENSION ABX (JIX)
    _____


    Main program
    _____

    COMMON JIX
    JIX =
    CALL EXAMPL (X)
```

Questions and problems

1   The programmer got confused. To fix the program, declare all integer variables in a program to be real and all real variables to be integer.

2   Code declaration and input/output to:
    (*a*) Read a double-precision variable and print it.
    (*b*) Read a complex variable and print it.
    (*c*) Read a logical variable and print it.

3   Write a program segment to define the day names, SUNDAY, etc., for the first week in October 1978 and to compare a character input data item (say MONDAY) to find out which day it is.

4   Write FORMAT statements to read and/or write to produce stated results.

Data		Output
(*a*) Input on cards as 45 13		45.13
(*b*)	0.1765E15	17.65E + 13
(*c*)	347.0	+ 347.
(*d*)	78	0078
(*e*)	.TRUE.	T

5 Explain the use for:
- (*a*) PARAMETER
- (*b*) PROGRAM
- (*c*) IMPLICIT
- (*d*) Logical equivalence
- (*e*) Alternate entry for subprograms and return for subroutines
- (*f*) SAVE statement
- (*g*) ASSIGN statement (with FORMAT statements)

chapter **7B**

Example programs and programming exercises using additional features

The example programs illustrate the use of some of the additional data types and other features not frequently used in FORTRAN programs, but which may sometimes be useful or necessary.

General notes on Chapter 7 examples

Type declarations such as REAL and INTEGER allow the use of variable names that more clearly identify what they represent or how they are used without regard to the first letter. In some instances, double-precision variables may be required to get sufficient accuracy. Special intrinsic functions and data representations will be required for double-precision computations. The P edit descriptor is used to move the decimal point in the output.

General program example 7 — Manhattan Island

This program uses double-precision computations in order to accurately find the value of an amount of money compounded over a long period of time. Depending upon the computer on which it is run, this may make a significant difference in the accuracy of the result.

Problem description for general example 7

The program is to compute the amount to which the original $24 paid for Manhattan Island in 1626 would have grown by a given year and assuming various interest rates. It is to compare the results obtained by both single- and double-precision computations. Input consists of a year and an interest rate.

Program documentation for general example 7

Full documentation is not given because of the simple nature of the program. The program listing is given in Figure 7-2. The sample input data has not been shown because it is printed as part of the output listing (Figure 7-3).

Notes on general example 7

REAL, INTEGER, and DOUBLE PRECISION type statements are used to indicate the nature of several of the variable names (lines 1–3). Several other variables (for example, DOLLAR) use the implicit type denoted by the first letter of their names. Double-precision constants are found in line 14. Note that $0.4D+1$ is equivalent to $4.0D+0$; either could be used. The exponent (line 14) need not be double precision to achieve a double-precision result. The intrinsic function DBLE is used in line 5 to obtain a double-precision equivalent of a single-precision variable.

Use of the format edit descriptor P is shown in the second and third lines of the FORMAT statement on line 16. In order to print out the decimal fraction percentage interest rate in the common form of a number greater than 1, a '2P' is used to modify the F5.1 edit descriptor. In order to restore the multiplier to normal for the rest of the values printed out, '0P' must be inserted before the next descriptor—E20.14 in the third continuation line.

Figure 7-2
Program listing for general example 7—Manhattan Island.

```
**********          PROGRAM IDENTIFICATION          **********
*                                                             *
*        MANHATTAN ISLAND PROGRAM CALCULATES THE AMOUNT TO WHICH *
*        THE $24.00 INVESTED IN 1626 TO PURCHASE MANHATTAN ISLAND *
*        WOULD HAVE GROWN BY A GIVEN YEAR, ASSUMING SOME INTEREST *
*        RATE AND COMPOUNDING QUARTERLY.  INPUT YEARS LESS THAN *
*        1626 OR RUNNING OUT OF DATA CAUSE PROGRAM TERMINATION. *
*        BOTH SINGLE AND DOUBLE PRECISION COMPUTATIONS ARE MADE. *
*        WRITTEN BY T. HOFFMANN 08/08/1977                     *
*                                                             *
***************************************************************
*                                                             *
**********          VARIABLE IDENTIFICATION         **********
*                                                             *
*        YEAR   = YEAR TO WHICH TO COMPOUND                   *
*        IRATE  = INTEREST RATE                               *
*        DIRATE = INTEREST RATE (DOUBLE PRECISION)            *
*        NYEARS = NUMBER OF YEARS TO COMPOUND                 *
*        AMOUNT = COMPOUND AMOUNT                             *
*        AMTDBL = COMPOUND AMOUNT (DOUBLE PRECISION)          *
*        DOLLAR = AMOUNT PAID FOR ISLAND = $24.00             *
*        DBLDOL = DOLLAR EXPRESSED IN DOUBLE PRECISION        *
*                                                             *
***************************************************************
*                                                             *
**********   TYPE DECLARATION AND STORAGE ALLOCATION  **********
*
1.          REAL IRATE,NYEARS
2.          INTEGER YEAR
3.          DOUBLE PRECISION DIRATE,AMTDBL,DBLDOL
4.          DATA DOLLAR/24.0/
*                                                             *
***************************************************************
*                                                             *
**********          INITIALIZATION BLOCK            BLOCK 0000
*                                                             *
5.          DBLDOL = DBLE(DOLLAR)
6.          WRITE(6,3)
7.        3 FORMAT('1',6X,'MANAHATTAN ISLAND PROBLEM')
*                                                             *
***************************************************************
*                                                             *
**********          INPUT AND COMPUTATION           BLOCK 0100
*                                                             *
8.      101 READ(5,102,END=301) YEAR,IRATE
9.      102 FORMAT(I4,F3.2)
10.         IF(YEAR .LT. 1626) GOTO 301
11.         NYEARS = FLOAT(YEAR-1626)
12.         DIRATE = DBLE(IRATE)
13.         AMOUNT = DOLLAR*(1.0 + IRATE/4.0)**(4.0*NYEARS)
14.         AMTDBL = DBLDOL*(1.0D+0 + DIRATE/0.4D+1)**(4.0*NYEARS)
*                                                             *
***************************************************************
*                                                             *
**********          OUTPUT BLOCK                    BLOCK 0200
*                                                             *
15.         WRITE(6,202) DOLLAR,YEAR,IRATE,AMOUNT,AMTDBL
16.     202 FORMAT(//5X,'$',F6.2,' INVESTED IN 1626, COMPOUNDED QUARTERLY ',
       1        'THROUGH',I5,', AND'/5X,'AT A RATE OF',
       2        2PF5.1,' PERCENT, WOULD AMOUNT TO'/
       3        1X,'$',0PE20.14,' OR, MORE PRECISELY, $',D30.24)
*                                                             *
*           GO BACK TO READ ANOTHER DATA CARD                 *
*                                                             *
17.         GOTO 101
*                                                             *
***************************************************************
*                                                             *
**********          TERMINATE                       BLOCK 0300
*                                                             *
18.     301 STOP
19.         END
```

Two sets of results from two different computers are given in Figure 7-3—the IBM System/370 and the Control Data Cyber computers. The results from double precision and single precision on the Control Data Cyber computer do not differ as much as the two results on the IBM System/370. These differences reflect the different precision built into the computer designs. The Cyber computer was designed for high-precision, scientific processing;

Figure 7-3
Output using two different computers for Manhattan Island problem with double-precision processing.

OUTPUT FROM CONTROL DATA CYBER—VERY HIGH PRECISION

```
     MANAHATTAN ISLAND PROBLEM

     $ 24.00 INVESTED IN 1626, COMPOUNDED QUARTERLY THROUGH 1976, AND
     AT A RATE OF  6 0 PERCENT, WOULD AMOUNT TO
  $ .27081355025273E+11 OR, MORE PRECISELY, $ .27081355025255549784147073E+11


     $ 24.00 INVESTED IN 1626, COMPOUNDED QUARTERLY THROUGH 1976, AND
     AT A RATE OF  7.0 PERCENT, WOULD AMOUNT TO
  $ .84800087010391E+12 OR, MORE PRECISELY, $ .84800087010592263148473E+12
```

OUTPUT FROM IBM SYSTEM/370—MEDIUM PRECISION

```
     MANAHATTAN ISLAND PROBLEM

  $ 24.00 INVESTED IN 1626, COMPOUNDED QUARTERLY THROUGH 1976, AND
  AT A RATE OF  6.0 PERCENT, WOULD AMOUNT TO
  $0.27058163712000E 11 OR, MORE PRECISELY, $0.2708134250148970000000000D 11


  $ 24.00 INVESTED IN 1626, COMPOUNDED QUARTERLY THROUGH 1976, AND
  AT A RATE OF  7.0 PERCENT, WOULD AMOUNT TO
  $0.84790371942400E 12 OR, MORE PRECISELY, $0.8479987837387943000000000D 12
```

the IBM computer was designed as a general-purpose computer without a need for high precision in most situations. In a problem of this type, the double precision is very important for the medium-precision IBM System/370 and less important for the high-precision Cyber.

It is not meaningful to print out as many digits as are shown. In a problem with figures in the billions, showing data beyond the nearest dollar (or perhaps hundreds of dollars) cannot be justified. The results, however, show the high precision of the CDC machine and show how the IBM computer handles output beyond the data available in the computer. The double-precision results beyond 15 digits do not exist in the IBM computer, and thus they are replaced by zeros on output.

Statistical program example 7 — geometric series

This program example shows the use of a LOGICAL type variable as well as the REAL, INTEGER, and DOUBLE PRECISION types shown in the previous example program. It also illustrates the use of an expression in the output list, the PARAMETER feature, and use of a character constant to define format.

Problem description for statistical example 7

Compute the sum of a particular geometric series as well as its last term, given the form of the series and the number of terms. The series is

$$1 \ r \ r^2 \ r^3 \ \cdots \ r^n$$

where r is either e or $1/e$. If it is the latter, also compute the sum of the infinite series of terms. The number of terms is input; if it is negative, use the ratio of

Figure 7-4
Program listing for statistical example 7—geometric series.

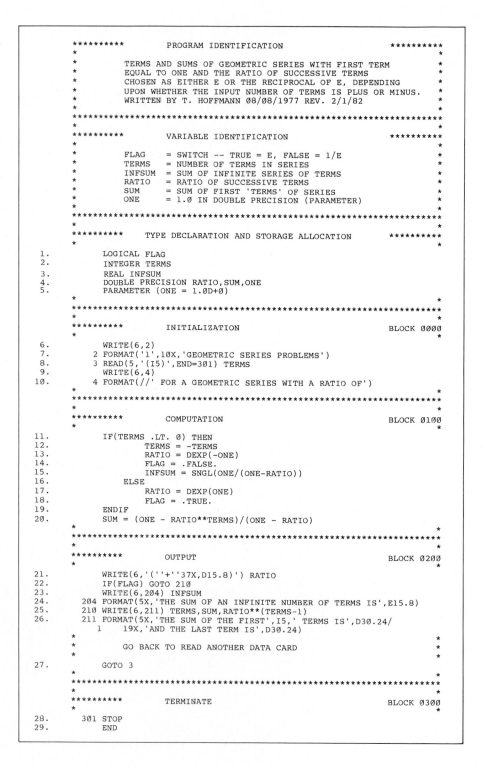

```
**********          PROGRAM IDENTIFICATION                    **********
*                                                                      *
*         TERMS AND SUMS OF GEOMETRIC SERIES WITH FIRST TERM           *
*         EQUAL TO ONE AND THE RATIO OF SUCCESSIVE TERMS               *
*         CHOSEN AS EITHER E OR THE RECIPROCAL OF E, DEPENDING         *
*         UPON WHETHER THE INPUT NUMBER OF TERMS IS PLUS OR MINUS.     *
*         WRITTEN BY T. HOFFMANN 08/08/1977 REV. 2/1/82                *
*                                                                      *
************************************************************************
*                                                                      *
**********          VARIABLE IDENTIFICATION                   **********
*                                                                      *
*         FLAG    = SWITCH -- TRUE = E, FALSE = 1/E                     *
*         TERMS   = NUMBER OF TERMS IN SERIES                          *
*         INFSUM  = SUM OF INFINITE SERIES OF TERMS                    *
*         RATIO   = RATIO OF SUCCESSIVE TERMS                          *
*         SUM     = SUM OF FIRST 'TERMS' OF SERIES                     *
*         ONE     = 1.0 IN DOUBLE PRECISION (PARAMETER)                *
*                                                                      *
************************************************************************
*                                                                      *
**********     TYPE DECLARATION AND STORAGE ALLOCATION        **********
*                                                                      *
1.          LOGICAL FLAG
2.          INTEGER TERMS
3.          REAL INFSUM
4.          DOUBLE PRECISION RATIO,SUM,ONE
5.          PARAMETER (ONE = 1.0D+0)
*                                                                      *
************************************************************************
*                                                                      *
**********          INITIALIZATION                     BLOCK 0000 **********
*                                                                      *
6.          WRITE(6,2)
7.        2 FORMAT('1',10X,'GEOMETRIC SERIES PROBLEMS')
8.        3 READ(5,'(I5)',END=301) TERMS
9.          WRITE(6,4)
10.       4 FORMAT(//' FOR A GEOMETRIC SERIES WITH A RATIO OF')
*                                                                      *
************************************************************************
*                                                                      *
**********          COMPUTATION                        BLOCK 0100 **********
*                                                                      *
11.         IF(TERMS .LT. 0) THEN
12.             TERMS = -TERMS
13.             RATIO = DEXP(-ONE)
14.             FLAG = .FALSE.
15.             INFSUM = SNGL(ONE/(ONE-RATIO))
16.         ELSE
17.             RATIO = DEXP(ONE)
18.             FLAG = .TRUE.
19.         ENDIF
20.         SUM = (ONE - RATIO**TERMS)/(ONE - RATIO)
*                                                                      *
************************************************************************
*                                                                      *
**********          OUTPUT                             BLOCK 0200 **********
*                                                                      *
21.         WRITE(6,'(''+''37X,D15.8)') RATIO
22.         IF(FLAG) GOTO 210
23.         WRITE(6,204) INFSUM
24.     204 FORMAT(5X,'THE SUM OF AN INFINITE NUMBER OF TERMS IS',E15.8)
25.     210 WRITE(6,211) TERMS,SUM,RATIO**(TERMS-1)
26.     211 FORMAT(5X,'THE SUM OF THE FIRST',I5,' TERMS IS',D30.24/
        1      19X,'AND THE LAST TERM IS',D30.24)
*                                                                      *
*         GO BACK TO READ ANOTHER DATA CARD                            *
*                                                                      *
27.         GOTO 3
*                                                                      *
************************************************************************
*                                                                      *
**********          TERMINATE                          BLOCK 0300 **********
*                                                                      *
28.     301 STOP
29.         END
```

Figure 7-5
Sample output from geometric series problem with double-precision results.

```
                GEOMETRIC SERIES PROBLEMS


FOR A GEOMETRIC SERIES WITH A RATIO OF .27182818E+01
     THE SUM OF THE FIRST     2 TERMS IS .37182818284590452353602␥E+01
                       AND THE LAST TERM IS .2718281828459␥452353602␥E+01


FOR A GEOMETRIC SERIES WITH A RATIO OF .27182818E+01
     THE SUM OF THE FIRST    20 TERMS IS .28235484213␥226283815603E+09
                       AND THE LAST TERM IS .17848230␥963187260844910E+09


FOR A GEOMETRIC SERIES WITH A RATIO OF .36787944E+00
     THE SUM OF AN INFINITE NUMBER OF TERMS IS  .15819767E+01
     THE SUM OF THE FIRST    20 TERMS IS .15819767␥360862940440787E+01
                       AND THE LAST TERM IS .56␥27964375372675400129␥E-08


FOR A GEOMETRIC SERIES WITH A RATIO OF .27182818E+01
     THE SUM OF THE FIRST    10 TERMS IS .12818308␥5␥5246␥42100284E+05
                       AND THE LAST TERM IS .81␥3␥839275753840␥77100␥␥E+04


FOR A ␥EOMETRIC SERIES WITH A RATIO OF .36787944E+00
     THE SUM OF AN INFINITE NUMBER OF TERMS IS  .15819767E+01
     THE SUM OF THE FIRST    10 TERMS IS .1581904885237948669␥7859E+01
                       AND THE LAST TERM IS .1234␥98␥4␥8667954497637E-03
```

$1/e$. Compute both single- and double-precision values for the finite sum and the last term.

Program documentation for statistical example 7

Only the program listing (Figure 7-4) and the output (Figure 7-5) are given. Input data can be inferred from the output values.

Notes on statistical example 7

In reviewing the program listing, the following points are of interest:

1 The variable FLAG is declared to be a logical variable (line 1). It is set to .FALSE. in line 14 or .TRUE. in line 18. The logical variable FLAG is tested for the true condition in line 22 by the statement IF(FLAG). . . . FLAG is used as a program switch to determine whether the infinite sum line (lines 23 and 24) should be printed.

2 The variable TERMS is declared as integer and INFSUM as real (lines 2 and 3). In line 4, RATIO and SUM are declared to be double precision.

3 A character constant is used as FORMAT specification in the input statement (line 8).

4 A double-precision constant of 1.0 is given the name ONE by a PARAMETER statement (line 5).

5 The expression with RATIO (line 13) uses a double-precision exponential function DEXP and a double-precision constant ONE.

6 INFSUM is a real, single-precision variable, and thus double-precision results to be stored there are explicitly converted to single precision in line 15 by the SNGL conversion function.

7   The computation of the last term in the series is written in the output list as (RATIO**(TERMS-1)) in line 25.

8   A character constant is used to specify a format in the output statement in line 21. Note the character output of + in column 1.

Programming exercises

Description of assignment

Select one or more problems (or take the problems assigned by your instructor). Write each of the programs so as to use features described in this chapter. Follow the style guidelines and prepare the following:

1   Pseudocode description.

2   Program flowchart.

3   Program listing.

4   List of test data and expected results. Test for both valid and invalid data.

5   Output including testing for error conditions.

Mathematics and statistics

1   Refer to problem 4-1. Make use of at least the FORMAT specifications in the read statements.

2   Refer to problem 4-2. Make use of at least the character functions and FORMAT specification in character storage to print the output in the usual equilateral triangle shape.

3   Refer to problem 5-3. Make use of at least the statement function.

Business and economics

4   Refer to problem 6-4. Make use of at least the LOGICAL type statements and logical variables.

5   Refer to problem 4-5. Make use of at least the P format edit descriptor and the PNYRND function subprogram of general example 6 as a statement function.

6   Refer to problem 5-6. Make use of at least the statement function.

Science and engineering

7   Refer to problem 4-7. Make use of at least the LOGICAL type statement.

8   Refer to problem 5-9. Make use of at least the PARAMETER statement and the statement function.

9   Refer to problem 6-9. Make use of FORMAT specifications in input/output statements or in character storage.

Humanities and social sciences

10   Refer to problem 4-11. Make use of at least the index function and character substrings.

11   Refer to problem 5-11. Make use of at least the DOUBLE PRECISION type statement and corresponding double-precision intrinsic functions and the statement function.

12   Refer to problem 6-12. Make use of at least the LOGICAL and IMPLICIT statements.

General

13   Refer to problem 6-13. Make use of at least the LOGICAL and IMPLICIT statements.

14   Refer to problem 5-14. Make use of at least the IMPLICIT statement.

15   Refer to problem 6-15. Make use of at least the IMPLICIT statement, alternate entry feature, and SAVE statement.

appendix **A**

How to use the card punch

Students of computer data processing frequently need to be able to operate the key-driven card punch, either to keypunch their programs or to make corrections in previously punched card decks. The purpose of this appendix is to aid these activities; therefore, it covers only the basic elements of using the card punch. There are many features for facilitating its use that will not be explained. A person learning to be a keypunch operator needs additional training information not contained here.

The three most common card punches are the IBM Model 129, the IBM Model 29, and the IBM Model 26 printing card punches (Figure A-1). The Model 26 was the standard card punch until 1960; the Model 29 was introduced in 1960 in conjunction with IBM's System/360 computers; the Model 129 is similar to the 29 in keyboard but uses an internal buffer (memory) to hold the card contents as they are being keyed. In the Model 129 (and other buffered card punches), when the keying of data is complete for a card (and corrections have been made, if necessary), the card is punched from the data in the buffer. The punching occurs while the next card is being keyed, thus reducing the waiting time found on the nonbuffered 26 and 29 models. The features of the Model 129 buffered card punch are most significant for commercial keypunching. Occasional users are more likely to use a Model 29 (or a Model 26 because many of these older units are still in service). Other vendors supply keypunches with the same (and additional) features. The explanation in this appendix will concentrate on the Model 29 but give some attention to the IBM Model 26.

The alphabetic characters on the keypunch keyboard are identical to those on a typewriter. This means that a person who can type can keypunch alphabetics without learning any new keying (Figure A-2). The numbers 1 to 9 are arranged so they can be punched with three fingers of the right hand.

There are differences between the Model 29 (and 129) and the older Model

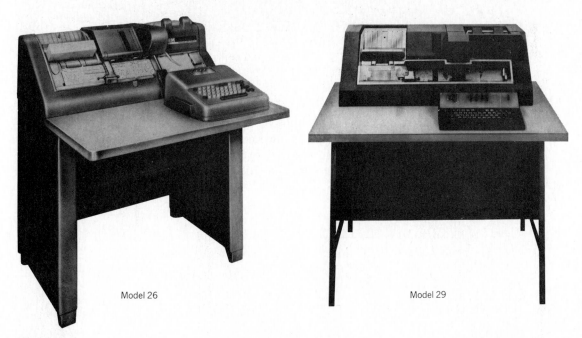

Model 26   Model 29

Figure A-1
IBM Model 26 and Model 29 card punches. (Courtesy of International Business Machines Corporation.

Figure A-2
Keyboards of IBM Model
29 and Model 26 card
punches.

Model 29

Model 26 with scientific keytops

26; these are differences in punching of the special characters. On Models 29 and 129 there are different punch patterns for each of 28 special characters, and each character has a unique position on the keyboard. The Model 26 has only 11 special characters with the same punch codes being used for five pairs of different characters—one set of characters termed *commercial* and the other set identified as *scientific*. The differences in the keyboards for Model 26 are as follows:

MODEL 26 KEYBOARD AND
PRINTING CHARACTERS

Commercial	Scientific (FORTRAN)
#	=
&	+
%	(
☐	)
@	' (apostrophe)

The punches are the same for either of each pair of characters; the only difference is the keytop character and in the printing character that is printed on top of the card when it is punched. This means that a user needing to punch the FORTRAN statement IF(X.GT.Y)X = 0 on a Model 26 commercial keyboard can get the correct punches by punching IF%X.GT.Y ☐ X#0.

The use of the card punch is facilitated by features that perform functions that otherwise must be done manually. The beginner may wish to start out by doing punching without using these features and then, as more proficiency is developed, begin to use these aids to increase punching speed. The use of the card punch will therefore be described at three levels:

1   Punching without making use of the automatic features.
2   Punching with use of the automatic feed but not using a program card.
3   Punching with a program card.

Punching without use of automatic features

The "on-off" switch for the card punch is on the inside of the right leg for the Model 29 and at the upper left in the card stacker for the Model 26.

On the panel directly above the keytops, there are six toggle switches on a Model 29 and three switches on a Model 26 (Figure A-3). Turn the AUTO SKIP DUP and AUTO FEED switches off (down). Turn the PRINT switch on. On a Model 29, the LZ print should be on; the PROG SEL and CLEAR are not used. In the upper part of the card punch, directly below the window showing a cylinder (program drum), there is a small program-control lever. Depress this lever to the right to deactivate the program-card mechanism.

Blank cards to be punched are placed in the card hopper at the upper right;

Figure A-3
Functional control switches for Model 29 (below) and Model 26 (above) card punches.

Model 26

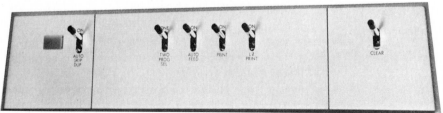

Model 29

Figure A-4
Path of card through the
card punch.

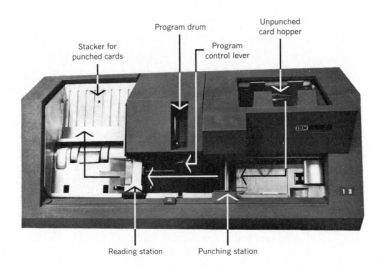

Stacker for
punched cards

Program drum

Program
control lever

Unpunched
card hopper

Reading station   Punching station

cards that have been punched are moved by the card punch into a card stacker, at the upper left, from which they can be removed. The path of a card through the card punch is shown in Figure A-4.

In Figure A-2, note the three keys at the right-hand side of the keyboard labeled REL, FEED, and REG. These are the release, feed, and register keys. Using these keys, punching a card is performed as follows:

1 Press FEED key to move one card from the card hopper to the entrance to the punching station.

2 Press REG key to move the card into position for punching.

3 The card is punched serially (column by column) by striking the proper keys. The keyboard operates normally in alphabetic mode (the bottom character is punched if more than two are shown on a keytop). To obtain the upper character, which includes all the numerics, the numeric shift key at the lower left of the keyboard must be depressed while striking the keys. Columns may be skipped by depressing the space bar.

4 When all punching has been performed, the card is moved to the reading station by pressing REL.

5 If only one card is to be punched, immediately pressing REL and REG will move the card from the reading station to the card stacker where it can be removed.

If a card needs to be corrected or duplicated, or a damaged card needs to be replaced, the card to be reproduced is manually inserted against the card hopper by depressing FEED (or a card is inserted manually at the punching station). Pressing the REG key will then register both cards. Depressing the DUP (duplicate) key will cause the punches in the card at the reading station to be punched into the card at the punching station. If one or more columns are to be omitted or altered from what is found in the card being reproduced, the operator depresses the space bar or keyboard characters instead of the duplicate key for the columns to be omitted or altered. The next column to be punched or duplicated is read from the column indicator in the opening that contains the program control drum.

Punching with **AUTO FEED**

If many cards are to be punched, the feeding of cards can be speeded up by using the AUTO FEED option. When this is on, it causes a new card to be automatically fed and registered each time the card being punched is released. Since this provides a continuous supply of cards at both the punching and reading stations, it is turned off in order to insert a card to be duplicated or corrected.

Punching with a program card

In punching applications, there are repetitive operations—for example, the starting of the punching of a field at a certain column, the duplication of certain information from the previous card, or the switching to numeric or alphabetic for a group of columns. The program card allows these functions to be done automatically.

The program card is a regular punched card that is wrapped around the program drum. Control punches in the top five rows are read by program star wheels (Figure A-5) and cause certain functions to be automatically performed. On a Model 29 a second program may be punched lower in the same card. The second program is selected by the PROG SEL switch. This should be on ONE to use the control cards explained here. A small lever on the keypunch is depressed to the left to activate the program card and to the right to deactivate it. Some common control punches are shown at the top of the next page:

An example will illustrate the use of a control card. In punching a FORTRAN program, the first column is used to indicate a comment line, the next four columns are for a statement number (numeric). Column 6, indicating a continuation of a statement, is rarely used. Columns 7–72 are for alphanu-

Figure A-5
(a) Program drum and (b) program drum in place. (Courtesy of International Business Machines Corporation.)

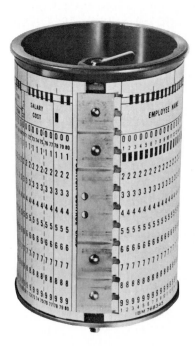

Punch	Function
none	Beginning of numeric field to be manually punched.
1	Beginning of field and shifts keyboard to alphabetic mode with program control; the card places the keyboard in numeric mode unless this control punch is used. Used like a typewriter tab stop.
0	Starts automatic duplication (0 plus 1 starts automatic duplication of alphabetic field—punched as /). ⎫ AUTO SKIP DUP toggle switch must be "on" for duplication or skipping.
11 (minus punch)	Starts automatic skipping. ⎭
12 (& punch or + on Model 26 scientific)	Defines the columns for which the preceding punches apply. An & is used for a numeric field and A for alphabetic field (12 and 1 punches).

meric punching, with alphabetics most common. Columns 73–80 are for identification (optional).

A control card for punching a FORTRAN program will illustrate the use of control cards and will make it easier to punch the FORTRAN programs assigned in this text using the suggested style.

Columns	
1	Used to indicate a comment line by a C or *.
2–5	Used on some statements for a numeric statement label (except for comment cards).
6	Used very infrequently to indicate continuation. The control card will skip past it; if there is to be a punch in column 6, backspace one space.
7	Start of punching for statements.
11	Start of punching for indented statements and for imbedded comments.
72	Last usable column for statement. If comment line is a comment block, an asterisk is punched (for style in this text).
73–80	Either duplicate an identification or skip. The sample control card duplicates an identification into each card (say the programmer's initials and problem number or identification).

See Figure A-6 for an example control card. The FORTRAN control card causes the card to be in alphabetic mode for column 1 and in numeric mode for columns 2 to 6. Pressing the SKIP key repeatedly moves the card first to position 7, to 11, to 72, and finally to 73. When 73 is reached, the next six positions are automatically duplicated. When punching FORTRAN under program card control (and with the AUTO SKIP DUP switch on), there will be no need to manually skip the card to margins. The first column has an *, C, or a space. If punching is to start in column 7, pressing the SKIP once will position the card at that margin. If the FORTRAN statement is to be indented at column 11 or a comment is to be punched, pressing SKIP again will move the card to column 11. After punching the statement or comment, pressing SKIP again will move the card to column 72 (where, if it were a comment, an * would be punched). Pressing the space bar once moves the card to column 73, at which point the next eight columns are duplicated, the card is moved out, and a new card is brought into place.

Figure A-6
Example of program card
for punching FORTRAN
programs.

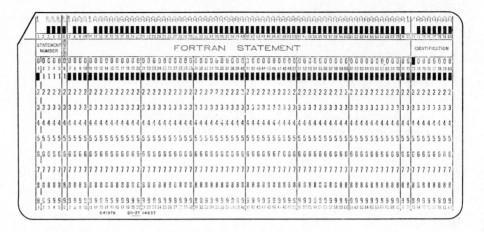

Other keys and controls

The MULT PCH (multiple punch) key is used when a punch combination not found for the machine is to be punched. If, for example, an 11, 5, 8 punch combination is to be punched on a Model 26, the MULT PCH key is depressed, and 11, 5, 8 are punched. The multiple punch key keeps the card from advancing to allow the three digits to be punched in one column.

The backspace control is a small rectangular button between the reading station and the punching station. Depressing the control backspaces one column.

On a Model 29 (but not on a Model 26) there are two additional switches not normally used by the student. If the LZ PRINT is OFF, it suppresses the printing of leading zeros in a field. The switch should usually be on for the student user. The CLEAR switch is a spring switch that causes all cards then in process to be moved through to the stacker without feeding any new cards.

FORTRAN
programming from
a terminal

The trend in programming is toward the use of terminals by both programmers and users. The terminal may be a teletypewriter or a visual display unit (often called a *CRT*). The terminal may be used for one or more of the following:

1   Original entry of program statements
2   Correction of a program already entered (through the terminal or by separate input on cards)
3   Data input
4   Instructions to execute (run) the program
5   Output of messages from program and operating system
6   Output of results from program

The advantages are reductions in elapsed time for programming, faster corrections and checkout cycles, etc. The disadvantages are a somewhat less efficient use of computer resources and a tendency to rely too heavily on the computer to do debugging.

FORTRAN at a terminal is essentially the same as with cards; the major differences are the result of the difference in physical characteristics between terminals and line printers. Terminals are limited to a line width of 72, 80, or 120 positions. They print at speeds of 10, 15, 30, or 120 characters per second in contrast to line printer speeds of 1 to 4 lines per second where each line may be up to 120 or 132 characters wide. In addition, for some implementations, the terminal does not have vertical spacing control based upon the character (0, +, 1) in column 1; hence, column 1 is available for printing.

In an effort to overcome the limitations and capitalize on the advantages of interactive terminals, various compiler writers have modified the FORTRAN standards. There is no standard to cover these modifications, and hence the following remarks describe typical features, but anyone using FORTRAN from a terminal should refer to the local documentation for specific instructions.

Following are some major features of terminal (timesharing) FORTRAN.

1   Each line of the FORTRAN program must be assigned a sequencing line number (different from the optional FORTRAN statement labels). Generally, this is a five-digit number between 00001 and 99999. In other words, the sequencing line number precedes the FORTRAN coding on each line.

Line
No.   FORTRAN statement

| 00100 | 1 | 3 | 7 | X = Y + Z |
| 00110 | | | | R = 1.75 * SQRT(X) |

These line numbers are usually spaced (10, 20, 30, etc.) to allow insertion of correction lines or additional code lines. The system rearranges FORTRAN statements in numerical order by sequencing line number before compilation. This means that statements may be inserted between others or in place of others in a program merely by entering a statement with a line number that is in the desired sequence.

For example, if a line coded X = X + 1.0 is to be inserted between the two lines just shown, it can be coded later in the program as:

00105	X = X + 1.0

The system will sequence the statements before compilation, and thus line 105 will be inserted between lines 100 and 110.

2   The second major difference is that free-form input is allowed. That is, the convention of using columns 2–6 only for statement labels and 7–72 only for statement code is relaxed. If the column immediately following the line sequence number contains a plus sign, it is considered a continuation of the previous line. If it contains anything else except a blank, it is interpreted as a comment line. If it is blank, then the balance of the line is considered a FORTRAN coding line. Immediately following the blank may be either a statement label or a FORTRAN statement. For example, a short program might be entered as follows; note comment lines, continuation (lines 110 and 120), and statement label (line 100).

```
00080* THESE COMMENT LINES DESCRIBE
00090* THE FOLLOWING CODE. NOTE THE
00095* FREE FORM INPUT.
00098 READ *, Y, Z
00100 105 X = Y + Z
00110 R = 1.75*
00120+ SQRT(X)
00130 PRINT*, Y, Z, R
00140 STOP
00150 END
```

3   The number of characters available in a line of FORTRAN coding may still be 72 (as with a standard manual coding form), but the characteristics of the terminal and compiler may make this smaller or larger.

4   Data to be entered from a terminal for program execution should generally use a list-directed input; it is difficult to format input data using a terminal, since it usually does not indicate the column position of a character being entered. For each READ statement the system generates a question mark (or other prompt character) at the terminal to prompt the user for input data. To assist the user in responding to the READ, a message should be printed by the program before the READ. To enter data in response to the request for input, the value is keyed in and the "return" key is pressed. No data, but just a return may be interpreted by some systems the same as an end of file (or end of data) in a card (batch) system.

5   Output to a terminal may be formatted, but the area available for output is often limited to only 72 or perhaps 80 characters per line. However, some newer terminals do have full line-printer-width carriages. Using the terminal requires additional system-specific information, which therefore cannot be included in this text. There is a place on the last page of the book to record the information for your system. These specifications generally include procedures to:

Figure B-1
Listing of a FORTRAN program entered at a terminal.

```
00100*****     PROGRAM IDENTIFICATION
00110*
00120*    THIS PROGRAM COMPUTES THE AMOUNT TO WHICH AN INITIAL
00130*    PRINCIPAL COMPOUNDS AT VARIOUS INTEREST RATES.
00135*    WRITTEN BY T. HOFFMANN 08/07/1977
00140*
00150*****     VARIABLE IDENTIFICATION
00160*
00170*    PRINCE = INITIAL PRINCIPAL
00180*    RATE   = INTEREST RATE
00190*    YEARS  = NUMBER OF YEARS TO COMPOUND
00200*    FREQ   = ANNUAL  FREQUENCY OF COMPOUNDING
00210*    AMOUNT = COMPOUND AMOUNT AFTER YEARS
00220*
00230**********
00240*
00250*****     BLOCK 0100     READ IN DATA
00260*
00270 101 PRINT *, 'WHAT IS YOUR PRINCIPAL AMOUNT'
00280 READ(5,*,END=401) PRINCE
00290 IF(PRINCE .LE. 0.0) GOTO 401
00300 102 PRINT *, 'WHAT IS THE INTEREST RATE'
00310 READ *, RATE
00320 IF(RATE .GE. 1.0) GOTO 901
00330 PRINT *, 'FOR HOW MANY YEARS, AND HOW OFTEN PER YEAR'
00340 READ *, YEARS,FREQ
00350*
00360*****     BLOCK 0200     COMPUTE COMPOUND AMOUNT
00370*
00380 AMOUNT = PRINCE*(1.0 + RATE/FREQ)**(YEARS*FREQ)
00390*
00400*****     BLOCK 0300     PRINT RESULTS
00410*
00420 WRITE(6,310) PRINCE,RATE,YEARS,FREQ,AMOUNT
00430 310 FORMAT('$',F8.2,' AT RATE OF',F6.4,' FOR',F4.0,
00440+    ' YEARS, COMPOUNDED',F3.0,' TIMES PER YEAR',/6X,
00450+    ' AMOUNTS TO $',F10.2//)
00460*
00470*    GO BACK TO READ MORE DATA
00480*
00490 GOTO 101
00500*
00510*****     BLOCK 0400     TERMINATION MESSAGE
00520*
00530 401 PRINT *, 'NORMAL STOP.'
00540 STOP
00550*
00560*****     BLOCK 0900     ERROR MESSAGE
00570*
00580 901 PRINT *, 'INTEREST RATES MUST BE LESS THAN 1.00'
00590*
00600*    GO BACK TO RE-READ INTEREST RATE
00610*
00620 GOTO 102
00630*
00640 END
:
```

(a) Log onto the terminal. This includes user number, user password, etc.
(b) Specify that the statements to follow will be a FORTRAN program and give it an identifying name.
(c) Enter statements.
(d) Specify compilation and execution of the program.
(e) Specify correction of statements in a program.
(f) Specify corrected program execution.
(g) Input data as needed.

Figure B-1 shows a listing of a simple program as written at a terminal and Figure B-2 shows the dialog between a programmer at a terminal and the computer (command to run, input of data, and output).

Free-form entry of the FORTRAN coding lines at the terminal includes a relaxation of some of the style features associated with card input. In Figure

Figure B-2
Dialog at execution of
program from a terminal.

```
User      { RUN
command

System    { 82/02/12. 11.46.10.
response  { M77TS      PROGRAM    TSPROG


           WHAT IS YOUR PRINCIPAL AMOUNT
         ? 1000
Note       WHAT IS THE INTEREST RATE
error    { ? 6
handling   INTEREST RATES MUST BE LESS THAN 1.00
           WHAT IS THE INTEREST RATE
         ? .06
           FOR HOW MANY YEARS, AND HOW OFTEN PER YEAR
         ? 5,4
         $ 1000.00 AT RATE OF .0600 FOR  5. YEARS, COMPOUNDED 4. TIMES PER YEAR
                 AMOUNTS TO $    1346.86


           WHAT IS YOUR PRINCIPAL AMOUNT
         ? 5000
           WHAT IS THE INTEREST RATE
         ? .055
           FOR HOW MANY YEARS, AND HOW OFTEN PER YEAR
         ? 3,4
         $ 5000.00 AT RATE OF .0550 FOR  3. YEARS, COMPOUNDED 4. TIMES PER YEAR
                 AMOUNTS TO $    5890.34

Note use
of value  { WHAT IS YOUR PRINCIPAL AMOUNT
to end    { ? -1
program     NORMAL STOP.

           SRU     0.510 UNTS.
System    { RUN COMPLETE.
message
```

B-1 note the reduced number of asterisks on comment headings and the location of the block number designation. The free form of the code lines is especially illustrated in lines 270, 280, 360, and 440. In line 270, the FORTRAN statement label starts in column 7; in line 280, the instruction itself starts in column 7. In line 360, the asterisk in column 6 (it could have been a C) means that the entire line is a comment; in line 440, the + sign in column 6 indicates the continuation of the previous line.

When the program is run, the PRINT statement in line 270 is executed first to ask for the data to be input, and the READ statement in line 280 causes a question mark to be printed. Since the user may not have control over the printing of the question mark, it is good style to write all the print statements preceding requests for input as questions rather than declarative sentences ("What is. . . ," rather than, "Enter data") so that the question mark makes grammatical sense to the user. See this in Figure B-2.

As suggested, list-directed input (lines 280, 310, 340) is used for input, and a format-directed output statement is used for printing the results (line 420). The program terminates on either an END condition caused by an end-of-file condition (line 280) or a negative input value for the principal (line 290).

The execution of the program is illustrated in Figure B-2. After typing in RUN, the system responds with the date, time, compiler, and program names before compiling and executing the program. This response is somewhat different for every time-sharing system. At the conclusion of the program, the system prints the message 'SRU 0.510 UNTS.' and 'RUN COMPLETE'. These system-dependent responses indicate how much computer system resource units were consumed and that the system considers the job run to be complete.

If, at attempted execution, a program error were detected, an error message would print. A program correction can be made immediately by typing the line number to be corrected and the revised FORTRAN statement. If execution is then specified, the revised statement is inserted by the system and the corrected program is compiled and executed.

The 1966 American National Standard FORTRAN was a landmark in the development of the FORTRAN language because the language, which began in the late 1950s, was codified into a standard version. During the period 1966 to 1977, many implementors of FORTRAN made enhancements to the language. Among the most significant developments were WATFOR and WATFIV, student-oriented FORTRAN compilers developed by the University of Waterloo in Ontario, Canada, for use on IBM 360 and 370 computers. A student-oriented FORTRAN comparable to WATFIV, called MNF, was also developed at the University of Minnesota for use on large-scale Control Data computers. Another interesting development is WATFIV-S, a special version of WATFIV containing instructions for use in structured programming. The 1977 FORTRAN can be viewed as an enhancement of the 1966 standard FORTRAN, including most of the added features in WATFOR, WATFIV, MNF, and other compilers. The 1977 standard has a simplified version called Subset FORTRAN. After the introduction of the 1977 standard, MNF was replaced by M77, which adheres to the standard.

This appendix summarizes the language changes and enhancements from 1966 to 1977 standard FORTRAN, and compares the subset version with the full 1977 FORTRAN. It also compares both WATFOR/WATFIV and M77 with the fundamental features of 1977 FORTRAN presented in Chapters 1–5 of the text. The WATFOR/WATFIV and M77 comparison does not include the less commonly used file processing, and other instructions described in Chapters 6 and 7. The features of WATFIV-S are described and compared with the standard. In general, a programmer is advised to check the reference manual for the compiler being used to learn the specific, current implementation of new features.

Differences between 1977 Standard FORTRAN and 1966 Standard FORTRAN

The 1977 American National Standard FORTRAN specifications are used in this text. The updated standard is generally compatible with the 1966 standard, but there are a few conflicts. Also, new features have been added. These differences and additions are listed in relationship to the text chapters.

Text chapter	Feature in 1977 FORTRAN	Conflict	New feature
1	List-directed input/output		X
2	Use of generic intrinsic function names		X
	Generic names MAX and MIN		X
	Block IF(IF . . . THEN . . . ELSE . . . ENDIF)		X
	Mixed-mode expressions allowed		X
3	READ *fs*, list and PRINT *fs*, list		X
	Apostrophe edit descriptor		X
	T edit descriptor		X
	END for end of data and ERR for data error		X
	The + or − required before exponent in E field	X	X
	Dropping of implied method for handling character (Hollerith) data	X	

Text chapter	Feature in 1977 FORTRAN	Conflict	New feature
	Dropping of Hollerith constant using H statement	X	
	CHARACTER data type		X
	Expression in output list		X
4	Use of any integer arithmetic expression for subscript (limited to i ± k, k * i, and k * i ± k in 1966 FORTRAN)		X
	Upper and lower bounds for dimensions		X
	DO loop control variable can be integer or real variable (instead of only integer variables)		X
	DO loop parameters may be negative, real variable, or integer or real expression (instead of only an integer or integer variable)		X
	If DO loop termination parameter value is greater than initial value, loop will not be executed (undefined previously)		X
	Comma in DO statement after statement number allowed but optional, for example, DO s [,]i = m_1, m_2, m_3		X
	Transfer of control into range of a DO statement not allowed	X	
5	Comma optional before control variable in computed GOTO, for example, GOTO(s_1,s_2)[,]i		X
	Any integer expression allowed as index for computed GOTO		X
6	OPEN, CLOSE, and INQUIRE statements		X
	UNIT = and FMT = control specifiers		X
7	Additional intrinsic functions—ACOS, ANINT, ASIN, CHAR, COSH, DACOS, DASIN, DCOSH, DDIM, DNINT, DPROD, DSINH, DTAN, DTANH, ICHAR, IDNINT, INDEX, LEN, LOG, LOG10, NINT, SINH, and TAN		X
	IMPLICIT declaration		X
	Dropping of reading into Hollerith format descriptor	X	
	Concatenation operator		X
	Substrings		X
	Lexical relationship functions—LGE, LGT, LLE, and LLT		X
	Additional format edit specifications BN, BZ, Ew.dEe, Iw.m, Gw.dEe, TRc, TLc, S, SP, SS, and :		X
	FORMAT specifications in character storage		X
	FORMAT in input/output statement		X
	PARAMETER statement		X
	Exclusive OR (EQV and NEQV)		X
	PROGRAM statement		X
	SAVE statement		X
	Alternate entry and alternate return points for subroutines		X
	Variable dimensions		X
	INTRINSIC statement		X

Full 1977 FORTRAN features not included in 1977 Subset FORTRAN

The differences between the full FORTRAN and Subset FORTRAN will generally be significant for smaller computers. The differences are arranged by book chapter.

Chapter	Feature not included in Subset
1	List-directed input and output
2	Generic function name
3	ERR specifier READ *fs*, list and PRINT *fs*, list Tc format edit descriptor Expressions in output list
4	More than three subscripts (full FORTRAN allows seven subscripts) Array element reference or function reference in subscript Upper and lower bounds for array declarator DO loop control variable can be real variable DO parameters can be integer or real expressions Implied DO loops in DATA statement (also, DATA statement must follow specification statement but precede executable statements in Subset) Real variables allowed in implied DO loop as control and parameters
5	Index expression of a computed GOTO may be an integer expression BLOCK DATA subprogram
6	Formatted direct-access records CLOSE statement INQUIRE statement OPEN (except for use with ACCESS = DIRECT and RECL = record length)
7	Double-precision and complex types Double-precision and complex expressions and intrinsic functions LEN, CHAR, and INDEX functions Unequal length for character variables Asterisk length specifier for character functions Character functions Substring Concatenation operator FORMAT edit descriptors—Iw.m, Dw.d, Gw.d, Gw.dEe, Ew.dEe, Tc, TLC, TRC, S, SP, and SS Format scan terminator (colon) UNIT= and FMT= control specifiers Use of character variables or array elements as FORMAT specification PARAMETER statement SAVE statement without a list ENTRY statement Alternate return from subroutine

Differences between WATFOR/WATFIV and 1977 Standard FORTRAN for Chapters 1–5

WATFOR is a more restricted version of FORTRAN than WATFIV. The differences between these two versions and 1977 FORTRAN are summarized only for Chapters 1–5 of the text; most of the features in Chapters 6 and 7 are available (such as sequential file instructions and the explicit method of character variable definition, but for the new or advanced features, the user needs to have access to the specific installation specifications.

Chapter	Comments on WATFOR and WATFIV
1	List-directed input and output is written in WATFIV without an asterisk, for example, READ,list. WATFIV allows multiple assignment statements of the form v1 = v2 . . . = expression on one line. This is not allowed by the 1977 standard.
2	The block IF is not supported by WATFIV.
3	WATFIV (but not WATFOR) allows list-directed I/O statements of the form READ(unit,*,ERR = s,END = s) list and WRITE(unit,*) list. These are the same as the 1977 standard. The WATFIV statements DUMPLIST and ON ERROR GOTO are not allowed in the 1977 standard. The implied method of defining character variables is permitted; the explicit method (Chapter 3) is also available
4	Full FORTRAN allows real control variable in a DO loop and real or integer expressions as DO parameters; these are not allowed by WATFOR or WATFIV. It is possible to end a DO loop on a transfer of control in WATFOR/WATFIV. This not allowed in 1977 FORTRAN. The WATFIV statement NAMELIST// is not allowed by 1977 FORTRAN.
5	Variables in both blank and named (labeled) COMMON can be initialized by DATA statements; in 1977 FORTRAN, only named COMMON can be initialized by DATA statements and only with a BLOCK DATA subprogram.

Differences between M77 and 1977 Standard FORTRAN for Chapters 1–5

M77 replaces the earlier compiler MNF. Both M77 and MNF allowed all standard features described in Chapters 1–5, except that MNF did not have CHARACTER type. M77 was designed to conform fully to the 1977 standard. It also accepts Hollerith statements and implied character variables to allow compatibility with the 1966 FORTRAN standard and has numerous interesting extensions to the standard.

Structured instructions in WATFIV-S

WATFIV-S is a structured programming version of WATFIV. It contains six sets of instructions to program the structured patterns described in Chapter 1 in FORTRAN without using GOTO instructions. Only one of these structured instructions, the block IF, has been incorporated in 1977 Standard FORTRAN (but slightly altered). The remaining instructions are therefore nonstandard, and our recommendation is not to use nonstandard instructions.

Structured instruction	Format of instruction

1 Block IF or IF DO instruction	IF (condition) THEN DO
	    statements
	ELSE DO
	    statements
	END IF

2 WHILE DO loop instruction	WHILE (condition) DO
	    statements
	END WHILE

3 DO CASE statement	DO CASE 1
	    statements for $case_1$
	CASE
	    statements for $case_2$
	CASE
	    statements for $case_3$
	CASE
	    statements for $case_n$
	IF NONE DO
	    statements for case greater than n
	END CASE

4 A block of code in a program is given a name by the REMOTE BLOCK statement and the end of the block is delineated by an END BLOCK statement	REMOTE BLOCK name statements in block END BLOCK
The block is executed by an EXECUTE statement	EXECUTE name-of-block
5 WHILE EXECUTE instruction	WHILE (condition) EXECUTE block name
6 AT END DO instruction When the end of file or end of input is detected, the program executes the block of code between AT END DO and END AT END	READ( ) AT END DO statements END AT END

Form for relating your FORTRAN compiler to the 1977 standard FORTRAN in the text

FORTRAN COMPILER DEPENDENT SPECIFICATIONS FOR CHAPTERS 1 THROUGH 5

		Typical	My compiler			Typical	My compiler
1	Maximum size of real constant	8 digits	_____	5	Standard unit numbers for		
2	Maximum size of integer constant	6 digits	_____		(a) Card reader	5	_____
3	Maximum precision for real variable (in digits)	8 digits	_____		(b) Printer	6	_____
4	Maximum magnitude of real variable (maximum size of exponent)	±39	_____	6	Limit on number of subscripts	3 or 7	_____
				7	Other specifications		_____

Chapter first used		Inclusion of features checklist for Chapters 1 through 5	YES	NO	IF NO, THEN
1	1	List-directed (format-free) input and output	☐	☐	See pages 35–36
		(a) If yes, is form READ*, list and WRITE*, list	☐	☐	Use form of free format instruction specifications for your compiler
1	2	Asterisk allowed in column 1 instead of C for comment line	☐	☐	Use C
2	3	Block IF allowed (IF...THEN...ELSE...ENDIF)	☐	☐	Use sets of regular logical IFs
2	4	Generic name for intrinsic functions, especially MAX, MIN, REAL, and INT	☐	☐	Use specific names
3	5	Name description form allowed for input and output, e.g., READ 701, A, B, C and PRINT 702, A, B, C	☐	☐	Use regular I/O statements
3	6	Apostrophe edit descriptor for Hollerith output	☐	☐	Use H edit descriptor
3	7	Tc edit descriptor (tabulate)	☐	☐	Use Xn edit descriptor
3	8	Character data defined as CHARACTER v*length	☐	☐	Use implicit method described in text (check specifications for length implied by your compiler)
3	9	END specification in input statement	☐	☐	Use special end-of-data record and test for it
3	10	ERR specification in input statement	☐	☐	No alternative in program; handled by operating system
3	11	Expression allowed in output list	☐	☐	Compute expression separately
4	12	Real variable allowed as DO loop index and real expressions allowed as DO loop parameters	☐	☐	Use only integer variable for index and integer constant or variable for loop parameters
4	13	Implied DO loop in DATA statement	☐	☐	Initialize with DO loop
4	14	If DO loop termination value is less than initial value, loop is not executed	☐	☐	If a problem, code an IF statement to test for the condition and prevent execution
4	15	Upper and lower bounds for dimensions	☐	☐	Calculate a subscript within dimension limits that start at 1
5	16	Block data subprogram	☐	☐	Initialize in program with assignment statements
5	17	Computed GOTO index can be integer expression	☐	☐	Use integer variable only

Index

List of 1977 American National Standard FORTRAN statements and specifications

SYMBOLS USED IN LIST OF STATEMENTS

Shaded	Not included in 1977 Subset of standard FORTRAN	n	An integer number of five or less digits or a character constant
A	Name of an array	s	Statement label
d	Places to right of decimal in FORMAT	st	Statement
e	Expression	u	Unit designator (integer constant or variable) for I/O statement
f	Subprogram name or statement function name		
fs	FORMAT statement label	v	Variable name (either real or integer)
i	Integer variable	vk	Variable or constant (either real or integer)
ie	Integer variable or integer expression		
ik	Integer variable or integer constant	vek	Variable or expression or constant (either real or integer)
iek	Integer variable, integer expression, or integer constant	w	Field width in FORMAT statement
k	Constant of any type	x	Dummy arguments in subprogram declaration
		[ ]	Optional item in statement

EXECUTABLE STATEMENTS

Reference in text	Description of statement	Form	Example
	ASSIGNMENT		
	Assignment	$v = e$	
	operators		
	+ addition		
	− subtraction or negation		
	* multiplication		
	** exponentiation		
	// concatenation		
	where $e =$		
30–32, 61–63	arithmetic expression		X = 5.0 + Y*Z**2
335–336	character string		NME = 'NAME'
336	character substring		STRNG = SUB1 // SUB2
333	logical variable		SWITCH = .TRUE.
350	Assignment of statement label	ASSIGN s TO i	ASSIGN 210 TO ILABEL
	TRANSFER OF CONTROL		
77	Unconditional GOTO	GOTO s (or GO TO s)	GOTO 910
254–257	Computed GOTO	GOTO $(s_1,s_2, . . .,s_n)[,]i$	GOTO(210, 260, 320), INDX
		GOTO $(s_1,s_2, . . .,s_n)[,]ie$	GOTO(210, 260, 320), I + (3 * J)
350	Assigned GOTO	GOTO $i(s_1,s_2, . . .,s_n)$	GOTO ILABEL(320, 415, 210)
79–80	Arithmetic IF	IF (e) s_1, s_2, s_3 (s_1 if e is negative, s_2 if zero, s_3 if positive)	IF(SIN(X) + 0.3) 250, 350, 210
78–79	Logical IF	IF (e) st where e is a relational expression or logical expression	IF (A .EQ. 0.0) B = B + 1.0
			IF (SWITCH) STOP
69–70		Relational operators:	IF(X .GT. Y) GOTO 350
		.LT. Less than	IF(X .LE. Y) Z = Z + 1.0
		.LE. Less than or equal to	
		.EQ. Equal to	
		.NE. Not equal to	
		.GT. Greater than	
		.GE. Greater than or equal to	

70–71	Logical operators:	
	.NOT.	Logical negation
	.AND.	Logical conjunction
	.OR.	Logical inclusive disjunction
	.EQV.	Logical equivalence
	.NEQV.	Logical nonequivalence

342

```
IF(X.GT.Y.AND.Y.LT.17.0) GOTO 260
```

68–69 Block IF

```
IF (e) THEN
   statement block
ELSE
   statement block
ENDIF (or END IF)
```

```
IF (IVAR .GE. JVAR)THEN
   J2 = J2 + 1
   K2 = J2**2
ELSE
   KIX = JIX / 2
ENDIF
```

71–73 Nested Block IF

```
IF (IVAR .GE. JVAR)THEN
   J2 = J + 1
   KJ = J2**2
ELSE
   KIX = JIX / 2
   IF (KIX .EQ. 0)THEN
      PRINT *, KJ
   ELSE
      PRINT *, J2
   ENDIF
ENDIF
```

73–75 Nested IF tests

```
ELSEIF (e) THEN
   (or ELSE IF)
```

```
IF (X .LT. 3.5)THEN
   KTR = KTR + 1
   Y = SIN(B)
ELSEIF (X .GT. 4.7)THEN
   NTR = NTR + 1
   Y = COS(B)
ELSE
   Y= TAN(B)
ENDIF
```

32–33 Stop with no restart

```
STOP [n]
```

```
STOP or STOP 3 or STOP 'ERROR'
```

349	Pause with restart	PAUSE [n]	PAUSE or PAUSE 2
32, 242, 249	End of program unit	END	END

LOOP

187–194	Establishing loop parameters, subset / full	DO s[,]i = ik$_1$, ik$_2$, [ik$_3$] / DO s[,]v = vek$_1$, vek$_2$, [vek$_3$]	DO 210 I = 1, N3 / DO 210 X = .01, 3.0*Y, .05
189–191	Define end of DO loop	s CONTINUE	210 CONTINUE

INPUT AND OUTPUT

25–26, 29–30	Read, list-directed and predefined unit	READ *[,list]	READ *, X, I
122	Read, list-directed	READ (u,*)[list]	READ (5, *)X, I
120–123	Read, format directed	READ (u,fs)[list]	READ (5, 160)X, E
122–123	Read, format-directed and predefined unit	READ fs[,list]	READ 160, X, I
140–142 299, 302	Read, with control list specifiers / For full list, see Chapter 6	READ (u,fs,control specifiers)[list] / Examples are END = s and ERR = s	READ (5, 160, END = 510, ERR = 920)
296	Read, unformatted (from files on external storage)	READ (u)[list]	READ (10)X, I
26–29	Write, list-directed and predefined unit	PRINT *,[list]	PRINT *, X, I, 'TOTAL'
122	Write, list-directed	WRITE (u,*)[list]	WRITE (6, *) X, I, 'TOTAL'
120–123	Write, format-directed	WRITE (u,fs)[list]	WRITE (6, 210)X, X**2, 3, 14
122–123	Write, format-directed and predefined unit	PRINT fs[,list]	PRINT 210, X, I
298, 301–304	Write, with control list specifiers / For full list, see Chapter 6	WRITE (u,fs,control specifiers)[list]	WRITE (7, 210, REC = 12)X, I
146–147	List (for any WRITE) may include constants and expressions	WRITE (u,fs)vek$_1$, vek$_2$. . . vek$_n$	WRITE (6, 210)X, X**2, 3, 14.4)
296	Write, unformatted (to files on external storage)	WRITE (u)[list]	WRITE (10)X, I
298–305	Files on external (auxiliary) storage (see text for details)	REWIND, BACKSPACE, ENDFILE, OPEN, CLOSE, and INQUIRE	REWIND 7 / ENDFILE 8

FORMAT SPECIFICATIONS

Both Subset and Full FORTRAN

Reference in text	Specification symbol	Form	Specifies
125–131	F	Fw.d	Real data
125–131	E	Ew.d	Data in exponent form
125–131	I	Iw	Integer data
139–140	A	Aw	Character data, specified field width
139–140	A	A	Character data, field width based on data
133	X	wX	Skipping of field
142–143	/	/// . . . /	Skip to next unit record, or skip over n − 1 unit records
135–136	H	nH . . .	Hollerith character (n = number of characters following H)
134–136	' '	'characters'	Hollerith
338	L	Lw	Logical data
339	B	BN	Blanks on input ignored
339	B	BZ	Blanks are input as zero
339	P	nP	Scaling (nP precedes F, E, D, or G specification)

Full FORTRAN only

Reference in text	Specification symbol	Form	Specifies
339	E	Ew.dEe	Exponent of e digits
340	I	Iw.m	Integer data with at least m field length
338	G	Gw.d	Either E or F edit depending on data
339	G	Gw.dEe	Exponent of e digits
338	D	Dw.d	Double-precision data
133	T	Tc	Tabulate to column c
339	T	TLc	Tabulate backward c position from current position
339	T	TRc	Tabulate forward c positions from current position
340	S	S, SP, SS	SP = print plus, SS = do not print +, S return to processor option
339	: (colon)	:	Terminates FORMAT control if no more data items in list

CONTROL CHARACTERS FOR VERTICAL SPACING

Character in position 1 of output	Vertical spacing before output
Blank	One line (single space)
0 (zero)	Two lines (double space)
1	To first line of next page
+	No advance

NONEXECUTABLE SPECIFICATIONS OR DECLARATIONS

Reference in text	Description of specifications or declaration	Form	Example
124–125 340–341	FORMAT of data statement In input/output statement	$ƒs$ FORMAT (specifications) (see specifications list) '(specifications)'	210 FORMAT(F10.0, 2X, 'TOTAL') WRITE(6,'(F10.0, I6, 'NONE')')X,IX
200–201	Initialization of data	DATA $v_1,v_2, \ldots / c_1,c_2, \ldots /$ $k * c$ represents k values of c Implied DO loop in DATA statement	DATA X, Y, Z, A / 1.0, 3.5, 2*0.0 / DATA (G(I), I = 1, 10) / 10 * 0.0 /
183–184	Dimension of maximum size of array	DIMENSION $A_1(k_1)$, $A_2(k_1,k_2)$, $A_3(k_1,k_2,k_3)$, . . . Limited to three dimensions in Subset and seven in full FORTRAN	DIMENSION A(100), B(5, 15, 3)
183–184	Upper and lower bound for a dimension	DIMENSION $A_1(k_1:k_1)$, $A(k_1:k_1,k_2:k_2)$, . .	DIMENSION D(3:12)
342	Constant expression	DIMENSION $A(k \pm$ or $**k)$	DIMENSION B(3+2, 5**2)
250–251	Define data names in blank common storage	COMMON [/] v_1,v_2, A(k), . . . For A(k) k is dimension	COMMON A, B, I or COMMON // A, B, I COMMON A(100), B, I
251–253	Define data names in named COMMON storage	COMMON / name / $v_1, v_2, \ldots$	COMMON / ABLOCK / X, M, W
252–254	Define different variables to use same storage	EQUIVALENCE $(v_1, v_2, \ldots), (v_3, v_4, \ldots) \ldots$	EQUIVALENCE (C, D), (I, N)
64–67, 334	Define type of data	type $v_1, v_2, \ldots v_n$ v can be in form A(k) INTEGER REAL COMPLEX LOGICAL DOUBLE PRECISION	INTEGER G, ZED, ALPHA(5,6) REAL IX, JON(50) COMPLEX C, DX(5) LOGICAL SWITCH DOUBLE PRECISION A, X, YR(10)
63–67	Define type and length	CHARACTER name*length, name*length CHARACTER[*length,]name$_1$,name$_2$, . . .	CHARACTER BETA*5, GRW*7 CHARACTER *10, LNAME, ALPHA
334–335	Define first letter as type	IMPLICIT type $(a_1,a_2, \ldots a_n)$ or $(a_1 - a_n)$	IMPLICIT INTEGER (A, B, R – T)
342	Equate constant and name	PARAMETER (name = constant)	PARAMETER (FIVE = 5.0)
342–343	Main program (optional)	PROGRAM name	PROGRAM XAMPLE

SUBPROGRAM SPECIFICATIONS OR DECLARATIONS

Reference in text	Description of specification or declaration	Form	Example
350–351	Statement function declaration	$f(x_1,x_2, \ldots ,x_n) = e$	CALC (A, B) = A**2 + SIN(B) / 4.0
340–343	Function subprogram	[type] FUNCTION $f(x_1,x_2, \ldots ,x_n)$	FUNCTION EOQ(S, C1, C2, CP)
245–249	Subroutine without arguments	SUBROUTINE f	SUBROUTINE X
245–249	Subroutine with arguments	SUBROUTINE $f(x_1,x_2, \ldots ,x_n)$	SUBROUTINE X(A, I, M)
343–346	Subroutine with alternate returns	SUBROUTINE $f(x_1,x_2, \ldots ,*, *, \ldots)$	SUBROUTINE XED(X, I, *, *)
	Variable dimensions for dummy arrays in subprogram:		
345	Assumed size equal to calling program array	In subprogram DIMENSION $A_1(*)$, $A_2(k,*)$	DIMENSION ALPH(*), BETA(10,*)
345–346	Adjustable array equal to value of integer variable in calling list or in COMMON	In subprogram SUBROUTINE $f(A_1,A_2,i, \ldots)$ DIMENSION $A_1(i)$, $A_2(i, i)$	SUBROUTINE BEST (D, KX, MB, L, IX) DIMENSION D(MB), KX(L, IX)
251–253	Block data subprogram	In calling program CALL $f(A_1,A_2,i \ldots)$ BLOCK DATA [name]	CALL BEST (G, MX, 10, 5, 7) BLOCK DATA A1
343–344	Optional entry point into subprogram	ENTRY $f[(x_1,x_2, \ldots ,x_n)]$	ENTRY N1(X, ALPHA)
343	Save data from subprogram	SAVE or SAVE list	SAVE X, L, M
346	Define external function names to be used as arguments	EXTERNAL list of routine names	EXTERNAL MYFUN, YOURFN
346	Define intrinsic function names to be used as arguments	INTRINSIC list of intrinsic functions	INTRINSIC SIN, COS

399

STATEMENTS TO USE SUBPROGRAMS AND TO RETURN TO USING PROGRAM

Reference in text	Description of statement	Form	Example
	SUBPROGRAMS		
240–243	Transfer to function	Use function in statement	$X = MYFNCT(Y, M) + 3.175$
245–249	Transfer to subroutine, no argument with argument list	CALL subroutine	CALL DOIT
		CALL subroutine (argument list)	CALL DONT(X, I, J)
343–346	Transfer to subroutine with alternate returns	CALL subroutine (argument list with *s for each alternate return statement number)	CALL STAT(A, Y, *210, *340)
247–249	Return to calling program	RETURN	RETURN
343–346	Alternate returns n = 1, 2 . . . n	RETURN n	RETURN 2
343–344	Transfer to subroutine with alternate entry	CALL entry name (argument list)	CALL ALT3(GEORGE)

Index